FIND, FIX, FINISH

FIND, FIX, FINISH

INSIDE THE COUNTERTERRORISM
CAMPAIGNS THAT KILLED BIN LADEN AND
DEVASTATED AL-QAEDA

AKI PERITZ & ERIC ROSENBACH

PUBLICAFFAIRS
New York

Published in the United States by PublicAffairs™,
a Member of the Perseus Books Group

PublicAffairs books are available at special discounts for bulk purchases in the U.S. by corporations, institutions, and other organizations. For more information, please contact the Special Markets Department at the Perseus Books Group, 2300 Chestnut Street, Suite 200, Philadelphia, PA 19103, call (800) 810–4145, ext. 5000, or e-mail special.markets@perseusbooks.com.

Book Design by Brent Wilcox

Library of Congress Cataloging-in-Publication Data
Peritz, Aki.
    Find, fix, finish : inside the counterterrorism campaigns that killed Bin Laden and devastated Al Qaeda / Aki Peritz & Eric Rosenbach.—1st ed.
        p.   cm.
    Includes bibliographical references and index.
    ISBN 978-1-61039-128-3 (hbk.)—ISBN 978-1-61039-129-0 (electronic)
    1. Terrorism—United States—Prevention.   2. Terrorism—Government policy—United States.   3. Qaida (Organization)   4. Intelligence service—United States.   5. United States—Military policy.   I. Rosenbach, Eric B.   II. Title.
    HV6432.P47 2012
    363.325'160973—dc23

                                                                    2011043638

First Edition
10 9 8 7 6 5 4 3 2 1

For Dana

—A. P.

To my family, because they put up with a lot

—E. R.

Safety from external danger is the
most powerful director of national conduct.

–ALEXANDER HAMILTON, 1787

CONTENTS

PREFACE   ix

CHAPTER 1   Fire from the Sky: The Find-Fix-Finish Doctrine in Action   1

CHAPTER 2   Atrophy: National Security Before 9/11   13

CHAPTER 3   The Search for Mr. #3   35

CHAPTER 4   The Finishing Never Ends: How Far Will America Go?   57

CHAPTER 5   Interrogations, Intelligence, and War   79

CHAPTER 6   Counterterrorism in a War Zone   107

CHAPTER 7   Bojinka Redux: The Need for Good International Cop Work   135

CHAPTER 8   An Increasing Preference for Lethal Ends   149

CHAPTER 9   The Enemy Within   167

CHAPTER 10   America's Future: Shadow Wars in Yemen and Somalia   185

CHAPTER 11   Geronimo   207

CHAPTER 12   To Thine Own Self Be True   219

ACKNOWLEDGMENTS   239
APPENDICES   241
NOTES   253
INDEX   297

PREFACE

Terrorism is a political tornado that has the capacity to wreck lives and disrupt societies. For those unlucky bystanders caught up in its path and for those who have lost loved ones in attacks, terrorism is a random, unforgivably cruel turn of fate. The specter of terrorism causes people to think twice about normal social activities: joining a crowd, idling at a café, boarding a plane, and taking the subway. Terrorists fray the intangible ties that bind, causing otherwise rational individuals and modern civilizations to act in irrational, medieval ways.

Al-Qaeda has been the world's foremost purveyor of this particularly lethal form of social mayhem. Its 9/11 operation was notable not only for its destructive capacity but also for its audacity, striking the heart of the world's superpower on a sunny Tuesday morning. And, unlike many terror groups that have focused on regional and parochial interests, al-Qaeda has taken its cause worldwide. Al-Qaeda members have attacked New York City, Madrid, London, Amman, Istanbul, Islamabad . . . the list goes on and on.

For all the rhetoric that followed 9/11, America did not possess a fully formed, off-the-shelf strategy to disrupt, dismantle, and defeat al-Qaeda. Rather, on September 12, the US began the first of a series of painful, halting steps to confront this determined adversary. America's counter-terrorism policy is a dense web of interconnected stories of men and women making tough choices and authorizing risky decisions. It is a complex series of tales filled with victories as well as defeats, resolute behavior, bureaucratic compromises, paths taken and those not.

As we enter the spring of 2012, America's leaders insist that al-Qaeda is on the ropes. Upbeat evaluations have been the hallmarks of American policymakers even in the worst of times. "I'm convinced," defense secretary Leon Panetta said in mid-2011, "that we're within reach of strategically defeating al-Qaeda." Michael Vickers, who a generation ago provided creative solutions in the covert war against the Soviets in Afghanistan, expanded this sentiment, noting that "within 18 to 24 months core al-Qaeda cohesion and operational capabilities could be degraded to the point that the group could fragment and exist mostly as a propaganda arm." Thankfully, this optimism may be merited. While al-Qaeda has proven itself a resilient and resourceful foe, America's ability to track and destroy al-Qaeda operatives anywhere on earth has never been better.

BOTH AUTHORS served in sensitive US government positions. As such, various publication review boards have examined this manuscript. Some redactions remain as blacked-out text in the final version of this book. Uncle Sam also asked to include the following text: *In the interest of full disclosure, this publication was submitted for pre-publication reviews to the Central Intelligence Agency to ensure that no classified information was accidentally disclosed. However, the CIA's review did not shape the case study's scope, tone, or subject material; rather, the authors remain solely responsible for this publication's content.*

CHAPTER 1

FIRE FROM THE SKY

The Find-Fix-Finish Doctrine in Action

The crisp, clear morning of August 5, 2009, was the last one of Baitullah Mehsud's life.[1] The grim leader of Tehrik-e-Taliban Pakistan (TTP)—more commonly known as the Pakistani Taliban—had been responsible for Prime Minister Benazir Bhutto's assassination and dozens of gruesome suicide attacks in Afghanistan and Pakistan. On that sunny morning Mehsud was lounging on the roof of a squat house in South Waziristan. Without warning, two missiles streaked through the sky and slammed into the house.[2] Mehsud, like many of his victims, never saw his enemy until it was too late.

What happened? Two days earlier, Central Intelligence Agency (CIA) employees, stationed thousands of miles away in suburban Virginia, had identified Mehsud in surveillance footage and ordered the lethal Hellfire missile strike via an unmanned aerial vehicle (UAV). After the dust settled, the video feed indicated that Mehsud had been sliced in half and was unquestionably dead.[3] A week later, President Barack Obama reported that "we took out" Mehsud, confirming it was indeed the US that felled the Taliban commander.[4]

In contrast to the many sanitized Hollywood storylines of American officials ordering precision air strikes against dastardly terrorists, eliminating

Mehsud had been a lengthy, messy process of trial and error for the US government. The *Washington Post* called finding Mehsud an "obsession" for the CIA; this was the sixteenth drone strike that the Agency, with explicit White House blessing, had executed intending to neutralize him.[5] In pursuing Mehsud, the US had killed an estimated two hundred other individuals—combatants and noncombatants alike—since 2008.[6] Not trusting just one method, American officials beginning in early 2009 even took a parallel approach, advertising a $5 million bounty for information leading to Mehsud's death or capture.[7]

Mehsud's death exemplified not only the capacity to hunt individuals in the remote badlands of Pakistan without committing ground forces to the area, but also American willingness to allocate resources to finding and killing one man—spending eighteen months, multiple strikes, significant analytical and operational capital, and countless personnel hours to do so. The death of Baitullah Mehsud was the culmination of a learning process for the US, and evidence of a new approach to countering America's terrorist enemies in remote parts of the world.

The tenure of Baitullah Mehsud's successor, Hakimullah Mehsud, lasted less than five months. It was cut short by another UAV strike, which severely wounded Hakimullah and occurred only five days after a video surfaced on Al Jazeera showing the new TTP leader seated beside a Jordanian militant who had just killed eight CIA officers in a suicide bombing in Khost, Afghanistan. The quick turnaround time from the video's emergence to Hakimullah's neutralization sent a clear message: the US was rapidly perfecting its ability to eliminate those who seek to harm America.

This energetic national security capability, which did not exist a decade before, now stands as a core component of the strategy the US deploys to defeat its adversaries. The new doctrine for national security is based on dramatically improved drone technology, close cooperation by civilian and military organizations and with host-nation intelligence services, lethal Special Forces, and a modern interpretation of the law of war that allows for the targeting of militants. The attacks on 9/11 were the catalyst for a radical restructuring of America's attitudes toward security and stability, especially toward the protean threat of international terrorism. The revolution in counterterrorism operations began in 2001 with the invasion of Afghanistan, which demonstrated the power of coordinated intelligence and military operations. Later, both Afghanistan and Iraq served as the laboratories for developing the capacity to suppress terrorism abroad and at home.

THE COLOSSUS SHIFTS ITS FOOTING

For much of American history, when the US looked to take on foreign threats it focused on the menace of hostile nation-states. With rare exceptions—such as when Thomas Jefferson sent US naval forces to battle the Barbary pirates in the early nineteenth century, or when Woodrow Wilson authorized the US Army to (unsuccessfully) hunt for Pancho Villa in Mexico in the early twentieth century—the US has understood the primary threat to its security interests as coming from national adversaries.

No longer. The 9/11 attacks brutally exposed an inability to detect and disrupt a small, highly disciplined, well-trained group of individuals bent on massive destruction. Understandably, America's efforts in the decade since have been refocused on targeting people and small groups who seek to find ways to disturb America's advantaged position.

This shift, however, has affected US national security strategy beyond the immediate concern of eliminating the so-called terrorist threat. Developing the ability to target individuals has proven critical to achieving other national security priorities. The policy debate about the future of Afghanistan policy that occurred within the Obama administration in 2009 represented the formal arrival of a new strategic option: focused, small footprint counterterrorism operations aimed at crippling al-Qaeda in Pakistan and Afghanistan. In the end, President Obama chose to pursue a more expansive counterinsurgency (COIN) strategy. The COIN strategy in Afghanistan, or some variant, was appropriate to achieving a long-term solution to a conflict. But it required—more than guns, troops, or briefcases of cash—a long-term commitment from the American people. But polling in 2010 suggested that public support for the fight was declining, and by 2011 President Obama had announced the beginning of a complete withdrawal from Afghanistan.

Yet the terrorism threat emanating from South Asia did not simply evaporate. Until 2011 COIN represented the strategy for the main effort, but parallel targeted counterterrorism operations increased dramatically on both sides of the Afghanistan-Pakistan border whose object was to find, fix, and finish the adversaries that threatened America's national interests.

FIND, FIX, AND FINISH

The idea of "find, fix, finish" is not new, Indeed, it has a classic American military heritage. In the 1950s General Matthew Ridgway rallied his demoralized troops during the Korean War by repeatedly exhorting his commanders to "Find them! Fix them! Fight them! Finish them!"[8] Ridgway reportedly based his maxim on a study of General Ulysses S. Grant, who said, "The art of war is simple enough. Find out where your enemy is. Get him as soon as you can. Strike at him as hard as you can as often as you can, and keep moving on."

Following the Korean War, General Ridgway's exhortations evolved into national security policy during the cold war:

FIND: Find the enemy
FIX: Ensure the enemy stays (is fixed) in that location
FINISH: Defeat the enemy

The find-fix-finish mantra helped shape the cold war worldview of the adversary: the Soviet Union and its proxies. A bipolar world was a simple world, and the long-term US goal was to defeat the USSR, or at least hold Soviet power in check. The intelligence community knew its targets and its mission: finding and fixing Red Army divisions, strategic bombers, nuclear assets, and the like. Locating the enemy was the easy part; the Soviet Union had cities, citizens, and interests to defend. Finishing the Soviet Union militarily was a much greater challenge, one the US never undertook because of the threat of mutually assured destruction.

But once terrorist groups, not nations, were viewed as the main threat, the rules of engagement that had evolved under the bipolar system of nuclear powers—deterrence, containment, reassurance—were less relevant. There was no tangible adversary, no army of uniformed soldiers, no arsenal regulated by carefully negotiated arms agreements, and certainly no state leader with whom to negotiate.

The fundamental assumption of the cold war—that neither side wanted to risk annihilation—was null and void, since the terrorists were willing to martyr themselves. Since the adversaries had changed, the find-fix-finish doctrine had to evolve as well. Now finishing the enemy would be relatively simple, but finding and fixing an individual or small cell became devilishly hard.

A number of intelligence professionals had begun to draw attention to this shift in strategic thinking. "For most of, certainly, my professional life, most of our work was out there on fix and finish," said former CIA director Michael Hayden in 2007. "The world has turned upside down . . . the finishing is relatively easy. In this world it's the finding that's the hardest-to-do function, it's the intelligence thing. And we now have to treat those sources and methods with the same almost sacred respect we treated the secrecy of troops movements and operational plans in the '40s, '50s, '60s, '70s, and '80s, because it's those things at the front-end, the fine point, that have become the critical piece of that 'find, fix, finish' equation."[9]

The current director of national intelligence, Lt. General James Clapper, elaborated on this point in mid-2009. "Many aspects of the intelligence community today, including some investments and practices, are legacies of the Cold War era and anachronistic," mused Clapper. "Nowadays, with the kind of targets being pursued, the antithesis is true. Today's targets are very elusive and therefore quite hard to find, yet once they are found, they are very easy to finish. This reality has a very profound effect on the way intelligence is done today."[10]

Find

Finding potential threats—figuring out who they are and where they are—is a core requirement of the new doctrine and has proven to be the most difficult aspect of counterterrorism. The intelligence and law enforcement communities have struggled to find regular criminals within American borders. Internationally, locating threats is an even greater task.

In order to accomplish these goals, the intelligence, military, and law enforcement communities have evolved significantly in both mind-set and allocation of resources since 2001. Within American borders, the new nature of the threat led to the creation of the Department of Homeland Security (DHS) and a radical restructuring of the intelligence community, including the establishment of the National Counterterrorism Center and the position of the director of national intelligence (DNI). Controversially, law enforcement officials have additionally been given new powers in regard to electronic and physical surveillance.

Intelligence officials have strengthened working relationships with other nations' intelligence and security services, arguing that the US cannot eliminate the global terrorist threat by itself. In 2005, CIA deputy director for operations Jose Rodriguez told Congress that nearly every capture or killing of a suspected terrorist outside Iraq since 9/11—more than 3,000 in all—was the result of CIA cooperation with foreign intelligence services.[11] One CIA official who worked with Pakistan claimed in late 2009 that the country's Inter-Services Intelligence Directorate (ISI) had captured or killed over six hundred US targets.[12]

Navigating the new challenges to finding terrorists has not been without incident. Revelations that the Bush administration launched controversial counterterrorism programs such as a warrantless electronic surveillance program riled an already tumultuous political environment. The operational necessity for extensive electronic surveillance of individuals within the US who have connections to terrorists abroad is clear; however, the murky legality of the Bush-era Terrorist Surveillance Program resulted in political controversy that distracted national security professionals from their core mission. Finding the enemy is essential, but at what political, moral, or legal price?

Fix

In a global war against small groups of extremists, the US now more than ever places a premium on "actionable intelligence" and has developed new mechanisms to collect fresh tips and refine its dissemination. Whether this perishable information comes from signals intelligence or imagery analysis, from drone-based cameras or from human assets' lips, US forces require precise input to be proactive. Since the targets are not lumbering armies but highly mobile individuals, the instantaneous and momentary nature of the threat requires much greater speed to generate and synthesize this information than in the past.

The US and other countries struggled for years to "fix" Abu Musab al-Zarqawi, a Jordanian militant who arguably became the single most important instigator of sectarian carnage in Iraq from 2003. The fix did not occur until June 2006, three long, bloody years later.

The success was the result of years of trial and error that demanded a massive bureaucratic shift, which has not been fully completed. During the cold war, the intelligence community relied heavily on expensive satellite systems to clarify the capabilities and intent of America's adversaries. Despite the enormous cost of these systems, disproportionate to their utility in locating terrorist individuals and small groups, the intelligence community has struggled over the past decade to reallocate its resources and budgets.

Technical methods can generate excellent intelligence, but satellite systems and electronic surveillance cannot see into men's souls or divulge their exact location. Human intelligence is a crucial aspect of the effort to fix terrorists, and the US had to significantly improve its capacity in this area. In 2001, CIA had limited ability to operate in significant terrorist hotspots, including Afghanistan, Lebanon, Somalia, and Yemen. By the late 1990s, for example, the US still had not replaced intelligence officers in Afghanistan, all of whom had left when the US embassy in Kabul was evacuated in 1989. But over the past decade, the intelligence community has dramatically bolstered the cadre of collectors and informants in the toughest parts of the world. They focus on developing local sources that help the spies attack terrorist cells and provide the actionable details necessary to support capture or kill operations.

The US ability to act swiftly on this information is also rapidly evolving. The need for focused military action in combating smaller targets has led to the rising importance of the Joint Special Operations Command (JSOC) and counterterrorism task forces that combine a wide range of military and intelligence resources. For instance, JSOC, with CIA assistance, has increasingly exploited the use of on-the-ground technical analysis of cell phones, computer hard drives, and documents in combination with the debriefing of captured militants to quickly locate new targets for attack.[13]

Finish

US decision makers have struggled, not only to establish a new paradigm for finding and fixing terrorists, but also new strategies for "finishing" them. The US now attempts to neutralize its targets using special military forces, an integrated group of military operators and analysts, high technology, and severe legal sanctions—which keeps US and civilian casualties to a minimum. The mechanics of finishing terrorists may include a combination of lethal action, physical detention, and prosecution. Terrorist suspects are successfully finished when they no longer represent a physical or ideological threat to US interests, not just when they are killed by military strikes or by covert action.

Many intelligence and military officials argue that detaining and interviewing terrorist suspects is the most effective way to finish them, since they can provide information that will allow the find-fix-finish cycle to begin again; the debriefing of one suspect can aid in locating, isolating, capturing, or killing others. After Khalid Shaykh Mohammed (KSM) was arrested in Pakistan, he provided actionable intelligence that was used to arrest the leader and several top members of Jemaah Islamiya, an extremist group in Southeast Asia.[14] Still, the brutal circumstances under which KSM provided certain information—for example, after being tortured—proved controversial.

Also notorious was the case of Ibn al-Shaykh al-Libi, a Libyan militant captured by the Pakistani military and turned over to the US, which "finished" him by guaranteeing that he remained confined for the rest of his life within US, Egyptian, and Libyan facilities. While al-Libi is better known for providing erroneous information that Saddam Hussein and al-Qaeda had a high-level relationship prior to Operation Iraqi Freedom, he did provide actionable intelligence about pending attacks against US interests at the beginning of his detention.

Lethal action, as in the case of Baitullah Mehsud, and rendition, as with KSM and al-Libi, remove individuals from the global battlefield and prevent them from harming US citizens and interests. Lethal action may also disrupt ongoing or imminent terrorist planning, as critical individuals are removed from future plots.

The mechanics of finishing terrorists is easier than ever before, but significant legal, ethical, and political complications remain. Some of the complications of nonlethal methods were demonstrated in the cases of al-Libi and KSM. Once a terrorist suspect is in custody, US officials must decide how to proceed with his incarceration. One option is to bring the terrorist suspect to trial, but this obliges American officials to provide some sort of legitimate legal process. Another option is to detain him indefinitely, which, beyond the likely unconstitutionality of this alternative, begs thornier questions of where to imprison him and under what conditions. US officials can deport a detainee to a third country, as in the case of Osama bin Laden's driver Salim Hamdan. After spending time in the detention center at the Guantanamo Bay naval base, he was deported and is today living quietly in Yemen. But freed individuals may then engage in terrorism or militant activity, as was the case for former Guantanamo Bay detainees Said Ali al-Shihri, who became the al-Qaeda in the Arabian Peninsula (AQAP) leader, and Abdullah Ghulam Rasoul, who became a Taliban commander.[15]

American attempts to adapt the find-fix-finish paradigm to a new era have not come without high political costs. The Bush administration famously stated that the war on terror should not be fought as a law enforcement exercise; at the same time, President Bush claimed that terrorists would be "brought to justice." If we measure justice in terms of fair trials and convictions, the US has fallen short of that standard. Despite more than three hundred convictions for terrorist-related offenses in civilian courts and a handful in military courts since 9/11, the US has yet to place a single al-Qaeda leader on trial, let alone obtain convictions and sentences. Moreover, the ongoing debate inside and outside the Obama administration over whether al-Qaeda and Taliban militants should be tried in civilian or military courts—as well as other festering issues, such as the ongoing inability to shutter Guantanamo Bay—demonstrates the hard decisions Americans face in determining the appropriate manner of finishing the threat. The US continues to grapple with the thorny political, legal, and moral problems, seeking clear-cut answers that will maintain its legal and ethical footing in very uncertain, constantly shifting political terrain.

IN SEARCH OF MONSTERS

Some might argue that America's new national security paradigm ignores the warning that President John Quincy Adams uttered in 1821 and makes it a nation that goes abroad "in search of monsters to destroy." Whether the US has the foresight to cease, as Adams said, involving itself "beyond the power of extrication, in all the wars of interest and intrigue, of individual avarice, envy, and ambition, which assume the colors and usurp the standard of freedom" remains up for debate. In an interconnected world, however, some of the monsters have the will to journey here unless they are stopped.

The ability of some organizations to create havoc should not be underestimated, especially when they have indicated a strong desire to procure chemical, biological, and nuclear weapons. Osama bin Laden said in 1998 that it was his obligation in furthering jihad to acquire weapons of mass destruction; this public statement followed al-Qaeda's various attempts to procure uranium since the early 1990s.[16] Beyond al-Qaeda, other terrorist groups, such as Egyptian Islamic Jihad, Jemaah Islamiya, Aum Shinrikyo, and Lashkar al Tayyib, have tried to acquire weapons of mass destruction.[17] Indeed, the possibility of WMD—especially nuclear weapons—falling into the wrong hands is, as then-Senator Obama said in 2008, "the gravest danger" the US faces today.[18]

Pursuing an effective national security strategy abroad in the post-9/11 era also requires a new approach to political consensus at home. Given the controversial nature of many of the tools now routinely used by the US government to protect our interests, it is critical to receive the support of Congress and the public at large. The hyperpartisanship displayed on various issues must not hinder our ability to pursue new threats to American security in an ethical and legal manner.

More importantly, scoring cheap political points at the expense of national security corrodes the public's faith in the government's ability to protect it from attack. What America sorely needs is an adult, bipartisan consensus within the legislative branch on how to proceed on security issues that brings legitimacy, intellectual rigor, and a sense of permanence to our often ad hoc security system. A new national security consensus will also allow the US to better appreciate the intelligence and military costs of these efforts, as well as rein in future leaders guided by a misplaced zeal to protect the country from attack.

Finally, to confront security threats in the twenty-first century, the US will require a more nuanced approach to the world, as foreign liaison relationships, particularly with Middle Eastern and South Asian countries, become instrumental in isolating and ending terror networks. A standoffish attitude toward international laws and norms jeopardizes international relationships and the nation's moral standing. Furthermore, using the new tactical tools in a sloppy manner—such as rendering people to noxious countries like Syria or firing Hellfire missiles into dwellings in Pakistan without regard to civilian casualties—will undermine these methods politically and morally, and make protecting US interests more difficult. By revealing how America reinvented its approach to security after 9/11 and by showing its successes and failures, we hope to contribute to a wiser, safer future for the US and its allies.

CHAPTER 2

ATROPHY

National Security Before 9/11

On December 21, 1998, the head of the CIA's Osama bin Laden unit grumpily wrote to Gary Schroen, the CIA's chief of station (COS) in Islamabad, that he had been unable to sleep the night before. "I'm sure we'll regret not acting last night," he told him in an e-mail. Faced with a National Security Council (NSC) "obsessed" with convincing the Saudis, Pakistanis, and Afghan tribal members to "do what we won't do"— capture or kill Osama bin Laden—he was feeling very frustrated.[1]

The day before, the administration's top national security and intelligence officials had assembled in response to intelligence indicating that bin Laden would be spending the night at the Taliban governor's residence near Kandahar, Afghanistan. The question was whether or not to strike the house with a cruise missile, thereby ending the threat posed by bin Laden.

By this point, the NSC wanted to eliminate bin Laden. Just over four months earlier, al-Qaeda had simultaneously bombed the US embassies in Kenya and Tanzania, killing over two hundred and wounding thousands more. Still, top officials debated whether to support and authorize a strike against bin Laden. Available analysis indicated that an air strike against him might kill hundreds of innocent people and damage a neighborhood mosque. Doubting the reliability of the intelligence—there was only a 50 percent chance it was accurate—the NSC decided that the plan was too risky and nixed it.[2]

This was not the first time the NSC had declined an opportunity to target bin Laden, nor would it be the last. By 1997, the intelligence community (IC) had recognized the magnitude of the threat he posed and had begun developing plans to capture or eliminate him. They took these proposed operations to President Clinton and NSC members. Following the 1993 attack on the World Trade Center in New York City and the 1996 attacks on the Khobar Towers military housing complex in Saudi Arabia, they recognized the necessity of acting against terrorist networks.

By all accounts, President Clinton approved the plans that were placed before him and authorized the IC to carry them out.[3] Still, various members of the intelligence, military, and policymaking communities opposed the implementation of almost every capture or strike proposed against bin Laden, claiming each time that the chances of success were too low and the risks associated with failure were too high.[4] Thus no matter how firmly the Clinton White House publicly stated its intention to counter the threat posed by bin Laden, little direct action—with the exception of one round of cruise missile strikes in 1998—was taken against him before 9/11.

The options, it seemed, were simply not good enough. Two days before the African embassy bombings, a note taker at a meeting of the NSC's Counterterrorism Security Group scribbled that when it came to how the government should confront bin Laden, "there was a dearth of bright ideas around the table, despite a consensus that the [government] ought to pursue every avenue it can to address the problem."[5]

In fact, a dearth of ideas wasn't the problem; it was that for every plan there was a risk-averse counterreaction. In 1997 the CIA had begun developing plans to render bin Laden from Afghanistan and bring him to the US. These plans did not envision CIA operatives entering Afghanistan at all. Rather, the CIA would recruit and instruct members of the anti-Taliban Northern Alliance to conduct the operations.

However, CIA leadership rejected one such plan—allegedly the most detailed proposal prior to 9/11—three months before the African embassy bombings: the risks were seen as too great considering the low chances of success.[6] All future plans to send US forces after bin Laden would similarly be rejected by CIA's leadership, often in conjunction with members of the NSC, for a laundry list of reasons: al-Qaeda might retaliate against US interests; Afghan tribal elements or Northern Alliance forces might prove unreliable; there might be a lack of prosecutable evidence against bin Laden and the US might fail to convict him once he was captured; the operation, if discovered, might be misconstrued as an illegal assassination attempt; the financial cost might be too great; killing or capturing bin Laden might bring more extremists flocking to al-Qaeda's cause.

The CIA could have eliminated one of the above objections—the unreliability of the Afghans—by sending a team from its Special Activities Division to hunt bin Laden. Doing so, however, would certainly have increased the risks associated with failure. Possessing relatively little capacity or will for paramilitary action and still reeling from budget cuts, personnel losses, and a decade of drifting leadership, the Agency was reluctant to risk yet another failed covert action.

Before 2001 the military was hesitant to conduct operations, despite the fact that it had some capacity to do so. Since the founding of Joint Special Operations Command (JSOC) in 1980, the military had been honing a special operations capability for counterterrorism. Following the 1998 embassy bombings, it had developed plans for capture or kill operations against terrorist targets including bin Laden. Still, the military leadership remained hesitant to authorize complex quick-strike operations deep in hostile territory, pointing repeatedly to the disastrous effects of the 1980 hostage rescue attempt in Iran and the 1993 battle of Mogadishu memorialized in the book and movie *Black Hawk Down*. To complicate matters further, the military had no suitable bases in the region from which to conduct operations against bin Laden or maintain backup and search and rescue capabilities if the operation went poorly. US relations with Afghanistan's neighbors Iran and Pakistan were, to put it charitably, somewhere between strained and nonexistent, and the closest US military bases were a thousand miles away in the Persian Gulf.[7]

So despite the administration's numerous requests for more options to eliminate bin Laden and al-Qaeda, launching cruise missiles from offshore naval vessels was the only one to satisfy everyone's need to minimize risk. Unfortunately, even this effort by the Clinton administration failed to achieve its objective.

ADRIFT IN THE POST-COLD WAR ERA

"What are you going to do now that you've lost your best enemy?" Mikhail Gorbachev laconically inquired of national security advisor Colin Powell in April 1988.[8] Although he was referring to the introduction of glasnost and perestroika in the Soviet Union, Gorbachev's query suggested the problems top US policymakers would face when the USSR collapsed three years later. The shattering of the two-superpower framework of the previous half century left the US leadership struggling to construct a new national security strategy.

"The end of the Cold War was followed by a period of strategic drift," remarked Brent Scowcroft, who took over as national security advisor in 1989.[9] The first Bush administration promised that the period following the demise of the Soviet Union would provide a "peace dividend," implying that the implosion of America's greatest enemy had left the US with no tangible existential threats—and that a more peaceful world would emerge, with America as the undisputed beneficiary.

It was a hopeful time.

President George H. W. Bush had a full plate of foreign affairs conundrums, including managing the fallout from the collapse of the Soviet Union, the weakening of communism throughout Eastern Europe, and the first US confrontation with Saddam Hussein. However, Bush had no formal policy on counterterrorism because none seemed necessary. When Clinton took office in 1993, he similarly lacked a solid counterterrorism agenda. "The notion that terrorism might occur in the United States was completely new to us," wrote Richard Clarke, head of the NSC's Counterterrorism Security Group. "The National Security Council staff, which I had joined in 1992, had only ever concerned itself with foreign policy, defense, and intelligence issues."[10]

Although the world had changed, the US government hadn't. Congress did not reorganize its national security functions, and congressional committees did not change the way they handled foreign policy, defense, and intelligence. Emerging issues like international terrorism, which fell under the jurisdiction of fourteen different committees, fell between the cracks. Later, the 9/11 Commission concluded that terrorism was a "second- or third-order priority within the committees of Congress responsibility for national security," including the Senate and House Armed Services, Foreign Relations, and Intelligence Committees.[11]

One month after the Clinton administration took office, however, an event occurred that proved a harbinger of the changing nature of threats to the US. On February 26, 1993, a bomb placed beneath the North Tower of the World Trade Center in New York City ripped a hole through four stories, killing six people and injuring over a thousand. The damage, however, was not as great as the attackers intended. The leader of the attack, Ramzi Yousef, would later state he had hoped to collapse the towers into each other and kill some 500,000 people.[12]

FBI agents quickly deduced that a vehicle-borne explosive had caused the explosion. In fact, a truck containing over 1,300 pounds of explosive material detonated in the public parking garage. Sifting carefully through the debris, they discovered parts from the truck that had carried the bomb and traced the vehicle to a Ryder rental facility, where records indicated that Mohammad Salameh had rented the truck. Salameh, a cost-conscious international terrorist, attempted to reclaim the security deposit for the truck eight days later. Authorities quickly arrested him, and the FBI took three other conspirators into custody and, two years later, would catch up with Ramzi Yousef in Pakistan.

In hindsight, a speedy end to the 1993 WTC bombing had its disadvantages. Because the FBI quickly located and arrested the conspirators, and because the bombs killed relatively few people, many officials assumed that existing counterterrorism systems would effectively protect Americans. "It seemed like the counterterrorism machinery was working well," wrote Richard Clarke. "It wasn't. The FBI and CIA should have been able to answer my questions, 'Who *are* these guys?' but they still could not."[13] Because the IC did not fully identify the threat, neither the public nor the policy community could galvanize to counter it.

In the aftermath of the attack, the White House made no distinguishable policy shift regarding terrorism. "Clinton was aware of the threat and sometimes he would mention it," said Leon Panetta, Clinton's first-term chief of staff, who would lead the CIA and the Pentagon under Obama. But the big issues at the time were "Russia, Eastern bloc, Middle East peace, human rights, rogue nations and then terrorism."[14]

Complicating the issues, the White House maintained some distance from its intelligence bureaucracy, preferring to focus on domestic programs. Few major counterterrorism initiatives were proposed, and those that were—such as the FBI counterterrorism center—were not thoroughly implemented. President Clinton infamously avoided contact with CIA for almost two years after the bombing, not once meeting privately with CIA director James Woolsey. Woolsey later recalled that in 1994, when a two-seater Cessna aircraft crashed onto the White House lawn, administration staffers joked, "That must be Woolsey still trying to get an appointment."[15]

PICKING UP THE PACE

President Clinton announced in January 1995 that he would introduce "comprehensive legislation to strengthen our hand in combating terrorists, whether they strike at home or abroad." In February, he worked with Congress to introduce legislation targeting terrorist financing and easing restrictions on deporting terrorists.

A bitter wind arrived later that year when two separate incidents vaulted terrorism into the public view and onto the list of US government priorities. In March, members of the Japanese cult Aum Shinrikyo released sarin gas into three different lines of the Tokyo subway system, killing twelve and injuring over a thousand. Japanese authorities later discovered that the cult was capable of producing enough sarin to kill over 4 million people.[16] For the US government, the event demonstrated that a small group—with limited means and without backing from any nation—could develop its own chemical or biological weaponry and pose a significant threat.

In April, Timothy McVeigh, assisted by Terry Nichols, detonated a truck bomb in the Alfred P. Murrah federal building in downtown Oklahoma City and killed 168 people. It was the worst attack on American soil to date, and made a strong impact on the American psyche. One month later, the Clinton White House strengthened the proposed legislation, adding provisions boosting FBI surveillance authority and providing new money to the IC.

June 1995 brought the most significant change yet. That month, President Clinton issued Presidential Decision Directive (PDD) 39—"US Policy on Counterterrorism." The directive delineated the responsibilities of the various government agencies in deterring and responding to terrorism and stipulated that they give "the highest priority to developing effective capabilities to detect, prevent, defeat and manage the consequences of nuclear, biological, or chemical materials or weapons use by terrorists." PDD 39 also specified that terrorism should be viewed as a "threat to national security as well as a criminal act,"[17] a declaration that assigned the counterterrorism portfolio to the NSC, Department of Defense, and the CIA as well as specific law enforcement agencies.

The directive also led to the expansion of the CIA's rendition program, which empowered the agency to remove suspects from foreign countries without the benefit of the formal extradition process and bring them outside the country, even if that country did not officially approve of the transfer. "If we do not receive adequate cooperation from a state that harbors a terrorist whose extradition we are seeking, we shall take appropriate measures to induce cooperation," read the PDD. "Return of suspects by force may be effected without the cooperation of the host government."[18]

CIA Director John Deutch's 1996 speech "Worldwide Threat Assessment Brief" recognized a shift in the general nature of threats facing the US. "The potential for surprise is greater than it was in the days when we could focus our energies on the well-recognized instruments of Soviet power."[19] However, Deutch mentioned terrorism as a threat to US security only after he concluded his remarks on India-Pakistan, China, North Korea, Russia, Iraq, Iran, Bosnia, Libya, Sudan, Mexico, Haiti, Cuba, and WMD proliferation. Accordingly, by 1996, President Clinton sought assurances from other countries that they would not provide safe haven to terrorists and directed the IC to target al-Qaeda specifically, despite neither the CIA nor the administration considering the organization the biggest terrorist threat to the US at the time. According to the worldwide threat assessment, Iran was still the main terror threat to the US.[20]

These changes would spur Congress to stabilize the CIA budget and increase the FBI's starting in 1996. Also that year, Congress passed some of Clinton's proposals as the Antiterrorism and Effective Death Penalty Act. This legislation banned fund-raising by groups that supported terrorists or terrorist activities. It required all plastic explosives to contain chemical markers that indicate the presence of a bomb, expanded federal jurisdiction to prosecute and deport terrorist suspects, and strengthened penalties for terrorism. The bill, however, lacked a number of provisions requested by President Clinton, including increased wiretap and surveillance authority for the FBI.[21] Most of the act's provisions once again treated counterterrorism as a law enforcement activity, strengthening investigations that would occur *after* an attack.

In 1998, President Clinton signed PDD 62 and PDD 63, which reaffirmed the provisions set out in PDD 39. These two PDDs attempted to further define the role of governmental agencies in preventing and responding to terrorist attacks, sketched out recommendations regarding critical infrastructure protection, and promoted Clarke to national coordinator for security, infrastructure protection, and counterterrorism.[22] Although Clarke would become a major advocate of find-fix-finish operations against terrorists, particularly bin Laden, his new position only allowed him to "provide advice regarding budgets for counterterrorism programs and lead in the development of guidelines that might be needed for crisis management."[23]

TRIAL AND ERROR

The new presidential directives would soon be tested in real life. On August 7, 1998, less than three months after the signing of PDD 62 and 63, al-Qaeda struck American embassies in Kenya and Tanzania with simultaneous suicide bombings, events that together proved a watershed for all organizations working in the area of counterterrorism. While the US first assumed that it was the work of Iran-backed Lebanese terror group Hizbollah—Iran was implicated in the Khobar Towers bombing in Saudi Arabia two years before—and sent CIA experts on Hizbollah to inspect the bomb sites,[24] US intelligence eventually linked the bombings to al-Qaeda and bin Laden, and, almost as quickly, received information that several hundred terrorist leaders, including bin Laden, might be meeting at a training camp near Khost, Afghanistan.

In the months before the bombings, the Pentagon was asked to prepare a potential plan of attack on bin Laden and the al-Qaeda network. At the time, officials had suggested firing Tomahawk cruise missiles to destroy a series of targets. After the embassy bombings, that plan would become the NSC's main retaliatory option. On August 20, cruise missiles launched from US vessels in the Arabian Sea struck the terrorist camp near Khost, several other terrorist training camps, and one target in Sudan: al-Shifa, a pharmaceutical plant US intelligence suspected was producing chemical weapons materials.

Although most missiles hit their intended targets, the strike failed to injure bin Laden and was almost immediately criticized both domestically and internationally as an overly aggressive move by the White House. Ahmad Kamal, Pakistan's UN ambassador, warned that "such action, if condoned, acts as a precedent which can encourage other countries to pursue aggressive designs against their neighbors on flimsy or unsubstantiated pretexts."[25] The media scrutinized the motivations and evidentiary support for the decision, particularly after it was discovered that the intelligence on which the strikes had been based was "less than ironclad" by then CIA director George Tenet's own admission—a category into which almost all intelligence falls.[26] The *Economist* argued that "if it resorts to punishment raids without the best of reasons, and without the best of evidence, America risks finding itself increasingly friendless in truly important disputes."[27] Many alleged that President Clinton had attempted to use the strikes to distract attention from his dalliance with intern Monica Lewinsky.[28]

Following the initial strikes, the military developed plans for another round of missile attacks, code-named Operation Infinite Resolve. Other members of the NSC rejected all options for an ongoing campaign, pointing to the lack of political popularity of the strikes, worrying that such attacks would create increased Islamic extremism, and invoking a common argument of this era: that the targets were not worth the price of the expensive missiles needed to destroy them.[29]

The lack of sustained cruise missile strikes, however, did not indicate a lack of concern on the part of the government or of the IC. Fear of future terrorist attacks rose exponentially with the embassy bombings, and the analysis of the identity of the enemy shifted to more accurately reflect the threat from nonstate sponsors of terrorism, primarily al-Qaeda. The NSC called for other options for dealing with terrorism from both the IC and the military.

The Clinton administration ended with an event that illuminated the government's inability to neutralize the emerging threat. In October 2000 an al-Qaeda attack in Yemen killed seventeen Americans aboard the naval destroyer USS *Cole*. The NSC rejected a plan to strike al-Qaeda assets in Afghanistan in retaliation. Michael Sheehan, the State Department's counterterrorism coordinator, then made the now infamous remark: "What's it going to take to get them to hit al-Qaeda in Afghanistan? Does al-Qaeda have to hit the Pentagon?"[30]

President George W. Bush took control of national security concerns after a month of intense legal wrangling over his election results; the thirty-six days it had taken for the Supreme Court to decide to halt the recount of Florida ballots and declare Bush the winner cut the traditional presidential transition period in half. Already falling behind in hiring staff, his administration delayed establishing a terrorism policy, particularly as it related to Afghanistan, until regional policies could be established. Bush, like Clinton at the beginning of his term, had other concerns upon entering office. No al-Qaeda-focused NSC meeting would occur until September 4, 2001. Out of one hundred NSC meetings held by the NSC prior to 9/11, only two dealt with terrorism.[31]

Bush's national security advisor, Condoleezza Rice, wrote an article for the Jan/Feb 2000 issue of *Foreign Affairs*, "Promoting the National Interest." It foreshadowed the NSC focus on strategic relationships with the world's major state actors, including China and Russia.[32] "American policies must [maintain] a disciplined and consistent foreign policy that separates the important from the trivial," wrote Rice; terrorism, mentioned only briefly in the article, seems to have belonged to the latter in her opinion. Likewise, for the first months of the administration's tenure, substate actors attracted attention only from the members of the foreign policy team, which, in the words of General Don Kerrick, had the "same strategic perspective as the folks in the eighties" in how they thwarted "rogue state" actors.[33]

The NSC had debated the use of unmanned aerial vehicles throughout the summer and approved a draft of a presidential decision directive establishing a three-year strategy against al-Qaeda. That strategy, however, would never be adopted, and one week after the draft was approved, on 9/11, it would become obsolete. Both the Bush and Clinton administrations failed to act aggressively against nonstate actors, pointing to not only a lack of political will on the part of the executive branch but also to the CIA, the military, and the FBI being either ill equipped or unwilling to carry out the proposed actions.

BLEEDING THE CIA

In 1991, after the fall of the Soviet Union, some members of Congress proposed abolishing the CIA,[34] and although they were unsuccessful, in 1992 Congress made deep cuts to the IC budget.

As the Commission on the Roles and Capabilities of the United States Intelligence Community found, the cuts were significant. The overall intelligence budget declined by billions of dollars in the 1990s. While the exact amount remains classified, former DCI George Tenet claims that the CIA budget declined by about 18 percent overall.[35] In 1995, the FBI allegedly had more special agents in New York City than the CIA had case officers in the entire world.[36]

The limited funds made cold war–era satellite architecture an increasingly larger part of the intelligence budget. As staff levels fell, the IC fought to continue all proposed satellite projects—partly to take advantage of staggering advancements in satellites that could produce incredibly sharp images, and partly to satisfy the powerful military (and intelligence) industrial complex.[37] The National Reconnaissance Office (NRO) received an estimated $5 to 7 billion annually during the 1990s— an amount twice CIA's budget. In 1995 the *Washington Post* reported that the NRO had approximately $1 billion in *excess* funds.[38]

It was these funds that some members of Congress had intended to cut when they reduced overall IC funding; they argued that tracking troop and missile movements should no longer be the IC's main priorities. For example, the chairman of the Senate Select Committee on Intelligence (SSCI), David Boren, argued that the IC should focus on human intelligence: "A satellite photograph cannot detect the actions of a terrorist making explosive devices in an abandoned building."[39]

In fact, the CIA's capacity for HUMINT collection—which would aid in tracking individual substate actors such as al-Qaeda and Hizbollah— substantially decreased during the 1990s.[40] The CIA shuttered multiple stations and bases, including fifteen in Africa,[41] and the Agency was forced to shift its dwindling numbers of analysts and case officers from threat to threat. Shifting from crisis to crisis to attempt to put out fire after fire—or to prevent new fires from flaring—distracted the CIA from some big-picture concerns. The loss of personnel, combined with a lack of understanding about future threats, left it increasingly unable to create the capabilities necessary for the new era's challenges.

By the end of the 1990s, an executive branch increasingly aware of the threat of terrorism and al-Qaeda in particular would task the CIA to take the lead in actions it proposed against terrorism. From at least 1997 onward, the Agency emphasized counterterrorism issues, directing analysts to focus on tracking bin Laden and disrupting al-Qaeda's activities. In December 1998, DCI George Tenet wrote a directive to top CIA staffers: "We are at war. I want no resources or people spared in this effort, either inside CIA or the [Intelligence] Community."[42]

Yet few resources were actually shifted as a result of this directive. Although the Agency developed numerous proposals for aggressive operations against bin Laden and provided the targeting information for potential cruise missile strikes against al-Qaeda, almost all of these proposals remained just that: proposals. Before 9/11, the CIA never sent its own case officers after bin Laden, and, as Tenet would later admit, it was the CIA's seventh floor leadership who would halt almost all of the plans to capture or kill bin Laden, deeming the risks too great.[43]

A lack of resources was certainly part of the problem. Facing a dwindling staff and fewer assets abroad, HUMINT capabilities withered. And, despite an increase in resources and importance in the late 1990s, the CIA's Counterterrorist Center (CTC) remained a relative backwater in the Agency, vying with several competing intelligence priorities.[44] Those working in the CTC's Alec Station—the CIA's first "virtual station" founded in 1996 to deal solely with bin Laden—were considered obsessive in their concerns regarding al-Qaeda and criticized for their "crazed alarmism" regarding terrorism.[45] Underscoring that they were not taken seriously, the CIA placed an analyst from the Directorate of Intelligence to serve as the first head of Alec Station—a bureaucratic no-no, given that COS slots were almost exclusively reserved for officers from the Directorate of Operations. CIA veteran Robert Baer, who worked at the Agency from 1976 until 1997, claimed Alec Station "was the Siberia of CIA, located in a bleak office building in Tysons Corner, Virginia." He recalled, "If you needed someone important to pay attention to you, you had to drive down Route 123 to the main building in Langley. And even then you'd be lucky to get fifteen minutes of anyone's time."[46]

When the executive branch demanded action at the end of the decade, there would be other impediments as well, including the Agency's oft-cited inability to act decisively. The CIA recognized the threat posed by al-Qaeda, but by 1999 had neither infiltrated nor cultivated sources inside the group. CIA personnel complained about John Deutch's requirement that they had to get special permission if they intended to recruit assets who were under suspicion of substantial criminal activity—a serious impediment since most people willing to betray secrets usually had other skeletons in their closet. Moreover, Cofer Black, the CTC director in 1999, allegedly told Richard Clarke that he had to get special permission each time he wanted to send a case officer to Afghanistan, even into those regions friendly to the United States.[47]

Some called this caution practical and even necessary. Covert action, after all, had generated most of the CIA's bad publicity, despite the fact that it had consumed only a small percentage of the Agency's activities throughout its existence. Ill-starred operations such as the 1980s mining of Managua harbor in Nicaragua had taught CIA leaders that risk taking without appropriate political cover could land them in a hostile congressional hearing or behind the defendant's table in a courtroom. This had been the case with the Church and Pike committees, which investigated CIA participation in the overthrow of foreign governments, botched assassinations, the Watergate affair, and other Agency activities of the 1960s and 1970s. George Tenet pointed out the inconsistency: "A succession of administrations would tell them that they were expected to take risks and be aggressive. But if something went wrong, Agency officials faced disgrace, dismissal, and financial ruin."[48]

Agency staffers remember this as a time of frustration, for although the sense of urgency regarding terrorism continued to increase, no viable plan of action emerged. Agency operatives and management were uncertain whether they had the legal authority to try to kill bin Laden. Although President Clinton had, in fact, signed a memorandum of notification (MON), the CIA still believed that any operation against bin Laden must aim to capture him and could only kill him as an unintended side effect. These real and perceived legal impediments made planning against him more complicated, as Agency assets in Afghanistan—the Northern Alliance—found the proviso inhibiting to almost every plan they developed.[49]

An additional option that the NSC considered would later become a centerpiece of US strategy in the Middle East and South Asia: unmanned aerial strikes. At the time, however, when—and whether—to deploy armed unmanned aerial vehicles (UAVs), originally developed for reconnaissance purposes, was a titanic struggle among the CIA, the military, and the NSC leadership.[50]

In September 2000, the CIA and the military jointly launched a test run of the unarmed Predator drone over Afghanistan. The results were promising. The UAV's cameras twice spotted a tall man in white robes at bin Laden's compound, Tarnak Farms. But after the Afghan media and the Taliban took note of the drone's appearances, CIA leadership expressed concern. Agency officers concluded that they would only be able to conduct another five missions before the Taliban shot down a drone, and, according to a deal they reached with the Air Force, the CIA would foot half the bill, or $1.5 million, of any lost aircraft.[51] For the CIA, this made reconnaissance flights too costly, and the NSC, the military, and the CIA decided to put off further test runs until the UAV could be outfitted with lethal weaponry.[52]

The CIA's reticence to engage in the project likely slowed the pace of drone deployment and indicated the bureaucracy's aversion to counterterrorism innovations.[53] According to most accounts, some Agency officers and members of senior leadership (who would eventually go along with the plan) were wary of deploying an armed drone until they understood who would fire the missiles and what the chain of command would be for strike authorization.[54] One CIA official claims that the general perception at the Near East Division of the program was "Oh, these harebrained CTC ideas. This is going to be a disaster."[55]

INSTITUTIONAL INERTIA AT FBI

While the CIA attempted to combat terrorists abroad, the FBI, as the premier US law enforcement agency, took the lead in domestic counterterrorism operations. This area—as compared to foreign intelligence and military operations—was found by the 9/11 Commission to have "the most serious weaknesses in agency capabilities." Two bureaucratic issues emerged repeatedly as root causes of this lack of preparedness: culture and resources.

The Clinton administration viewed the FBI as integral to counterterrorism efforts but prioritized collecting evidence for the prosecution of terrorist attack perpetrators over stopping them before attacks happened. Before 9/11, the FBI possessed a weak domestic counterterrorism intelligence capability. The Bureau employed underqualified intelligence analysts, developed only a small number of intelligence sources, conducted limited intelligence-related surveillance, employed few translators, and maintained "woefully inadequate" information-sharing systems.[56]

Ironically, this phenomenon was exacerbated by FBI successes. As well as the 1993 World Trade Center attack, the FBI had successfully investigated the 1988 bombing of Pan American Flight 103 over Lockerbie, Scotland, in which the strength of the Justice Department's evidence forced Libya to admit responsibility, demonstrating that the FBI could root out those responsible for an attack and giving the appearance that the FBI could protect US citizens from terrorism. The decade prior to 9/11 also saw the successful conviction of five of the perpetrators of the first WTC bombing; Timothy McVeigh of the Oklahoma City bombing; and Omar Abdel-Rahman, also known as the "Blind Sheik," who had encouraged his followers to attack various New York City landmarks.

Although the Foreign Intelligence Surveillance Act (FISA) of 1978 authorized the Bureau to surveil "agents of a foreign power" for the purpose of collecting foreign intelligence information, a series of procedures and institutionalized beliefs led many agents to believe that passing intelligence to other agents conducting criminal investigations—let alone other agencies, such as the CIA—was impermissible. Many agents claimed this phenomenon, informally referred to as "the wall," compromised key investigations. According to Attorney General John Ashcroft, "the wall specifically impeded the investigation into Zacarias Moussaoui, Khalid al-Midhar and Nawaf al-Hazmi.[57] Records indicate that after the FBI arrested Moussaoui, agents became suspicious of his interest in commercial aircraft and sought approval for a criminal warrant to search his computer. The warrant was then rejected because FBI officials feared breaching the wall."[58]

Within the FBI, terrorism investigations received relatively little attention.[59] FBI agents were rewarded in large part on the basis of arrest, prosecution, and indictment statistics. Counterterrorism operations provided few opportunities to achieve high numbers in these areas, particularly operations that were disruptive or preventative. Most staff and resources were, therefore, assigned to the Bureau's traditional activities targeting organized criminal syndicates, violent individuals, and drug-related crime where agents routinely conducted physical and electronic surveillance operations, developed sources and informants, ran undercover operations, and invested significant resources to develop an understanding of traditional criminal organizations.[60]

This is not to say, of course, that no attempts were made to shift away from the law enforcement paradigm. After the 1993 World Trade Center bombing, FBI director Louis Freeh increased the number of legal attaché offices abroad, created the FBI counterterrorism division, and arranged for exchanges and cooperation between the FBI and the CIA. He argued that "merely solving this type of crime is not enough; it is equally important that the FBI thwart terrorism before such acts can be perpetrated."[61] Unfortunately several of Director Freeh's other policies hindered his counterterrorism goals, including his emphasis on a decentralized FBI characterized by strong local efforts but little information sharing.

In May 1998, three months before the African embassy bombings, the FBI would again attempt to force institutional change, announcing a strategic five-year plan that made national security and counterterrorism its top priorities. The plan stipulated that the Bureau shift resources to bolster its preventative counterterrorism capability, including intelligence collection, analysis, dissemination, and nationwide information sharing. To meet these goals, the FBI created new investigative services, counterterrorism, and counterintelligence divisions in 1999, oblivious to the findings of internal reports that 66 percent of analysts were not qualified to perform their job. The Department of Justice's inspector general would later find that although the Bureau's counterterrorism *budget* tripled during the mid-1990s, counterterrorism *spending* had remained relatively flat during the late 1990s, and by 2001 only 6 percent of the Bureau's personnel worked in counterterrorism.[62] Unsurprisingly, by 2003, many facets of the reorganization had not been implemented and of those that had, several had fallen short of the mark.

The FBI had other institutional and bureaucratic demons to conquer. In 2000, the Bureau began its ill-fated Trilogy project, an attempt to update its information management and sharing systems, which had been designed and installed in 1995 using technology from the 1980s. These shockingly deficient systems were critical to the ability of FBI agents to collect the necessary information to identify and communicate threats within US borders. Before 2001, FBI agents had little ability to effectively search or store information or intelligence contained in its files within and across field offices, severely hampering its ability to identify and track potential challenges.[63] Director Freeh infamously avoided using computers as much as possible. As such, after the 9/11 attacks, the FBI had to send photos of hijackers by mail as they were unable to email them.[64] After the project started, however, the Bureau discovered that its computers were in even worse repair than originally anticipated, and, by 2003, the project was declared a "large disaster" by the chair of the Senate Appropriations Committee: "FBI software and hardware contracts for Trilogy have essentially become gold-plated. The cost is soaring. The schedule is out of control."[65] By 2005, the Bureau gave up and scrapped the project.

TAKING THE CONVENTIONAL ROAD AT THE PENTAGON

As early as 1996, the US armed forces were asked to craft a plan to eliminate bin Laden. In response, the Joint Chiefs presented the NSC with a plan to strike a number of buildings in Sudan where bin Laden was supposedly living at the time. While still outlining the plan, however, the military briefer conducting the presentation reported that the Pentagon recommended against it. In response, national security adviser Anthony

Lake allegedly told the briefer, "I can see why. This isn't stealth. There is nothing quiet or covert about this. It's going to war with Sudan." The briefer allegedly replied, "That's what we do, sir. If you want covert, there's the CIA."[66]

For the military, the bureaucratic lanes in the road were clear. "The Pentagon wanted to fight and win the nation's wars, as Colin Powell used to say," said Michael Sheehan, a former counterterrorism coordinator at the State Department. "But those were wars against the armies of other nations—not against diffuse transnational terrorist threats. So terrorism was seen as a distraction that was CIA's job, even though terrorists were attacking military targets and personnel. The Pentagon way to treat terrorism against Pentagon assets abroad was to cast it as a force protection issue."[67] The military waged war and war had traditionally been fought with state actors—not with nebulous terrorist organizations. During the late 1990s, the military would accordingly focus on the war in Kosovo and the Desert Fox bombing campaign against Iraq, "traditional" conflicts using conventional capabilities against troops and weapons systems.

Many officials argued that the use of military might to target terrorist cells presented a serious problem of scale. Former defense secretary William Cohen and former chairman of the Joint Chiefs General Hugh Shelton told the 9/11 Commission that cruise missiles were too expensive to be used against the "jungle gym" terrorist training camps built from "rope ladders" in Afghanistan.[68]

This does not mean, of course, that the military did not have to grapple with terrorism. Its forces had sustained a number of terrorist attacks during the 1980s and 1990s, including devastating attacks on barracks in Beirut, Lebanon, in 1983 that killed hundreds of US and French servicemen. On June 25, 1996, assailants attacked the Khobar Towers housing complex in Khobar, Saudi Arabia, killing nineteen Americans. Although Iran was suspected of having a part in the bombing, the military took no retributive action it would characterize as "counterterrorism." Instead, the military focused on defensive measures, force protection, and consequence management.[69]

Indeed, the military would take steps to improve force protection after the Khobar Towers attack and the later bombing of the USS *Cole*, but some officials believed that these attacks were an unfortunate consequence of being the last superpower standing. One "very senior [Special Operations Forces] officer who had served on the Joint Staff in the 1990s" allegedly said that he had often been told that terrorist strikes were "a small price to pay for being a superpower."[70]

The inevitability of terrorist attacks and the Pentagon's conception of the pursuit of terrorists as inappropriate would mean that political concerns often overrode a need for retribution. For example, after the Khobar Towers attacks, US officials took no action against Iran for its complicity in the attack. Ten years after the bombing, Louis Freeh would write in a *Wall Street Journal* opinion piece, "Mr. Clinton and his national security advisor, Sandy Berger, had no interest in confronting the fact that Iran had blown up the towers." They did not want to take on Iran and risk being forced into military intervention.

Other sources agree that more traditional political and diplomatic concerns triumphed in this case. According to the conservative *Weekly Standard*, when an aide presented a plan for a series of retaliatory military strikes to a high-level meeting in the Pentagon, one senior policymaker allegedly responded: "Are you out of your mind? You're telling me that our Middle East policy is not important and that it's more important to go clean out terrorists? Don't you understand what's going on in terms of our Middle East policy? You're talking about going after terrorists backed by Iran? You just don't understand."[71]

That particular plan included a significant reliance on Special Operations Forces (SOF), the capability the Pentagon would have deployed had it attempted a kill or capture operation. Highly trained and elite, Special Operations units, under the command of the US Special Operations Command (SOCOM), included 45,000 active and reserve personnel, 2 percent of US military personnel overall, by 2001.[72]

SOCOM was created in the aftermath of the disastrous operation in Iran commonly referred to as Desert One, when military personnel attempted to rescue fifty-two hostages trapped in the American embassy. The ad hoc operation ended in tragedy when eight US servicemembers died in a midair collision. The military hoped that the new SOCOM would enable more effective cooperation between the branches of the US services to avoid such disasters in the future. They weren't entirely successful, as subsequent US operations in the early 1990s in Somalia would prove. In front of the 9/11 Commission, military authorities would repeatedly reference the two operations in their explanations as to why the military sought to avoid smaller, unsupported military operations in the 1990s.

The military preferred to respond to terrorism conventionally, retaliating against the state sponsors of terrorism as opposed to the substate actors, a strategy that—unlike special ops—appeared to work. In 1986, a bomb planted in a German disco killed two US servicemen and injured fifty others. Within days, the Reagan administration had linked the bombing to Muammar Qadhafi's Libyan state and, in retaliation, launched air strikes against the Libyan cities of Tripoli and Benghazi. Although later intelligence would indicate that Qadhafi's interest in terrorism continued after the attack, the strikes were declared successful at the time.[73]

Experience from the early Clinton administration reinforced the apparent efficacy of a conventional response. In April 1993, days before George H. W. Bush was to visit Kuwait, the country's intelligence officials discovered a car bomb allegedly intended to assassinate the former president. In the months following, the FBI linked the plot to the Iraqi Intelligence Service (IIS), and President Clinton ordered a cruise missile strike on IIS headquarters. US intelligence discovered little direct Iraqi involvement in international terrorism from that point on.[74] For the military the lessons of the 1990s were clear: conventional action works, and covert action doesn't.

Even as the executive branch began to recognize that the threat of nonstate organizations required the conceptualization of new military options, the Pentagon continued to recommend against the deployment of special operations personnel. Some military leaders doubted the ability of special operations teams to successfully conduct counterterrorism operations. More often, however, senior military brass intent on keeping the military's role limited to traditional war-fighting activities relied on a false belief in Washington that the military had no authority to conduct covert operations.

Because the FBI had defined counterterrorism for many years as a law enforcement issue, some Defense Department officials claimed that the military could not intervene. "If you declare terrorism a criminal activity, you take from Defense any statutory authority to be the leader in responding," said one official. "Lawyers at the Defense Department . . . argued that we have no statutory authority because this is essentially a criminal matter."[75]

The basis of this belief rests in an interpretation of law: whereas military operations are authorized in Title 10 of the US Code, covert action is covered in Title 50, which deals with the IC. As a result, many military leaders, policymakers, and national security lawyers have concluded that the CIA had sole responsibility for covert action. Moreover, the military required special authorization from the president or Congress to use force outside of specified combat zones and, with the exception of the missile strikes in Sudan and Afghanistan, prior to 9/11, this authorization was not forthcoming.

Even at the time, however, this interpretation rested on poor analysis, as Title 50 states that the written finding used to support each covert action "shall specify each department, agency, or entity of the United States Government authorized to fund or otherwise participate in any significant way in such action"—it does not specify that only the CIA can carry out covert actions.[76] But according to one member of the NSC's counterterrorism group, the military would not budge from this understanding; even when presented with a legal opinion to the contrary, the NSC member said, "They would say, 'Well, we're not going to do it anyway. It's a matter of policy that we don't.'"[77] Some argued that the military only made the legal argument to provide justification to decline sending SOF to combat terrorism. "The Joint Staff was very happy for the administration to take a law-enforcement view," said one Pentagon official. "They didn't want to put special ops troops on the ground."[78]

Even though the military had conceived of SOF as small, stealthy, and independent units, after the Mogadishu imbroglio, the military demanded better force protection for special ops, including air support. But there were few bases that could provide the necessary logistical support for operations against terrorist hotspots such as Afghanistan and few allies that would allow US forces to cross their airspace.

Although the lack of infrastructure would hinder SOF deployment, many at the Pentagon would argue that poor intelligence collection posed an even bigger challenge. SOF employed an "intelligence drives operations" approach[79]—the information generated the operational possibilities and not the other way around. Since the CIA was not producing the appropriate type of intelligence, the Pentagon's objections created the intellectual architecture that made it all but impossible to deploy special operations forces to track down terrorists who had attacked Americans.[80]

Officials on both sides of the political fence would present the military as a force of obstruction in its stalwart support of cruise missiles as the only option. At least one Pentagon official agreed, claiming that "the Joint Staff was the biggest foot-dragger on all of this counterterrorism business."[81] The 9/11 Commission report concluded, "At no point before 9/11 was the Department of Defense fully engaged in the mission of countering al-Qaeda, though this was perhaps the most dangerous foreign enemy then threatening the United States."[82]

THE EFFORTS of every agency within the US government to develop and deploy a robust counterterrorism strategy prior to 2001 was ultimately stymied by a host of creative, bureaucratic, and political hurdles. Institutional inertia and culture, lack of political and public will, legal concerns, limited resources, and an ill-aligned infrastructure would combine to create an environment in which the executive was denied options to counter the new threat. Nothing seemed likely to change the state of affairs short of a severe shock to the political system—one that occurred on a bright blue Tuesday morning in September 2001.

CHAPTER 3

THE SEARCH FOR MR. #3

We are at war.

—GEORGE W. BUSH, SEPTEMBER 12, 2001

The attacks on New York City and Washington DC, and the crash near the small town of Shanksville, Pennsylvania, rocked America and its political leaders. With further terror strikes possibly on the horizon, Congress prepared to respond with legislation. But what were legislators responding to and what laws should they pass?

The White House, with the Pentagon still smoldering across the Potomac, provided a quick answer: on the night of September 12, the Bush administration handed Congress a forcefully worded document that called for unlimited preemptive authority to attack America's enemies. Not only did it call for the authority to crush the terrorists involved in the attacks that had occurred the day before, but it also authorized the president to "deter and preempt any future acts of terrorism or aggression against the United States."

To its credit, Congress balked at the unprecedented power grab and on September 14 responded by excising that phrase in its sweeping Authorization for Use of Military Force (AUMF), allowing America to pursue al-Qaeda worldwide.

The final wording of the legislation was both short and vague. It authorized the president:

> To use all necessary and appropriate force against those nations, organizations, or persons he determines planned, authorized, committed, or aided the terrorist attacks that occurred on September 11, 2001, or harbored such organizations or persons, in order to prevent any future acts of international terrorism against the United States by such nations, organizations or persons.

The AUMF is the primary legal infrastructure—along with a classified Presidential Finding that authorized the CIA to capture or kill al-Qaeda members—that undergirds America's fight against al-Qaeda. But despite its ambiguities, this document did not authorize endless war or limitless executive authority. In fact, one could view the Bush administration's prosecution of al-Qaeda not simply as a response to the terrorist attacks but also a reaction to, and restructuring of, blurry legal boundaries to accommodate the modern terrorist threat.

As Mieke Eoyang, defense policy adviser to the late Senator Ted Kennedy, remarked, "In the days after 9/11, people went 'big and broad' because we didn't know what we wanted, what we needed."[1] Eoyang continued, "When Congress passed AUMF, they had no way of knowing how the Bush Administration would stretch that document."[2]

In fact, the White House tried a final fast grab for authority after the Senate passed its version of the legislation. As Senator Tom Daschle recounted years later, "Literally minutes before the Senate cast its vote, the administration sought to add the words 'in the United States' and after 'appropriate force' in the agreed-upon text. This last-minute change would have given the president broad authority to exercise expansive powers not just overseas . . . but right here in the United States, potentially against American citizens."[3]

FIRST STEPS

The war was now on, and America's major effort to disrupt and destroy al-Qaeda centered on the group's leadership. This, of course, meant targeting

Osama bin Laden and his deputy, Ayman al-Zawahiri, who were chased by the CIA and Special Forces into the caves of Tora Bora as the Taliban regime in Afghanistan that had permitted al-Qaeda to operate uninhibitedly.

After 9/11 bin Laden and Zawahiri mainly provided motivation and strategic guidance. The day-to-day work of approving and organizing new terrorist operations as well as training recruits and inserting them into action fell to al-Qaeda's operational commander—its number 3 in the public's perception—the point of contact between the organization's strategic and tactical wings.

The US initially had two interconnected objectives in its counterterrorism strategy: disrupting and dismantling al-Qaeda's operations worldwide, and capturing or killing the leaders responsible for the attacks on New York and Washington. Tracking down the number 3 leader was the key to achieving both. As head of operations, he would know the details and the timing of future attacks, as well as the locations and identities of cells worldwide. And as the organization's most active senior leader, he would be one of a few who knew the location of al-Qaeda's top men.

Following the US invasion of Afghanistan, al-Qaeda's operational commander became even more important as bin Laden and Zawahiri most likely took refuge in the mountainous, ungoverned area in the northwest of Pakistan. Fearing discovery by US and allied intelligence agencies, bin Laden and Zawahiri were reduced to issuing ad hoc video recordings and communicating via human courier to the rest of their global operation. As they focused on their own safety, the operational number 3 commander became responsible for planning, funding, and coordinating the attacks that would eliminate apostate regimes throughout the world and establish a new global caliphate.

Organizing al-Qaeda's various cells required internal and external communication efforts, and communication meant vulnerability. Again and again, the US tracked al-Qaeda's commanders through their communications systems—by cell phone, satellite phone, e-mail, landline, facsimile, and even face-to-face meetings.[4] No medium was safe. To make matters worse for al-Qaeda in the early days of 2002, the US was offering millions of dollars in the form of bounties for information on its leaders' movements and whereabouts; one good tip had the potential to yield more money than most families in South Asia would see in a lifetime.

The pressure from the US put the number 3 man in a precarious position: the more active he was in directing operations, the more targeting information he provided potentially endangering himself and others. But the more he stayed hidden, the more the movement risked becoming paralyzed and irrelevant.

However, the US initially faced several disadvantages. First, US analysts had only a rudimentary understanding of the organization, still needing to sort through information on key personnel and operations—to say nothing of what any given person actually looked like. Second, US military forces were trained in fighting conventional wars against conventional armies, and that was reflected in America's force structure, chain of command, and combat regulations. Even when resourceful commanders were prepared to adapt to the new enemy, they remained ensnared within a massive bureaucracy that had been shaped around a different kind of threat. Finally, the US was constrained by concerns that had little relevance for al-Qaeda, including international law, questions of sovereignty, winning elections, and layers of bureaucratic oversight.

Over time, however, the balance shifted. Both civilian and military personnel became more seasoned in the tactics and organization of al-Qaeda, and began working more closely together to develop a template for tightening the noose around senior leaders. Military and intelligence personnel were freed from some of the legal and bureaucratic constraints that hindered them. This led to faster operations and enhanced cooperation with countries such as Pakistan and Yemen that put pressure on the safe haven that al-Qaeda's commanders initially enjoyed. Fresh espionage sources and cutting-edge surveillance tools such as armed UAVs created an aura of insecurity around operational leaders and their entourages, forcing them to devote their time and energy to avoiding detection and rooting out security leaks. Eventually, the once coveted job of al-Qaeda's operational commander seemed like a certain death sentence.

EARLY WINDFALL: MOHAMMAD ATEF (KILLED, NOVEMBER 2001)

The first of bin Laden's top lieutenants to be eliminated after 9/11 was Mohammad Atef (Abu Hafs al-Masri), an operational commander and trusted aide. Quiet, cautious, and determined, Atef was well-known to US intelligence at the time of the 9/11 attacks. He was a founding member of al-Qaeda and was widely believed to have had a major role in the 1998 suicide attacks on the US embassies in Kenya and Tanzania.[5] He had been on the FBI's most wanted list for three years and had a $5 million price on his head.[6]

Atef was killed, along with his guard Abu Ali al-Yafi'i and six others, in an air strike on a house near Kabul on November 15, 2001, probably while attending a meeting with Taliban leaders. He was in his early- to mid-fifties at the time of his death—a thirty-year veteran of terrorist campaigns against the Soviet Union, Egypt, the US, and other "apostate regimes" around the world.

Atef began his career as an Egyptian policeman before falling sway to radical ideas. According to one of bin Laden's sons who knew him personally, Atef became disgruntled with Egypt's sclerotic political landscape and joined the Egyptian Islamic Jihad (EIJ).[7] At least one source claims he was expelled from the police force for suspected fundamentalism.[8] Sources disagree as to whether he met EIJ's leader, Ayman al-Zawahiri, while still in Egypt[9] or after he left to join the fight against the Soviet invasion of Afghanistan in the mid-1980s.[10] Either way, it was Zawahiri who introduced Atef to bin Laden. Atef went on to forge close ties with the organization during campaigns in Afghanistan, Sudan, and Somalia[11] and became the deputy military commander of al-Qaeda in Africa in the early 1990s, allegedly helping to organize and arm part of the anti-US forces in Somalia in 1992.[12] He took the role of al-Qaeda's military leader after the accidental drowning of Ali Amin Rashidi in 1994, and was in charge of its Afghan training camps until the time of the 2001 attacks, according to Egyptian security sources.[13] Atef also appeared to be in charge of bin Laden's physical security and conducted searches of journalists meeting bin Laden in 1998.[14]

Despite his size—at 6 foot 4, he was a tough, physically formidable figure—Atef was described as "a very quiet man," "modest," "devout," "serious-minded," and "disciplined."[15] Numerous observers commented on Atef's intelligence, including bin Laden himself.[16] According to one account, Atef was being groomed to take over al-Qaeda in the event of bin Laden's death. In early 2001 Atef's daughter married one of bin

Laden's sons in a move that was intended to seal his succession within the group.[17]

Atef was concerned with operational security. In 1994, for instance, he refused to inform American double agent Ali Mohammed of the name and passport he would be using at any given time,[18] and in 1998 he warned a Palestinian journalist not to photograph anyone at the camp other than bin Laden and Zawahiri for security reasons.[19] As a strategist, Atef demonstrated a nuanced understanding of al-Qaeda's enemies and world politics. While in Sudan, he conducted a study which concluded that aircraft hijackings were a bad idea, as they were engineered to allow the negotiation of hostages in exchange for prisoners rather than inflicting mass casualties.[20] In another study, he analyzed the Taliban leadership, recognizing their common background and loyalty, but acknowledging their weaknesses as well.[21] He speculated on the strategic role that the Afghan Arabs and Taliban could play in toppling the regimes of Pakistan and Iran,[22] and concluded that strategic interests would lead the United States to favor an oil pipeline through Afghanistan in the near future.[23]

A CIA Predator UAV initiated the attack on Atef from high overhead.[24] The UAV's pilot noticed a convoy of vehicles stopped at a ramshackle three-story structure near Gardez; operators observed several other pickup trucks, military vehicles, and guards idling in the parking lot. According to one report, the CIA knew that a secret meeting with Taliban leaders would be held at that location but not the time.[25] With the arrival of the VIP convoy, the time was ripe to strike. The Predator relayed imagery of the location to CIA officers, who then coordinated with the military to call in strikes from Navy F/A-18s operating from an aircraft carrier in the Gulf.[26] The planes arrived in position and dropped two or three GBU-15 smart bombs guided by infrared cameras in their noses. After the strike, the Predator surveyed the damage, firing Hellfire missiles into the target as survivors emerged, then circled again over the area to confirm the job was complete.[27] According to one account, close to one hundred people were killed.[28] The armed Predator had only been operational for about a month; this may have been one of the first strikes to target al-Qaeda leaders directly.[29]

The loss of Atef was not just symbolic; he was a key source of experience, insight, and intelligence for al-Qaeda.

The successful tracking and elimination of a key al-Qaeda commander was a remarkable victory for the US, coming only two months after the attacks in New York and Washington and only one month after military operations began in Afghanistan. Atef was not a household name like bin Laden, but he was important within the organization as the mind behind much of al-Qaeda's strategic and operational planning. And yet the strike may have been mostly luck.

The Pentagon described the strike as a "pre-planned mission"—one of many on a list[30]—and secretary of defense Donald Rumsfeld seemed unprepared to discuss Atef's death the following day.[31] US intelligence analysts probably knew that they were tracking down al-Qaeda and Taliban leaders, but not specifically focusing on Atef.[32] It was only when the US later intercepted communications from al-Qaeda members lamenting Atef's death, that they deduced the identity of their victim.[33] According to one British official, an al-Qaeda operative broke security protocol after the attack and used a satellite phone to report on the casualties, a call that was intercepted by US and British signals intelligence.[34] Atef's death was separately confirmed by a human source,[35] and the Taliban ambassador to Pakistan publicly announced it on November 18.[36] Even so, for months after the strike Atef remained on the FBI's and the CIA's list of most wanted al-Qaeda leaders—suggesting that they remained unsure about who had died.[37]

Atef's elimination may be linked to the defection of Mullah Mohammed Khaksar, once the Taliban's deputy interior minister and head of the Taliban's intelligence service, who was later gunned down in Kandahar in 2006.[38] Khaksar remained in Kabul as the rest of the Taliban fled—having negotiated a deal to switch sides before the Northern Alliance took the city—and had offered to help the US oust Taliban leadership even before 9/11.[39] He almost certainly had credible information on safe houses, communications networks, escape routes, and operating procedures, and had probably maintained a secret dialogue with the Northern Alliance and, to a lesser degree, the CIA.[40] In 2002 Khaksar complained that while he was ready to pass information on top al-Qaeda leaders and hideouts in Afghanistan to the US, nobody ever contacted him.[41]

While the US had been lucky in fixing Atef, the means of finishing him may not have been ideal. A key element in the intelligence cycle is to debrief captured terrorist leaders. As one node reveals another, the whole network can be mapped out and taken down. Atef would have made an attractive capture for interrogation; as al-Qaeda's senior operational planner, he would have known a wide section of the organization and had insight into all of its operations and capabilities. However, Atef was a hardened ideological fighter with few readily apparent weaknesses that might be exploited for advantage. He thoroughly believed in the cause, and possessed both a powerful physique and a formidable mind likely able to weave a web of deception even under duress.

THE WRONG GUY: ABU ZUBAYDAH (CAPTURED, MARCH 2002)

If Atef's death appeared to demonstrate the power and reach of the US, the months to come seemed to highlight its limitations. Uncomfortable questions began to emerge: What would American forces do with individuals caught on the battlefield? Given the running conflict in Afghanistan, and the AUMF that authorized the almost unfettered ability for the US to prosecute the metastasizing war on terror, American forces, military or civilian, would inevitably capture more than a few suspects. Where would they go?

Two months after the 9/11 attacks saw allied Afghan and American forces shattering Taliban defenses in and around the capital, Kabul, and the final showdown with al-Qaeda was thought to be imminent. Bin Laden was still loitering in the city during the first week of the month, and even gave an interview to a Pakistani journalist Hamid Mir on November 8.[42] "Mark my words," the al-Qaeda chief said, "[the Americans] can kill me anytime but they cannot capture me alive; they can claim victory only if they get me alive but if they will just capture my dead body, it will be a defeat."[43] Four days later, Kabul fell to the Northern Alliance, but bin Laden and his al-Qaeda comrades managed to escape the tightening vise around the city and fled east toward Jalalabad. America's endgame in Afghanistan was in sight—or so President Bush thought. The pivotal battle for Tora Bora, where bin Laden and his colleagues would slip away and eventually traverse the mountains into neighboring Pakistan—was still a month away.

Bush decided to answer one of the questions by casting battlefield-captured individuals into a legally ambiguous space. On November 13, the day after Kabul fell to the Northern Alliance, he signed a classified order—drafted by the vice president's gruff, politically conservative adviser David Addington and White House counsel Alberto Gonzales a week before—authorizing military commissions to hold and interrogate the hundreds of men captured on the battlefield.[44]

The order's wording allowed great latitude and was remarkable for its underlying belief in maximalist executive power. The resulting military commission system could cast a wide net for individuals who were linked to al-Qaeda or conspired to participate in acts of terrorism. A panel would determine what sort of evidence was admissible, and decisions it made were final.[45] Detainees could be put to death if found guilty. Gonzales later wrote in a memo "this new paradigm renders obsolete [the Geneva Conventions'] strict limitations on questioning of enemy prisoners."[46]

These legal deliberations—the first of many—occurred behind closed doors while news of terror suspects being transferred soon spread. After 9/11, the White House was still stumbling to determine how to solve this new national security challenge but also saw an opportunity to concentrate diffused national security power in the hands of the president—to a degree not seen since the scandals of the Vietnam era.

More than one commentator found this disturbing, as the legal paradigm for prosecuting this new conflict continued to be hidden from view. "In the beginning," recalled Mieke Eoyang, "it was all about theory. But when theory met reality, it was way outside what was the normal operating procedure for the US government."[47] Perhaps the president relied on goodwill from a scared public amenable to his secrecy and overreach? "9/11 was not an excuse for what happened afterwards," retorted Eoyang. "Remember, all this happened outside of public debate. There was no reason to create a legal framework in secret—the implementation can be secret, but the law itself should never be secret."[48]

And where would this exciting new legal paradigm unfold? The Pentagon selected America's oldest overseas military base—the Guantanamo

Bay naval station in Cuba—as the final stop for its captives in this shadowy conflict. Newly captured individuals, clad in orange jumpsuits, taken directly from the faraway battlefields of Afghanistan, began arriving at this tropical facility in early January 2002.

WILLIAM ARKIN, a military consultant to Human Rights Watch and instructor at the US Air Force's School of Advanced Airpower Studies, said that in the first two weeks of bombing, fewer than 10 percent of strikes directly targeted al-Qaeda; the campaign was set up as if the enemy were Iraq or Russia.[49] The US was trying to fight a conventional war against an unconventional foe. The Pentagon's tactics had been strikingly effective in defeating the Taliban on the battlefield, but were much less effective in identifying senior leaders or eliminating al-Qaeda as a movement. "The inability to neutralize the core leadership of al-Qaeda and the Taliban in the first six months . . . is clearly the war on terrorism's single biggest failure," wrote Rohan Gunaratna, a consultant to the United Nations on terrorism.[50]

CIA and other members of the IC still knew little about the identities and roles of key individuals in the organization—information that could only be gathered through human or technical means, not by killing prisoners outright. Detractors further complained that Special Forces frequently arrived too late in areas where al-Qaeda fighters had been hiding, and that the overreliance on local Afghan allies probably allowed bin Laden and other senior leaders to escape.[51]

US military officials defended their strategy: the war had successfully ousted the Taliban, destroyed al-Qaeda's safe haven, and deprived the terrorist network of the freedom to operate, train, and meet in Afghanistan.[52] This was true to an extent, but many intelligence analysts believed that the damage had been insufficient to cripple the terrorist network. "As people have been killed or captured, we have seen temporary blips in al-Qaeda operational activity, but not an overall decline," said one American official.[53] After a leader was eliminated, another one stepped in to take his place and the organization remained strong.

Based on the organizational structure of al-Qaeda that was known at the time, several sources believed that Egyptian national Saif al-Adel would inherit Atef's duties as operational commander.[54] Formerly a colonel in the Egyptian army, al-Adel was an experienced operative and had risen to become Atef's right-hand man, as well as Zawahiri's personal friend. Operational duties were often passed within narrow ethnic cliques; since al-Adel was Atef's deputy and, like Atef and Zawahiri, an Egyptian, the fit made sense. But by early 2002, al-Adel had seemingly disappeared into Iran, and US officials were focusing on Palestinian Abu Zubaydah (Zayn al-Abidin Muhammad Husayn) as the new number 3.[55]

Abu Zubaydah grew up in a middle-class Palestinian family in Saudi Arabia. As a teenager he relocated to the West Bank to join the Palestinian uprising against Israel.[56] There he became enamored with militant causes. Too young to be a veteran of the struggle against the Soviets, he traveled to Afghanistan in 1991 and apparently fought in the civil war that followed the Soviet retreat.[57] It was during this internecine conflict in Afghanistan that bin Laden came to know him and, over the next ten years, he acted as an administrator and facilitator for camps and guesthouses serving bin Laden's network.[58] He also recruited Arab fighters in Pakistan and arranged their travel to various training camps and the frontlines of Bosnia and Chechnya.[59] By mid-2001, the CIA was tracking him as a senior al-Qaeda operative—citing his actions in pre-9/11 briefings to national security adviser Condoleezza Rice.[60]

CIA agents would later describe him as intelligent, confident, self-assured, and disciplined; a "highly self-directed individual who prizes his independence."[61] They maintained he was the coordinator of al-Qaeda's unsuccessful millennium plot, a key planner in the 9/11 attacks, and, with Zawahiri, one of bin Laden's top deputies.[62] They knew he acted as a freelance human resources officer, keeping a list of members and screening new recruits for operational training.[63] Some said he was *the* central link between the senior leadership and multiple operational cells overseas.[64]

At the time of his capture, Abu Zubaydah was described as the highest-ranking al-Qaeda leader to fall into US hands, the "key terrorist recruiter and operational planner and member of bin Laden's inner circle."[65] US analysts may have believed this due to the frequency in which his name turned up in intelligence traffic—a side effect of his role as a travel and training coordinator—which left them with the impression that he was a major figure in the terrorist hierarchy.[66] President Bush named Abu Zubaydah as "one of the top three leaders" and "al-Qaeda's chief of operations."

Later evidence, however, seemed to indicate Abu Zubaydah was not nearly as important as they then assumed; he was more of a fixer for jihadist groups, not a formal member of al-Qaeda and certainly not the number 3 in the organization.[67] Some even said that he had severe mental problems, a war-wounded schizophrenic who was trusted with little more than making hotel and plane reservations.[68]

Despite his dubious credentials as a terrorist mastermind, Abu Zubaydah was still a hard target. He had lived in Pakistan for years and had a myriad of contacts; he knew safe houses and travel routes. As al-Qaeda's supposed travel and operations coordinator, he spoke several languages and had access to extensive resources, including false passports and aliases.[69] He was smart; he moved around frequently and covered his tracks, avoiding patterns.[70] The CIA discussed for months how to get rid of him.[71]

But Abu Zubaydah made a mistake somewhere, perhaps not realizing the additional resources and momentum that the US had gained in Afghanistan. The CIA had begun to track and profile him as they catalogued his various aliases and associates, using information from captured documents, hard drives, maps, training manuals, intercepts, and former terrorist operatives. By understanding how he operated and with whom he associated, analysts could better fix his possible location. It would take time to decode, process, and piece together so much information but, by March 2002 the US had a much sharper picture of the terrorist network and had increased communications surveillance on many newly discovered al-Qaeda nodes overseas.[72]

In late February 2002, CIA officers stationed in Islamabad received word from Agency headquarters that Abu Zubaydah was in Pakistan, probably in the dusty, overgrown city of Faisalabad.[73] According to one account, this initial break came from Pakistani ISI, who had noticed a caravan of very tall burqa-clad "women" (actually male operatives) traveling from the militant tribal area and had bribed the driver to learn their destination.[74] Using this information, the US mounted a major surveillance operation in the area, with sophisticated electronic equipment scanning the airwaves and teams of translators and analysts pouring over every fragment of intercepted communications. To parse the large amount of information being gathered, a Washington-based targeting analyst flew out to work with CIA field officers, and together they narrowed down the list of suspected hideouts to fourteen sites stretched across two cities.[75] Most were mud huts with thatched or corrugated tin roofs, but one—a modest middle-class residence identified as "Site X"—seemed to be especially important.[76] Realizing that it was understaffed for tackling fourteen safe houses simultaneously, the CIA assembled a larger team of FBI and Agency personnel and contacted ████████████ ████████ to plan a raid.

The plan was to use teams of US and Pakistani officers to hit all the sites simultaneously at 2:00 AM—the first time an ambitious joint operation of this nature between the two countries had been attempted since 9/11. The Pakistanis would do the dangerous work of breaking down the doors and capturing the men inside; CIA and FBI officers would then join them to sort through the prisoners and the evidence, sweeping up computers, phones, weapons, and documents. The CIA planned the raids but worked closely with the Pakistanis to coordinate the teams.[77] To build trust, and deferring to their Pakistani colleagues who were risking their lives, CIA case officers on the ground revealed the name of their target.[78] Both sides knew it would be a key test of the new cooperation the US and Pakistan had forged after 9/11; its success—or failure—would set the tone for the future.

When the strikes commenced, the team at Site X encountered stiff resistance. The battering ram they carried bounced off a steel-reinforced door, alerting the people inside and resulting in a protracted firefight.[79] In the resulting chaos, three men ran onto the roof in an attempt to flee, but Pakistani soldiers had them in their sights when they tried to jump to the house next door. One was killed instantly; another was seriously wounded in the leg and a third was wounded in the stomach, groin, and leg.[80] Once the apartment was secured, the FBI and CIA moved in and found bomb components and a map locating the British School in Lahore—evidence that suggested they were planning an attack that might have killed women and children. They also recovered a treasure trove of "pocket litter"—incriminating documents and debris that helped paint a more robust picture of Abu Zubaydah and his confederates.

Outside, Pakistani officers found a man they identified as Abu Zubaydah. By the time American officers reached him, he was unconscious and close to death. He had been shot three times.[81] He looked nothing like his picture—he was forty pounds heavier, had different hair, and was covered with blood. His identity was confirmed through pictures of his ears. Concerned with the possibility of having a key intelligence source die as soon as they captured him, CIA officers at the house negotiated with the ranking Pakistani military officer and hauled the unconscious terrorist to the closest hospital in the back of a Toyota pickup. Startled doctors performed emergency surgery to stop the bleeding, and CIA officers began a twenty-four-hour watch over their captive until he could be turned over and rendered from the country.[82] At one point, Abu Zubaydah reportedly woke up and saw his American captor standing over his bed in a SpongeBob Squarepants shirt. His heart rate soared and he nearly died again.[83]

Meanwhile, back in the US, CIA deputy director John McLaughlin arranged for a US trauma surgeon to fly to Pakistan to keep Abu Zubaydah alive.[84] After he was stabilized, he was loaded aboard a CIA plane and flown out of the country: probably to the remote island of Diego Garcia in the Indian Ocean and later to a secret facility in Thailand where he could be interrogated.[85]

Americans had Abu Zubaydah—but now what would they do with him?

By April 2002 the battle against the Taliban was basically over, but the cat-and-mouse war to eviscerate al-Qaeda was just beginning. The administration needed a victory to show progress in the war—and Abu Zubaydah's capture fit the bill. But even more, Americans needed an intelligence coup to start turning the tables on their nimble foe. US intelligence officers needed to discern the significance of raw data gathered from the captured hard drives, paper, and communication devices recovered in the raid, before the enemy adapted and the information became useless. To achieve that level of operations, top officials argued, they would need to change the rules of the game.

Initially Abu Zubaydah wouldn't cooperate.[86] CIA director George Tenet recounts that he tried to outsmart his interrogators by giving nominal bits and pieces of information, without really compromising anything important.[87] Nevertheless, he began yielding useful information that expanded CIA's map of the al-Qaeda network and provided new targets for intelligence collection.[88] He quickly identified Khalid Shaykh Mohammed (KSM) as a key leader and the mastermind of the 9/11 attacks, and revealed one of his aliases: "Mukhtar."[89] At the time, KSM was known but "did not even appear in [the CIA] chart of key al-Qaeda members and associates."[90] This new information allowed analysts to comb through previously collected intelligence and opened new leads that, in a roundabout way, helped lead to KSM's capture.[91]

By late April, analysts had verified the accuracy of some of Abu Zubaydah's information, and counterterrorism officials were cautiously issuing alerts based on his description of proposed attacks on US banks and other financial institutions.[92] During one interrogation he accidentally revealed the existence of an al-Qaeda associate whose physical description matched that of American José Padilla, leading to Padilla's arrest in May 2002.[93] By mid-June, information from Abu Zubaydah—along with triangulated data from his cell phone, computer, bank cards, and documents—led to the capture of at least two senior al-Qaeda operatives, Abu Zubair al-Haili and Mohammed Haydar Zammar in Morocco.[94]

Still, the White House wanted more. Abu Zubaydah was the highest-ranking al-Qaeda leader captured to date and they believed he was withholding important information on imminent attacks. He had also stopped cooperating[95] and according to a report by CIA officials, had "become accustomed to a certain (controlled) level of treatment," displaying no signs of disclosing further information.[96] CIA officers knew from recovered training manuals that al-Qaeda operatives received counterinterrogation training[97] and believed that Abu Zubaydah was applying that training to keep investigators at bay. There was intense pressure from the highest levels of government for new and actionable information, and a growing sense within the CIA that American lives were at stake.[98]

CIA officials had already begun discussing options for new "enhanced" methods of extracting information from captured operatives before Abu Zubaydah's capture,[99] but now they sat down with the National Security Council (NSC) and the Justice Department's Office of Legal Counsel (OLC) to seek direct guidance on how to proceed. On July 24, 2002, the CIA received oral guidance from OLC head Jay Bybee, and on August 1 formal written guidance—the so-called Bybee memo that authorized the "enhanced interrogation techniques" that the CIA requested with Abu Zubaydah in mind.[100]

US government employees and subcontracted personnel would eventually subject Abu Zubaydah to close confinement, extreme cold, forced stress positions, as well as waterboarding at least eighty-three times to force him to surrender information.[101] In addition to the special interrogators trained in the new techniques, detainees like Abu Zubaydah were questioned by CIA subject matter experts—individuals who claimed deeper knowledge about al-Qaeda—allowing for an accelerated pace of questioning.[102]

Concerns about the techniques used to interrogate him started early. In a press briefing, Secretary Rumsfeld flatly denied that administration officials were considering torture as a way to extract information, and dismissed claims that Abu Zubaydah was being relocated to a foreign country where the legal restrictions against torture could be skirted.[103] CIA officials later briefed senior lawmakers on his interrogation thus far, and did so again after they received approval from the White House to use the enhanced measures—seeking to ensure that the interpretation of the law the CIA had received was known and approved by all parts of the US government.[104]

The US denied access to high value detainees to groups such as the International Committee of the Red Cross, and the CIA later destroyed the tapes that documented its interrogation of Abu Zubaydah and another prisoner.[105] Sharp interagency disputes broke out regarding the legality and utility of such harsh methods. The FBI, which had initially been cooperating with the CIA to debrief Abu Zubaydah and other captives, eventually became so concerned that it required its interrogators to separate itself from "other agencies" (i.e., the CIA) that did not use FBI-approved interrogation methods.[106]

Later, the OLC would disavow the Bybee memo and experts would question whether Abu Zubaydah actually provided critical information to US interrogators after they adopted the enhanced interrogation techniques.[107] According to senior US officials and newly declassified memos, Abu Zubaydah provided the most useful information prior to being subjected to harsh measures, and no significant plot was thwarted due to information gathered through enhanced interrogation.[108] Some claimed that CIA officials ordered the enhanced methods to be used based on a highly inflated assessment of his importance, even after investigators said they believed he had already told them all he knew.[109] CIA officials—most notably George Tenet—dispute this, insisting that Abu Zubaydah was an important player and that the information he provided led to the disruption of several attacks as well as the capture of other terrorist leaders.[110]

The focused precision of the operation to find and capture him proved that the US was still discovering how to apply the find-fix-finish doctrine in the new counterterrorism setting. There was one other important detail in his capture that many overlooked, however: the safe house where he was found belonged to the Pakistani terror group Lashkar-e-Taiba (LeT), which had been closely managed and funded by Pakistan's spy agency.[111] Like the Taliban, LeT was an outgrowth of the ISI program to cultivate militant proxies who would carry the fight to Pakistan's enemies—in this case, India—without being directly affiliated with the Pakistani government.

The fact that Abu Zubaydah was captured in a LeT safe house indicated that he and other al-Qaeda leaders were cultivating relations with other groups in Pakistan.[112] It probably also indicated that the ISI sold them out. Finally a deal was struck: the CIA paid Pakistan some $10 million to help it find Abu Zubaydah, which the ISI then used to construct a beautiful new headquarters on thirty-five pristine acres outside Islamabad.[113]

A GIFT FROM A FRIEND:
ABU FARAJ AL-LIBI (CAPTURED, MAY 2005)

Khalid Shaykh Mohammed (KSM) became the number 3 man in al-Qaeda after Atef's death, and when Mohammed was captured in March 2003 (see the next chapter) he was succeeded by his deputy, Libyan national

Abu Faraj al-Libi (Mustafa Muhammad al-Uzayti).[114] An experienced paramilitary operative, Abu Faraj appears to have been a second-tier operative who received a field promotion—a sign that the US strategy of eviscerating the senior leadership was working.

Abu Faraj first met bin Laden in Sudan or Afghanistan and, by the mid-1990s, had become an early sworn member of al-Qaeda.[115] He became expert at using explosives, helping administer and train operatives at several al-Qaeda-affiliated training camps in Afghanistan.[116] He may also have worked as bin Laden's personal assistant, a key step that would have smoothed his way up the chain of command. In Afghanistan, he learned to speak Pashto and Urdu and married a Pakistani woman, making him an ideal liaison for extremist groups in both countries.

When Kabul fell to the Northern Alliance in 2001, Abu Faraj fled to Pakistan, moving between Karachi, the Punjab, and the Northwest Frontier Province.[117] During this period, he probably kept track of the families of al-Qaeda operatives and assisted in the vetting and transportation of al-Qaeda fighters to Afghanistan.[118] Shortly after KSM was captured, Abu Faraj took operational command; in December 2003 he met with other jihadists in Pakistan to plan operations against US forces in Afghanistan, and in September 2004 traveled to Syria to discuss a variety of operations against the US, Europe, and Australia.[119] He was also entrusted with serving as the conduit between bin Laden and lower-level al-Qaeda leaders, receiving couriered messages and public statements from bin Laden and transmitting messages back as appropriate.[120] Given the sensitivity of the communications, the US believed that his position within the organization almost certainly required personal meetings with bin Laden or Zawahiri—a privilege reserved for only the most trusted members of the group.[121]

Although he communicated with the top leadership, senior Pakistani officials later characterized him as more of a "regional commander" rather than an international terrorist in KSM's mold.[122] As an operational commander, Abu Faraj lacked the strategic depth exhibited by Mohammad Atef and KSM. Furthermore, he did not have direct experience with the West useful for training al-Qaeda operatives for overseas missions.[123] Finally, his distinctive appearance put him at a disadvantage; a relatively tall individual, he had discolorations on his face and arms that made him easily recognizable.[124]

It was only in late 2003 after al-Qaeda tried to kill Pakistani president Pervez Musharraf twice that he attracted the full attention of the Pakistani government. Al-Qaeda had been badly damaged by the new US-Pakistan relationship, and the organization apparently hoped that assassinating Musharraf would throw the country into political chaos and remove President Bush's only real ally in Pakistan. Abu Faraj was ideally suited for such an operation, due to his connections with both Pakistani terrorist groups and members of the armed forces—some of whom were successfully recruited for the mission.[125] Abu Faraj and his confederates planned two independent strikes: one designed to blow up a bridge while the president drove past it, and the other with two suicide bombers driving vehicles packed with explosives into Musharraf's motorcade. Both missed assassinating the head of state, but the second effort killed nineteen people and exposed the weakness in Pakistan's internal security net.[126] Abu Faraj and his associates soon became some of the most hunted men in Pakistan.

With significant US help, Pakistani intelligence traced the vehicles and phones used in the attack and arrested one of Abu Faraj's associates, Salahuddin Bhatti. According to Pakistani officials, it was Bhatti who first revealed Abu Faraj's position in the al-Qaeda hierarchy.[127] Computer expert Muhammad Naeem Noor Khan (a.k.a. Abu Talha) confirmed Abu Faraj's role, while also revealing a hidden terror network in Britain.[128] Later analysis of files and e-mails seized from Abu Talha's computers uncovered detailed surveillance of financial institutions in New York City, Newark, and Washington, and demonstrated that the Pakistan-based wing of al-Qaeda—under Abu Faraj's management—communicated with cells in the UK, and countries in both South and Southeast Asia.[129]

After winning a hard-fought reelection campaign in November 2004, the Bush administration was looking for another quick "victory" in the war on terror—and Pakistani officials, eager for further American financial and technological counterterrorism support, had incentive to paint Abu Faraj as one of al-Qaeda's most important operatives. Pakistani officers finally apprehended Abu Faraj some thirty miles north of Peshawar on May 3, 2005. By the time he was captured, both US and Pakistani officials described him as al-Qaeda's third most senior leader, subordinate only to bin Laden and Zawahiri, and director of all operations against the US and UK.[130]

Pakistani intelligence had missed catching Abu Faraj twice before. In the first instance, in April 2004, they had tracked down and arrested his driver. The interrogation led them to a man in the Punjab who had served as both a courier and host for the terrorist leader.[131] The man told them that he had rented a house for Abu Faraj in nearby Abbottabad—the same city where American forces would discover bin Laden several years later. The Pakistanis raided the one house they had uncovered, but the wily terrorist operative moved between three houses to avoid discovery and was safely somewhere else.[132] The second time, Pakistani intelligence was alerted to a meeting between two high-level al-Qaeda leaders at another house in Abbottabad, and set up an elaborate ambush to intercept them. But Abu Faraj cleverly sent a decoy ahead to test the waters and, when this individual approached the house, he triggered the ambush. In the resulting firefight, Pakistani officers killed the decoy and Abu Faraj, safe in his observation point, again escaped unharmed.[133]

By early 2005, the ISI managed to capture and recruit one of Abu Faraj's Pakistani accomplices, giving them a key penetration into the organization. The asset gave the Pakistanis a critical advantage: they were able to set the stage for the encounter, rather than waiting for information on his location and hoping they could respond in time. Even so, Abu Faraj proved to be a cautious foe.

The recruited source arranged to meet Abu Faraj at 4:30 PM. Pakistani intelligence knew that he often traveled by motorbike with a driver, and so three officers on motorbikes planned to intercept him at the designated rendezvous point. Abu Faraj called his contact repeatedly to confirm the meeting but then declined to show up—perhaps wary of just such a setup. The next morning, however, Abu Faraj called to reschedule, giving Pakistani officers another slim shot. The source agreed to meet him at a famous shrine on the outskirts of the town of Mardan, some two hours west of Abbottabad, providing cover for both the elusive terrorist and the intelligence service. Preparing for the operation, several officers dressed as women in burqas and placed themselves among the crowd. At exactly 9:30 AM, Abu Faraj arrived wearing sunglasses and a cap and approached the ISI asset. As he passed by one of the disguised men, the officer jumped up and wrestled Abu Faraj to the ground.[134]

Some disagreement remains about what degree American cooperation contributed to Abu Faraj's capture. In his memoirs, Musharraf paints the operation as a unilateral Pakistani success that came as a welcome surprise when he told Bush of the capture, and seems to make a point of downplaying the value of US technical assistance.[135] But Pakistan may have been acting on American-provided information.[136] A senior Pakistani intelligence official confirmed that the US had provided communications intercepts and information gathered in Afghanistan.[137] Also, the US tracked Abu Faraj to Mardan through his satellite phone.[138] There was reportedly disagreement between the CIA and ISI on how long to watch him once he had been fixed to some degree of precision. The Pakistanis were intent to apprehend the man who had tried to kill Musharraf, while the Americans hoped he might lead them to bin Laden—who might have been in Abbottabad by early 2005.[139]

With the capture of Abu Faraj, US intelligence officials believed they had a key source of new intelligence on al-Qaeda's plans and operations. Unlike most other operatives, he was computer savvy and was believed to have detailed insight into how al-Qaeda units used coded and hidden communications to coordinate attacks.[140] He was also a key contact for the top leadership; Abu Faraj eventually told interrogators that he was in contact with bin Laden through couriers, and that the last letter he had received was in December 2004.[141]

Pakistan took the first crack at his interrogation. According to Pakistani officials, they asked only two questions: "Where is bin Laden?" and "What are your plans?"[142] It remains unclear whether the Pakistanis acquired any useful information during these initial rounds of questioning, despite the physical pressure they exerted. By tracing contacts on his mobile phone, however, Pakistani operatives uncovered and detained more than two dozen other al-Qaeda suspects in the subsequent weeks.[143] Bowing to US pressure, Pakistani intelligence soon turned Abu Faraj over to American officials.

The capture of Abu Faraj was unquestionably a victory in the conflict with al-Qaeda. "If he's a big fish, it's because it's a much smaller pond," commented terrorism expert Bruce Hoffman at the time. Then again, "this movement has a knack for replacing serious operatives."[144] The war against al-Qaeda would continue.

THE REMOVAL of the al-Qaeda number 3s represented significant signs of progress for the US—hard men were off the streets. But in its quest to crush al-Qaeda, America made some hard choices.

CHAPTER 4

THE FINISHING NEVER ENDS

How Far Will America Go?

Every thing secret degenerates, even the administration of justice; nothing is safe that does not show how it can bear discussion and publicity.

—LORD ACTON

Rawalpindi, March 2003. The prisoner blinked unsteadily at his captors. Unshaven, obese, the man had been pulled out of bed by heavily armed intruders—but not before popping off a rifle round at his assailants, hitting one in the foot. As the prisoner was being dragged from the building, a photographer snapped a few photos. The prisoner was then stuffed into the black maw of a waiting vehicle.

So began Khalid Shaykh Mohammed's long journey into the American justice system.

Mohammed—better known in the Western press by his initials, KSM—is the most important terrorist in US custody to date. The mastermind of the 9/11 attacks, KSM was also a significant player in half a

dozen attempted attacks on US and allied sites and personnel dating
back to the mid-1990s, including plots to assassinate President Clinton
and Pope John Paul II. KSM was a one-man terrorist wrecking ball.

While a number of his colleagues, such as Mohammad Atef, met fiery
ends courtesy of missiles launched from overhead aerial platforms, KSM
was captured alive, allowing US authorities to use newly expanded national security tools such as rendition, enhanced interrogation techniques, and military commissions against him. US authorities have had
some short- and medium-term successes likely attributable to KSM's
capture—terror plots halted in early stages, lives saved, and terror suspects removed from the streets. But his incarceration has also led to long-
term political, legal, and ethical conundrums. How long can the US
detain an individual without trial? Can the US legitimately use brutal
methods, including torture, to elicit information from suspects, and then
use that information—the fruit of the poison tree—against them in a
court of law? Does KSM's evolving legal status matter? And what does
the treatment he receives at the hand of US authorities acting in an official capacity mean for the future of US national security actions against
other suspected terrorists—or even US citizens?

The way KSM has been treated in US custody has become a
Rorschach test for people discussing finishing techniques. Either he's a
terrorist of the first order, and nothing should be off-limits to extract
intelligence or achieve justice (or revenge), or he's the most famous
victim of an overbearing, overreaching counterterrorism program that
has shredded the US Constitution and has trampled on American values and decency. The example of KSM—and the treatment he received in US custody—serves as a cautionary tale about the ongoing
issues that America's new national security posture has brought. The
fires and the fears of another attack following 9/11 have long since re-
ceded, but the US is now left with the consequences of its decisions
from that time.

ORIGINS

Khalid Shaykh Mohammed was born in Kuwait on April 24, 1965,
to Baluchs from Iran. His father, a conservative cleric, moved to the

Persian Gulf in the early 1960s to take advantage of the riches found under the ground, but died when KSM was four years old.[1] KSM and his nephew, future 1993 World Trade Center attack mastermind Ramzi Yousef, were precocious expat kids and second-class citizens in the oil-rich Middle East. Drifting and searching for an identity, KSM reportedly joined the Muslim Brotherhood at age sixteen in what the CIA termed "an expression of his defiance against the secular world he saw around him."[2]

KSM enigmatically attended Chowan University, a small religious institution in North Carolina with a mission to provide "a caring environment characterized by Christian values and intellectual freedom in which students can gain the knowledge, skills, creativity, and ethical values they need to flourish in a rapidly changing, culturally diverse global society." Chowan was not a good fit for the radical son of a Baluch cleric, and within a year KSM had transferred to another unlikely fit, the predominantly African American North Carolina Agricultural & Technical State University (NCA&T) across the state in Greensboro. KSM graduated from NCA&T in 1986 with a degree in mechanical engineering. During this time, he came to the conclusion, much as his Islamist predecessor Sayyid Qutb had a generation before, that the US was a racist, corrupt, debauched society. His impression of the country was not helped by a stint in a North Carolina jail cell over unspecified financial issues.[3]

After graduation KSM left America to battle the Soviets in Afghanistan, drawn to the concept of violent jihad and the possibility of participating in it. There he linked up with the tireless purveyor of jihad, Abdullah Azzam, and the charismatic warlord Abdul Rasul Sayyaf, who had recently founded Ittihad-e-Islami and may have been the person who invited Osama bin Laden to Afghanistan.[4] Sayyaf, later a member of the Afghan parliament, was a major player in the Soviet-Afghan war, receiving funding from the Saudis and the US to fight the Red Army, and known by CIA case officers as one of the "seven dwarves."[5]

In late November 1989 a massive car bomb in Peshawar turned Azzam and his two sons into smoke, leaving KSM only one mentor. KSM would then exclusively work with Sayyaf, spending the next few years straddling the porous borderlands between Pakistan and Afghanistan.

Ramzi Yousef's intense interest in striking the World Trade Center in New York City was pivotal in convincing KSM to attack the US. KSM backed Yousef financially, offering $1,000 to fund his WTC attack.[6] In an operation designed to blow up passenger aircraft in midair in the Philippines, KSM played a larger operational role alongside his nephew and made it onto the American intelligence radar screen. The US in the late 1990s considered a military option to nab KSM in Qatar where the minister of religious endowments, Shakyh Abdullah bin Khalid al-Thani, provided a measure of safe haven to Islamic militants. But the Qatari government dithered and delayed helping the US, and KSM was able to flee the country.[7]

The irrepressible KSM was interested in securing capital and access to men willing to follow his command. In 1996 he made his way to Afghanistan for an audience with bin Laden, who had heard about his exploits in Southeast Asia. The two men, along with Mohammad Atef, met in bin Laden's camp in the mountain redoubt of Tora Bora on the borderlands of Pakistan and Afghanistan. There, in the narrow paths where bin Laden and his crew would eventually flee after September 2001, he laid out plans to strike the US homeland. Since the mid-1990s, he had constructed a plan to hijack ten planes simultaneously, crash them into sites in California, Washington State, nuclear power plants, CIA and FBI headquarters, the World Trade Center, the Pentagon, and the Capitol building.[8] KSM would save the most operatic aspect for himself. He would personally hijack the last plane, murder all the male passengers, make a speech denouncing the US, then land the aircraft and turn himself in to law enforcement. Being caught and executed by US authorities was always his master plan, allowing KSM to become the martyr of martyrs.[9]

At the time, bin Laden was not impressed with the plot, and shelved the "planes operation." Evidently KSM was convincing enough, however, for bin Laden to ask him to swear *bayat* to him, but KSM refused. To him, al-Qaeda's leaders would be the venture capitalists, the "angel investors" who would provide funds and suicide personnel but not serve as his board of directors. KSM also maintained close relations with Sayyaf, who was aligned with Ahmad Shah Masood, leader of the anti-Taliban, anti-al-Qaeda Northern Alliance.[10] This proved to be politically problematic. KSM's relationship with Sayyaf and Masood would make him think twice before aligning himself with their deadly rivals—and Masood's later assassins.

Al-Qaeda's 1998 attack on the US embassies in Kenya and Tanzania convinced KSM that the group was dedicated to broad anti-US efforts. Soon he reconnected with bin Laden and Atef and put the planes plan into motion in the spring of 1999. KSM was in the driver's seat, and the trio—but, surprisingly, not Ayman al-Zawahiri—picked the targets and selected the operatives for the mission.[11] Since KSM had the most experience abroad, he instructed the operatives on culture and travel in the US, collecting information on flight schools—even purchasing computer flight simulator software for his students.[12] KSM was so singularly focused on the planes operation that he did not swear allegiance to bin Laden until *after* 9/11 so that he could ignore a directive from al-Qaeda to halt the plot in the event that the group got cold feet.[13]

On that crisp Tuesday morning in September 2001, KSM, and his compatriots Ramzi bin al-Shibh, Mustafa Ahmed Hawsawi, Anmar al-Balochi, and Jaffar al-Tayer, met in an Internet café in Karachi, Pakistan, watching their cruel handiwork unfold in New York and Washington DC in real time.[14] They then went to a safe house to observe the aftermath on satellite TV. They repeatedly congratulated themselves on how well their plot had unfolded. They had carried out the most devastating attack on US soil ever, and they were about to become the most wanted men on earth.

In spite of his central role in the most devastating attack in US history, KSM was not well-known outside of intelligence circles. Indeed, it was not until Abu Zubaydah's capture by US and Pakistani forces in March 2002 and subsequent debriefings that the US knew for sure that KSM was 9/11's mastermind, according to a June 2005 CIA intelligence assessment.[15]

KSM dropped out of sight after the 9/11 attacks and the fall of al-Qaeda's Afghan sanctuary, spending much of 2002 helping operatives obtain safe passage from their collapsing bases in Kandahar and elsewhere into Pakistan and the Middle East.[16] Still, he planned other follow-on plots during this time, including hijacking airplanes to slam into London's Heathrow airport. Given the fierce US counterattack after 9/11 and the need for increased security, however, these plots didn't progress beyond the planning stage.

But KSM and some of his colleagues could not resist a taste of the media spotlight. In April 2002 he contacted and met with Yosri Fouda of the Al Jazeera satellite channel in Karachi to discuss the 9/11 attacks. Fouda later recalled that he "looked Khalid in the eye and asked: 'Did you do it?' But Khalid didn't flinch [replying,] 'I am the head of the al-Qaeda military committee . . . and Ramzi [bin al-Shibh] is the coordinator of the Holy Tuesday operation. And yes, we did it.'"[17]

Despite America's expensive high-tech infrastructure, it was an old-fashioned personal betrayal that allowed security services to sweep in and grab KSM. An informant—a walk-in who would receive $25 million for his efforts and a new life in America—met with KSM in Rawalpindi, Pakistan in March 2003. At one point, he excused himself to use the toilet, where he feverishly sent a text message to authorities: "I am with KSM."[18]

Who could have gotten so close to a paranoid sociopath like KSM? His identity remains a closely guarded secret, but chances are that it wasn't a member of al-Qaeda, for the US has not had much luck recruiting members of the group. The limited reporting on his identity suggests he was "a little guy who looked like a farmer."[19] George Tenet insisted that the asset betrayed KSM because he was motivated by religious zeal—although the $25 million bounty must have been a fine incentive, too.

This individual would not have belonged to KSM's inner professional circle, as those people would have given him up a long time ago had they had the chance or the inclination, but perhaps an individual who had a tangential relationship to KSM or his family. Given the ties that bind the Baluchs to the land, it might have been a person of consequence, such a religious figure from KSM's ancestral hometown, and it would have been considered rude of the terrorist to refuse to break bread with him.

A little before two in the morning in early March, several heavily armed Pakistani officers broke down the door and ran upstairs to find the sleepy 9/11 mastermind along with his colleague Mustafa al-Hawsawi in one of the rooms.[20] In the ensuing struggle with the elite Pakistani forces, KSM shot one of the officers in the leg. Ultimately KSM and al-Hawsawi were overwhelmed and dragged away.[21]

RENDITION

After his arrest, US authorities whisked KSM from Pakistan outside the usual mechanisms of extradition—stopping at Bagram air base in Afghanistan, and the little-used Syzmany airport outside of Warsaw, among other places—in the finishing mechanism termed "rendition."

Rendition, a controversial but productive national security tool, has been utilized by the US government to disrupt terror networks. A rendition occurs when the US, working in concert with another country, transfers a captured fugitive or suspect to another country without performing the formal diplomatic mechanisms of extradition.[22] The captured individual may be transferred from the country where he was captured either to the US directly or to another foreign country (e.g., Pakistan to Egypt). George Tenet testified that prior to 9/11 the US rendered seventy individuals and brought at least twenty to the US for trial.[23]

President Ronald Reagan authorized the first rendition in 1987 when he green-lighted the capture of Fawaz Younis, a Lebanese national implicated in the 1985 hijacking of TWA Flight 847 and the death of a US Navy diver. US officials tricked Younis into sailing to a boat into international waters, where waiting FBI agents (with CIA assistance) detained and rendered him to the US for trial and subsequent conviction.[24]

The rendition program became an important counterterrorism tool in the mid-1990s, when President Bill Clinton, in a series of presidential decision directives (PDDs), established terrorism as a top intelligence priority and mandated that the intelligence community increase efforts to capture terrorists abroad.[25] For example, the Pakistani authorities captured and then handed over KSM's nephew Ramzi Yousef without formally extraditing him. Another person, Egyptian militant Talaat Fouad Qassem, was wanted in connection with the assassination of Egyptian president Anwar Sadat in 1981. The Croatian services discovered and detained him in 1995, then asked their US counterparts how to proceed. Since there was an outstanding warrant for his arrest in Egypt, the US served as the go-between for the Croats and the Egyptians, quietly delivering Qassem to the Egyptians. Egypt was extremely pleased to welcome the prisoner home. Qassem disappeared into the bowels of the Egyptian security system and was never heard from again.[26]

Under Clinton-era rules, nominal safeguards generally made sure that prisoners were not abused in foreign custody. For instance, the foreign country to which a suspect was rendered had to have a legal case pending against the suspect prior to rendition.[27] Rendered individuals were, furthermore, supposed to be treated in accordance with international human rights norms within US and non-US custody.[28] Furthermore, the US abstained from sending people to countries with poor human rights records.[29] But these safeguards, it seems, were not always observed.

EXTRAORDINARY RENDITIONS

An "extraordinary rendition" occurs when American authorities render an individual without the consent of the host country. An Office of Legal Counsel (OLC) opinion from 1989 stated that the executive can authorize US officials to violate the territorial sovereignty of a country that has contravened international legal norms. Given the complex logistics required for their execution and the diplomatic fiascos they can create, however, extraordinary renditions are a rarely used tool. Daniel Benjamin, the State Department's counterterrorism coordinator, claimed the US never carried out an extraordinary rendition before 9/11.[30]

At least one case seems to undermine Benjamin's assertion. President George H. W. Bush authorized the rendition of Dr. Humberto Alvarez Machain from Mexico after he was implicated in the torture and murder of a DEA officer.[31] After being brought across the US-Mexico border, the doctor was later acquitted in federal court due to a lack of evidence. Had the CIA captured bin Laden in 1998 from Afghanistan and brought him to the US that, too, would have been an extraordinary rendition.[32]

Renditions, extraordinary or otherwise, have advantages. First and foremost, rendition is one way of removing terror suspects from the streets. Captured and rendered terror suspects cannot harm US citizens and interests. The act of rendition may also disrupt terrorist plots in their planning phases, as individuals critical to the successful planning of a terrorist operation are incapacitated. KSM's activities in South Asia and the Middle East were brought to a halt after his arrest.

Rendition also opens doors to intelligence gathering. The US can glean time-sensitive information by interrogating rendered individuals.

According to George Tenet, after KSM was arrested and handed over to US custody for interrogation, he quickly provided actionable information that was used to arrest the leader and several top members of Jemaah Islamiya, an extremist group based in Southeast Asia.[33]

Once individuals leave US custody, American authorities lose the ability to control and monitor their treatment. "We have a responsibility of trying to ensure that [detainees] are properly treated," former CIA director Porter Goss told the Senate in 2005. "And we try and do the best we can to guarantee that. But, of course, once they're out of [our] control, there's only so much we can do. But we do have an accountability program for those situations."[34] Notably, this has not stopped the US from rendering individuals to countries with lackluster human rights histories.

Finally, the US legal system has strict standards governing the admission of evidence. One of the thorniest problems facing prosecutors of rendered suspects is that critical evidence is inadmissible either because it is classified or because it was acquired outside of constitutional evidence-gathering procedures. Conversely, as Georgetown University professor Daniel Byman has noted, "Many US allies in the Middle East have a far lower standard of evidence and are willing to bend what rules they have in response to a US request."[35] Rendering individuals to nations with lower evidentiary standards at trial maximizes the likelihood of long-term incarceration and diffuses the threat to American citizens and interests, while at the same time ensuring that US intelligence sources and methods remain secret.

In spite of these advantages, renditions pose legal, ethical, and political problems. Whereas formal extradition requires a warrant subject to independent review by both the State and Justice departments, the rendition process lacks this accountability.[36] Renditions undermine the notion that the US is a nation of laws that adheres to global norms of conduct. As such, the act of rendition irritates US allies and can undermine otherwise friendly international relationships.

The US also occasionally renders innocent individuals. Since intelligence is almost always based on incomplete, perishable information, the US sometimes renders the wrong people. Such mistakes make the US intelligence bureaucracy—specifically the CIA—look foolish and undermine the technique's legitimacy. Perhaps the most egregious example was the rendition of Khaled al-Masri, a Lebanese-born German citizen who was mistaken for an al-Qaeda operative and rendered to Afghanistan. He was held for months under unpleasant circumstances before US officials recognized the mistake.[37] In response to his kidnapping, al-Masri has filed several diplomatically embarrassing lawsuits against the US and Germany.[38]

The US has been accused of rendering suspects to countries with dubious human rights records, including Egypt, Jordan, Morocco, Syria, and Libya.[39] These countries are known to use techniques outlawed in the US to elicit information during interrogation, up to and including torture. The United Nations Convention Against Torture, to which the US is a signatory, guarantees that "no State party shall expel, return ('refouler') or extradite a person to another State where there are substantial grounds for believing that he would be in danger of being subjected to torture."[40] However, one former CIA analyst involved in the rendition program dismissed these efforts as a "legal nicety" and admits that interrogations performed by foreign officers "might yield treatment not consonant with United States legal practice."[41]

KSM's journey from Pakistan to Bagram air base in Afghanistan, then to a disused airfield in Poland, and finally in 2006 to the Guantanamo Bay prison facility in Cuba was, according to US law, completely legal.[42] The ability of US officials to transfer a suspect from a country—with permission from that country's government but without adhering to strict extradition procedures—has been authorized by multiple White House directives since the mid-1980s, and Congress has been regularly briefed on this procedure.[43]

In the weeks and months that followed 9/11, American intelligence officials scrambled to obtain accurate information on the nature of the threat and, more importantly, whether new attacks were going to be launched. According to former CIA director Michael Hayden, questioning detained al-Qaeda militants as they were captured worldwide quickly became the preferred method of eliciting vital intelligence information.[44] Hayden believed that the intelligence gleaned from these captured militants was "absolutely irreplaceable" and formed "more than 70 percent of the human intelligence" that became the basis of at least one national intelligence estimate on terrorism.[45]

The number of suspects rendered since 9/11 remains classified, but Columbia Law School adjunct professor Scott Horton estimated roughly 150 individuals were rendered between 2001 to 2005.[46] In 2007 CIA director Hayden admitted as much: "apart from that 100 that we've detained, the number of renditions is actually . . . mid-range two figures."[47] Since most, if not all, of the individuals who were incarcerated in the Guantanamo Bay prison facility after 9/11 arrived there outside a formal extradition process, it stands to reason that they were obtained through rendition or in a rendition-like manner.

The US rendition program began to run into serious issues when, after 9/11, it became a favored tool to deal with terror suspects captured in foreign countries and so grew exponentially. While many rendered suspects were most likely part of terrorist groups, their subsequent legal-limbo status—whether ultimately detained under US custody or by a foreign country—has proven problematic for the US justice system, causing what one former lawyer at CIA's Office of General Counsel called "a nightmare."[48]

High-profile counterterrorism actions have political consequences. US officials could not have believed that the ramped-up use of a counterterrorism tool, especially one that has as many legally and ethically gray areas as rendition, would remain secret for long. They must have realized that KSM and others in the al-Qaeda constellation in American custody would have their day in court, exposing the rendition process, as well as the sizable logistical apparatus and international cooperation needed to carry it out.

INTERROGATING A TERRORIST

KSM's knowledge about the world of al-Qaeda was a gold mine for US authorities. According to declassified CIA intelligence from mid-2005, KSM began to spill secrets to his interrogators pretty quickly. "Uncharacteristic for most detainees, KSM almost immediately following his capture in March 2003 elaborated on his plan to crash commercial airlines into Heathrow Airport."[49] This information, in the words of one 2004 CIA analytical product, "shed light" on al-Qaeda's "strategic doctrine, plots and probable targets, key operatives and the likely methods for attacks in the US homeland," "dramatically expanded [the US] universe of knowledge" of al-Qaeda's plots, and "provided leads that assisted directly in the capture of other terrorists."[50]

His debriefings also provided information used to capture and incarcerate al-Qaeda operatives in the US, including businessmen and explosives smugglers Sayfullah Paracha and his son Uzair, al-Qaeda operatives Saleh Almari and Majid Khan, and Iyman Faris, an Ohio-based truck driver who schemed to destroy the Brooklyn Bridge with a blowtorch.[51] A number of these men were captured and sent to Guantanamo Bay to await trial.

Despite its successes, the KSM interrogations are best known for the liberal use of brutal methods—enhanced interrogation techniques (EITs) in CIA documents. The Obama administration's attorney general would later refer to them as "torture" in his confirmation hearings. According to Amnesty International, KSM claimed that during his first week in the facility in Poland, he was "waterboarded five times, beaten including by having his head repeatedly banged against a wall and deprived of sleep and clothes and when not being interrogated, was forced to stand for prolonged periods, shackled to the ceiling and floor."[52] Even his food allotment was calibrated to get him to talk.[53]

EITs used on KSM included the old Bolshevik technique described in *Darkness at Noon* of keeping the prisoner awake for 180 hours and the 1950s Chinese technique of waterboarding some 183 times.[54] Why did US government employees—likely decent Americans worried about their mortgages, kids, and retirements—utilize methods that the attorney general of the United States would cite as worse than those used by the Khmer Rouge, the Inquisition, and the imperial Japanese army and were considered prosecutable offenses in World War II and Vietnam?[55]

Someone must have never understood the overall purpose of interrogating a suspect. The goal of interrogations is to "obtain the maximum amount of usable information . . . in a lawful manner, in a minimum amount of time."[56]

This is nothing new. In the Pacific Theater during World War II, the US Marine Corps established an interrogation program based on establishing rapport with captured Japanese prisoners. This program proved so successful that in June 1944 the Marines provided US commanders with the complete Japanese order of battle within forty-eight hours of arriving on the islands of Saipan and Tinian.[57] In the current conflicts in Iraq and Afghanistan, CIA,[58] military,[59] and FBI[60] teams have interrogated thousands of individuals without the use of coercive or harsh techniques.

Prior to 9/11, the CIA had a checkered past concerning interrogation, and few officers had ever interrogated anyone. During the 1960s, the Agency published the KUBARK manuals that described various forms of coercion that can elicit information, such as "threats and fear," "pain," and "debility."[61] By the 1980s, as a means to improve foreign liaison relationships, the CIA dusted off the manuals—subsequently amended to state that certain practices are both illegal and immoral—to help train foreign interrogators under the euphemistic title of the Human Resource Exploitation program. According to the CIA's inspector general, political sensitivities at the time caused the deputy director to forbid the use of the word "interrogation."[62] The CIA shuttered the whole program in 1986 after allegations surfaced that the Agency had trained certain Latin American intelligence services in the fine art of interrogation—with which CIA had little actual experience—that was then used to commit widespread human rights violations.[63]

Then 9/11 happened and the White House pressured the Agency to crack heads and get answers. "The gloves came off," as former CTC head Cofer Black famously quipped. But which gloves came off, and what did that mean from an operational perspective once al-Qaeda members were apprehended? Could government employees use the full range of methods handed down from antiquity on these individuals? Surely, there were legal and ethical redlines not to be crossed that would wall off what US interrogators could and could not do.

In the months following the 9/11 attacks, political leaders and the IC felt pressure to take steps necessary to prevent future—and possibly imminent—terrorist attacks. After receiving permission from the White House and the Justice Department, the CIA began using alternative interrogation techniques to gather intelligence from so-called high value al-Qaeda detainees—individuals like Abu Zubaydah and KSM.[64] The subsequent disclosure of these techniques to the public fueled an ongoing debate over whether these interrogation techniques are effective and ethical.

The Agency went to the White House legal team for guidance. Ultimately, the case was decided by a team of lawyers in a small office in the Department of Justice: the Office of Legal Counsel (OLC). OLC had the responsibility to provide "authoritative legal advice to the President and all the Executive Branch agencies."[65] After 9/11, the office was charged with determining the government's stance on the legality of coercive interrogation techniques.[66] In 2002, through a series of classified memoranda, OLC drafted findings stating that the CIA's enhanced interrogation methods were permitted, providing legal cover to interrogators utilizing enhanced interrogation techniques.

All of these memos were subsequently retracted, but at the time they provided legal justification for enhanced interrogation techniques. For example, an August 2002 memo gave approval for specific coercive techniques, including waterboarding, on grounds that they were not "specifically intended" to cause "severe physical or mental pain or suffering."[67] Furthermore, three May 2005 memos found that waterboarding and other harsh techniques, whether individually or in concert, did not violate the federal criminal prohibition against torture since the CIA had implemented certain safeguards and limited the techniques. However, a footnote in one of the memos admitted that, according to the CIA's inspector general, these rules were not always followed.[68]

In addition to this enhanced interrogation regimen, President Bush also authorized the creation of a secret CIA prison system specifically designed for the detention and debriefing of high value al-Qaeda members like KSM.[69] The program reportedly involved the operation of "black sites" in eight foreign countries where high value al-Qaeda detainees were held incommunicado and subjected to coercive interrogation techniques.[70] The Agency also reportedly operated a prison in northern Afghanistan where, in November 2002, a detainee of little intelligence importance froze to death after a CIA case officer ordered prison guards to strip him naked and chain him to a concrete floor overnight.[71] Due to popular pressure and the *Hamdan v. Rumsfeld* Supreme Court ruling, the Bush White House closed these legally dubious sites in 2006 and transferred the remaining prisoners to the Guantanamo Bay military complex.

ARE COERCIVE INTERROGATIONS EFFECTIVE?

Anecdotal experiences of some in the intelligence and law enforcement fields claim that physical pressure on detainees is, at least in the short run, an occasionally effective means to generate data. For example, during the brutal conflict between France and the terrorist Front de Libération Nationale in Algeria in the 1950s, the commander of the French paratroopers routinely and successfully used torture to extract information, crushing the enemy, at least temporarily.[72] More recently, the lead police officer who in 1993 and 1994 solved a series of bomb blasts in and around Bombay after a brutal sectarian bloodletting was quite open about his methods to elicit intelligence. In *Maximum City: Bombay Lost and Found*, Suketu Mehta describes how the officer, when presented with a detainee, cracked the case:

> The suspect is deprived of sleep for a whole week. Usually, neither party has that luxury. So another method is to take two ends of an old style telephone wire and apply it to the arms or the genitals; a portable dynamo is whirled, and a powerful electric current is generated . . . fear of death is the most effective. During the bomb blasts I just took a few of the suspects to Borivali National Park and fired a few bullets past their ears.

But with many of these suspects, ordinary violence wouldn't work. There had to be special methods.

> Those who have no fear of death also have no fear of physical pain. For them we threaten their family. I tell them I'll plant some evidence on their mother or their brother and arrest them. That usually works.[73]

Nonetheless, coerced confessions have also led to poor analytical outcomes and disastrous policy decisions. Psychologists and other specialists commissioned by the Intelligence Science Board issued a report in 2007 claiming there was little evidence that harsh interrogation methods produced better intelligence than traditional interrogation techniques.[74] When asked in 2008 whether any attacks on US soil had been thwarted due to enhanced interrogation techniques, FBI director Robert Mueller replied, "I'm really reluctant to answer that . . . I don't believe that has been the case."[75]

Controversial methods in intelligence can additionally generate terrible political fallout. Much like how the use of *la question* stained the honor of the French military for years after Algeria, the CIA program—where KSM became the cause célèbre—spawned multiple investigations and the possibility of prosecutions. In August 2009, the Justice Department appointed a special prosecutor to conduct a preliminary investigation into allegations of abuse by CIA interrogators that first surfaced in a 2004 CIA inspector general report.[76] The decision to open the probe was controversial and opposed by several former directors.

The legal terrain of interrogation is complex, and there is ongoing debate about which laws apply to agents of the US government. In any given context, the actions of US interrogators may be constrained by international treaties such as the Geneva Conventions and the Universal Declaration of Human Rights; US statutes such as the War Crimes Act and the Detainee Treatment Act; judicial doctrine, such as *Hamdan v. Rumsfeld*; or executive orders.[77] Government employees who participated in this CTC program were concerned with their actions. The CIA's inspector general recognized this fear as early as 2004, and wrote in scathing detail:

> A number of Agency officers of various grade levels who are involved with detention and interrogation activities are concerned that they may at some future date *be vulnerable to legal action in the United States or abroad and that the US Government will not stand behind them.* Although the current detention and interrogation Program has been subject to [Department of Justice] legal review and Administration political approval, it *diverges sharply* from previous Agency policy and practice, rules that govern interrogations by US military and law enforcement officers, statements of US policy by the Department of State, and public statements by very senior US officials, including the

President, as well as the policies expressed by Members of Congress, other Western governments, international organizations, and human rights groups.[78] [Emphasis added.]

As many have found out, political winds can become unfavorable, exposing them to future sanction. These unnamed officers instinctively grasped the long-term consequences:

> Officers are concerned that future public revelations of the CTC Program is inevitable and will seriously damage Agency officers' personal reputations, as well as the reputation and effectiveness of the Agency itself. . . . The Agency faces potentially serious long-term political and legal challenges as a result of the CTC Detention and Interrogation Program, particularly its use of EITs and the inability of the US Government to decide what it will ultimately do with terrorists detained by the Agency.[79]

In 2008 one official told a reporter, "I'm worried that the next administration is going to prosecute the guys who got involved, and there won't be any presidential pardons at the end of it. It would be O.K. if it were [former attorney generals] John Ashcroft or Alberto Gonzales. But it won't be. It'll be some poor GS-13 who was just trying to do his job."[80]

THE 2004 CIA inspector general's report proved to be prescient in another way: the US government remains unable to decide what to do with many of the individuals detained by American forces in the global conflict against al-Qaeda.

Some have argued in favor of trying these individuals in military commissions. Military commissions are not regularly constituted military courts; instead, they are ad hoc institutions first used by the US during the Mexican-American War and subsequently in every major war.[81] In 1942, the Supreme Court unanimously upheld the constitutionality of military commissions in *Ex Parte Quirin*.[82] Specifically, the Court held that a military commission had jurisdiction over eight German saboteurs caught on US soil for violating the laws of war because they failed to wear military uniforms.

In November 2001, President Bush announced that he was authorizing the trial by military commission of noncitizens suspected of terrorism.[83] Whereas US federal courts have stringent rules for the admission of evidence—hearsay and evidence gathered unconstitutionally are strictly prohibited—military commission rules drafted by the Bush administration allowed evidence to be admitted provided "the evidence would have probative value to a reasonable person."[84] The Bush administration also exempted military commissions from review by most US courts. Finally, if national security requires, prosecutors were given the right not to inform defendants of evidence against them, as well as the ability to exclude defendants from attending their own trials. Congress further diminished protections for defendants tried by military commissions when it passed the Detainee Treatment Act of 2005. The majority of the act relates to the interrogation of prisoners, but it states that only the Court of Appeals for the District of Columbia can review military commission decisions and hear habeas corpus petitions of military prisoners challenging their detention.

In 2006, the Supreme Court held in *Hamdan v. Rumsfeld* that certain military commission procedures violate international and domestic law.[85] Specifically, the Court ruled that prohibiting a defendant from attending his own trial, admitting testimony obtained through coercion, and denying the defendant access to classified information violate both the Geneva Conventions and the US military's Uniform Code of Military Justice (UCMJ). Based on these violations, the Court found that the military commissions as they were constituted at the time were unlawful.

Reacting to the *Hamdan* decision, Congress passed the Military Commissions Act in 2006 explicitly authorizing trials by military commission for "unlawful enemy combatants," including members of the Taliban and al-Qaeda. The act strengthened procedural protections for defendants in military commissions. The act also included a double jeopardy prohibition barring a defendant from being tried more than once for the same crime. However, the act further limited the jurisdiction of the civilian court system to hear appeals; beyond reaffirming that only the Court of Appeals for the District of Columbia could hear military commission appeals, it barred all other civilian courts from reviewing detainees' habeas corpus petitions.

In 2008, the Supreme Court in *Boumediene v. Bush* struck down as unconstitutional the act's ban on detainees' habeas corpus rights.[86] The Court ruled that Guantanamo Bay is similar enough to US territory that detainees have a constitutional right to petition for habeas corpus. Justice Kennedy's majority opinion noted, "Within the Constitution's separation-of-powers structure, few exercises of judicial power are as legitimate or as necessary as the responsibility to hear challenges to the authority of the Executive to imprison a person."[87]

During this time, KSM was brought before a military commission. He refused legal representation and, along with Ramzi bin al-Shibh, Mustafa al-Hawsawi, Walid bin Attash, and Ammar al-Baluchi, attempted to plead guilty and request the death penalty.[88] Despite his hopes, death by execution was not in the cards at this juncture for KSM and his comrades, as the military commissions were suspended pending indefinite review by the incoming Obama administration.

During the 2008 presidential campaign, President Obama sharply criticized the military commission system and declared that, if elected, he would "reject the Military Commissions Act."[89] "By any measure," then-Senator Obama said in June 2008, "our system of trying detainees has been an enormous failure." In the days immediately following his inauguration, President Obama followed up on his pledge by issuing Executive Order 13492, directing the secretary of defense to immediately take steps to halt all referrals to military commissions and to stay all pending proceedings.[90]

Nevertheless, the Obama administration's Guantanamo review panel believed certain individuals could not be tried in civilian court.[91] During mid-2009, an interagency task force of attorneys determined which detainees were to be tried in a new military commissions system.[92] President Obama noted, "Military commissions have a long tradition in the United States. They are appropriate for trying enemies who violate the laws of war, provided that they are properly structured and administered."[93] Lawyers worked under the presumption that detainees would be tried in civilian court unless they found a compelling reason not to permit a civilian trial. The president tasked Attorney General Eric Holder with making a final determination of which system each detainee would see during his day in court.[94]

In late 2009, the attorney general announced that KSM and four others accused of planning the 9/11 attacks would be tried in civilian court in New York City. He added that five other detainees accused of planning the October 2000 attack on the USS *Cole* would receive trials by military commission. One of the rationales offered publicly for using different trial systems for the two groups of detainees was that the USS *Cole* was a military target, thereby making the attack a crime subject to military trial. As noted by former top Justice Department officials Jack Goldsmith and James Comey, this rationale failed to acknowledge that the Pentagon itself, targeted on 9/11, could be considered a military target. Goldsmith and Comey speculated that the true reason for using different trial systems for the two groups of suspects is that the limited evidence against the *Cole* suspects admissible in federal court was much weaker.[95] Both decisions proved controversial.

Intense national political pressure, questions about cost and security, and parochial concerns derailed the civilian trial in New York. The list of prominent lawmakers who opposed putting KSM on trial in New York included the governor of New York, the mayor of New York City, and several senators from both sides of the aisle.[96] Mayor Michael Bloomberg said on television, "There are places that would be less expensive for the taxpayers and less disruptive for New York City. For example, military bases away from central cities where it is easier to provide security at much less cost."[97] NYPD commissioner Ray Kelly raised the prospect that a trial would require the installation of some 2,000 checkpoints.[98] Finally, the question remained, If KSM were acquitted, what would happen? Would he be released a free man on the streets of the United States?

Since many US allies view the military commissions system—even with procedural protections in place—as less than completely legitimate, trying detainees by military commission had the adverse effect of decreasing the likelihood that other countries would cooperate by providing critical legal assistance. In 2009, when federal prosecutors began to build a criminal case against KSM for a civilian trial, they found far greater cooperation from US allies; Germany, France, and Great Britain volunteered evidence and witnesses for the trial.[99]

Furthermore, military commissions have not yet been successfully employed on a broad scale to try suspected terrorists and other enemy combatants. For instance, only a handful of people have been convicted by the US through military commission trials. In contrast, hundreds have been convicted in federal court of terrorism-related crimes. To add injury to insult, sentences handed down by military commissions tend to be lighter than civilian ones.

At the time of this writing, efforts to identify a suitable location for KSM's trial in either civilian or military court remain ongoing.

SOME OF the changes to the Military Commissions Act desired by the Obama administration were codified into law in the Military Commissions Act of 2009, passed as part of the National Defense Authorization Act of 2010. The new law established that statements obtained through torture or cruel, inhuman, or degrading treatment are to be excluded from evidence.[100] Defendants are granted the right to attend their complete trials and examine all evidence presented against them. Furthermore, military lawyers were required to disclose any exculpatory evidence to the defense.

Although they acknowledged that the amendments offered significant improvements, civil liberties groups remained unsatisfied with the changes. The American Civil Liberties Union still asserts that the military commissions system represents a "second class system of justice," and that the commissions are "not only illegal but unnecessary."[101]

SO, WHAT to make of the brutalized, sociopathic 9/11 mastermind, languishing in legal limbo in an island prison complex that probably should have been shuttered years ago? Finishing al-Qaeda leaders by taking them alive exposes the contradictions and compromises of the ad hoc post-9/11 US system. The usual linear progression of capture, interrogation, court trial, conviction, and incarceration, which worked to successfully and legitimately disarm terrorists such as Ramzi Yousef, shoe bomber

Richard Reid, Timothy McVeigh, and others, has been compromised by some of the short-term actions taken by the US government.

KSM was not forsaken by his comrades-in-arms—bin Laden and Ayman al-Zawahiri mentioned him throughout the years in their various media submissions, underscoring his continuing propaganda value for al-Qaeda. Since his capture, KSM has grown a long beard and has chosen Middle Eastern clothing over Western attire. Gone is the man who made the headlines in 2003 and in his place is a man who, consciously or unconsciously, has modeled himself after his chief financier, bin Laden. What differentiates KSM from al-Qaeda's former leader, however, is that KSM does not seem interested in the fantastical reestablishment of the caliphate but is motivated by anti-American sentiments and a desire to strike the US, whatever the consequences.

He is single-minded, and that makes him dangerous. If released, he will likely continue to pursue violent anti-American activities; if imprisoned without trial, he will become the preeminent symbol of an American legal system gone badly awry. The status quo, then, may be the "least worst" option for the US government. This most indefensible of defendants will most likely remain incarcerated without trial for the rest of his natural life, a thorn in the side of the White House and a stain on America's honor.

CHAPTER 5

INTERROGATIONS, INTELLIGENCE, AND WAR

A little more than a month after the US launched Operation Enduring Freedom and invaded Afghanistan, Pakistani security forces patrolling the rugged terrain of western Pakistan's Kurram valley apprehended a senior al-Qaeda operative. Ibn al-Shaykh al-Libi—not to be confused with Abu Faraj al-Libi or any of the other Libyans in al-Qaeda—whose given name was Ali Abdul-Hamid al-Fakhiri, was detained as he attempted to cross over the border into Pakistan to escape American military operations targeting Osama bin Laden in Tora Bora.[1]

Over the next eight years, officials would transfer custody of al-Libi at least three times, though the US government has never confirmed the exact destinations.[2] First detained and interrogated by the military, FBI, and CIA in Afghanistan, al-Libi was subsequently imprisoned in Egypt,[3] again in Afghanistan, and eventually in the US detention facility in Guantanamo Bay, Cuba.[4] In 2006, US officials transferred al-Libi from Guantanamo Bay to Libya, his country of birth, where he remained imprisoned until his death—allegedly a suicide—in May 2009.[5]

Al-Libi, who had been the emir of the Khalden military training camp in Afghanistan, initially tricked his Pakistani captors into thinking he was a mere refugee fleeing the conflict in Afghanistan. After approximately two weeks of interrogation, however, Pakistani forces determined that he held a senior position in al-Qaeda and turned al-Libi over to the US military. American intelligence officials in Kandahar air base in Afghanistan soon determined al-Libi's true identity and value as a source of detailed intelligence information about al-Qaeda operations.[6] He certainly was a catch: Al-Libi was one of the top twelve al-Qaeda terrorists initially targeted by President Bush after 9/11.[7] At the time, few would have guessed that the subsequent transfer and interrogation of the first official high-value detainee would eventually result in one of the most controversial episodes in the global war against al-Qaeda.[8]

Al-Libi's case raises key questions concerning the analysis and use of intelligence in policymaking. Despite some intelligence officials' initial doubts about the accuracy of the intelligence produced by interrogations of al-Libi,[9] several senior political leaders, including President Bush and Secretary of State Colin Powell, exploited the information he provided to construct the case for the 2003 Iraq invasion.[10] The intelligence later came under scrutiny after the links between al-Qaeda and the Iraqi WMD program asserted by the Bush administration proved overstated and incorrect. Such an outcome raises questions: How should intelligence agencies ensure that only the most reliable intelligence goes to senior policymakers? And to what degree was the al-Libi case politicized to achieve purely partisan objectives?

Even before he began working with al-Qaeda, al-Libi had been long involved with radical Islam. Born in 1963 in Ajdabiya, Libya, al-Libi ("the Libyan") left his homeland in the mid-1980s for Syria, where he studied engineering.[11] Al-Libi then moved to Afghanistan, where he became a bombmaker[12] and then a commander in the twilight struggle against the Soviet army.[13] Later, al-Libi joined the radical Libyan Islamic Fighting Group (LIFG)[14] before training hundreds of mujahideen as the emir of the Khalden training camp in Afghanistan.[15]

According to his associates, al-Libi's subordinates respected his leadership and intellectual abilities. In his book detailing his experiences training with al-Qaeda at the Khalden camp, Omar Nasiri called al-Libi an "intellectual" who obviously "read and thought very deeply." Citing his "extraordinary charisma," Nasiri wrote that al-Libi "spoke more intelligently and eloquently than anyone else at the camp" and that "all the brothers listened to him with rapt attention."

Soon after the Pakistanis turned him over to US authorities, al-Libi was transferred from Kandahar to Bagram air base, where CIA, FBI, and military officials interrogated him.[16] From the start, the FBI and the CIA had different perspectives on the most appropriate and effective method of interrogating al-Libi. No agency, it seemed, was without its problems.

The military's interrogation (or "strategic debriefing") capabilities focused on providing tactical commanders on the ground the intelligence necessary to successfully accomplish their mission on the battlefield. As one interrogator described it, military officials typically look for tactical information such as "the location of the next IED, the next arms cache"—that is, "immediately actionable information"—and not larger objectives like the structure of a terrorist organization.[17]

FBI special agent Russell Fincher and New York Police Department detective Marty Mahon were among the first sent to Bagram to interrogate al-Libi. "What I was hearing from Russell [Fincher] about al-Libi's vetting in Bagram, during his initial intake session, highlighted the many inefficiencies of this whole process," said Jack Cloonan, a senior FBI counterterrorism agent who was supporting Fincher and Mahon from New York City. "It was clear that the military investigators vetting al-Libi didn't have a clue what they were doing."[18]

The interrogation of terrorist suspects and al-Qaeda members was not traditionally the CIA's responsibility. As Kenneth J. Levit, former special counsel to the CIA director argued, the organization's future "lead responsibility for al-Qaeda interrogation" represented "a departure from the Agency's previous counterterrorism role." Because the "job of interrogating terrorist operatives is distinct from the typical elicitation and information gathering traditionally associated with intelligence service responsibilities," Levit viewed "significant changes in training and mindset" as a necessity.[19]

On the other hand, the FBI's Counterterrorism Division began interrogating members of al-Qaeda as far back as 1996, when President Clinton took the first steps to identify and target bin Laden, Zawahiri, and the rest of al-Qaeda network. After identifying hundreds of key al-Qaeda operatives, the FBI succeeded in capturing and interrogating a few lower-level individuals. To build rapport, the FBI utilized the traditional law enforcement framework of carrots and sticks: suspects who cooperated were rewarded with favors. According to Cloonan, these methods were successful, enabling the FBI to find both al-Qaeda's weapons suppliers and supporters.[20]

But interrogation in Afghanistan post-9/11 was very different. Cloonan later said, "We had to work within the military chain of command, and no one really knew what was going on or how the detainees were being picked up. Many of the detainees the military zeroed in on were strap hangers—these [detainees] clearly didn't know much if anything. The military guys didn't really understand how the training camps worked."[21]

In 2001, there were over 120 such military training camps in Afghanistan and Pakistan.[22] Though many had been established in the 1980s during the Soviet occupation to train troops, bin Laden directed some of these camps to exclusively train al-Qaeda operatives. In his testimony on March 27, 2007, Abu Zubaydah provided the following history of the Khalden camp—of which al-Libi was emir:

> The Khalden camp has been around since back when Russia was considered our enemy due to their invasion of Afghanistan. The mission of this training camp was for the purpose of training Muslim brothers for defensive jihad. Defensive jihad means that if an aggressor or invader invades Muslim lands, no matter where, then it is every Muslim's duty to defend the land against the invader.[23]

According to Omar Nasiri, al-Libi agreed with the camp's purpose as described by Abu Zubaydah and "spoke mostly of jihad, and the duty of Muslims all over the world." He explained to the men "the difference between the *faridat al-jihad* and the *kifayat al-jihad*—the obligatory or defensive jihad and the offensive or preemptive jihad, respectively. All of us, he explained, were fighting the *faridat al-jihad*, the battle to reclaim the lands of the caliphate from the infidels."[24]

Still, Cloonan argued, the Khalden camp was of "low importance," since it was "well-infiltrated by Saudi, British, and some US agents, and the terrorists knew this." At such an inconsequential camp, the only person of significance would have been the emir, who was responsible for identifying talented trainees, testing their commitment to the cause, and then sending them to specialized training camps. This, according to Cloonan, was al-Libi's primary role.[25]

INITIAL INTERROGATIONS

After vetting al-Libi, CIA agents concluded that he had important information but was hiding it.[26] On the FBI's behalf, Fincher and Mahon took charge of the investigation. Fincher began his interrogation by offering al-Libi coffee and attempting to build up his ego as a jihadist commander.[27] Knowing that al-Libi was a religious man, Fincher asked him whether he prayed, to which al-Libi replied, "of course."[28] Fincher then explained that he, too, was a man of faith, though a Christian. The two men prayed together and discussed religion over numerous cups of coffee. Soon al-Libi began to open up about his history and his contacts, at which point Fincher showed him photos, and al-Libi identified US terrorist suspects who had been at the Khalden camp.[29] "Russell [Fincher] went through a basic interview, and before they finished, al-Libi says two important things: he knew Zacarias Moussaoui and he knows Richard Reid," recalled Cloonan.

Both Reid and Moussaoui were significant terrorist suspects in US custody at the time. Reid, widely known as the shoe bomber, was later convicted of attempting to destroy American Airlines Flight 63 en route to Miami from Paris in December 2001 by igniting explosives embedded in his footwear. His al-Qaeda colleague Zacarias Moussaoui had trained to be a pilot and was thought at the time to have been the 9/11 attacks' intended twentieth hijacker. Though authorities had already arrested him in Minneapolis in August 2001, the FBI had little evidence directly connecting Moussaoui to al-Qaeda—until al-Libi provided it.

"Neither the Moussaoui or Reid cases were a slam dunk for the FBI," said Cloonan. "I told Russell he needed to preserve this guy and his info, and treat him accordingly. I told him to read him his Miranda rights in Arabic and English so the whole thing was preserved if he goes before the court."

Fincher continued to interrogate al-Libi for the next few days, playing on al-Libi's religious motivation to build rapport.[30] In return, al-Libi continued to provide valuable, actionable intelligence, including details about al-Qaeda training camps and recruits.[31] But when pressed for insight into a connection between al-Qaeda and Iraq, al-Libi said he had no information.[32]

Al-Libi also said that he had never really liked bin Laden. Although bin Laden wanted al-Qaeda fighters to be trained for the offensive *kifayat al-jihad*, and insisted that the Khalden camp be used to train only al-Qaeda fighters,[33] al-Libi preferred to train those underneath him in the defensive *faridat al-jihad*. Both he and Abu Zubaydah disagreed with bin Laden on these doctrinal points.[34]

But as the FBI proceeded to extract information from al-Libi, tension rose among the FBI, CIA, and military officials.[35] Continuing fear of another terrorist attack inside the US put pressure on the entire IC to generate results—though they disagreed as to the best method to do so. As one of the first high-value detainees to be interrogated after the 9/11 attacks, al-Libi became a focal point of the tensions, and FBI director Robert Mueller and the Bagram military commander were among the first to intervene.[36]

Both supported the idea that the FBI and the military should work in concert.[37] It made sense for the two organizations to cooperate in interrogations, not only because "some of the military guys at Bagram were reservists who had been cops or detectives in their former lives," but also because "Mueller and others felt that al-Libi was for real, and that he wanted to cooperate. We wanted a prosecutable case on bin Laden and [Moussaoui and Reid]." The FBI, accordingly then, wanted to maintain custody of al-Libi and incarcerate him in a federal prison to serve time for aiding terrorist activities—while testifying against other terrorist suspects.[38]

CIA officials disagreed, according to Cloonan. "Russell began explaining to me what was going on vis-à-vis the military and the CIA at Bagram.[39] The Commanding General of the 10th Mountain Division at Bagram was in favor of working with the FBI on interrogations. The CIA, however, didn't want the FBI involved and didn't want to get the lawyers involved. They didn't want to go through the formal channels of investigation. To them, it was 'gloves off' and 'do what it takes' to get these people interviewed."[40]

CIA felt strongly that al-Libi was withholding information about other key al-Qaeda leaders and potential attacks against the US. To further press al-Libi for this information, they wanted him transferred from FBI custody.[41] The dispute quickly escalated, and the White House decided that the CIA should receive custody of al-Libi. Unlike FBI director Mueller, CIA director George Tenet had a seat at the decision-making table.[42]

"The bottom line is that we lost to the CIA," said Cloonan.[43]

On the night al-Libi was transferred to CIA custody, Fincher and Mahon met with him one final time. According to Cloonan, "Al-Libi knew that he was about to be transferred." A few days earlier, a CIA agent had visited al-Libi, intending to intimidate him by announcing that he was being sent to an Egyptian prison.[44]

On January 8, 2002,[45] al-Libi was transferred from Bagram air base to the USS *Bataan,* where US authorities further interrogated him.[46] This time, he provided information about an alleged al-Qaeda plot to blow up the American embassy in Yemen. In response, the US embassy in Yemen was shuttered for a week. Al-Libi also disclosed that al-Qaeda planned to bomb the US Navy base in Bahrain[47] and provided specific information about the location of Abu Zubaydah,[48] who was then believed to be the third- or fourth-highest ranking member of al-Qaeda. Abu Zubaydah had also been on the initial US list of twelve suspected terrorists whose assets were frozen following 9/11.[49] US and Pakistani forces captured Abu Zubaydah a few months later.

In late January 2002, US officials rendered al-Libi to Egypt.[50] Three years after his rendition, President Bush defended the practice: "In the post-9/11 world, the United States must make sure we protect our people and our friends from attack. That was the charge we have been given. And one way to do so is to arrest people and send them back to their country of origin with the promise that they won't be tortured."[51]

But was al-Libi tortured?

In Egypt, al-Libi was held in the ████████ maximum security compound known as al-Aqrab, or Scorpion.[52] Although little was known about al-Libi's detention there at the time, two other prisoners detained in this facility—Ahmed Agiza and Mohammed al-Zery—have recounted stories of horrific treatment, being incarcerated in freezing cold cells, receiving beatings routinely, and being electrocuted through electrodes clamped to their genitals.[53]

Still, it would be another two years before al-Libi's treatment in Egyptian custody would surface publicly.

American intelligence analysts who reviewed al-Libi's interrogation transcripts from Egypt believed that the information he provided on potential terrorist attacks against the US was generally credible but lacked specificity. In April 2002, for example, al-Libi declared that al-Qaeda planned to attack financial institutions in the northeastern and mid-Atlantic US,[54] a threat confirmed by Abu Zubaydah. US homeland security officials then raised threat-warning levels around the country.[55] But American officials could not independently verify al-Libi's claims, and were left wondering if al-Libi had made up his threats.[56]

While in Egyptian custody, al-Libi also began to claim that al-Qaeda had sent two operatives to Iraq for training in chemical and biological weapons (CBW)—despite the fact that he had initially denied any knowledge of a link between al-Qaeda and Iraq.[57] This information, of course, piqued the interest of intelligence analysts for an obvious reason: the idea that if al-Qaeda had acquired training in weapons of mass destruction it would have posed a clear and immediate threat to US interests.

Both the CIA and the DIA (Defense Intelligence Agency) noted these new declarations in their respective reports with varying degrees of uncertainty as to their accuracy.[58] In the September 2002 and January 2003 versions of the *Iraqi Support for Terrorism* report, CIA analysts assessed al-Libi's interrogation information as "credible," but noted that he "did not know the results of the training" and that he "was not in a position to know if any training took place."[59] DIA analysts reviewing the same information doubted al-Libi's statements on the Iraq/al-Qaeda WMD relationship. A DIA daily intelligence summary, or DITSUM, reported al-Libi lacked specific details about the relationship and stated that while the information from al-Libi's interrogation was possibly true, it was "more likely that [he] was intentionally misleading debriefers."[60]

DIA analysts at the time further questioned the overall idea of a relationship between al-Qaeda and Iraq. Saddam Hussein was a secular leader and wary of Islamic revolutionary movements; he was unlikely to assist a group such as al-Qaeda that he could not control.[61] Later DIA reports, however, failed to question the veracity of al-Libi's claims.

BUILDING THE CASE FOR WAR AGAINST IRAQ

During the scorching summer of 2002, political momentum in Washington began to build for military action against Iraq. As Congress prepared for the upcoming November elections, they debated the necessity and justification of a military invasion. Several key Democratic leaders, including Senator Joe Biden—at that time chairman of the Senate Foreign Relations Committee—felt the US must ultimately eliminate an Iraqi nuclear threat. "The question is the means by which we eliminate the threat," said Biden in early August, "and the means by which you build support to be able to do that."[62]

Through the fall, Vice President Dick Cheney and Secretary of Defense Donald Rumsfeld began building a public case justifying a preemptive invasion.[63] On September 8, Cheney appeared on NBC's *Meet the Press*, declaring Iraq a "mortal threat" and claiming that there was increasing intelligence that Saddam Hussein intended to acquire equipment for enriching uranium and, eventually, nuclear weapons.[64] When asked if there was a direct link between al-Qaeda and Iraq, Cheney responded ambiguously. That same morning, the *New York Times* published an article about Iraq's nuclear ambitions that pointed to the recent acquisition of high-strength aluminum tubes as evidence that Hussein was seeking to rebuild Iraq's nuclear program.[65] Political commentators began discussing the possibility of an Anglo-American invasion of Iraq.

As public information about Iraq's alleged nuclear weapons program and a potential link between al-Qaeda and Iraq mounted, Democratic senators on the Senate Select Committee on Intelligence (SSCI)—Dick Durbin, Carl Levin, Bob Graham, and Dianne Feinstein—each sent letters to CIA director Tenet and President Bush, requesting a national intelligence estimate (NIE) evaluating Iraq's WMD capabilities and potential connections with terrorist organizations.[66] "There has not been a formal rigorous IC assessment, such as a National Intelligence Estimate, addressing the issues relating to Iraq, and I deeply believe that such an estimate is vital to Congressional decision making," wrote Senator Feinstein.[67] The IC then rammed the Iraq NIE through the system in a record-breaking three weeks—a process that normally takes months—and delivered the document to Congress on October 1, 2002.

Throughout the autumn, several intelligence officials testifying before Congress used al-Libi's statements as evidence—albeit imperfect—of a link between Iraq and al-Qaeda. Tenet testified on September 17 before the SSCI that "Iraq provided training to al-Qaeda members in Iraq—of most concern, in the area of chemical and biological agents," a statement directly stemming from al-Libi's assertions.[68] He continued:

> There is evidence that Iraq provided al-Qaeda with various kinds of training—combat, bomb-making, and chemical, biological, radiological and nuclear. Although Saddam did not endorse al-Qaeda's overall agenda and was suspicious of Islamist movements in general, he was apparently not averse, under certain circumstances, to enhancing bin Laden's capabilities. As with much of the information on the overall relationship, details on training are second-hand or from sources of varying reliability.

In another classified SSCI briefing on October 2, 2002, senators questioned deputy director of Central Intelligence John McLaughlin about Iraq's links to al-Qaeda. Using information gleaned from al-Libi's Egyptian interrogation, McLaughlin said that "we have credible reporting that al-Qaeda leaders sought contacts in Iraq who could help them acquire WMD capabilities. The reporting also stated that Iraq has provided training to al-Qaeda members in the areas of poisons and gases and making conventional bombs."[69]

Al-Libi's statements even surfaced in speeches and interviews with Bush administration officials. National security advisor Condoleezza Rice cited al-Libi's statements when making the case for an al-Qaeda–Iraq link during a September 25 interview on PBS *NewsHour*:

We clearly know that there were in the past and have been contacts between senior Iraqi officials and members of al-Qaida going back for actually quite a long time. We know too that several of the detainees, in particular some high-ranking detainees, have said that Iraq provided some training to al-Qaeda in chemical weapons development. So, yes, there are contacts between Iraq and al-Qaeda.[70]

Later, on October 7, 2002, just as Congress prepared to vote on a joint resolution authorizing war against Iraq, President Bush outlined his case for invasion in a key speech in Cincinnati. To support an al-Qaeda–Iraq connection, President Bush referenced al-Libi's statements yet again,[71] claiming "we've learned that Iraq has trained al-Qaeda members in bomb-making and poisons and deadly gases."[72]

Three days later, the die was cast. The House of Representatives passed a joint resolution authorizing President Bush, acting alone if necessary, to use military force against Iraq. The Senate approved the resolution the following day.

Shortly thereafter, following the November midterm elections, the Republican Party maintained its majority in the House of Representatives and regained control of the Senate. The landslide Republican victory was viewed by many as an overwhelming vote of confidence in the Bush administration's handling of the post-9/11 era and lead-up to the Iraq invasion. Likewise, the United Nations Security Council appeared supportive of the invasion, voting unanimously to adopt UNSC Resolution 1441, which declared Iraq in material breach of its cease-fire agreements and offered Saddam Hussein's regime one last chance to disarm, as stipulated by previous UN resolutions.

Less than one week before he was to make the final US presentation arguing for the legitimacy of war against Iraq to the UNSC, US secretary of state Colin Powell seemed frustrated, according to Colonel Larry Wilkerson, Powell's chief of staff.[73] Poring through the reports that served as the basis for his speech, Powell thought the intelligence provided to him lacked substance.[74]

"In preparing to argue the case for war, we wanted to cover three main areas: the threat of WMD, the Iraq-al-Qaeda terrorist connection, and human rights," recalled Wilkerson. "The human rights portion was clear-cut. For the other two sections, we received a 48-page paper from Scooter Libby and the Vice President's Office on WMD and a 25-page paper from the CIA on the terrorist portion."[75] According to George Tenet, the CIA drafted only the terrorism section of the speech after Powell "promptly dismissed" a forty-page document "of unknown origin" provided by Scooter Libby and the vice president's office. "They kept suggesting language so far over the top (for example, suggesting possible Iraqi-9/11 connections)," wrote Tenet in his memoirs, "that I finally pulled aside Phil Mudd, the then deputy chief of our Counterterrorism Center, and told him to write the terrorism piece himself."[76]

Before building his presentation, Powell asked Tenet to make sure every fact had "three, preferably four, independently corroborating sources."[77] After reading the forty-eight-page paper from the vice president's office, however, Powell realized that the paper's intelligence lacked corroboration. In fact, the document had no sources at all.[78]

Despite the rewrite, "Colin was really uncomfortable with the CIA-provided intelligence on al-Qaeda's connections to Baghdad as well," recalled Wilkerson. "'This is nothing more than a genealogy,' he said, 'like something from the book of Genesis. This is not intelligence. It's a chronological history of potential contacts between potential terrorists and the Mukhabarat[79] in Iraq, and there's no solid evidence.' Colin and I discussed the information, and he decided that he wasn't going to argue the connection between al-Qaeda and Iraq. There just wasn't enough evidence."[80]

Tenet was also skeptical of the information provided by the vice president's office, rejecting a great deal of the draft as exaggerated.[81] "Much of our time in the run-up to the speech was spent taking out material, including much that had been added by the policy community after the draft left the agency, that we and the Secretary's staff judged to have been unreliable," McLaughlin later stated.[82]

Because of all these doubts, Powell instructed his speechwriter, Lynne Davidson, to strike all information about the al-Qaeda–Iraq connection from the speech, and instead include information from the October 2002 Iraq national intelligence estimate. "We didn't know at the time how flawed that NIE was," claimed Wilkerson.

While Davidson rewrote the speech, the rest of the team selected graphics and photos for inclusion in the secretary's presentation. In a February 1 meeting with advisers at CIA headquarters,[83] Powell, Wilkerson, McLaughlin, and other intelligence officials were selecting aerial photographs and architectural sketches when Tenet interrupted the meeting.[84] "George walked into the room and said, with a grin on his face, 'We have learned we have a source who can provide us with contacts for the [al-Qaeda] chemical and biological weapons training in Iraq,'" said Wilkerson. "'We have training locations, descriptions, and names.' The Secretary asked him if this was corroborated and certain, and George said 'yes.' After some conversation, the Secretary asked us to refashion his remarks again to include the al-Qaeda–Iraq relationship. It wasn't until months after the presentation that we learned that this source was al-Libi."[85]

Davidson and Wilkerson spent the next thirty-six hours finalizing Powell's speech. The entire team then flew to New York City and set up a mock UN room, where Powell practiced his presentation. Around 10:30 on the evening of February 4 at the conclusion of his final practice round, Secretary Powell sat down for a break. Tenet sat directly behind him.

According to Wilkerson, "The Secretary turned his head slightly and said to George, 'You stand behind everything, Mr. DCI?' George replied 'yes,' that it was the best they had. 'I'll have to stand before my oversight committees in the Congress and explain why if it isn't.'"

The following morning, before the UN, Powell argued for the necessity of invading Iraq; Tenet again sat directly behind him. In his speech, which lasted approximately an hour and a half, he outlined Iraq's history of hiding weapons material and thwarting inspections; provided intelligence concerning Iraq's biological, chemical, and nuclear weapons program; and described the links between al-Qaeda and Iraq.

Arguing that Iraq had trained al-Qaeda operatives in chemical weapons, Secretary Powell referenced intelligence gleaned from al-Libi's confessions:

I can trace the story of a senior terrorist operative telling how Iraq provided training in these weapons to al-Qaeda. Fortunately, this operative is now detained, and he has told his story. I will relate it to you now as he, himself, described it.

This senior al-Qaeda terrorist was responsible for one of al-Qaeda's training camps in Afghanistan.

His information comes firsthand from his personal involvement at senior levels of al-Qaeda. He says bin Laden and his top deputy in Afghanistan, deceased al-Qaeda leader Mohammed Atef, did not believe that al-Qaeda labs in Afghanistan were capable enough to manufacture these chemical or biological agents. They needed to go somewhere else. They had to look outside of Afghanistan for help. Where did they go? Where did they look? They went to Iraq.[86]

After Powell made the case, the American team promptly returned to Washington. "He [Powell] gave everyone who worked on the speech an award," said Wilkerson. "I told him I didn't want one. I didn't think the speech was as powerful as it needed to be."

The secretary's speech received generally favorable reviews. For many Americans, even those skeptical of the case for declaring war, Powell provided the Bush administration the political cover for the necessity of military action against Iraq. Senate Minority Leader Tom Daschle wrote a press release that said Powell made a "powerful and compelling case about Iraq's failure to comply with its obligation to disarm."[87] Other Democratic lawmakers found the presentation "compelling."[88] "The evidence proves that Saddam Hussein has a loaded gun pointed at the civilized world," stated House Speaker Dennis Hastert. "It is time to take that loaded gun away from this evil tyrant."[89]

Other lawmakers remained skeptical about the necessity of an invasion. "There are more immediate threats to security around the globe," argued West Virginia senator Robert Byrd.[90] House Minority Leader Nancy Pelosi, who otherwise believed that Iraq must disarm, said, "The question is whether war now is the only way to rid Iraq of these deadly weapons. I do not believe it is."[91]

Powell's performance received mixed reviews from other countries. "The clear and present danger posed by Saddam's regime requires a united response from the community of democracies," wrote the foreign ministers of Albania, Bulgaria, Croatia, Estonia, Latvia, Lithuania, Mace-

donia, Romania, Slovakia, and Slovenia in support of Powell's presentation and US policies toward Iraq.[92] "Our countries understand the dangers posed by tyranny and the special responsibility of democracies to
defend our shared values."[93] Britain and Spain also strongly supported
Powell's presentation. British foreign minister Jack Straw called the presentation "powerful," and Spanish foreign minister Ana Palacio found the
evidence Powell presented "compelling."[94]

France and Germany remained skeptical, arguing that they needed
more time to review the evidence. Both countries reiterated their preference for strengthening weapons inspections as a critical next step.
"The use of force can only be a final recourse," said French foreign minister Dominique de Villepin. "We must move on to a new stage and
further strengthen the inspections."[95] German foreign minister Joschka
Fischer concurred: "The dangers of a military action and its consequences are plain to see. We must continue to seek a peaceful solution
to this crisis."[96]

No matter. The US continued to move forward with preparations to
invade Iraq. On March 16, during a conference in the Azores, President
Bush and the leaders of Great Britain, Portugal, and Spain announced
that Iraq had twenty-four hours to fulfill all previous UN resolutions
for disarmament and come into full compliance with UNSC Resolution 1441, which had been adopted in November 2002. Iraq failed to
act accordingly. In response, President Bush authorized air strikes on
targets around Baghdad on March 19. When Iraq did not take action
again, US-led coalition forces launched nine hours of bombing and missile strikes, and ground forces entered Iraq. Operation Iraqi Freedom
had begun.

Over the following weeks, US-led coalition troops marched to Baghdad, encountering less opposition from Iraqi troops than initially anticipated. On April 9, coalition troops entered Baghdad and pulled down a
large statue of Saddam Hussein in celebration. Coalition troops had successfully taken Baghdad; however, they had uncovered no weapons of
mass destruction along the way.

The search for alternate explanations was on. "As it became increasingly clear that the US forces in Iraq were unlikely to find any WMD
stockpiles or any substantial nuclear program," explained Wilkerson, "the

Bush Administration began to search for ways to explain its errors. The principal response the administration came up with was that Saddam Hussein had every intention of stockpiling WMD once the sanctions were lifted and the international focus was off."[97]

In the meantime, Tenet and McLaughlin made calls to Powell and his deputy, Richard Armitage, about Powell's UN presentation. "We got several things right in that speech," recalled McLaughlin. "We were correct about Saddam Hussein's intent—he wanted to use the threat of nuclear weapons to deter Iran. And, we were right about the delivery systems. Iraq was in violation of the UN agreements—they had illicit weapons systems."[98] However, McLaughlin continued, "What we were wrong on was the stockpiles of chemical and biological weapons. They were not there. We had never said they had nuclear weapons—only that they might be able to obtain them in 5–7 years. And the al-Qaeda–Iraq connection had never been strong. The CIA produced two reports on the connections between al-Qaeda and Iraq and both concluded there was no operational relationship between them."[99]

During this same period, the CIA commenced a six-month internal investigation into prewar intelligence collection and analysis. "In June when it was becoming increasingly clear that we were not going to find any WMD in Iraq, [the CIA] put fifteen of our sharpest people in a room together and asked them to look at what went wrong," said McLaughlin. "They reviewed every report, every email going day-by-day, report-by-report and did a scrub of everything. In January 2004, they presented their final report documenting our errors and tracing them back so that we could better understand why they occurred."

"The first thing that collapsed was the nuclear program," Wilkerson said. "The information about the mobile labs was the last to collapse in August. But from about late April until June, evidence began to surface that there was some dissent on the verifiability of al-Libi's information."

As al-Libi languished in Egyptian custody, intelligence analysts from the CIA and DIA disagreed about the validity of his statements. "Well after Secretary Powell's UN presentation, I learned that there was a DIA report that consisted of that agency's dissent on the al-Libi interrogation," said Wilkerson. "When we asked CIA officials why this DIA dissent wasn't brought to our attention previously, the official answer was 'a computer glitch.' The CIA claimed that the file wasn't properly coded so they weren't able to find it in the system."[100]

According to Wilkerson, no DIA representatives were included in Powell's preparation sessions.[101] Other senior intelligence officials have reported, however, that senior DIA representatives in fact reviewed Powell's speech and did not object to including information provided by al-Libi.[102]

As the search for Iraqi WMD continued fruitlessly into the summer of 2003, the Senate launched a unified and bipartisan oversight effort to investigate the quality, reasonableness, and objectivity of prewar intelligence. As the situation in Iraq rapidly deteriorated and the WMD search failed to uncover anything of significance, the Bush administration attempted to head off these inquiries with a full-throated defense of the policy decisions. In late October, undersecretary of defense for policy Douglas Feith sent SSCI a classified report, *Summary of Body of Intelligence on Iraq-Al-Qaeda Contacts (1990–2003)*, that outlined fifty prewar links between al-Qaeda and Saddam Hussein's regime.[103]

The report was originally produced by a small group of intelligence analysts in a project called the Policy Counter Terrorism Evaluation Group (PCTEG) that became generically known as the Office of Special Plans (OSP). It was founded by Feith and deputy defense secretary Paul Wolfowitz in September 2002, and headed by Feith until its dissolution in mid-2003. Established to provide the Bush administration policymakers with analysis of "raw" intelligence—intelligence that the IC had neither completely vetted nor analyzed—the OSP was controversial. Composed of Pentagon policy and intelligence analysts, the OSP produced assessments that contradicted analysis of the greater intelligence community about the relationship between Saddam Hussein and al-Qaeda.[104]

One Pentagon adviser who worked closely with the OSP said, "Special Plans was created in order to find evidence of what Wolfowitz and his boss, Defense Secretary Donald Rumsfeld, believed to be true—that Saddam Hussein had close ties to al-Qaeda, and that Iraq had an enormous arsenal of chemical, biological, and possibly even nuclear weapons that threatened the region and, potentially, the United States."[105] The adviser further argued that the Pentagon believed the CIA misinterpreted the situation. "The [CIA] was out to disprove linkage between Iraq and terrorism. That's what drove them. If you've ever worked with intelligence data, you can see the ingrained views at CIA that color the way it sees data."[106]

Many intelligence officials did not approve of OSP's activities. "Feith and company would find little nuggets that supported their beliefs and seize upon them, never understanding that there might be a larger picture they were missing," noted Tenet. "Isolated data points became so important to them that they would never look at the thousands of other data points that might convey the opposite story." When he first heard the reports produced by Feith's team, Tenet allegedly told DIA head Vice Admiral Jake Jacoby, "This is entirely inappropriate. You get this back in intelligence channels. I want analysts talking to analysts, not people with agendas."[107]

On November 24, journalist Stephen Hayes of the conservative *Weekly Standard* published portions of the classified summary in his article "Case Closed: The US Government's Secret Memo Detailing Cooperation Between Saddam Hussein and Osama Bin Laden."[108] That same day, the Pentagon issued a press release, stating that the "classified annex was not an analysis of the substantive issue of the relationship between Iraq and al-Qaeda, and it drew no conclusions."[109] The CIA also sent Feith a list of corrections and disputed the reliability of several of the reports he cited.[110]

AL-LIBI RECANTS

Sometime in 2003, al-Libi was returned from Egyptian to US custody.[111] The exact details of his detainment remain hidden from public view. According to some reports, al-Libi was transferred from Egypt to Afghanistan and then sent to the detention center in Guantanamo Bay, Cuba, in the spring of 2004.[112]

In January 2004, likely while in US custody in Afghanistan,[113] al-Libi began to recant his previous testimony that Iraq had provided chemical and biological weapons training to al-Qaeda operatives.[114] On February 4 and 5, soon after he was transferred to Guantanamo, interrogators sent a series of cables detailing al-Libi's new claims to CIA headquarters.[115] These cables reported that al-Libi asserted he was recanting because he "had a strong desire to tell his entire story and identify why and how he fabricated information since his capture." He said that Iraq had never trained al-Qaeda in chemical or biological weapons—"to the best of his knowledge."[116]

Why did he go back on his testimony? Al-Libi claimed that in 2002, while in US custody in Afghanistan, his debriefers threatened to make him sleep on the floor of his cold cell and to transfer him to a third country for interrogation if he did not cooperate.[117] After his debriefers made him remove his socks and gloves and placed him on the cold floor of his cell for fifteen minutes, al-Libi claimed he decided to fabricate information in order to obtain better treatment. "Once al-Libi started fabricating information, his treatment improved and he experienced no further physical pressures from the Americans."[118]

Later, after he had been transferred to Egypt, al-Libi explained that his Egyptian interrogators pressed him repeatedly about an al-Qaeda–Iraq connection.[119] Al-Libi claimed that "this was a subject about which he said he knew nothing and had difficulty even coming up with a story."[120] Allegedly dissatisfied with his response, his Egyptian interrogators shoved him into a container twenty square inches tall and held him there for some seventeen hours.[121] When he was released from the box, al-Libi continued, the Egyptians gave him a final opportunity to "tell the truth" and then knocked him to the floor where he was pummeled for fifteen minutes. Al-Libi stated that his interrogators then pressed him again for an al-Qaeda–Iraq connection. This time, he claimed, he concocted a story about three al-Qaeda operatives who went to Iraq to receive some manner of nuclear weapons training. Allegedly he used the names of actual al-Qaeda members so he could recall details of his tale and make it more believable to his Egyptian questioners.[122]

According to al-Libi, the Egyptians asked him about training in anthrax and biological weapons several days later. Again, al-Libi at first claimed he "knew nothing about a biological program and did not even understand the term biological."[123] But when he could not conjure up a story, al-Libi declared, he was "beaten in a way that left no marks."[124]

Senior US officials learned about al-Libi's recantation in a report issued on February 14.[125] The CIA was sharply divided on al-Libi's reversal and reviewed all reports related to him.[126]

Despite the new information pouring forth from al-Libi, the White House still defended the analysis of a strong link between Iraq and al-Qaeda. On June 17, four months after receiving al-Libi's recantations, Vice President Cheney told Gloria Borger of CNBC's *Capitol Report* that the evidence supporting the connection was firm. "There clearly was a relationship," said Cheney. "It's been testified to. The evidence is overwhelming. . . . The notion that there is no relationship between Iraq and al-Qaeda just simply is not true. I mean, there are reams of material here. Your show isn't long enough for me to read all the pieces of it."[127]

The media did not learn of al-Libi's reversal until July 2004, when Michael Isikoff first reported it in *Newsweek*.[128] In contrast to the information al-Libi provided to debriefers in 2002 on Iraq's ties to al-Qaeda, he "subsequently recounted a different story," a US official told Isikoff. The bottom line: "It's not clear which version is correct. We are still sorting this out."

In his memoirs, George Tenet wrote, "Al-Libi's story will no doubt be that he decided to fabricate in order to get better treatment and avoid harsh punishment. He clearly lied. We just don't know when."[129] Officials accordingly asked, Did al-Libi lie initially when he said Iraq trained al-Qaeda operatives in weapons of mass destruction? Or did he lie when he went back on his earlier statements in order to receive better treatment once he returned to US custody? "A recantation would restore his stature as someone who had successfully confounded the enemy,"[130] said Tenet. In other words, did al-Libi lie? Or did he lie about lying? And what role did his alleged torture play in his claims that he lied? The CIA sought to determine what was true and what was false.

"Many of the HVDs (high-value detainees) recanted information,"[131] said Rolf Mowatt-Larssen, the former head of the WMD branch of the CIA Counterterrorism Center.[132] "This is why all of this intelligence couldn't be corroborated. This is also why we began from the assumption that al-Libi was lying, and we only considered his intelligence to be true if we could corroborate it amongst several sources. For example, by playing al-Libi and Abu Zubaydah in sequence, we were able to cross-check the two."[133]

"We know that torture affects the quality of intelligence, the strongest correlation of accurate intelligence comes from willing debriefees," continued Mowatt-Larssen. ███████████████████████████████████████ ███████████████████████ The CIA also strongly suspected that al-Qaeda was trying to acquire chemical, biological, and/or nuclear weapons. Iraq already had a well-established history of developing poisons and chemical weapons and had proven that it would use them—even against its own citizens.

After al-Libi recanted in early 2004, CIA's internal review of intelligence failures in the lead-up to Iraq expanded to include his case. "We had several lessons learned from al-Libi's case, which resulted in changes in our standard operating procedures," said McLaughlin. "First, we must be very careful when relying on foreign intelligence services for information. Second, analysts need to have greater transparency behind reporting in order to better understand the sourcing of reports and assess their confidence in the information. And lastly, if the descriptor on a source includes language that suggests caution, this must be conveyed to the recipient of the analysis. We need to be clear about the provenance of information and let people know if we have direct access to the source or not."[134]

The SSCI released its first report on the IC's assessments leading up to the 2003 invasion of Iraq. The 511-page *Phase I* report, released on July 9, 2004, pointed to failures in the IC's analysis—failures that led to serious errors of judgment in the October 2002 Iraq NIE. The report also contended that the IC's assessments about Iraq's biological and chemical WMD capability, as outlined in the 2002 NIE, were not supported by the underlying information.

The SSCI assessed that for the WMD portions of Powell's speech to the UN, "much of the information provided or cleared by the CIA for inclusion in Secretary Powell's speech was overstated, misleading, or incorrect."[135] Although the committee considered the IC's assessment of the links between al-Qaeda and Iraq to be reasonable, the report found that in a post-9/11 environment, analysts "were under tremendous pressure to make correct assessments, to avoid missing a credible threat, and to avoid an intelligence failure on the scale of 9/11" and be "bold and assertive."[136]

In February 2004, the SSCI voted to include several key issues, including the IC's prewar assessments about postwar Iraq, postwar findings about Iraq's WMD and links to terrorism, and a review of statements by senior policymakers to determine if those statements had been substantiated by available intelligence in a follow-up report that came to be called *Phase II*.[137] Accordingly, at the release of the report, Vice Chairman Jay Rockefeller recognized that "there is a real frustration over what is not in this report, and I don't think it was mentioned in [SSCI] Chairman Roberts' statement, and that is about the—after the analysts and the IC produced an intelligence product, how is it then shaped or used or misused by the policymakers?" Senator Rockefeller pointed out several other concerns left unaddressed and expressed his desire to see the second phase of the investigation begin quickly so that it might fill in these gaps.[138]

THE POLITICS OF INTELLIGENCE

Nearly a year and a half after the release of the SSCI's *Phase I* report, some Democrats argued that the Republican-controlled committee under Roberts wanted to delay the second phase of the investigation until after the November congressional midterm elections in 2006. California Senator Dianne Feinstein sent a letter to Chairman Roberts on August 2, 2005, stating:

> I am increasingly dismayed by the delay in completing the Committee's "Phase II" investigation into intelligence prior to the Iraq War. As you know, the Committee voted unanimously on February 12, 2004, to investigate five questions on pre-war intelligence, including use of intelligence by policymakers. Nearly eighteen months later, much work remains before these questions will be satisfactorily answered.[139]

Democratic senators as well as the Armed Services Committee continued to examine prewar and postwar intelligence, investigating whether the Bush administration had misused intelligence data to deceive other policymakers and the country into invading Iraq. Al-Libi's case appeared to provide such evidence.

Accordingly, in October 2005, SSCI members Jay Rockefeller and Carl Levin sent a letter to DIA requesting that specific sections of a DIA report based on al-Libi's interrogation in Egypt in 2002 be declassified.[140] Specifically, the senators highlighted the following excerpt from the report:

> This is the first report from Ibn al-Shaykh [al-Libi] in which he claims Iraq assisted al Qaida's CBRN efforts. However, he lacks specific details on the Iraqis involved, the CBRN materials associated with the assistance, and the location where the training occurred. It is possible he does not know any further details; it is more likely this individual is intentionally misleading the debriefers. Ibn al-Shaykh has been undergoing debriefs for several weeks and may be describing scenarios to the debriefers that he knows will retain their interest. Saddam's regime is intensely secular and is wary of Islamic revolutionary movements. Moreover, Baghdad is unlikely to provide assistance to a group it cannot control.[141]

Later that month, DIA declassified relevant portions of DITSUM 044–02.[142]

The national media eventually took note of the declassified report, and Democrats used the report as evidence that the White House had misused prewar intelligence. "This newly declassified information provides additional, dramatic evidence that the administration's prewar statements were deceptive," said Senator Levin. "More than a year before Secretary Powell included that charge in his presentation to the United Nations, the DIA had said it believed the detainee's claims were bogus."[143]

In response, some Republicans accused Democrats of attempting to use the al-Libi case for partisan purposes. After Democrats forced Republicans into a highly unusual closed session of the entire Senate to review the report and secure assurances that Phase II would be completed, GOP Senator Orrin Hatch called the move "a political stunt."[144] "Whether [the intelligence] is from defense intelligence, whether it's from the CIA, whether it's from other sources around the world, we need to get that right to make the right decisions," opined Senator George Allen. "But what we don't need is a bunch of partisanship."[145]

PHASE II COMPLETED

In early September 2006, just two months before the November midterm elections, SSCI released the first two parts of the Phase II investigation, titled *Postwar Findings About Iraq's WMD Programs and Links to Terrorism and How They Compare with Prewar Assessments,* and *The Use by the Intelligence Community of Information Provided by the Iraqi National Congress.* The reports documented the numerous disputes among analysts within the various intelligence agencies over both Iraq's WMD capabilities and the links between al-Qaeda and Iraq.

Given al-Libi's prominence in providing WMD-related intelligence, SSCI scrutinized his debriefing materials. The *Postwar Findings* section zeroed in on CIA's analysis in 2002 and 2003 of al-Libi's assertions that al-Qaeda received chemical and biological weapons training in Iraq.[146] *Postwar Findings* similarly drew attention to 2002–2003 DIA reports that expressed doubt about al-Libi's statements—citing his lack of knowledge about the details of the weapons training—as well as the suggestion that al-Libi was "intentionally misleading his debriefers."[147]

The report also outlined changing assurances from officials about al-Libi's information. For instance, it referenced Tenet's testimony before the SSCI from September 2002. At that time, Tenet recognized the supporting evidence might be wrong: "As with much of the information on the overall relationship, details on training are second-hand or from sources of varying reliability." Tenet did not discuss the "varying reliability" of the IC's sources; still, when he testified again in February 2003, he claimed that "[Iraq] has also provided training in poisons and gases to two al-Qaeda associates. One of these associates characterized the relationship he forged with Iraqi officials as successful."[148]

After the two reports were released, the media focused on the partisan rancor of the debate over prewar intelligence. For instance, White House spokesman Tony Snow dismissed the findings in the reports as old news, declaring, "If we have people who want to re-litigate that, that's fine."[149] Senator Carl Levin on the other hand pointed to the reports' continuing relevance: "The President is still distorting [the truth]. He's still making statements which are false."[150]

After the 2006 midterm elections, Democrats gained a majority in both the Senate and the House—the first time that Democrats had controlled both chambers of Congress in twelve years. Democrat Jay Rockefeller took control of SSCI, and the former chairman, Senator Pat Roberts, decided to leave the committee.

After al-Libi recanted his statements in early 2004, his whereabouts became largely unknown to the general public for the next two years; no Bush administration official mentioned his name again. Human rights organizations in the US and UK, however, continued to attempt to track detainees like al-Libi who had been rendered to third countries and dubbed them "ghost detainees" or "ghost prisoners." Without access to the detainees themselves or to the classified intelligence reports concerning them, however, they found the task of accounting for all detainees and pressing the US government for greater transparency and accountability an enormous challenge.

Even members of the US Congress could not confirm al-Libi's whereabouts. In a May 2007 letter to President Bush, Representatives Edward Markey, William Delahunt, and Jerrold Nadler requested a "detailed account of al-Libi's whereabouts since he was first detained by Pakistani authorities.[151] They sent the letter several months after Markey introduced the Torture Outsourcing Prevention Act, which aimed to prevent the rendition of US detainees to foreign countries, particularly countries in which torture or other inhumane treatments were known to occur.

The letter also asked the Bush administration to clarify how and why it transferred al-Libi to Egypt, when the US government first learned that al-Libi claimed to have been tortured, and how the administration verified al-Libi's information while he was in Egyptian custody.

The congressmen never received a response.

In early 2006, al-Libi arrived in Libya, where he fell ill with tuberculosis.[152] Following 9/11, US-Libya relations had improved dramatically. Libyan president Muammar Qadhafi, attempting to improve relations with the US and the European Union, renounced Libya's WMD program in December 2003, and the US reestablished diplomatic relations with Tripoli in 2004. Later that year, as the Bush administration sought to reduce the number of detainees held in Guantanamo Bay, Libya began taking back Libyan detainees. Later in 2006, al-Libi was tried before the State Security Court and then detained in the infamous Abu Salim prison.[153]

A sojourn in a Libyan jail must have been much worse than incarceration in Guantanamo Bay. "Abu Salim and Ain Zara prisons are run by Libya's internal security agency and are not under the jurisdiction of the Libyan Ministry of Justice like other prisons in Libya," said Heba Morayef, a researcher from Human Rights Watch. "Abu Salim is usually where the Libyan government places anyone suspected of being affiliated with or involved in Islamist activities. Members of the Libyan Islamic Fighting Group are all kept there."[154]

Morayef and a colleague from Human Rights Watch visited Abu Salim in April 2009. Human rights organizations had long suspected that al-Libi was imprisoned there, but up to this point, had never been granted access to the prison or to al-Libi. One day, however, prison authorities gave Morayef and her colleague access to several Libyan detainees, including al-Libi. The first four prisoners claimed they had been arrested, detained, and tortured by US forces in Thailand and Pakistan and claimed they had also been detained in Bagram.[155] They described these experiences to Morayef and claimed the CIA had questioned them throughout their detention.[156]

"We learned that most of the prisoners had been before the Libyan State Security Court and not given a fair trial," Morayef explained. "Some said they didn't have a lawyer, and those that did said they weren't able to meet with their lawyer before their trial. We realized that they were taking significant risks in even telling us that much."

After the two researchers spoke with the first four prisoners, the prison guards brought al-Libi to meet them. "He could walk fine, slowly, but unassisted. Although we only saw him for about three minutes, there were no obvious signs of scarring or recent harm that we could detect. He looked thin and gaunt, but not seriously ill," reported Morayef. Al-Libi, she said, was wearing a blue jumpsuit. According to the prisoners, a blue jumpsuit meant a sentence of life in prison. Red jumpsuits indicated a prisoner had been sentenced to death.[157]

"Al-Libi sat farther away from us," explained Morayef. "His movements were angry and agitated, and he glared at us. [My colleague] explained that we were there to hear al-Libi's story and explain to the world what has happened to him, and I translated it into Arabic." But when they explained they only interviewed prisoners with their consent, al-Libi abruptly stood up and said, "Where were you when I was being tortured in American prisons?" and walked away.[158]

"We never expected that we would be allowed to meet al-Libi," recalled Morayef. "They could have so easily refused us access—they refused to allow us to meet seven other prisoners we asked to meet. They brought him out because they wanted us to see him. The only way I can explain the fact that he was immediately so angry with us, before we even said anything, is that he must have been forced to come out and tell us that he didn't want to speak to us."[159]

On May 11, two weeks after Morayef's visit, al-Libi allegedly killed himself.[160] *Oea*, a Libyan newspaper founded by Qadhafi's son, Saif al-Islam, first reported al-Libi's death. Al-Libi's family was told that he had committed suicide by hanging himself with a bed sheet, though his friends apparently doubted a man of such conservative religious conviction would commit suicide, a practice prohibited in Islam.[161]

Others apparently doubted that al-Libi's death was a suicide as well. For example, al-Libi's family told Libyan friends that in a recent visit al-Libi had appeared positive and thought there was a chance he might be released from Abu Salim.[162] Abu Zubaydah's defense attorneys had also recently attempted to arrange to talk with al-Libi.[163] Brent Mickum, Abu Zubaydah's lawyer, said, "The timing of this [was] weird."[164]

Accordingly, human rights organizations called for an immediate investigation into al-Libi's death. Human Rights Watch called on Libyan authorities to conduct a full investigation, adding that the authorities should also reveal what they knew of al-Libi's treatment while he was in Egyptian and US custody.[165] In the US, officials appeared to take al-Libi's death seriously, stating that they were looking into the situation and were working with the US embassy in Tripoli.[166]

THE STRANGE case of Ibn al-Shaykh al-Libi highlights troubling aspects of the limitations of intelligence and the intelligence community—if top policymakers are dead-set on one course of action, enablers can take

highly classified information and massage it to their liking. The business
of intelligence is to provide the leadership of a country the most accurate
view of the way the world works, but ultimately it is up to the civilian
leadership to accept, reject, or exploit it for its own ends. When intelligence is murky—and it usually is—the conclusions of the professional
bureaucracy can be jettisoned for the political requirements of the elected
(and unelected) few.

Intelligence officers have been aware of this for generations. Dick
Helms, who headed the CIA from 1966 to 1973 and who was caught
up in an imbroglio over conflicting loyalties and convicted of lying to
Congress, wrote that "public debate lessens our usefulness to the nation
by casting doubt on our integrity and objectivity. If we are not believed,
we have no purpose."[167] The intelligence analysis that led up to the Iraq
war severely tarnished the overall credibility of the IC. The attributes
that Helms held dearly—integrity and objectivity—were trampled in the
rush to war.

CHAPTER 6

COUNTERTERRORISM
IN A WAR ZONE

War is a series of catastrophes that results in a victory.

—GEORGES CLEMENCEAU

"**O**h shit." Those were the last words uttered by Sergio Vieira de Mello, the Brazilian United Nations secretary-general special representative to Iraq, before a massive truck bomb ignited in frightful luminescence underneath his personal office. The explosion caused the UN Baghdad compound at the Canal Hotel to pancake and crumble on the afternoon of August 19, 2003.[1] The envoy had just begun a meeting with colleagues and outside researchers when the force of the explosion caused the roof, walls, and floors in his wing of the building to buckle and disintegrate, leaving a large tan and gray concrete jumble where the UN's mission—and its top man—had stood moments before.

The bombing would eventually claim some two dozen lives—UN officials, independent researchers, and local nationals dedicated to forging a better future for Iraq. After another suicide strike against the Canal Hotel a month later, the UN decided to pull out of Iraq. One organization single-handedly forced the humiliating withdrawal of the UN—an organization that had maintained a steadfast presence in Iraq throughout the punishing years of sanctions during the 1990s.

It was the handiwork of relatively little known terrorist Abu Musab al-Zarqawi and his group Jama'at a-Tawhid wa Jihad (JTJ). He and his organization would eventually go by a number of names. In October 2004 it evolved into Tanzim Qa'idat al-Jihad Fi Bilad al-Rafidayn (Organization of Jihad's Base in the Country of the Two Rivers, or QJBR), better known as al-Qaeda in Iraq (AQI). Zarqawi would prove to be a master of mayhem, battering away at the US mission in Iraq, and acting as the bogeyman most responsible for spurring the sectarian carnage that engulfed the country after 2003. After Saddam Hussein was captured, Zarqawi became high value target number 1 for the US. And despite intense efforts to track him down, Zarqawi remained beyond the reach of American and Iraqi forces for years while his group engaged in some of the most gruesome terror attacks against civilian targets in recent memory.

The hunt for Zarqawi was characterized by numerous near misses. Before the US invaded Iraq, the failure to neutralize Zarqawi was largely political. The Pentagon had actionable intelligence on Zarqawi's whereabouts, but was held back by the White House out of a need to build support for the impending conflict. Following the invasion until mid-2005, most near misses stemmed from poor operational planning, thin intelligence, conflicting military objectives, and bad luck. During this time, Zarqawi demonstrated an evolving understanding of the US approach to capturing or killing him; over time, he and his henchmen learned to improve their personal operational security while exploiting weaknesses in the US approach. Zarqawi commanded support in key parts of the local Sunni populace and benefited from the foreign fighters flowing into Iraq, using them for protection and cover, as well as a force multiplier for his terrifying suicide operations.

Besides demonstrating the challenges faced by US forces, the story behind Iraqi, Jordanian, British, and US attempts to find, fix, and finish a terror leader like Zarqawi provides a compelling case study in the importance and the complexities of integrating human intelligence and military resources in conducting counterterrorism operations in a war zone. It also raises questions about the role of technology in intelligence gathering, as well as the possibilities for cooperation with foreign intelligence services. Finally, the hunt for Zarqawi shows that a small group of vicious, committed killers can destabilize a country.

ZARQA

Zarqa, Jordan, is a noisy, sprawling urban area of factories, low-slung buildings, and petty domestic intrigues—a developing city of dusty brick and concrete apartments and narrow, rutted streets. The local government functions poorly: "The smell of backed-up sewage clouds the city because the government will not improve the inadequate drainage system."[2] Like many grim factory towns the world over, the young men of Zarqa have few job opportunities beyond working in the many sweatshops and workshops scattered throughout the city. It's a Middle Eastern version of a Bruce Springsteen song—a land of deferred and broken dreams. This was the world Abu Musab al-Zarqawi entered on October 20, 1966.

Hailing from the Bedouin Bani Hassan tribal confederation, Zarqawi—born Ahmad Fadil Nazal al-Khalayleh—grew up in the dilapidated but not destitute Masoum district of the city. Like many kids, Ahmad Fadil enjoyed kicking around a soccer ball and picking fights more than finishing his homework, and left school in the ninth grade. He found employment in a paper factory, then as a municipal functionary, but was fired from both jobs due to his chronic absenteeism and his knack for stirring up trouble.

After his two years of mandatory military service in the Jordanian army, the young Zarqawi returned to Zarqa and a life of drugs and petty crime. One report suggests he sexually assaulted a teenager, although that was never proven.[3] In 1987 he stabbed a man but escaped severe legal sanction with the payment of a stiff fine.[4] As one Western reporter noted years later, Ahmad Fadil was by all accounts "a bully and a thug, a bootlegger and a heavy drinker, and even, allegedly, a pimp in Zarqa's underworld."[5] This was a strange beginning for an international terrorist who would eventually terrify millions.

Ahmad Fadil's mother, fearing that her son's thuggish ways would mean disaster for his family, enrolled him in the late 1980s in the al-Hussein Ben Ali mosque in Amman.[6] There he would at least receive some sort of spiritual guidance. Sending the thug to a Salafist mosque was in hindsight a poor choice, as he fell in with a group of individuals who filled Ahmad Fadil with such religious zeal that he yearned to leave the humdrum confines of Jordan to pursue jihad abroad. Sometime in 1989, Zarqawi left Jordan for Afghanistan to battle the Soviet army.

Unfortunately for the Jordanian brawler, by the time he arrived in South Asia, the conflict between the mujahideen and the Soviets had more or less died down. Despite missing his first rendezvous with destiny, Zarqawi threw himself into the brutal internecine Afghan wars that erupted after the Soviet withdrawal.

Zarqawi also spent time in Pakistan, where he became fast friends with Palestinian jihadist thinker Abu Muhammad al-Maqdisi, whom the Combating Terrorism Center at West Point once called "the most influential living jihadi theorist." He wrote the Salafist textbook *The Creed of Abraham*. Maqdisi was extremely doctrinaire and may have been the one who encouraged Zarqawi to refine his burning hatred of his Shia coreligionists—a hatred that would play out more than a decade later in postoccupation Iraq. From a more practical perspective, Maqdisi gave Zarqawi the religious guidance to pursue his dreams of bringing jihad back to Jordan.[7] After a while, Zarqawi and Maqdisi returned to Jordan to overthrow the king.

The Jordanian spy agency, the General Intelligence Department (GID), began tracking Zarqawi in the 1990s.[8] Unlike most government bureaucracies in Amman, the GID is an aggressive, highly professional service, and one of the most loyal organizations serving the Hashemite Kingdom. A former French defense official described the GID as "topdrawer, probably the best counterterrorism force in the world. . . . Any network they put their mind to destroying is gone."[9] The GID was clearly not an organization that would suffer security threats to the country.

Zarqawi first encountered GID efficiency when he and Maqdisi formed Bayt al-Imam, a terrorist organization focused on attacking Israeli and Jordanian targets.[10] However, the GID broke up the cell in 1994 before it had conducted any major attacks. For their efforts, both Zarqawi and Maqdisi were imprisoned in 1996.[11]

In a stroke of luck for Zarqawi, in 1999 Jordan's King Hussein succumbed to cancer, and his son Abdullah II ascended the throne. In the tradition of extending royal amnesty for the forty days following a sovereign's death, and under pressure from the politically active Muslim Brotherhood, King Abdullah freed several low-level radicals, including Zarqawi. He had achieved precious little as a militant and did not appear to be a serious security threat. Nonetheless, the GID continued to monitor Zarqawi after his release. His mother claimed that the surveillance drove him from the country within a few months, again to Pakistan.[12]

Pakistan would prove to be almost as inhospitable as Jordan to the young militant. After a six-month stint in Peshawar, Zarqawi was thrown in prison for overstaying his visa. Faced with returning to Jordan and hostile GID surveillance, Zarqawi reluctantly crossed the border and connected with other Arab militants operating in the Taliban-controlled Islamic Emirate of Afghanistan.[13] Unlike many of the other Arabs living there from the Gulf States and North Africa, the former convict had few financial resources—but made up for these deficiencies with street smarts and a forceful personality, which made him stand out as a possible leader amid the motley crew of international jihadists.

In 2000, Zarqawi met Osama bin Laden in Kandahar. Bin Laden asked the Jordanian to pledge allegiance to him and al-Qaeda.[14] Reputedly, and surprisingly for a man with weak jihadist credentials and no committed followers, Zarqawi rebuffed bin Laden's advances over doctrinal issues. At the time, Zarqawi had no real interest in attacking the US in the so-called far jihad, preferring to wage the near jihad against the Hashemite Kingdom.[15] Bin Laden sent him packing. After a while, however, Zarqawi formed a small training camp near Herat in the western part of Afghanistan, for militants from the Levant, with $5,000 in seed money from Saif al-Adel, who sensed promise.[16]

The Herat camp was far away from other al-Qaeda camps, bin Laden, and the plotting that led to 9/11. Nonetheless, Zarqawi attracted a number of individuals to his spartan hideout, including many who would join him in the future fight in Iraq. After September 2001, however, he and his followers left the camp and disappeared—not with bin Laden's entourage in the mountains of Pakistan, where all the major figures of jihad migrated after the furious attack by US and Northern Alliance forces, but rather west to Iran, Iraq, and beyond.

Before 2002, despite running a militant facility in Afghanistan, Zarqawi was not a high priority for the US—just another terror suspect who had fled Afghanistan after the fall of the Taliban. Some sources suggested he meandered around the Middle East with his hardcore followers, mostly Jordanians and others from the Levant whom he knew from his days in Afghanistan.[17] Others claimed that he eventually moved to Iraqi Kurdistan, a region beyond Baghdad's grip, where he became involved with the al-Qaeda–associated Iraqi Kurdish terror group, Ansar al-Islam. The IC had lost sight of this Jordanian bit player, since he was not strongly associated with al-Qaeda's core group of individuals, most of whom were still in the crease between Pakistan and Afghanistan.

Nevertheless, by 2002, Zarqawi was garnering significant attraction from Jordanian authorities. That summer, GID asked its Iraqi counterparts (the IIS) to hunt down Zarqawi, as he was suspected in the assassination attempt against GID counterterrorism chief Ali Burjak in February 2002, when unknown individuals placed a bomb underneath his wife's car.[18] The bomb missed Burjak and his wife Yasmin but killed two unlucky bystanders. During this time, Zarqawi had also been sentenced in absentia for his part in the so-called Millennium Plot, which had targeted four sites in Jordan as well as the Los Angeles International Airport and the USS *The Sullivans*.[19] Jordanian officials wanted to reincarcerate, convict, and execute him.

On October 28, 2002, members of Zarqawi's group, looking for a target of opportunity, shadowed US Agency for International Development (USAID) official Laurence Foley, who was stationed in Amman. Ambushing Foley in his garage, Zarqawi's henchmen blasted him several times at close range with a silenced 9-mm pistol. In this way they showed themselves capable of "coordinating an operation from abroad and profoundly destabilizing his country of origin."[20] The GID quickly captured Foley's assassins, most notably Libyan national Salim bin Suwaid and Jordanian national Yasir Furaihat, who claimed they had been "recruited, armed, and paid" by Zarqawi.[21] These men were tried and executed for their crime in 2006, a death sentence extended to Zarqawi, again in absentia. He remained at large.

The American IC began to regard Zarqawi as an emerging threat. Still, American intelligence knew little, if anything, about Zarqawi and his activities. He might have been in Iraqi Kurdistan liaising with members of Ansar al-Islam, he might have been in Baghdad receiving unspecified surgery, or he might have been elsewhere. The US was guessing. However, everyone heard Zarqawi's name a few months later when US secretary of state Colin Powell cited his presence in Iraq as the clearest evidence of a link between Saddam Hussein and al-Qaeda in his address to the United Nations Security Council on February 4, 2003.

POWELL'S UN SPEECH

By early 2003, the US was banging the war drum to invade Iraq and overthrow the Saddam Hussein regime. While the Bush administration focused on Baghdad's supposed weapons of mass destruction (WMD) arsenal as the primary justification for invasion, Saddam's ties to terrorist groups were an integral part of the argument. While Baghdad had decades-long public ties to various Palestinian terror groups, the evidence tying Saddam's regime to al-Qaeda was thin. Without Zarqawi, Powell's slim presentation on Iraq's support for international terrorism could be whittled down to almost nothing.

Using linguistic sleight of hand, Powell only referenced Zarqawi's *associates* as closely allied with bin Laden. Powell outlined Zarqawi's associates' intentions and capabilities, most notably his relationship to WMD production at the Khurmal camp in Iraqi Kurdistan.

> When our coalition ousted the Taliban, the Zarqawi network helped establish another poison and explosive training center camp. And this camp is located in northeastern Iraq. . . . The network is teaching its operatives how to produce ricin and other poisons. Let me remind you how ricin works. Less than a pinch—imagine a pinch of salt— less than a pinch of ricin, eating just this amount in your food, would cause shock followed by circulatory failure. Death comes within 72 hours and there is no antidote, there is no cure. It is fatal. Those helping to run this camp are Zarqawi lieutenants operating in northern Kurdish areas outside Saddam Hussein's controlled Iraq.[22]

Of course, Zarqawi was famously *not* part of al-Qaeda, but Powell nevertheless painted a terrifying picture of a terror network spanning the globe and orchestrated by Zarqawi. Besides linking him to the Foley assassination, Powell said he had directed his associates to conduct terrorist acts throughout Europe and elsewhere:

> Zarqawi's terrorism is not confined to the Middle East. Zarqawi and his network have plotted terrorist actions against countries, including France, Britain, Spain, Italy, Germany and Russia. . . . Since last year, members of this network have been apprehended in France, Britain, Spain and Italy. By our last count, 116 operatives connected to this global web have been arrested.

To connect the Saddam regime to al-Qaeda, Powell pointed to the presence of two dozen al-Qaeda members in Baghdad, members he claimed first arrived during Zarqawi's two-month stay in that city in 2002 and with whom Zarqawi's "direct subordinates" maintained "regular contact." Suggesting that Baghdad must have known the terrorist's whereabouts during his time in the capital and in northern Iraq, Powell suggested that Saddam Hussein knowingly declined to capture Zarqawi or his associates:

> We asked a friendly security service to approach Baghdad about extraditing Zarqawi and providing information about him and his close associates. This service contacted Iraqi officials twice, and we passed details that should have made it easy to find Zarqawi. The network remains in Baghdad. Zarqawi still remains at large to come and go.

Powell's speech was an exercise in guilt by association, as he presented mostly circumstantial links between Zarqawi and Saddam's intelligence services. The US had thus far presented no hard evidence of an actual link between the two. Some questioned the administration's shaky analysis, noting that Zarqawi had few links to al-Qaeda and had not actually pledged himself to bin Laden through the Islamic custom of *bayat*. Finally, there was contention among analysts as to whether Zarqawi's camp even had any direct ties to Baghdad or al-Qaeda at all.[23]

Postwar findings—in particular the Senate Select Committee on Intelligence (SSCI) review, *Postwar Findings about Iraq's WMD Programs and Links to Terrorism and How They Compare with Prewar Assessments—*

eventually revealed many errors in the intelligence on which Powell's conclusions were based. Although Defense Intelligence Agency (DIA) analysis prior to hostilities indicated that Saddam's regime was aware of Ansar al-Islam's presence in Kurdistan,[24] Saddam's secular government, which was "firmly rooted in the separation between religion and state," had entirely different goals than Zarqawi's group of Islamic extremists.[25] As a result, some analysts concluded before the war that neither had an interest in working with the other; Zarqawi's cell considered Saddam's government apostate, while Saddam considered Zarqawi a "threat."[26]

Prior to the war, intelligence showed that Saddam appeared to have made a genuine effort to locate Zarqawi. These efforts by Saddam, for one reason or another, were unsuccessful in finding the Jordanian militant. In any case, the US, however, "overestimated" Iraqi intelligence capabilities.[27] While Zarqawi was probably somewhere in Iraq during the run-up to the invasion, now termed Operation Iraqi Freedom (OIF), the Baghdad regime was probably more preoccupied with preparing for war with the US and a countrywide occupation than with locating a middling terrorist who might or might not be in its territory.

Records seized after OIF revealed that Saddam took measures to catch Zarqawi. According to the SSCI review, Saddam's intelligence service, the Iraq Intelligence Service (IIS) "formed a special committee" to track down Zarqawi, but for one reason or another they could not locate him.[28] Even after Zarqawi was thought to have transited out of Iraq, the report concluded, Saddam continued to search, and in early 2003, the IIS managed to arrest one of the other individuals associated in the Foley murder, though Zarqawi remained at large.[29]

But these findings were developed three years after the invasion, written with the benefits of the full intelligence record and hindsight. In 2002–2003, the CIA Directorate of Intelligence had struggled to make sense of the scraps of information that argued for or against Saddam's supposed relationship with Zarqawi and al-Qaeda. The analysis by compromise would later emerge as CIA's *Iraqi Support for Terrorism* and *Iraq and al-Qa'ida: Interpreting a Murky Relationship,* among others.[30] Essentially, CIA analysts believed that "Iraq has had sporadic, wary contracts" with al-Qaeda, "[but] mistrust and conflicting ideologies and goals probably tempered these contacts and severely limited the opportunities for cooperation."[31] Furthermore, there may have been "limited offers of cooperation, training, or safe haven (ultimately uncorroborated or withdrawn)" between Saddam and al-Qaeda, but even this line of reasoning was tenuous at best.[32] As investigative journalist Michael Gordon later noted, this limp analysis was nevertheless "controversial within the agency" and that "the CIA ombudsman for politicization received a confidential complaint that the conclusion went too far."[33] Based on the heavily redacted version of the murky intelligence assessment released in 2005,[34] Zarqawi did not figure as a terribly prominent analytical data point in the case against Iraq.

While the US intelligence bureaucracy tied itself into knots creating pieces of paper, the action arms of the US government probably had several opportunities to finish Zarqawi prior to the outbreak of hostilities in Iraq. These included a June 2002 Pentagon-drafted plan to strike Zarqawi after intelligence revealed he had set up a bioweapons lab in Khurmal in northern Iraq to manufacture ricin and anthrax—the same camp Powell would refer to in his UN speech some eight months later.[35] The plan to attack the camp with cruise missiles and air strikes was debated to a standstill by the National Security Council (NSC) and ultimately shelved.

In October 2002, the Pentagon again advanced a plan after intelligence indicated that Zarqawi was planning to use manufactured ricin in terrorist attacks in Europe. According to former NSC member Roger Cressey, the NSC killed the plan because the administration was "more obsessed with developing the coalition to overthrow Saddam than to execute the president's policy of preemption against terrorists."[36] Former CIA analyst Michael Scheuer corroborated this account in a May 2006 interview, stating that the Bush administration was provided solid intelligence on Zarqawi's location in the year before the invasion but believed any unilateral military action would undermine support from key European allies, who might view the US as "gunslingers."[37] Nearing the eve of war, the NSC in January 2003 again nixed a Pentagon attack plan even after London police arrested six terror suspects and discovered a ricin lab connected to the Khurmal camp—apparently again fearing that destroying the terrorist camp would undercut the case for war against Saddam Hussein.[38]

So, prior to the outbreak of hostilities in March 2003, the Bush administration was able but unwilling to finish Zarqawi despite fixing him at various times in Iraqi Kurdistan and in Baghdad. Still, one of the first actions the US military took in Operation Iraqi Freedom was to obliterate Khurmal with a punishing weeklong aerial bombardment and a ground assault against the fanatical Islamists willing to fight to the death.[39] After the smoke cleared, the subsequent investigation indicated Zarqawi had long since left. American man-hunting forces shifted from finding this terrorist to targeting Baathists and Saddam supporters, allowing Zarqawi to take advantage of a distracted US overwhelmed by the task of occupying a country of 26 million people to develop his networks and lay the operational groundwork needed to unleash waves of punishing attacks against American forces and Shia groups.

Zarqawi's overall strategy was straightforward—ceaselessly attack US and Iraqi forces while murdering large numbers of Shia, causing them to react violently against their Sunni countrymen. The subsequent communal violence would then oblige the Sunni population—knowing that the Shia-dominated Iraqi government could not or would not protect them—to seek refuge with the only organization capable of protecting them: Zarqawi's group. US forces would get caught in a communal civil war, lose heart, and retreat, ceding the field to the jihadists. Zarqawi would then take advantage of the chaos to carve out an Islamic rump state while developing the capabilities to launch terrorist attacks outside the country. The crude, bloodthirsty strategy almost succeeded.

The US may have tracked Zarqawi periodically through early to mid-2003, but could not fix his location with any precision as he moved across borders to gather support and money for the insurgency in Iraq. The US believed that Zarqawi was one of many al-Qaeda leaders who crossed over to Iran as the Iraq ground war started, and was either in custody or considered a guest during major hostilities.[40] Sometime after the fall of Baghdad, Zarqawi began moving between Iraq and neighboring countries to gather men and materiel for the upcoming postconflict conflict, according to US officials.[41] As money, foreign fighters, and arms flowed into Iraq, Zarqawi probably set up a base of operations in the Sunni-dominated Anbar province where he could find protection.

Zarqawi likely enjoyed free range of movement following the invasion because American forces were preoccupied with the hunt for WMD and for Saddam. US military forces during this time were likewise focused on maintaining security, restoring basic services such as water and electricity, and pursuing the fifty-five members of "Iraq's most wanted" from the former regime. Defense secretary Donald Rumsfeld blithely dismissed concerns about the increasing anarchy in an unsecured Baghdad: "free people are free to make mistakes and commit crimes and do bad things . . . stuff happens."[42] Zarqawi was not unaware that US forces were overstretched; one of his top lieutenants—and key planner for the UN attack—Awwaz Abd al-Aziz Mahmood Sa'id (a.k.a. al-Kurdi) would later claim that, in the early days of the occupation, Zarqawi and he had no trouble meeting daily in Ramadi.[43]

Elite military units remained focused on capturing Saddam Hussein and his sons Uday and Qusay, not controlling the increasingly unstable political environment. Saddam's sons were killed in a firefight with US troops on July 22, and Saddam himself was captured in the famous "spider hole" on December 13. It is likely that US military planners refocused their efforts on the growing insurgency, spurred by the purging of Baath Party members from positions of power, as well as the disbanding of the Iraqi army, toward the beginning of 2004. The warning signs of a broader Sunni backlash went unheeded by most policymakers at the time.

In late summer 2003, Zarqawi struck. After a number of small-time attacks against Iraqi police stations, Zarqawi was responsible for a string of brutal bombings throughout August, including a car bomb outside the Jordanian embassy that killed seventeen; the aforementioned suicide bombing of the UN compound;[44] and an especially bloody suicide attack aimed at the revered Shiite clergyman and Supreme Council of the Revolution in Iraq (SCIRI) political leader Ayatollah Muhammad Baqir al-Hakim in Najaf. Zarqawi's father-in-law Yasin Jarad carried out the strike, killing Hakim and up to seventy-five bystanders.

Zarqawi's attacks directed attention at the insurgent leader, although Saddam remained the priority. Still, the US made some effort to quash Zarqawi's organization. Two wild firefights on September 16, 2003, in the towns of Ramadi and Khaldiyah between US forces and Zarqawi's men killed numerous terrorists—Iraqis and foreigners—and put a large dent in his plans. But Zarqawi escaped unscathed.

That same month the US Treasury listed his activities and locations at length to justify freezing his assets, but included no information at all after late 2002, when he traveled into Iraq to "initiate plans to smuggle additional small arms, explosives, and rockets . . . into Jordan for his terrorist cell."[45] By late October Washington announced a $5 million reward for information leading to his capture.[46] But as 2003 came to an end, the Sunni insurgency—Zarqawi was but one player, albeit the most bloodthirsty one—took root, and further bloodshed was in store for the US and Iraq.

The American IC and the military focused on Zarqawi more intensively in 2004 as his stature and effectiveness increased, but were ultimately kept at bay by his resourcefulness and support within the Sunni population. Throughout 2004 Zarqawi carried out a string of brutal attacks, from police assassinations, to car bombings, to coordinated attacks on civilian targets and US forces. In response, the US in February doubled its bounty on Zarqawi to $10 million, and in July increased it again to $25 million, the same amount it offered for information leading to the death or capture of bin Laden.

Zarqawi released his first audio statement in early January, attacking US forces and various Muslim clerics, and also challenging Sunni men to join his jihad: "Oh people, the wheels of war have begun to move; the caller has already declared *Jihad* and the gates of heaven are open [to the martyrs]. If you are unwilling to be one of the knights of war, make way for the women so they can run the war, and you take the cooking utensils and makeup [brushes] in their stead. If you are not women in turbans and beards, go to the horses and seize their harnesses and their reins."[47]

Increasingly, violence became the norm in Iraq, as hostile Sunni and Shia organizations quickly adapted to fighting the occupation. In March, four American contractors were slaughtered by local residents of the overwhelmingly Sunni city of Fallujah, and their charred bodies were hung from a bridge over the Euphrates River. Television crews would capture the scene and replay the images for worldwide audiences. The attack coincided with the deaths of five US soldiers from an improvised explosive device (IED), the weapon of choice for hit-and-run attacks by an evolving foe, on a dusty road near Habbaniyah, outside Fallujah.[48]

The reaction in Washington was fierce. In response to the slayings, President Bush would demand, "I want heads to roll."[49] Secretary Rumsfeld added "we have to pound these guys"[50] and authorized the siege and invasion of the "City of Mosques." Prior to deployment, commander of the Multi-National Force Iraq (MNF-I) General Ricardo Sanchez would authorize the US Marines to strike Fallujah with vengeance: "I don't mean any fucking knock-before-search, touchy-feely stuff."[51]

The subsequent Operation Vigilant Resolve (April) and Operation Phantom Fury (November–December) in Fallujah resulted in some of the most lethal urban combat that American forces had encountered since the 1993 engagements in Somalia. US, British, and Iraqi forces engaged in house-to-house fighting with Sunni militants holed up throughout the city. The two battles (the April engagements ended inconclusively) would level a large percentage of the city; over a hundred American servicemen and thousands of Iraqis lost their lives.

Eliminating Zarqawi and crushing his organization were top priorities both times, but as US forces hunted for him in the city,[52] he was nowhere to be found—although some later accounts say that US forces narrowly missed killing him. In 2005 a failed Saudi suicide bomber claimed that Iraqi security forces probably caught Zarqawi during the second assault on Fallujah in November 2004, but released him because they didn't know who he was.[53] US officials called the report "plausible" but refused to confirm it.

These early near misses indicated the US was on Zarqawi's tail, but also hinted at the early problems in synchronizing effective training of US and Iraqi forces. Using conventional military forces to hunt for a dozen hardened terrorists is like swinging a sledgehammer to smash a bee. Furthermore, there was probably not an effective system of coordinating information with US intelligence on high-value targets. Finally, this type of hunt relies on open communication and singular goals. The police force in Fallujah was almost certainly Sunni. While it is entirely possible that the police didn't recognize him, it is at least equally possible that someone did recognize him and either felt loyalty to him or did not want to incur his wrath.[54]

The members of the Fallujah police force had a right to be scared, as Zarqawi was perfecting his media strategy. In mid-2004, Zarqawi and his accomplices shocked the world by kidnapping foreign nationals, beheading them with a machete, then placing their execution videos online. Zarqawi released his first tape in May 2004, showing the murder of Philadelphia native Nicholas Berg. The films were released monthly through 2004 and into 2005 and 2006. As foreign nationals became more difficult to procure, Iraqi police and military personnel became the subjects in his gruesome canon.

Zarqawi finally cemented his relationship with al-Qaeda, pledging *bayat* to bin Laden in October 2004. By late December, bin Laden formally accepted his allegiance in a statement picked up by the Al Jazeera satellite channel. Bin Laden's statement from December 27 read, "We in al-Qaeda welcome your union with us . . . and so that it be known, the brother mujahid Abu Musab al-Zarqawi is the emir of the al-Qaeda organization in the land of the Tigris and the Euphrates and the brothers of the group in the country should swear to him an oath of obedience."[55] Zarqawi had received the blessings from on high, and his group, now renamed al-Qaeda in Iraq (AQI), instantly became the most lethal and financially profitable organization in the al-Qaeda franchise.

"TO DRINK FROM THE VARIOUS GOBLETS OF DEATH": 2005

In 2005 the US military struggled to define its mission in the quickly unraveling political landscape. Captain Piers Platt, who served in Iraq from 2004 to 2005 as a platoon leader with the US Army's 4th US Cavalry Regiment, 1st Infantry Division, recalled, "We never seemed to be doing anything besides treading water and waiting for our turn in theater to be up. All we did was protect US assets in theater. I know there was reconstruction work going on, and other units were working with Iraqis, but I got the strong sense we were doing as much harm as good. Combine that lack of strategy with a total lack of WMD and a couple poor commanders, and it made for a very frustrating year."[56]

Despite this overall strategic drift, as the year progressed, the US began to generate new opportunities to capture or kill Zarqawi through the use of smaller elite groups—rather than the broad and ineffective approach of committing large military forces to lay siege to a major urban area. During the deep night of February 20, 2005, a source within Zarqawi's network alerted an elite military unit to the AQI chief's whereabouts, including a time frame for when he would travel down a stretch of highway near the Tigris River.[57] The military established roadblocks along the road and deployed heavily armed elite forces for an ambush.

At one of the checkpoints, US troops detained a white truck deployed ahead as a scout, giving Zarqawi's driver time to make a U-turn and drive away. One Army Ranger reportedly had Zarqawi in his gun sights, but was denied permission to fire absent positive identification of the vehicle's occupants.[58] Elite military operators gave chase, but the driver drove the truck at great speed onto a secondary road. Zarqawi was able to escape by jumping out as it drove through an underpass, avoiding overhead UAV surveillance.[59] The pursuit was also stymied by a technical glitch: the operations staff lost sight of Zarqawi as the UAV's camera, situated on the bottom of the drone, switched from a tight focus to a wide-angle view.[60] In those precious seconds, Zarqawi unknowingly made decisive moves to avoid detection and flee the pursuing forces. The general chaos of a complicated nighttime operation—integrating Army Rangers, Navy SEALs, regular Army units, and overhead surveillance to capture a single individual—allowed AQI's top man to escape.

US Army Captain Eric Joyce, stationed in his battalion's tactical action center named Tal Afar Garage, later recalled that radio communications during the night were a constant stream of garbled messages: "We heard on the radio, 'Chase White!' 'Who got white?' 'Who is white?' 'Where do you need support?' 'What the hell is going on?'— what did it all mean? No one explained to us, for example, that 'white' meant 'white truck.' Not enough people in the Army knew how to use the radio and people kept jamming the net."[61] Furthermore, "We were essentially trying to deconstruct what [TF] 6–26 (Hunter), Air Support, our own brigade, battalion, and companies on site were trying to say all at once and make coherent orders in real time with no processing at this point."[62]

The intelligence distributed to the regular troops was pretty vague. Soldiers were supposed to look for a male or group of males with dark skin who appeared "Jordanian."[63] Complicating the mission was that US Special Forces "looked like natives—with beards and dirty clothes."[64] Since this was a high-priority mission, the troops had been awake for a long time. As Captain Joyce noted, "You're dead tired, you're scared, and you have little information from a tactical standpoint."[65] Moreover, "we knew something went wrong; we spent the rest of the night de-conflicting battle space to conduct appropriate searches, giving time to whoever it was we were chasing . . . [to] blend into the neighborhood."[66] Furthermore, without specific targets, the large number of poorly communicating US forces in a nighttime environment, and the overall jitteriness of the nineteen-and twenty-year-olds manning the checkpoints could have led to all kinds of friendly-fire casualties. The fact that no Americans were hit when gunfire inevitably rang out in the night may have been luck more than anything else.

While it was regrettable that the head of AQI was neither captured nor killed, the night proved fruitful nonetheless. US forces recovered Zarqawi's laptop, personal effects, pictures, thousands of euros, and various planning documents.[67] The abandoned computer provided a "treasure trove" of intelligence, according to one Pentagon official, including information on Zarqawi's medical condition and photos of him in the My Photos folder.[68] The US also captured his driver, Abu Usama, and his bodyguard,[69] yielding valuable intelligence that helped partially crack the network.[70] Zarqawi's brush with capture increased his wariness and scrutiny of intelligence leaks within his organization.

The cat-and-mouse game continued throughout 2005. US and Iraqi security forces narrowly missed capturing Zarqawi several times, in one case possibly wounding him.[71] According to one source, the increased American pressure on Zarqawi, as well as the killing or capture of several of Zarqawi's aides, had come about because of an increase in actionable intelligence gathered from both detainee interrogations and secular Iraqi insurgents who were increasingly resentful of the Jordanian's tactics and zealotry.[72]

In 2005 Zarqawi stepped up his attacks against the Shia, calling for a "total war" in his bid to fan the flames of sectarian conflict. In a September audio message, Zarqawi warned the Shia that "the mujahidin have prepared for you and for your soldiers, by Allah's virtues, a slashing

sword and lethal poison. Allah willing, you will be given to drink from
the various goblets of death, and the lands of the Sunnis will contain
your rotting corpses. Come, if you want, now or later."[73]

He called for the Sunnis to rise up, join AQI, and fight their apostate coreligionists: "Awaken from your slumber, and arise from your ap-
athy. You have slept for a long time. The wheels of the war to annihilate
the Sunnis have not and will not halt. It will reach the homes of each
and every one of you, unless Allah decides otherwise. If you do not join
the mujahidin to defend your religion and honor, by Allah, sorrow and
regret will be your lot, but only after all is lost."[74]

Zarqawi was on a roll. However, he was also becoming a public relations problem for his ostensible superiors in Pakistan because of his brutal exploits—so much so that in mid-2005 Ayman al-Zawahiri wrote
him a long letter asking him to reconsider some of his more bloodthirsty
tactics. Zawahiri implored Zarqawi to remember that terrorism is essentially a war for the hearts and minds of the populace and his tactics were
distasteful even to many hardened militants:

> Among the things which the feelings of the Muslim populace who
> love and support you will never find palatable . . . are the scenes of
> slaughtering the hostages. You shouldn't be deceived by the praise
> of some of the zealous young men and their description of you as
> the shaykh of the slaughterers, etc. They do not express the gen-
> eral view of the admirer and the supporter of the resistance in Iraq,
> and of you in particular by the favor and blessing of God. . . . I
> say to you: that we are in a battle, and *that more than half of this
> battle is taking place in the battlefield of the media.* And that we are
> in a media battle in a race for the hearts and minds of our Umma.
> [Emphasis added.][75]

Zawahiri's advice to tone down the carnage went unheeded. Later that
year, AQI committed a major strategic error that ended up alienating a
large swath of the Arab public. On November 9, Zarqawi sent four suicide attackers to the Radisson SAS, the Grand Hyatt, and the Days Inn
hotels in Amman, killing approximately sixty people, including many
Jordanians attending a wedding reception in the ballroom at the Radis-

son.[76] The fathers of both the bride and groom were killed, along with numerous women and children. The wedding ballroom victims also included Moustapha Akkad, the producer of the popular Jamie Lee Curtis horror vehicle *Halloween,* along with his daughter. Zarqawi proudly claimed credit for the attack, stating Jordan was "a backyard garden to the enemies of religion, Jews and crusaders . . . a filthy pasture to the apostate traitors."[77]

The visceral negative reaction to the attack surprised even the hardened AQI leader. Jordanians from all walks of life reacted immediately; sources reported that upward of 200,000 people demonstrated in Amman against the bombings, many displaying the names of their tribes in order to prove that they came from all over the kingdom.[78] Jordanian TV continuously reported news of the attack, especially after the GID apprehended one of the suicide bombers, middle-aged female Iraqi national Sajida al-Rishawi, who failed to detonate her suicide vest. Jordanian authorities then taped her showing off her (defused) suicide vest, which made for a riveting television broadcast on the evening news.

Zarqawi released a lengthy audio statement in his own voice on November 18, explaining that AQI was targeting US, Jordanian, and Israeli security services: "Know that we selected these hotels only after we learned—after scoping them out for over two months and collecting information from reliable sources inside the hotels [themselves]— that they have come to [serve] as headquarters for the Jewish, American, and Iraqi intelligence apparatuses. . . . Regarding the Radisson hotel— most of the people of the Israeli embassy stay there, as well as Israeli tourists, and this is also true for the Days Inn Hotel. As for Hyatt Amman, it is a den [of evil] for the Zionist, American, and Iraqi intelligence [services]."[79]

As for the attack on the wedding party, Zarqawi tried to backpedal, suggesting they were not the intended target, despite the fact that the suicide bomber had obliterated the banquet hall:

The brothers who carried out the martyrdom operation meant to target the halls which served as meeting places for intelligence officers of several infidel Crusader countries and countries allied with them. The people [at the wedding feast] were killed because part of the ceiling collapsed from the intensity of the blast, and it is no secret that this was not intended; it was an unintended accident, which had not been taken into account.[80]

However, the public relations damage had been done. Jordanian officials reported a surge in tip-offs about Zarqawi's whereabouts.[81] Members of Zarqawi's own tribe, including his brother and first cousin, denounced him in the newspapers: "We sever links with him until doomsday."[82] Even the Muslim Brotherhood, while making clear its continued support for those fighting against the US-led coalition in Iraq, called the terrorist attacks within Jordan completely unacceptable.[83] After Jordan's so-called 11/9, Zarqawi's capture became a goal shared by both the government and the general Jordanian population.

Despite—or perhaps because of—Zarqawi's notoriety, everybody wanted to claim credit for his death or capture. This resulted in a continuous stream of false claims from the Iraqi government that he had been killed, muddying the public's perception whether he was in fact alive or dead. In one such example, Iraqi foreign minister Hoshyar Zebari announced in late November 2005 that Zarqawi was killed in a coalition assault and subsequent firefight in Mosul.[84] Zebari's claim was apparently based on intelligence that the terrorist meeting might include Zarqawi,[85] a tip stemming from what a senior Iraqi military leader called a "credible source."[86] There was no confirmation that Zarqawi was even in the area.

The operation in Mosul also showed that US forces were often obliged to work jointly with Iraqi forces in the Zarqawi hunt. The fact that an Iraqi minister announced Zarqawi's possible death—apparently without coordinating with US officials—and that he was familiar with the source suggested that this operation stemmed from an Iraqi informant. Further, the combined Iraqi police, conventional and Special Operations forces used in the assault may have contributed to the messy and extended gun battle that followed: a six-hour firefight during which four Iraqi policemen and two US special operations officers were killed.[87] All the insurgents fought to the death. From an intelligence point of view, the raid was only a limited success since it yielded no surviving insurgents for interrogation and cost the lives of several team members. And Zarqawi was gone.

STUMBLING TOWARD CIVIL WAR: 2006

Beyond the hunt for Zarqawi, the overall US position in Iraq was becoming increasingly tenuous as a full-blown Sunni insurgency exploded all over the country. While the exact number of insurgents was debated (some believe it would exceed 200,000 people), what was clear was that attacks were on the rise.[88] During the winter of 2005–2006, US and allied forces reported 500 attacks per week; by summer 2006, it was up to 800.[89] One Army transportation battalion was hit 170 times out of 400 convoys between 2005 and 2006.[90] By midyear, the country's morgues were overflowing. For example, almost 2,000 bodies showed up in Baghdad's central morgue in July 2006, with some 90 percent of the deceased brought in due to a violent death.[91]

AQI's February 23 bombing of the al-Aksari Golden Dome shrine in Samarra revealed the depths of the sectarian conflict. A US serviceman stationed in Samarra recalled, "All eyes turned [toward] the explosion. You see this plume of smoke going up, and the plume of smoke was right next to the mosque. . . . You're thinking, What the heck happened there? . . . It was kind of a cloudy day, overcast. Now there's this huge plume of smoke, a monstrous cloud, and it's kind of yellowish and black."[92]

The attack on the shrine—one of the holiest pieces of real estate in Shia Iraq—was a bridge too far for many Shia Iraqis, who unleashed a furious response. Shia death squads greatly stepped up their murderous activities against terrified Sunni civilians, slaughtering hundreds if not thousands of Sunnis all over the country during the subsequent weeks. Baghdad's ethnic cleavages deepened quickly into Sunni and Shia enclaves hidden behind concertina wire and concrete blast walls. Suicide bombings in marketplaces became commonplace occurrences, tortured corpses littered the street, and the country lurched toward all-out civil war. Zarqawi's tactics had all but succeeded.

In 2006, AQI launched an online political front, the Islamic State of Iraq (ISI), placing an Iraqi with a rather bland name, Abu Umar al-Baghdadi, as its titular head. US and Iraqi forces could not figure out whether Abu Umar was a real person with actual responsibilities, a Iraqi puppet controlled by Zarqawi, an amalgam of individuals in the AQI/ISI hierarchy, or just a figment of someone's imagination. His death in April 2010 at the hands of Iraqi forces indicated he was a real person named Hamid Daoud Muhammad Khalil al-Zawi, but it remained doubtful whether he had meaningful power within the organization during his lifetime.[93]

Starting in March 2006, the US got closer to Zarqawi thanks to efforts made in large part by the US military's elite counterterrorism units from the Joint Special Operations Command (JSOC). These elite counterterrorism units were so secretive that recent operating titles have included Task Force (TF) 626, TF 121, TF 77, TF 145, and TF 16—numbers picked mostly at random.[94] These elite groups became the most lethal (and costly) light infantry units in the history of warfare.

An *Army Times* investigation from May 2006 provided specific details about the composition of the various TFs, reporting a hodgepodge of military and civilian personnel, including members of Delta Force, Navy SEAL Team 6, Air Force 24th Special Tactics Squadron, CIA officers, FBI agents, and civilian interrogators, among others.[95] Integrating these mixed components, the TFs were intended as a unique means of gathering and acting upon intelligence. Interrogators worked to extract information from detainees, immediately relaying any intelligence produced to the Special Forces members of the unit, who could then act on its basis. Unlike other military groups, JSOC units were authorized to work from raw intelligence and did not need to wait for authorization for follow-on strikes based on the acquired information.[96] This meant that JSOC could raid geographical units without consulting higher-ranking officials, a circumvention of the chain of command that enabled Special Forces to act on intelligence gathered by interrogators earlier that day.[97] Members of JSOC describe this fusion of intelligence and operations as "the unblinking eye."[98]

The JSOC commander, General Stanley McChrystal, was known to favor risk taking and held subordinates responsible for lack of results.[99] He demanded incremental fine-tuning of operational procedures. In an early 2006 internal memo, he wrote that "although initial structures and TTPs [tactics, techniques, and procedures] have evolved tremendously from where they were even two years ago, we are still operating with manning and operating processes that need to be improved . . . we will do everything to increase the effectiveness even in small ways."[100] An early 2010 profile of McChrystal characterized him as being so enthusiastic about JSOC and his ability to perfect his deadly arts that he had increased counterterrorism operations "to an industrial scale, with 10 nightly raids . . . 300 a month, that [he] . . . regularly joined."[101]

On April 16, 2006, JSOC raided a terrorist safe house in Yusifiyah and killed five Zarqawi associates.[102] Nine days later, JSOC killed twelve more AQI members in a shootout in another Yusifiyah safe house. Both raids sprang from the skillful interrogation of a Sunni insurgent in February, who revealed the existence of the residences.[103] Through the raids, a new group of midlevel AQI operatives was captured for interrogation and revealed that Zarqawi had been hiding just a few blocks away.[104]

Less evident but equally significant was the mounting pressure on Zarqawi as a result of effective US evisceration of his foreign leadership.[105] By May, US intelligence officials said they believed Zarqawi was beginning to run short of foreign fighters willing to conduct suicide missions.[106] Further, Zarqawi's micromanaging personality made him increasingly vulnerable to discovery, according to Jordanian intelligence officials.[107]

In late April, Zarqawi released what would be his final video statement. Zarqawi said that events were proceeding badly for the US, while hinting at future attacks outside Iraq. "Allah has given the mujahidin sons [of the nation] the strength to face the cruelest Crusader campaign, invading the lands of the Muslims. They have withstood this invasion for more than three years. . . . My dear nation, we in Iraq are but a stone's throw away from the place of the Prophet's ascension. We are fighting in Iraq, but our eyes are set upon Jerusalem, which will only be restored to us through the guidance of the Koran and the support of the sword."[108]

That month, JSOC raided an apartment in Yusifiyah, killing several people, including three suicide bombers.[109] Inside the apartment, JSOC found unedited footage of Zarqawi struggling to use an M249 SAW (squad automatic weapon) during the shoot for his last video production. The portly, white sneaker–clad AQI leader did not seem to be the cunning mastermind that some thought. Rather, he looked like a bungler. The US later released this footage, which came to be known as Zarqawi's blooper reel, to discredit him.

ENDGAME

A multiagency effort finally eliminated the AQI leader on June 7, 2006. Acting on information provided by ████████████ intelligence several months beforehand, US counterterrorism forces discovered a new name to work with: Shaykh Abd al-Rahman (a.k.a. Abu Amina).[110] Abu Amina was supposedly Zarqawi's spiritual adviser and met with the AQI head on a regular basis to discuss issues of Islamic jurisprudence.[111] Abu Amina's importance in the AQI hierarchy was unclear to the US until 2006, but subsequent painstaking sensitive site exploitation (SSE)—examining captured computer drives and the like—by a sharp-eyed analyst looking at the specific military raid designated "Arcadia 8," as well as detainee information, indicated that he was probably the best lead to find Zarqawi.[112] Furthermore, information from detainee debriefings and other HUMINT indicated Abu Amina's overall security rituals, including his attempt to shake off potential surveillance (called a surveillance detection route, or SDR) which allowed the US to track him and also build a picture of Zarqawi's movements.[113]

Having identified and corroborated his importance through multiple sources, US intelligence began tracking Abu Amina's movements and appointments via UAV and through his Thuraya satellite phone.[114] On June 3 or June 4, US forces followed Abu Amina as he traveled to a meeting with Zarqawi, but lost his vehicle in traffic.[115] On June 7 a UAV successfully tracked him as he drove to an isolated farmhouse outside the village of Hibhib near the city of Baquba.[116] Abu Amina had also been observed performing a SDR before arriving at the building, as would occur before meeting a high-level member of AQI. For the first time in many months, Americans thought they might have Zarqawi in their sights. But they could not be sure.

US civilian and military officials did not know who was in the building with Abu Amina. Compounding the dilemma, the video feed from the Predator overhead indicated there were women and children in the farmhouse, so any strike on the building would result in their grisly deaths.

After an agonizing debate in Baghdad and the main US military base in Balad over whether to or not to strike, the call was made to blast the house to smithereens. Commanders called in two nearby F-16s on routine patrol, but only one aircraft made the bombing run because the other was in the process of refueling.[117] The F-16's pilot set the fuse on the five-hundred-pound bomb to explode inside the house (rather than on contact) to collapse the structure, and then dropped a second bomb to complete the task.[118]

Unlike everyone else at the house, Zarqawi survived the blasts. US forces converged on the ruins to find the AQI head semiconscious and mumbling incoherently on the ground. Picking their way gingerly through the rubble, troops placed him on a stretcher. Zarqawi tried to get off to no avail, as his internal organs turned to jelly due to the over-pressurization waves caused by the high explosives.[119] The last few fading images the leader of AQI ever saw were of US soldiers, guns at the ready, standing over him. The hunt for the most wanted man in Iraq was finally over.

The success resulted from organizational momentum, a high tempo of both behind-the-scenes intelligence analysis and special operations actions running up to this event. US Army Major General William Caldwell later described Zarqawi's death as the culmination of "a very long, painstaking, deliberate exploitation of intelligence, information-gathering, human sources, electronic, signal intelligence that was done over a period of time."[120] Having identified Abu Amina, American civilian and military forces were able to triangulate and track his satellite phone.[121] The operation also demonstrated the combination of rapid action with luck—had Zarqawi not been in the farmhouse, the US would have instead shredded its best lead—Abu Amina—and ended up with a building full of dead women and children. If Zarqawi had once again escaped harm, the military and intelligence professionals who helped construct and authorized the military strike would have needlessly shed the blood of innocents instead of being lauded as the men and women who brought down a hard-core terrorist killer in a brutal conflict zone.

A review of US attempts to destroy Zarqawi reveals several key points about contemporary counterterrorism operations. First is the continued importance of painstaking research, interrogation, and human intelligence. Even though the US possessed some of the most advanced technology in the world, Zarqawi evaded American forces for over three years after he became a high-value target. In the February 2005 SUV chase, a combination of technology and military rules of engagement allowed Zarqawi to get away.

As wars and counterterrorism operations become increasingly asymmetrical and focused on breaking down small cells, human intelligence will become even more important. Even within the US, it is tricky to locate and finish one individual. For example, the individual responsible for the Centennial Olympic Park bombing during the 1996 Summer Olympics in Atlanta, Eric Rudolph, managed to hide in rural North Carolina for several years before being caught by a local police officer.[122] Small targets can evade detection easily. Human intelligence, broadly defined, decreases that advantage. Local sources can help officials attack cells from the inside out by guiding and directing a search that would otherwise prove impossible for outside forces. After all, before forces can fix or finish an objective, they need to first know where to look.

Still, despite the importance of developing human intelligence, the value of technology should not be underappreciated. Even though it may have failed at some key junctures in the search for Zarqawi, technology also proved invaluable to that search. Tip-offs and debriefings led US forces to Abu Amina, but technology helped track him. American technology taped his movements and intercepted his phone calls.[123] The US watched from a distance as Abu Amina led them straight to Zarqawi. Humans provided the direction, but technology ensured that their information could be fully captured and exploited.

By keeping all necessary components within relatively small, autonomous units, the US could gather and act on raw intelligence before the trail it provided went cold. Still, the importance of Zarqawi's case lies not only in the details but also the concept of organic integration. When potential terrorists organize into small units, they gain flexibility that makes them difficult to find, fix, or finish. The new, more nimble military intelligence groups, however, can return flexibility to the opposing force.

Of course, fixing and finishing Zarqawi did not mean that AQI had been crushed. The terror group's campaign of unremitting violence against the US, Iraq, and civilians escalated dramatically through the rest of 2006 and into 2007. Only after various Sunni tribes rose up against AQI and the Shia militant group Jaysh al-Mahdi led by Moqtada al-Sadr suspended political violence in mid-2007 did the violent fever in Iraq break significantly and some semblance of fragile peace return to the war-torn country. Strategic, long-term calculations by various political actors would ultimately bring Iraq back from the edge of all-out conflict.

CHAPTER 7

BOJINKA REDUX

The Need for Good International Cop Work

During the summer of 2005, London was on a knife edge. British citizens caught up in the nihilist ideology of al-Qaeda had twice attacked the bus and subway networks, killing dozens and bringing the horror and mayhem of international terrorism to the city's 7.5 million residents. Even the decades-long struggle with the Provisional Irish Republican Army paled in comparison. Al-Qaeda changed the equation; the point was not just to scare the British people but also to cause carnage in the name of religious ideals. And, in a video released after the July 7 bombings, the plot's ringleader, Mohammad Siddique Khan, promised more attacks:

> Your democratically elected governments continuously perpetuate atrocities against my people all over the world, and your support of them makes you directly responsible, just as I am directly responsible for protecting and avenging my Muslim brothers and sisters. Until we feel security, you will be our targets, and until you stop the bombing, gassing, imprisonment, and torture of my people, we will not stop this fight.[1]

Al-Qaeda's follow-up plot to the gruesome July transit attacks was even more daring and complicated: to destroy several transatlantic airliners in midflight, over American cities using a concoction of homemade chemicals. These acts of terror would kill several thousand civilians, cost billions of dollars, strain the Anglo-American relationship, bankrupt several airlines, severely damage the global civil aviation system, and cause untold ripples on the global economy.

But it never happened. The complicated plot involving dozens of individuals in multiple countries—dubbed Operation Overt by British authorities—was thwarted through the intimate cooperation of Britain, Pakistan, and America, as well as the largest surveillance operation in British history. Over a thousand British Secret Intelligence Service (SIS; a.k.a. MI6) agents, British Security Service (BSS; a.k.a. MI5) agents, undercover Metropolitan Special Branch officers, Thames valley police officers, and other officials worked for over a year with their US counterparts to crush the plot and bring the planners to justice.

Operation Overt is an excellent example of how the US finds and tracks potential threats, as well as how allied intelligence services can work together. It serves as a model case for both the US and UK in the prevention of large-scale terrorist attacks by demonstrating the importance of careful multinational intelligence work, robust information sharing, intricate diplomatic maneuvers, and good fortune. Operation Overt also instructs that solid detective work, long nights at the office, and luck—and not flashy counterterrorism actions or brutal methods—still serve as the primary mechanisms that thwart many terrorist acts.

IN THE BEGINNING: BOJINKA

A decade before Operation Overt, a group of disaffected individuals with no real connection to al-Qaeda hatched a similar plot in the Philippines known as Bojinka. Ramzi Yousef, the ringleader of the fizzled 1993 World Trade Center bombing in New York City, had fled to Southeast Asia and set into motion a plan to destroy in midair several commercial transpacific aircraft bound for American shores.

Proving that terrorism is often a family affair, Yousef and his co-conspirators lived in Doña Josefa Apartments in unit 603, a property owned by Yousef's uncle, Khalid Shaykh Mohammed (KSM).[2] The conspirators contemplated a variety of attacks, including assassinating US President Clinton and Pope John Paul II, as well as crashing a commercial plane into CIA headquarters, before settling on the idea of destroying multiple airplanes in flight over the Pacific.[3] The attack would be known as Bojinka—a nonsense word they made up—and would be carried out in January 1995.

Yousef had already proven capable of creating and smuggling explosives onto an international flight. In December 1994, Yousef, traveling under an alias, had boarded Philippines Airlines Flight 434 from Toyko to Manila. Bringing explosive material on board in his carry-on luggage, Yousef constructed a bomb in the airplane bathroom, placed it under his seat, and deplaned at a refueling stop before the aircraft began the second leg of its journey.[4] The subsequent explosion killed a twenty-four-year-old Japanese passenger, Haruki Ikegami, who had the misfortune to be sitting next to Yousef on the flight, and severely burned other individuals on board. The stricken plane's pilot landed safely in Okinawa without further loss of life despite a gaping hole in the fuselage.

For Yousef and his confederates, Abdul Hakim Murad and Wali Khan Amin Shah, the attack was a success. Yousef had succeeded in smuggling, assembling, and detonating a bomb on a commercial flight and could likely repeat the process. For its next attack, the trio decided to increase the bomb's explosive power tenfold.[5]

In the early morning of January 7, 1995, a member of the terrorist group accidentally ignited a chemical fire in the apartment's kitchenette, forcing the evacuation of the apartment complex. The police who responded to the scene found bomb-making equipment, bottles of liquid nitroglycerin, and computers with mysterious encrypted files in the apartment.[6] The officers arrested Abdul Hakim Murad—who, incidentally, had received training from various American flight schools—when he returned to the scene.[7] While Shah, who fled the scene, was caught in December in Malaysia,[8] Yousef evaded capture and made his way to Pakistan. Unfortunately for him, in February, Pakistani commandos acting on a tip caught up with him at an Islamabad guesthouse and rendered him to the US for trial.[9]

Despite its failure, the plan provided a clear template for future attacks. Yousef's December 1994 test run had shown that placing an incendiary device on an aircraft was relatively easy. The 9/11 attacks further proved that commercial aircraft could serve to cause mass death and widespread damage to civilian and military installations. This point was reaffirmed in 2001, when al-Qaeda-linked Richard Reid almost managed to detonate an explosive in his shoe during a transatlantic flight despite heavy post-9/11 security. After these attacks, al-Qaeda probably assessed that the mid-1990s plot—in which al-Qaeda had played no part—had fallen apart more because of the fickleness of fate than because of any inherent weakness in the plan. The key difference between the Bojinka test run and the 2006 plot was that the attackers would serve as suicide bombers.

The US first caught glimmers of the new Bojinka plot in 2005.[10] US interrogators learned from a detainee—Abu Faraj al-Libi, who had taken over the number 3 slot following KSM's detention in 2003[11]—the first clues.[12] This detainee provided the name of UK national Mohammed al-Ghabrah, who served as a banker of sorts to al-Qaeda and had a tangential relationship with the suicide attackers who struck London's transit system in July 2005.[13] Ghabrah, a chubby, unemployed Briton of Syrian descent, traveled to Pakistan to meet Abu Faraj al-Libi sometime in 2002, according to the US Treasury.[14] Since Ghabrah was on a terror list, it could be reasonably assumed that both the US and the UK began conducting physical and electronic surveillance on him in order to learn about their plan.

ENTER RASHID RAUF

The mastermind of Operation Overt turned out to be a young man of British Pakistani origin from Birmingham, England, with a history of violence, Rashid Rauf. He gained some notoriety in 2002, when he murdered his uncle, incited by a family problem with an arranged marriage.[15] At the time, he was twenty-one years old. Rauf then gave British authorities the slip and made his way to the dusty city of Bahawalpur in southern Pakistan. Since the UK and Pakistan lacked an extradition treaty,[16] Rauf was safe from British justice.

Rauf quickly aligned himself with one of the most hard-core jihadist organizations in the country, Jaish-e-Mohammed (JeM), by marrying the sister of its founder. Rauf likely had few delusions about the nature and extracurricular pursuits of his in-laws. A few months before Rauf entered Pakistan, JeM unleashed a brutal terror attack against the Indian parliament in Delhi that left a dozen dead and brought India and Pakistan to the brink of war.

These family ties gave Rauf the bona fides that allowed him to join extremist circles. In mid-2002, Rauf contacted al-Qaeda's chief in Pakistan, Amjad Hussein Farooqi, and the two men cemented a personal relationship that would last until Pakistani security forces killed Farooqi in September 2004.[17] At some point, Rauf also established contact with Abu Faraj al-Libi and al-Qaeda's master bomb maker, Abu Ubaydah al-Masri.[18]

Meanwhile, Rauf maintained associates in England—Abdulla Ahmed Ali and Assad Sarwar, two nondescript, twenty-something British Pakistani fellows—who would be his contacts in carrying out the attack. Notably, the duo traveled to Pakistan in February 2003 where Rauf met with them to discuss possible attacks in the UK.[19] At this point, Rauf had been serving as an interlocutor to the outside world for not only Abu Faraj but also Ayman al-Zawahiri.[20]

Ali returned to Pakistan a number of times over the course of 2004 and 2005.[21] At the same time, al-Qaeda's Abu Ubaydah al-Masri taught the future London transit attackers how to construct miniature hydrogen peroxide bombs, al-Qaeda's suicide weapon of choice for cramped quarters such as subways, trains, and busses.[22]

It remains inconclusive whether any other plane plotters received the same deadly training from Abu Ubaydah, but subsequent phone records linked Ali to the leader of the ineffectual July 21 follow-up bombing attack on London, Muktar Said Ibrahim.[23] Ali had also been in touch with the leader of the devastating July 7 bombings.[24] During the simmering month of June 2005—as Khan and Ibrahim prepared to blast their way into history and oblivion—Ali would return to Pakistan once more.

Sometime in 2005, one of Ali's confederates paid the equivalent of US$260,000 in cash for an anonymous-looking second-story apartment in Walthamstow, the largest Pakistani enclave in London.[25] Naturally, after the transport bombings, the neighborhood was on high alert for anything or anyone who would bring additional police pressure on the community. Perhaps in an effort to show the authorities their commitment to British safety, "several people" living in the neigh-borhood tipped off authorities to a "small group of angry young Mus-lim men" who had just moved into several rooms in a tan-colored row house along Forest Road.[26] Law enforcement officials would later call it the "bomb factory."[27]

Ali returned to Pakistan under the guise of helping the victims of the devastating October 2005 earthquake. This time, Arafat Waheed Khan—Ali's schoolmate whom MI5 once tried unsuccessfully to re-cruit as an asset[28]—and Assad Sarwar accompanied him. By April 2006, Sarwar drove to South Wales and used a false name to make his first purchases of hydrogen peroxide, the key bomb-making chemical used in the transit attacks the year prior.[29] Later that month, he pur-chased even more.

By 2006, Rashid Rauf was in constant e-mail and phone contact with Ali—which was intercepted by the UK's SIGINT collection or-ganization, the Government Communications Headquarters (GCHQ) and the NSA.[30] Since most of the world's electronic communications pass through the US, it would be a reasonable assumption that the US liber-ally utilized FISA-related warrants to collect and monitor Rauf, Ghabrah, Ali, and their widening circle of co-conspirators. Armed with eaves-dropping hardware, the US took the lead in electronically monitoring the plotters, and then NSA or CIA passed along the transcriptions to their British counterparts.

Ali and Sarwar departed for Islamabad to visit Rauf for the last time. Upon returning to London's Heathrow International Airport on June 24, British authorities, already keeping a sharp watch on the two, sur-reptitiously searched their belongings before they collected their baggage at the luggage carousels.[31] Inside, they found packets of Tang drink mix and a curiously large number of batteries—possibly the makings of a so-called Tang bomb.[32]

There is, of course, nothing illegal or unseemly about either the sug-ary orange drink mix or batteries. However, when mixed with purified hydrogen peroxide, the citric acid in Tang reacts and causes an explo-sion. According to Erroll Southers, the chief of intelligence and coun-terterrorism at Los Angeles International Airport, these bombs "are the weapon of choice in the Middle East," since "they leave no residue, they're extremely volatile, they're easy to make and they've been quite effective."[33]

With some trepidation, British authorities allowed the two bombers to leave the airport, since they had committed no crime at that point. But the investigation quickly expanded, consuming intelligence resources at an exponential rate.[34] Quickly taking precedence over the thirty other plots MI5 had been tracking at the time, Operation Overt became the only show in town.[35]

Ali soon noticed the increasingly invasive surveillance and e-mailed Rauf about it. Rauf dismissed his concerns, telling Ali not to worry, rather casually noting that "it's normal in summer time when it gets hot."[36] Still, a spooked Ali began to conduct meetings in public spaces such as restaurants, parks, and even a cemetery—locations where he believed that security officials would not be able to overhear him.[37] On July 4, Ali told Rauf he was ready for a test run.[38]

The authorities overheard Ali's words and more; they were monitoring some 200 individuals. By that time, 220 officers from across Britain were detailed to assist in the widening investigation.[39] Support was strong across the pond as well, as over 200 FBI agents and an unknown number of CIA and NSA officers combed through thousands of pieces of secret information from Britain and Pakistan to glean more information about the plot.[40]

MI5 decided to step up its efforts, planting listening devices and tiny cameras throughout the Forest Road apartment.[41] Their persistent surveillance revealed that the plot was nearing completion; a number of the bombers began to tape martyrdom videos for release on the Internet after the attack was complete.[42] In his video, Ali stated that he had desired martyrdom since he was fifteen years old.[43] Others thanked Allah and blamed American and British foreign policy for their actions, stating, "don't mess with the Muslims."[44]

On August 6, a plainclothes police officer observed Ali enter a local Internet café to research the departing flight schedules of major transatlantic flights leaving London for points in North America.[45] Ali made sure the flights were large passenger aircraft that would depart from Heathrow's Terminal 3 within a window of about two and a half hours— a short time that would allow bombers to board and detonate their lethal packages before the pilots or other passengers would become aware of their mortal situation.[46] And before they could fight back.

The bombs were crude but effective devices. The attackers planned to bring prepared soda bottles onto the flights in their carry-on luggage, as well as disposable cameras and regular batteries—probably the ones that some of the plotters had brought back from Pakistan in June—with their contents removed and replaced with explosives. To detonate the bombs on board, the conspirators would connect the bottle to the disposable camera via a small metal wire. When the camera flash went off, so, too, would the detonator and the explosive.

A number of the plotters tested the mixture somewhere in Pakistan and found that such contraptions could be effective.[47] The Forensics Explosives Laboratory in London later re-created the devices to measure and record the effects.[48] The resulting explosion destroyed one of the video cameras and sprayed the external sections of the laboratory with pieces of the reinforced protective walls meant to contain the detritus from the blast.[49] According to Sidney Alford, a British explosives engineer, the ensuing fiery explosion would have opened a gaping wound in the fuselage of the aircraft, causing significant pressure changes inside an aircraft traveling at high altitude.[50] "I wouldn't have liked to [have] been in that airplane," he said.

To smuggle the bombs on board, the conspirators enlisted a Heathrow airport security guard, Amin Asmin Tariq, to participate in the plot. Tariq planned to disguise the plotters as airport employees to allow the ringleaders to case Terminal 3. He also provided inside information about standard airport security procedures.[51] With this level of knowledge, the plotters may well have been able to pull off the operation.

Knowing these procedures, they planned to keep one unadulterated drink with them in case airport security officials asked them to taste the liquids inside.[52] To further confuse and embarrass airline security officials, the bombers planned to bring adult magazines and condoms with them in their carry-on luggage.[53] Ali took the preparations one diabolical step further than the others: he planned to bring his infant son on the suicide mission, so that the baby's bottle could be used to hold chemicals and deceive airport staff.[54]

The discovery of the second Bojinka plot raised the "strike versus develop" dilemma; officials had to decide whether to wait to gather more evidence or to sweep in and crush the menace. The precise series of events in the case remains unclear, and two competing narratives of the final days have emerged.

One possibility is that on August 6, Prime Minister Blair personally updated President Bush on the British investigation.[55] At this point, the British were still compiling evidence in expectation of an upcoming trial. The White House, however, wanted to move more quickly. President Bush later discussed Rauf's threat with American intelligence officers and policymakers—but not with the British prime minister.[56] Investigative journalist Ron Suskind suggested that Bush was acutely frustrated with British recalcitrance, as he saw it, in cracking down on the attackers and wanted to eliminate the threat then and there. He expressed this dissatisfaction to Vice President Cheney,[57] who then quietly ordered CIA's national clandestine service director, Jose Rodriguez Jr., to meet with ISI and take down Rauf—without informing the British.[58] According to Suskind, Pakistani officials already had Rauf under surveillance and arrested the al-Qaeda plotter on August 9.[59] There was no coordination within the CIA or with the United Kingdom until after the deed was done.

On the other hand, Jose Rodriguez might have been in Pakistan around August 9 and unilaterally authorized Rauf's arrest. During much of the past year, the US acted as the conduit between MI6 and ISI, as the two intelligence services had, for historical reasons, an extremely poor working relationship. Since both services trusted the CIA, however, it attempted to facilitate a free flow of information between the Pakistanis and the British. Still, not all information was always passed along.

In any case, Rodriguez was meeting with ISI's top leadership when he learned they had actionable intelligence on Rauf's whereabouts. US officials had previously believed Rauf might be in the Northwest Frontier Province, like bin Laden and Zawahiri.[60] After all, why would a top man in an imminent attack risk being in Pakistan proper—instead of the northern badlands—unless he felt secure from risk of arrest? It's possible that Rodriguez told his Pakistani counterparts to detain Rauf without

higher authorization. He was a top American official. Once back in secure communication with officials in CIA headquarters, Rodriguez
briefed them on ISI's actions; they would have then passed along the
message to British intelligence.[61]

Either way, Rashid Rauf's arrest in Pakistan forced London's hand in
rolling up the conspiracy—some say, before the British government
could fully construct its legal case. British officials knew that any delay
would either push the conspirators underground or oblige them to perform the operation the next day. One Pakistan-based militant arrested
days before had already sent a message to the UK plotters, urging them
to "do your attacks now."[62] Britain's Joint Terrorism Analysis Centre
(JTAC) ordered the country's threat level increased to its highest level,
reflecting the possibility of an imminent terror attack.[63] The top policymakers in the UK, including Prime Minister Blair, MI5 Director Eliza
Manningham-Buller,[64] and Home Secretary John Reid, among others,
convened to discuss the series of events. All in attendance agreed to take
down the network that night.[65]

Law enforcement spread out all over England to break up the conspiracy. By midnight on August 9, twenty-five people in Birmingham,
High Wycombe, and East London—including Ali and Sarwar—had
been arrested.[66] Outside the UK, Italian authorities arrested some forty
people, while Pakistan wrapped up several individuals.[67]

UK authorities then conducted nearly seventy independent searches,
netting some four hundred computers, two hundred cell phones, eight
thousand computer storage items, as well as several martyrdom videos
and bomb-making materials.[68] All told, officials retrieved over six thousand gigabytes of data pertaining to the investigation.[69] For American
officials, the arrests came none too soon. TSA quickly forbade all liquids
from being carried on planes—a restriction that more or less continues to
this day.[70]

Following the arrests, over a thousand flights were canceled to and
from the UK, affecting some 400,000 passengers; losses in revenue to
various airline companies may have topped $400 million.[71] Added to the
cost of adding security measures in other countries, the failed airline plot
easily caused cumulative worldwide costs to public and private groups
of almost US$1 billion.

In retrospect, British intelligence officials were probably relieved that their long surveillance operation did not go on longer despite the false start. Reportedly, the plotters were barely "two days away" from performing a test run and were planning to carry out the final attack within a week.[72]

THE FIRST TRIAL

In August, prosecutors charged the conspirators—Ali, Hussain, Sarwar, Muhammad Ghulzar, and six others—with various criminal offenses related to the failed airline plot. British prosecutors believed they had a good case against the defendants based on the assembled evidence even without the testimony of Rashid Rauf, who had escaped Pakistani police custody in December 2007 and disappeared. In addition to the chemicals and other bomb-making supplies that law enforcement had collected, the prosecution played the martyrdom videos as evidence of the plotters' intent. Prosecutors also claimed that Assad Sarwar was simultaneously developing plans to cripple other sites in England as well as inflight airliners.

Although several of the bombers pled guilty to lesser charges such as conspiracy to commit public nuisance and conspiracy to cause explosions, they fought the more serious charges, including conspiracy to murder using explosives on aircraft and conspiracy to murder persons unknown. They claimed that they wanted to cause a spectacle to protest British and US foreign policy but did not want to kill anyone. Ali even claimed that the bombs were just meant to frighten people as part of a political statement.

On November 8, 2008, after deliberating fifty hours, a jury convicted Ali, Sarwar, and Hussein of conspiracy to murder, but—incredibly— acquitted them of the crime at the heart of the plot: conspiracy to murder using explosives on an aircraft.[73] British authorities immediately declared that they would seek a retrial of seven suspects on all previous counts, as well as the conspiracy to detonate improvised explosive devices on transatlantic passenger aircraft. Unique among them, Mohammad Gulzar was cleared on all counts.

Several procedural and evidentiary reasons account for why British authorities failed to fully convict the plotters during this trial. The main reason prosecutors could not make the case against the ringleaders for conspiracy to commit murder using explosives on aircraft was their inability to include electronic communication intercepts as evidence. They could not exploit critical GCHQ and NSA intercepts as evidence because the UK and US governments thought that Rauf—who was still at large in Pakistan—might once again access his mail.yahoo.com e-mail account and reveal his location.[74] In the eyes of the British and US governments, intelligence gathering and protection of sources and methods trumped prosecutors' needs to make a convincing case based on all the evidence in open court.

RAUF'S DEMISE AND THE SECOND TRIAL

Rashid Rauf's life ended in mid-November 2008, soon after his British colleagues' first trial. Rauf was meeting with Egyptian al-Qaeda operative Abu Zubair al-Masri and al-Qaeda planner Abd al-Rahman Hussein bin Hillal in North Waziristan when a US drone fired a Hellfire missile into the building, reducing the structure to rubble.[75] His death paved the way for British prosecutors to produce his e-mails in the second trial. The judge in the second trial, Richard Henriques, later remarked that these e-mails were "a vital source of information as to the control, progress and scope of this conspiracy . . . they establish beyond question the ultimate control of this conspiracy lay in Pakistan."[76]

On February 17, 2009, the second trial began only to have the jury discharged a day later. Two weeks later, the trial resumed with a new jury. This new trial lasted for four months, with the prosecution arguing again that the plotters had indeed wanted to blow up commercial aircraft midflight. After deliberating for over fifty-four hours, the jury in early September delivered a guilty verdict for three of the main plotters—Ahmed Abdulla Ali, Assad Sarwar, and Tanvir Hussain—for conspiracy to murder involving liquid bombs and conspiracy to target airline passengers.[77]

On September 14, Judge Henriques called the plot the "most grave and wicked conspiracy ever proven within this jurisdiction."[78] Ali, Sarwar, Hussain, and Islam all received life sentences. A third trial, concluded in July 2010, convicted a further three Op Overt plotters of conspiracy to murder; they are currently serving long prison sentences.

Far from a clean sweep, however, some of the individuals implicated in the 2006 plot beat the rap. Mohammed al-Ghabrah, whose relationships in Pakistan gave authorities the initial leads to the plot, still walks the streets of East London. So does Mohammed Gulzar, a shadowy individual alleged to be a senior figure in the operation. He journeyed to UK from South Africa on a false passport to meet several times with Ali and Sarwar to discuss the plot.[79]

With multiple potential terror plots facing Great Britain in the summer of 2006, the embattled UK intelligence establishment enlisted the assistance of its well-financed American counterparts. By mid-August 2006, the US and UK intelligence communities worked and operated almost as a single entity with information-sharing reaching a new high. As CIA director Michael Hayden put it, "Nothing less than intensive cooperation with our overseas colleagues could have achieved such a complete success."[80] The cooperation occurred, not only at the highest levels, but also at multiple levels deep within the bureaucratic firmament of both countries. The US considered this plot to be the biggest operation since 9/11 and treated it as such.[81]

The fact that each nation used its strength—America's SIGINT capabilities alongside Britain's physical surveillance capability and combined ability to "flood the zone" with personnel—is remarkable. Operation Overt became the new gold standard in fighting international terrorism. On one hand, MI5 placed a still unknown undercover agent within the airline plot cell, while on the other, the CIA "provided critical help in identifying and tracking people involved in Pakistan"[82] related to the case. When the undercover British agent provided a scrap of information such as a name or a telephone number, US intelligence services could then leverage vast databases, information gleaned from detainee interrogations and signals intelligence capabilities, and provide even more e-mail addresses, phone numbers, and names to the British in return. This exchange was made over and over again, including when the NSA intercepted e-mails between Abdulla Ahmed Ali and Rauf in Pakistan and then shared them almost in real time with British authorities.[83]

The US also served as the conduit for information between the Pakistan's ISI and Britain's MI6.

Of course, with every relationship there are bumps and annoyances along the way. The most egregious one of these occurred when Rashid Rauf was originally detained in August 2006 without British knowledge—causing the whole arrest mechanism to begin prematurely in England. The intense media hubbub surrounding the arrests, as well as the media pronouncements by then-Homeland Security secretary Michael Chertoff and New York congressman Peter King, reportedly irked the British, who were hard at work laying the foundation for the upcoming court case and did not like crucial, potentially jury tampering information to emerge from the mouths of American policymakers. But in the end, these were small irritants in thwarting what could have been the worst terrorist attack in the post-9/11 era.

CHAPTER 8

AN INCREASING PREFERENCE FOR LETHAL ENDS

Hell is empty, and all the devils are here.

—THE TEMPEST

By the middle of the decade, the US had begun to shift strategically from capturing top al-Qaeda personnel to killing them. Technological dominance provided the US a critical advantage; mobile and satellite phone technology became increasingly fatal forms of communication and al-Qaeda personnel were forced to rely on human couriers and face-to-face meetings to transmit messages. Senior leaders were becoming so concerned about the risk of electronic interception that communication between remaining operational leaders became more and more restricted. US intelligence analysts were beginning to realize that al-Qaeda's hierarchy, like many Silicon Valley start-ups, had determined that a flatter management structure worked best, allowing them to adapt to the death or capture of senior leaders. But while al-Qaeda had regenerated each time, it had been forced to rely on leaders with less and less hands-on operational experience. Furthermore, fearing electronic interception, communication between bin Laden and remaining operational leaders had been increasingly restricted; each message spent months in the hands of couriers. In December 2005, US ambassador to Pakistan Ryan Crocker went as far as to claim that bin Laden no longer controlled operations and that al-Qaeda had "run into serious problems."[1]

A more lethal effort was now seen as the way forward to dismantle al-Qaeda in Pakistan.

AMERICAN UAVS, PAKISTANI SKIES: ABU HAMZA RABIA (KILLED, DECEMBER 2005)

Shortly after the capture of Abu Faraj al-Libi, the Bush administration launched a high-level internal review of its strategy against al-Qaeda. Behind the words "strategic approach to defeat violent extremism" was a commitment to pursue further capture/kill missions.[2] Since the bulk of the US military and intelligence efforts were tied up in the morass of Iraq, the US had few resources to dedicate to finding bin Laden and dismantling al-Qaeda in Pakistan. "There's been a perception, a sense of drift in overall terrorism policy. People have not figured out what we do next, so we just continue to pick 'em off one at a time," said Roger Cressey, a former NSC counterterrorism official.[3]

Al-Qaeda had some success cementing alliances with regional jihadist groups worldwide, granting them the al-Qaeda banner without much day-to-day input over their planning or operations. Zarqawi's bloodthirsty jihad in Iraq generated the most news, and al-Qaeda's leadership accepted him in light of the dramatic effectiveness of his campaigns. To the degree it still existed, however, the center of al-Qaeda's global operations remained in the border area between Pakistan and Afghanistan.

Abu Hamza Rabia (Muhammad Rabia Abdul Halim Shuayb) probably inherited the operational post by default when Pakistan captured Abu Faraj in May 2005. The thirty-something Rabia had been Abu Faraj's deputy and led al-Qaeda in Pakistan, helping plan the two assassination attempts on Musharraf in 2003.[4] He also had connections to fellow Egyptian Ayman al-Zawahiri; a Pakistani official said that Abu Faraj's interrogation had confirmed that Abu Hamza was in touch with al-Qaeda's deputy chief and "was an important connection between Zawahiri and various al-Qaeda cells."[5]

Abu Hamza was responsible for recruiting, training, and plotting large-scale attacks against US and European targets.[6] He possessed a wide network within the jihadist universe and was trying to reinvigorate al-Qaeda's terrorist operations.[7] An FBI official quipped to the *New Yorker* in 2004 that "if there is an attack on the US . . . [Abu] Hamza Rabia will be responsible."[8] Abu Hamza wanted to organize foreign fighters to fight and die in Iraq, but al-Qaeda's central command deemed him too valuable to be sent to the charnel houses of Baghdad and Mosul.[9]

As with Abu Faraj, US counterterrorism analysts could not determine with much degree of precision Abu Hamza's actual position within the organization. It was extremely difficult for analysts to establish exactly how terrorist leaders were related and who actually ran the show. Many counterterrorism officials had begun deemphasizing the importance of ranking al-Qaeda's leaders; the organization was increasingly hobbled in its ability to communicate globally and, to some degree, had reverted to operating under regional leaders. Neither Abu Hamza nor anyone else seemed to have any control over Zarqawi's operations in Iraq. Zarqawi operated independently, routinely ignoring advice from his supposed superiors in Pakistan.

While it was true that Abu Hamza's name was seldom mentioned by the US before his death, US officials eventually concluded that he was a senior terrorist leader[10] and Pakistani officials confirmed that he was on a CIA watch list.[11] Abu Hamza almost certainly was in the driver's seat in Pakistan, but there is little evidence to suggest that he directed global operations effectively. Abu Hamza had little time to gain experience, as he was killed after about six months on the job. At the time of his death, he had a US $5 million bounty on his head.

Abu Hamza had been playing hide and seek with American and Pakistani forces for months, transiting between the Pakistani tribal areas and the Afghan border.[12] He had been wounded in the leg in a UAV strike on November 5 that killed eight others—including his wife and eleven-year-old daughter.[13] Local residents said that UAVs had been flying around the clock in the border region before the attack,[14] and one reported that some of the men had arrived only a day before,[15] suggesting that the US was tracking Abu Hamza and his confederates as they traveled from place to place via signals intelligence.[16]

Finally, a missile from a UAV killed Abu Hamza on December 1, 2005, around 1:30 AM. He was taking refuge in the village of Asoray, near Miranshah, in North Waziristan. Besides him, the strike killed four others—two Arabs and the seventeen-year-old son and eight-year-old nephew of the man harboring them.[17]

Although the exact details of how the US tracked the terrorist leader remain shrouded in mystery, US intelligence probably had access to his cell phone through a British penetration of a terror cell in Manchester.[18] The Manchester police counterterrorism unit worked for three years to provide intelligence about who was directing and funding the operations in their city; senior officials later claimed that the investigation was instrumental in disrupting and destabilizing the senior levels of al-Qaeda.[19] Furthermore, given the two men's close relationship, Abu Faraj's debriefings doubtlessly provided crucial details in tracking Abu Hamza.

Islamabad initially denied reports that the Americans killed Abu Hamza, claiming instead that he had died accidentally while constructing a bomb.[20] But this story began to fall apart almost immediately. Several local residents told a Pakistani newspaper that a missile destroyed the house.[21] A Pakistani journalist shortly corroborated their account by taking a photo showing villagers with a piece of shrapnel with "AGM-114" (a Hellfire missile's designator) written on it.[22] Pakistani intelligence sources later also confirmed, anonymously, that a UAV felled Abu Hamza.[23]

Meanwhile, al-Qaeda flat-out denied that he died in the attack, claiming that he was safe and that the attack had killed mostly locals.[24] Their claims were buttressed by the fact that villagers had recovered the bodies from the rubble and turned them over to local militants, leaving little physical evidence.[25] President Musharraf responded in a fit of hyperbole, saying he was "200 percent certain" that Abu Hamza had been killed. Eventually Musharraf would amend his comments to say it was "500 percent confirmed."[26] American officials were more circumspect, having been previously fooled into prematurely celebrating a senior operative's demise. They refused to confirm Abu Hamza's death without physical evidence. However, US intelligence subsequently overheard lamentations shared between militants that seemed to confirm he was indeed dead.

Abu Hamza's killing was probably the result of intense US-Pakistani behind-the-scenes negotiations. US analysts had concluded that northwestern Pakistan served, not just as a hiding place for al-Qaeda leaders, but as an effective operational base, giving them the ability to coordinate and carry out attacks on the US.[27] Under pressure, the ISI was selectively cooperating—periodically tossing over a low-level terrorist to the Americans to keep Washington at bay—but failed to give the CIA the full access it needed.

The Pakistani military was similarly reluctant to overextend into a dangerous area where it could exert only marginal political control. After a brief push into the tribal agencies, the government brokered a truce: the army would not interfere as long as local leaders did not attack government officials, impede development projects, or allow foreign militants to operate within their territory. In the resulting power vacuum, al-Qaeda operatives moved freely and Taliban militants, distinctive with their dour expressions, unique headdresses, and lined eyes, moved against conciliatory tribal and religious leaders, kidnapped journalists, and imposed a brutal interpretation of Islamic law.[28]

Frustrated with the safe haven al-Qaeda enjoyed and by the inability or unwillingness of the ISI to pursue operations there, the Bush administration evidently struck a deal to allow occasional clandestine airspace access into the northwest of the country for armed American Predators to hunt down suspected terrorist leaders.[29]

Islamabad continued to deny that such cooperation existed, but several officials speaking under anonymity confirmed the agreement. Questioned about Abu Hamza's death, one official commented, "Here is what I can tell you: Our troops were not involved in the operation, but this is one of the areas where our intelligence and operational cooperation with US services is most intense . . . comments on media reports that it was a Predator strike would invoke sovereignty issues."[30] National security advisor Steven Hadley essentially confirmed the understanding: "There are conflicting reports as to what happened. . . . This is something that occurred on Pakistani soil. They obviously will be the ones to come forward and indicate how this happened."[31]

Pakistan's attempt at covering up its complicity revealed the concern senior officials felt over the potential for blowback in pursuing the new line of operations. There had been remarkably little controversy over the Abu Zubaydah capture; most Pakistanis were seemingly prepared to accept US assistance in combating foreign fighters on their soil, as long as Pakistan led the charge and civilian casualties were avoided. Abu Hamza's death, however, was different. His killing immediately triggered a political backlash. In the tribal regions, local militants responded by staging a series of bombings, striking out against pro-government leaders, and kidnapping paramilitary troops patrolling the area.[32] Musharraf's truce in the hinterlands was in jeopardy—and Musharraf was beginning to lose control over the increasingly jittery country.

THE SPOKESMAN: ABU LAYTH AL-LIBI (KILLED, JANUARY 2008)

By this point, the standard criticism to the strategy of killing any particular al-Qaeda leader was that the group would simply replace him with another person from within the organization.[33] To some degree, this was true. Without actually dismantling the al-Qaeda infrastructure, depriving the organization of a refuge, and countering the appeal of the jihadist ideology, isolated US successes could not eliminate the threat. Still, like waves crashing on the shore, the US campaign was wearing away al-Qaeda's effectiveness as a fighting force. Al-Qaeda still acted as a management structure for jihadist activities worldwide and, in this sense, depended on effective leadership to organize, motivate, and coordinate its personnel. With each leader the US successfully tracked down and neutralized, America further degraded its knowledge, experience, and connections in the terrorist underworld.

US intelligence experienced some setbacks but gained valuable new tools in 2006 and 2007 that allowed it to penetrate deeper into the terrorist networks threatening America and its allies. The Protect America Act of 2007 amended the Foreign Intelligence Surveillance Act (FISA) to further expand the umbrella under which the US could legally conduct wiretaps on international targets, asserting that agents did not need a warrant as long as there was sufficient justification and one side was "reasonably believed" to be outside the US.[34] The director of national intelligence—a position that had only come into existence a few years before—told Congress in early 2008 that the first six months of using these new authorities had already allowed the IC to better understand al-Qaeda's global network, identify key individuals at critical nodes, and disrupt terrorist attacks.[35]

By 2006, and probably as early as 2004, the US had begun operating armed UAVs from a secret air base in southwestern Pakistan.[39] The Shamsi air base—located in a secluded, windswept part of Baluchistan once used by Arab sheikhs for falconry expeditions—extended the reach of American find-fix-finish campaigns and allowed the US to launch a drone within minutes of receiving actionable intelligence on a leader's location. It was also about one hundred miles south of the border with Afghanistan, allowing US operators to squeeze al-Qaeda militants as they attempted to escape one area for the next.

Also in 2007, the US began deploying the MQ-9 "Reaper" UAV, a larger and more capable version of the MQ-1 Predator. It boasted an increased payload, better sensors, and a drastically improved range.[36] Whereas the original Predator was capable of flying 454 miles and had a maximum speed of 135 miles per hour, the new Reaper could travel 3,682 miles with a maximum speed of 300 miles per hour.[37] The significant improvement in reach and duration allowed near-constant overhead monitoring. It also added several cameras, including an improved synthetic aperture radar (SAR), allowing pilots to penetrate cloud cover and sandstorms—frequent obstacles in the South Asian battleground. The Reaper was especially attractive because it extended the operational advantages of the Predator but used the same control stations, allowing pilots to quickly adapt and put the new machine into service. According to the US military, the Reaper began operating in Afghanistan in September 2007 and made its first strike on enemy insurgents in October.[38]

The US now possessed the tools and the technology to maintain persistent overhead surveillance and rapidly strike within the al-Qaeda safe haven, but there were continuing strategic drawbacks. While the ability to strike without warning in northwestern Pakistan may have brought fear to the hearts of al-Qaeda members—perhaps forcing them to be even more careful in their communications and movements—it also cut the intelligence trail cold. With these strikes, there was little opportunity for the US to interrogate survivors, exploit recovered data, gather physical evidence, or manipulate enemy communications. The intensified reliance on UAVs as the primary tool for neutralizing terrorist leaders also emphasized the lack of other options. Finally, the psychic effects of the collateral damage were not limited to al-Qaeda's leaders. Broadcast every few weeks on the evening news and across the nation's newspapers, the images of devastation inevitably increased public hostility against US and Pakistani leaders in Pakistan, in particular against Musharraf.[40] At the extreme, it risked undermining support for the Pakistani government to the point of inviting a fundamentalist takeover—an al-Qaeda-influenced administration with access to nuclear weapons, Washington's worst fear.[41]

Despite these misgivings, the US forged ahead with its targeted killing program. US officials had identified the safe havens in Pakistan as the core of the al-Qaeda problem and, with Musharraf's cooperation, America's aerial platforms allowed them to reach deep into Pakistani territory. There were some early successes; based partially on intelligence from Abu Faraj: on January 13, 2006 the CIA thought it might have located Ayman al-Zawahiri.[42] This strike, however, killed as many as eighteen civilians, including women and children, and sparked protests across Pakistan.[43] By 2008 the campaign was flagging and US officials were voicing frustration with the results. Despite $10 billion in assistance to Islamabad—much of which went to upgrade conventional capabilities in order to fight Pakistan's real bogeyman, India—al-Qaeda had strengthened its position in the tribal areas and enjoyed the freedom to recruit, train, and plot new attacks.[44] Worse, al-Qaeda commanders—such as Abu Layth al-Libi—apparently traveled around Pakistan without fear of detection or capture.[45]

Abu Layth al-Libi (Ali Ammar Ashur al-Rufayi) was a longtime associate of bin Laden and joined al-Qaeda after 9/11.[46] Like many of his colleagues, he had come to Afghanistan in the 1980s to fight the Soviet Union.[47] In 1994, he returned to his native Libya and took part in an attempt to overthrow Muammar Qadhafi; when it failed, he escaped to Saudi Arabia. Following a bombing in 1995, he was imprisoned and probably tortured by Saudi security forces.[48] One report described him as a tall, burly man with scars on his back "as if beaten by a belt or wire."[49] After he was released or he escaped (the record is unclear), he returned to Afghanistan and rose to prominence after the US invasion.[50] He eventually became al-Qaeda's de facto spokesman, appearing on a Saudi-owned television channel in July 2002 to report that bin Laden and Taliban leader Mullah Omar were "in good health."[51] Another video showed him leading an attack on Afghan forces in 2004, and in 2006 he spoke to say that al-Qaeda was waging a holy war to restore the Taliban regime in Kabul.[52] In 2007 he appeared in a video with Zawahiri, indicating he maintained a close relationship with the top leadership.[53]

Abu Layth became an expert in explosives and guerrilla warfare, and played a pivotal role in recruiting and training operatives in the mountainous tribal areas of western Pakistan, according to US officials.[54] Unlike many others, he did not start as an al-Qaeda foot soldier; he had his own group of Libyan militants and was a leader of the Libyan Islamic Fighting Group (LIFG), an organization primarily dedicated to overthrowing Qadhafi.[55]

After Abu Hamza died, Abu Layth took over responsibility for Afghanistan and Pakistan, as bin Laden had become increasingly dependent on his organizing and military skills.[56] "[Abu Layth] al-Libi was the face of al-Qaeda for the past two years, practically commanding all operational activities," commented Ahmad Zaidan, Islamabad bureau chief for Al Jazeera.[57] He was the top ground commander, trainer, and coordinator, and a deputy to Zawahiri. "Operationally he was very competent," commented Henry Crumpton, former CIA official and counterterrorism coordinator for the State Department.[58]

Abu Layth earned a promotion to fifth place on the CIA's list, as well as a US $5 million bounty on his head, for his role in a February 2007 bombing attack on the Bagram air base in Afghanistan.[59] Al-Qaeda later claimed that it was an attempted assassination of Vice President Dick Cheney, who was visiting at the time. Cheney was unhurt, but the explosion killed twenty-three others.

Abu Layth hardly seemed ill at ease with the new attention. He felt secure enough to move about Pakistan, meet foreign officials, and visit wounded fighters as he planned further operations.[60] He was considered a "good and pious Muslim" by a few local politicians in Peshawar, and he met openly with a diplomat from Libya.[61] The fact that he could operate so freely for so long seemed to undermine the claim that Islamabad and the ISI were doing everything they could to hunt senior terrorist leaders.

Abu Layth was about forty years old when he, too, was cut down by a missile strike. In the predawn hours of January 29, 2008, a CIA-operated drone circled a safe house in the village of Khushali Torikel in North Waziristan.[62] The UAV focused its optical lens on a cluster of mud brick buildings a few miles from the town center, then fired its two Hellfire missiles—vaporizing Abu Layth and probably a dozen others inside the home of a local tribal leader.[63] It was the first successful operation against al-Qaeda's core leadership in more than two years.

Hours before the attack, assets on the ground alerted CIA to a convoy of vehicles moving through North Waziristan that strongly suggested the "signature" of al-Qaeda fighters.[64] Although the assets' identities remain veiled, they were probably well-paid informants from the local population, unconnected to the Pakistani army or intelligence service.[65] According to a former CIA officer who served in Waziristan, small American teams comprised of CIA and Special Forces officers had begun working from Pakistani military bases across the tribal belt, recruiting a network of paid informers to help the US find and target al-Qaeda operatives.[66] Tribal and religious leaders who had once embraced al-Qaeda increasingly viewed their presence with hostility, and had both a practical and financial motivation to sell them out. "All it takes," said one official, "is bags of cash."[67] CIA case officers had likewise begun equipping local tribesmen with electronic devices that they could plant near a militant's house, enabling US drones to quickly hone in on the signal.[68]

The American assets determined that the convoy carried up to seven al-Qaeda operatives and one unidentified high-ranking individual.[69] The CIA then followed the convoy using a variety of surveillance techniques through the town of Mir Ali into a walled compound.[70] As the UAV's pilot surveyed the scene, US intelligence zeroed in on Abu Layth and his associates through satellite phone signals emanating from the house.[71] With the importance of the target confirmed, the strike was approved, and the two buildings and their inhabitants went up in smoke.

Abu Layth's elimination occurred as the US was again escalating the drone program inside Pakistan's tribal areas. Several news sources reported that the strike had been unilateral; the Pakistani government was notified only as the operation was under way.[72] Having been denied permission for similar strikes in the past, the US now seemed to be demonstrating a willingness to act first and seek approval later. But this may have been a mutually convenient misperception. US operations against al-Qaeda depended on Pakistan's continued support, and three weeks earlier America's top two intelligence officials—DNI Mike McConnell and CIA director Michael Hayden—had traveled in secret to Pakistan to press for greater freedom for operations in the tribal areas.[73]

President Musharraf reportedly dismissed proposals for an overt American combat presence, but agreed to increase the number and scope of drone missions launched from the Shamsi air base inside Pakistan.[74] A secret agreement was probably reached to allow the US to strike important al-Qaeda targets without specific permission from the Pakistani military.[75] According to one report, the agreement included a tacit understanding with Musharraf and Pakistani chief of army staff Ashfaq Kayani that any strikes would be directed against foreign fighters operating in Pakistan, not the Pakistani Taliban.[76]

Shortly after Abu Layth's death, the Bush administration granted US officers greater freedom of action when attacking suspected al-Qaeda and Taliban fighters in the tribal areas.[77] In addition to grinding down enemy ranks, US officials hoped to collect new information on the senior leaders by continually harassing lower-level operatives to force them to move and communicate in ways that US intelligence could detect.[78] Previously, US officers were required to follow strict guidelines before striking, such as confirming the identity of a suspected militant before attacking. Now they were free to strike convoys of vehicles that bore the signature of al-Qaeda or Taliban leaders on the run, as long as they judged the risk of civilian casualties to be low.[79]

This new arrangement was shaped by intense political dynamics within the US and Pakistan. UAV pilots had been clamoring for years for greater freedom to strike at targets of opportunity, frustrated by what they saw as missed chances to take out enemy combatants because of bureaucratic and diplomatic niceties. "In the past, it required getting approval from the highest levels," noted one former US official, "you may have information that is valid for only 30 minutes. If you wait, the information is no longer valid."[80] CIA officials were likewise frustrated with the political stalemate in northwestern Pakistan, and worried that lukewarm cooperation from the Pakistanis would eventually lead to another successful attack against a US target. More importantly, 2008 was President Bush's final year in office, and there was intense pressure to track down bin Laden before he passed the baton.[81] The question of how to operate in Pakistan against al-Qaeda had become a political issue in the presidential campaign, and Bush administration officials hoped new tactical victories would validate their counterterrorism strategy.[82]

It was a dangerous compromise for Musharraf. Washington was ratcheting up the pressure even as he was fighting a protracted political battle over the domestic perception that the US could run roughshod over him. Former counterterrorism official Richard Clarke summarized the US approach: "The United States . . . sends a high-level delegation over to beat Musharraf up, and then you find that within a week or two a high-value target has been identified. Then he ignores us for a while until we send over another high-level delegation."[83] By agreeing to US quasi-unilateral strikes, Musharraf felt he could appease both the US and his own people by continuing to deny that the Pakistani government was approving US military strikes in the country.

But Musharraf nonetheless risked reaping the whirlwind. In March 2008 he suffered a political defeat that, among other national disturbances, would eventually lead to his forced resignation later that year.

THE ACCOUNTANT GETS A PROMOTION: SHAYKH SAID AL-MASRI (KILLED, MAY 2010)

UAV strikes accelerated throughout 2008, 2009, and 2010, taking out dozens of lower-level militants in an attempt to ravage the top tier of al-Qaeda's commanders.[84] As CIA director Hayden said at the time,

> By making a safe haven feel less safe, we keep al-Qaeda guessing. We make them doubt their allies; question their methods, their plans, even their priorities . . . we force them to spend more time and resources on self-preservation, and that distracts them, at least partially and at least for a time, from laying the groundwork for the next attack.[85]

Pakistan's political and military leaders continued to denounce the strikes in public, but in private provided intelligence for the missions and received collected surveillance data to aid their own operations.[86] In frustration, the Taliban began to kill more and more suspected spies, both villagers and fellow jihadists, in a frustrated effort to uncover the sources of the intelligence for the deadly and accurate new strikes.[87]

In May 2010, Shaykh Said al-Masri (Mustafa Ahmed Muhammad Uthman Abu al-Yazid)—one of the core founders of al-Qaeda promoted to fill a leadership gap created by the US campaign—was felled. He was fifty-four years old at the time of his death. He had long been the chief financial manager for bin Laden and was one of a dwindling number of veterans left from the pre-9/11 organization.

Like many Egyptian members of al-Qaeda, Shaykh Said cut his jihadist teeth with Egyptian Islamic Jihad (EIJ) alongside Zawahiri. As a young man involved in political Islam, he was imprisoned after Anwar Sadat's assassination in 1981.[88] His actual involvement in Sadat's murder was unclear, but his relatively short three-year sentence suggests the authorities were unable to link him directly to the operation or did not think he was particularly important. His Egyptian prison experience seemed to solidify his dedication to the global Islamist cause. After being released, he made his way to Afghanistan and eventually became a core member of al-Qaeda's advisory council.[89]

Shaykh Said followed bin Laden to Sudan, serving as accountant for the many businesses that served as both a front and a revenue stream for the terrorist enterprise.[90] In time, bin Laden allowed him to manage the organization's overall finances and help arrange funding for numerous worldwide operations. For instance, Shaykh Said supplied 9/11 lead hijacker Muhammad Atta with the money he needed to plan and carry out the operation.[91] Interestingly, recovered documents show that he opposed the 9/11 attacks, believing that the US response would endanger the movement.[92] This pragmatism does not appear to have damaged his credibility within the organization, however, for he was considered a trusted and popular member who could reconcile conflicting trends within Islamic fundamentalist thought.[93]

Shaykh Said largely disappeared from view after 9/11 but probably continued his role as al-Qaeda's money man. An accountant by training, he appeared to have little interest in military planning.[94] Some reports place him in Iran during this period along with several other al-Qaeda leaders, but there is no proof of this and he would later publicly denounce Iran.[95] He first reappeared publicly in May 2007 when he was named the operational commander for the struggle in Afghanistan in a video recording. This gave him the nominal authority to plan military attacks, but he seemed to indicate in the interview that he would continue to focus on fund-raising and personnel recruitment.

Shaykh Said was described by those who had met him as a spiritual leader with good management skills, but not a natural fit as a military commander.[96] He probably inherited al-Qaeda's number 3 spot to ensure some degree of continuity with the past, reinforce ties to the Taliban, and reassure supporters that, despite terrifyingly accurate US attacks, the organization remained strong and cohesive. He enjoyed a close personal relationship with bin Laden and Zawahiri and was a well-respected liaison with Taliban leader Mullah Omar, being fluent in Pashto as well as in Arabic.[97] As a core member of al-Qaeda, he had doubtlessly received training in field operations, weapons, and other skills. Still, al-Qaeda's ranks must have been badly depleted when the organization decided to place a middle-aged accountant with almost no military experience in the top operational command spot.

Shaykh Said began taping various propaganda videos and messages threatening the US and soliciting funds and fighters for the jihadist cause.[98] In July 2008 he even appeared in a television interview with Pakistan satellite channel *Geo TV*, condemning Danish newspapers that had published cartoons featuring the Prophet Mohammad. In September he claimed responsibility for the bombing of the Danish embassy in Islamabad.[99] The cartoon scandal proved remarkably successful in mobilizing Muslim youth, and in an elaborate fifty-five-minute video Shaykh Said urged European Muslims to plan similar operations against their own governments.[100] He garnered further attention in a June 2009 interview with Al Jazeera in which he promised that al-Qaeda would use Pakistan's nuclear weapons against the US once it gained access to them.[101]

Military affairs may not have been his strong suit, but he seemed a relatively successful organizer during his term. After the failed bombing attempt in New York City by Afghan immigrant and US permanent resident Najibullah Zazi, the US discovered that Shaykh Said had been in contact with Zazi through a middleman in the run-up to the operation.[102] By the end of 2009, he could claim credit for another major success: a suicide bomber struck the CIA's base at Khost, Afghanistan, killing multiple CIA officers and contractors, as well as a Jordanian case officer.[103]

In August 2008 Pakistani officials claimed Shaykh Said died in the Bajaur tribal area. But as the dust settled, it looked to be a different person with the same name. Shaykh Said the al-Qaeda leader later re-emerged unscathed.[104] Almost two years later, in May 2010, al-Qaeda announced that he had been killed in Pakistan along with his wife, three of his daughters, and several other men, women, and children.[105]

There is little public information available on how Shaykh Said was found, tracked, and subsequently eliminated. US officials only indicated that there was good reason to believe al-Qaeda's announcement was accurate, and that he was thought to have died in a missile strike sometime in late May.[106] This characterization suggests that either the CIA wanted to keep his death secret while monitoring militant communications, or that he was a victim of a strike under the new policy authorizing the Agency to eliminate targets that appear to be al-Qaeda. Two Pakistani intelligence officials later told the Associated Press that Shaykh Said had died on May 21 in North Waziristan, but that the bodies had not been recovered and that his death was confirmed only by local tribal elders and the Taliban.[107] Another Pakistani official said the drone attack had targeted a house owned by a tribesman some twenty-five kilometers west of Miranshah.[108]

As well as being, in the characterization of American officials, "the group's chief operating officer,"[109] Shaykh Said was the link between al-Qaeda and deep-pocketed donors in the Arabian Peninsula and elsewhere who kept the terrorist network in financial health. These supporters now lacked a trusted intermediary for their money—potentially isolating well-heeled extremist sympathizers unwilling to extend trust to an inexperienced replacement who might expose their involvement with a careless mistake.[110] The effect of the campaign to bring the hammer down on al-Qaeda and its top operatives extended into its Persian

Gulf–based financiers and facilitators, who feared being targeted for financial sanctions.

LESSONS FOR FUTURE FIND OPERATIONS

Two others additionally appeared on the roster of al-Qaeda's number 3: Abu Ubaydah al-Masri and Usama al-Kini. Each served as operational commander before and after Abu Layth, respectively. These two men caused great mayhem during their lives, and their dispatch was not a source of much lamentation, except among those in al-Qaeda. Abu Ubaydah played an integral part in the July 2005 London transit bombings, as well as the star-crossed Operation Overt, and al-Kini was integral to the 1998 attacks on the US embassies in Kenya and Tanzania.

Abu Ubaydah, an expert bomb maker, had the dubious distinction of being the only al-Qaeda number 3 who was neither captured nor killed by American ordinance. Rather, in late 2007, he died from complications from Hepatitis C, a particularly unpleasant way to die.[111]

Usama died on New Year's Day 2009 in much the same manner as his predecessors—via a Hellfire missile, courtesy of an American UAV. While he was certainly an ambitious leader—he tried to assassinate Benazir Bhutto and was responsible for the Islamabad Marriott bombing in September 2008 that left dozens dead, including the Czech ambassador to Pakistan[112]—relatively little is known publicly about him, aside from his being one of the few al-Qaeda members from Kenya.

The campaign to neutralize al-Qaeda's operational commanders forced the US to reorganize many of its existing structures to streamline the find aspect of the find-fix-finish doctrine. By pinpointing al-Qaeda's operational commander, the US successfully disrupted the organization and communicated the message that taking the reins of a terrorist campaign against the US is very dangerous.

The intense manhunts showed that finding and eliminating terrorist operatives from the sky offered operational ease but carried certain disadvantages. A militant target could be eliminated in a single operation, whereas on the ground several patient and methodical steps were usually required to get even marginally close to a target. Capture operations on the ground not only demand a greater cooperation with foreign partners and better operational security to prevent leaks, but also increased risk to the human beings involved. However, with aerial elimination there is greater risk of collateral damage, alienation of the local public, and the chilling of the intelligence trail. With the high value target eliminated, analysts lose the chance to repeatedly tap into their expertise and insight as new leaders appear or tactics change, and they have fewer means of reexamining the key assumptions under which they are crafting the analysis. Over the long run, this approach can make efforts to take down a large network increasingly difficult.

The second lesson is that technological dominance gives the US a critical advantage in cutting off al-Qaeda's ability to talk, travel, and broadcast its message. Mobile and satellite phone technology, key communication resources for anyone in the twenty-first century, can prove fatal to many in al-Qaeda. The combination of good targeting analysis, sophisticated remote sensors, on-the-ground assets, and persistent surveillance tools such as UAVs also made traveling a dangerous activity for al-Qaeda leaders. Propaganda efforts backfired when sophisticated voice analysis and computer-driven terrain mapping revealed key details about where and when a leader spoke.

The close integration of good collection and analysis can create an operational atmosphere so stifling that terrorist leaders spend most of their time in fear of discovery, rather than successfully carrying off attacks. The more varied the sources of information the US used in tracking wanted operatives—including paid informants, liaison intelligence exchanges, overhead surveillance, and electronic intercepts—the more raw information analysts found at their disposal to understand and dissect the threat.

Finally, cultivating effective counterterrorism cooperation with foreign partners remains critical to maintaining a decisive advantage and denying terrorists safe haven. It is often difficult work, and sometimes requires a clever mix of intimidation and accommodation. The 2008 escalation of the drone program put suffocating pressure on al-Qaeda but also stirred public resentment and sidestepped the systemic problem of forging a deeper working relationship with Pakistan. When it expanded the program from a narrow effort aimed at decapitating the al-Qaeda leadership to a large-scale campaign of air strikes based on signatures of convoys, safe houses, training camps, and weapon caches, the US waded into a much murkier area. Innocent civilians and marginally aligned militants became victims of US retaliation, significantly expanding the number of individuals who harbor anti-American feelings—individuals who, by the blood of their deceased relatives and the smoking wreckage of their destroyed homes, might later dedicate their lives to striking America. Any number of these people could and may, with time and training, become the next number 3.

CHAPTER 9

THE ENEMY WITHIN

In early September 2009, Najibullah Zazi, a citizen of Afghanistan and legal permanent resident of the United States, left his nondescript apartment in a sprawling outer suburb of Denver, nonchalantly climbed into a cheap rental car, started the engine, and headed east.[1] It was to be a long journey of almost 2,000 miles, from the foothills of the Rocky Mountains across much of the United States, already beginning to show its autumn colors. But this was not a pleasure trip. Rather, Zazi was dead set on arriving at his destination—New York City—and timing was key.[2]

Zazi didn't realize as he gunned the motor and headed past the Southland Shopping Mall, the Palms Tanning Resort, and the other forgettable big box stores that dotted the American landscape that the FBI was closely watching his every move. In fact, FBI agents had been monitoring him for months; they knew that he had traveled to a terrorist training camp earlier that year and had been stockpiling acetone and hydrogen peroxide, two base components for especially potent explosives. FBI electronic surveillance had also revealed that Zazi had been calling around to his accomplices trying to determine the right mixture to create an impactful explosion.[3]

Zazi was set to arrive in New York City right before the eighth anniversary of the 9/11 attacks, when President Barack Obama would give a speech near the open worksite where the World Trade Center towers once stood. A week later, the General Assembly of the United Nations would be in session.[4]

Before he could act, the FBI raided various homes and offices in Queens and Aurora, Colorado. By the end of the month, Zazi was in handcuffs, arrested and indicted for conspiracy to use weapons of mass destruction against persons or property in the United States and conspiracy to commit murder in a foreign country and providing material support to al-Qaeda. Zazi and two associates—pals from high school—had apparently intended to detonate bombs strapped to their bodies on the underground trains traveling the 1, 2, 3 and 4, 5, 6 lines of New York's subway system.[5] Striking these busy transit lines simultaneously would have caused mayhem and death, the type of coordinated attack that has been al-Qaeda's calling card.

The Zazi affair was the type of domestic terrorist plot the US government had galvanized to counter following the 9/11 attacks. In 2004 the domestic intelligence agencies had been told that they were the least prepared to handle individual threats prior to 2001. Although the efforts of the US law enforcement agencies to restructure and improve cooperation were by no means perfect, as the case of Zazi demonstrated, they had achieved some successes, particularly concerning interagency and international cooperation.

The year 1985 was one of the bloodiest in the Soviet-Afghan war. Mikhail Gorbachev had just come to power and had escalated the number of Soviet troops within Afghanistan with the hope of ending the war quickly and decisively. Reports from that year claim that more than half of the villages in Afghanistan were bombed, forcing millions of refugees across the border into neighboring Pakistan.[6] It was into this violent political maelstrom that Najibullah Zazi was born in Paktia province in eastern Afghanistan, the third of five children. His family remained in war-torn Afghanistan until 1992—the year the government of the Republic of Afghanistan collapsed, further escalating the conflict—before moving across the border to Peshawar, Pakistan.

Not long after the family's arrival in Pakistan, Zazi's father, Mohammad Wali Zazi, left for Flushing, Queens, where he worked as a taxi driver. When Zazi turned fourteen, his father succeeded in bringing the family to New York.[7] A jumble of American and Afghan influences thus defined Zazi's youth; according to his friends, he kept both a basketball and a prayer mat with him at all times.[8] He played video games, the lottery, and pool, but he also regularly prayed with his neighbors at the local Afghan mosque Masjid Hazrat Abu Bakr, where he would later volunteer as a janitor. Zazi was not a strong student—his father's step-uncle later told the press he was a "dumb kid." He quickly dropped out of high school to help his father support the family.[9]

Zazi turned sixteen shortly before the 9/11 attacks. His friends recall that he opposed terror throughout his teenage years and said after the attacks, "I don't know how people do things like this. I'd never do anything like that."[10]

But the young Zazi may have had contact with some who openly preached violence and extremism. Saifur Rahman Halimi, a chief representative of the powerful Afghan warlord Gulbuddin Hekmatyar, lived in the same building as Zazi's family and attended the same mosque in Queens.[11] Allegedly, Halimi championed Hekmatyar's cause in Queens and openly supported global jihad. But upon hearing about Zazi's arrest, Halimi said that he was shocked that Zazi heeded al-Qaeda's clarion call. Although he claims not to have spoken with Zazi or his family for six years, he told a reporter that Zazi "was not such a person. He was busy with his work."[12]

To help support his family, Zazi worked at a local supermarket and then began running his father's coffee cart, which stood only blocks from the World Trade Center site in Manhattan's financial district. One of Zazi's customers remembered him as a friendly kid: "He was well spoken. He always said good morning to everyone. He used to memorize what everyone needed in the morning."[13] Other customers also remember the "God Bless America" sign on his cart. At this point, according to his friend Ahmad Zaraei, he "wasn't that much into religion."[14] But, Zaraei continued, "that changed."

In 2006, Zazi flew back to Peshawar, where he wed his cousin in an arranged marriage.[15] His wife, who still lived in Pakistan and cared for their two children at the time of his arrest, had difficulty getting permission to accompany Zazi to the US.[16] Zazi visited her in Peshawar in 2007 and 2008. Mohammed Yousufzai, a fellow cart operator in the financial district, noted that after Zazi began traveling to Pakistan, he changed, growing out his beard, donning tunics instead of Western clothes, carry-ing prayer beads, and playing religious music.[17] Zazi's customers also no-ticed his increasing religiosity.[18]

After several visits to Pakistan Zazi encountered the demon of mod-ern American life: massive credit card debt. Between April and August 2008, he opened twelve credit card accounts and his expenses, reported as $1,108, exceeded his paltry $800 monthly income.[19] The following March, Zazi declared bankruptcy, citing some $51,000 in credit card debt.[20] He would later tell a US court that it was during this time—the spring and summer of 2008—he "conspired with others to travel to Afghanistan to join the Taliban and fight against the US military and its allies."[21]

On August 28, 2008, according to customs and border protection records, Zazi and a few others flew to Peshawar on Qatar Airlines Flight 84 from Newark via Geneva and Doha.[22] Peshawar was no more stable than it had been when the family departed years before.

There, as Zazi would later tell US authorities, he and a few others at-tended a terrorist training camp and "received instructions from al-Qaeda operatives on subjects such as weapons and explosives," according to prosecutors.[23] They had intended to join the Taliban to fight US-led forces in Afghanistan, Zazi claimed, but met with an al-Qaeda recruiter soon after arrival.[24] Al-Qaeda personnel had then brought Zazi and his associates to Waziristan, where they trained with a variety of weapons and Zazi received additional explosives training. After agreeing to con-duct suicide attacks in the US, they discussed possible targets, including subway trains.

Zazi made other friends during his time. Although the source and de-tails of the incident are unclear, Zazi may have met with US citizen Bryant Neal Vinas, along with other al-Qaeda members, to discuss po-tential attacks.[25] In 2009 Vinas pled guilty to conspiring to murder US nationals, providing material support to al-Qaeda, and rendering expert advice and assistance—including providing al-Qaeda information about the Long Island Rail Road. He described for the FBI what instruction in al-Qaeda terrorist training camps in Pakistan entailed. Between March and July 2008, Vinas, like Zazi, trained in Waziristan, taking three courses with ten to twenty students each. The first course introduced students to the staple of terrorists worldwide, the AK-47. The second class dealt with explosives; in fifteen days, students learned to make and test suicide belts and to handle explosives comfortably. The final class dealt with rocket-propelled grenades.[26]

Although the exact timing remains unclear, intelligence officials allege that a representative of al-Qaeda's then number 3, Shaykh Said, contacted Zazi. One of Zazi's associates would later tell law enforcement officials that Zazi and two others had met with both Saleh al-Somali, one of al-Qaeda's major international operations planners, and Rashid Rauf, the operative responsible for planning the 2006 thwarted transatlantic airliner plot.[27]

Before he departed the camp and left Pakistan, Zazi e-mailed himself a summary of what he had learned and provided al-Qaeda with money and computers.[28] If it wasn't already tracking him, the US was certainly paying attention, especially given the kinds of subjects that were discussed and the personalities involved. Furthermore, information from a separate British investigation known as Operation Pathway—a counterterrorism case that fell apart in April 2009 after an assistant British police commissioner was photographed leaving the prime minister's office holding top secret documents in plain sight—gave American officials confirmation that they had discovered a person of real interest.[29]

Returning to New York City from his adventures and training in Pakistan, Zazi journeyed westward to sprawling exurban Aurora, Colorado.[30] Zazi would later tell law enforcement officials that he moved to Aurora because it was cheaper than New York.[31] "Life is a little bit easier there," he had been told by a relative. "The living is cheaper."[32] Zazi also had family members in Aurora, and he would live with them until July 2009.

During this time, Zazi applied in Denver for a license to drive an airport shuttle. After passing a background and driving record check conducted by the Colorado Bureau of Investigation, he started work in April at the Denver International Airport.[33] Other drivers noted he was friendly and hardworking. "He talked to everyone," recalled one of his coworkers.[34] After he finished ferrying tourists and businessmen to their rental cars, Zazi set about gathering the primary materials for his bomb. Zazi searched online for sellers of hydrochloric acid, book-marking several sites that discuss its safe handling, and searched websites for other explosive chemicals.[35]

Zazi's e-mailed instructions specified that acetone can be found in nail polish remover and hydrogen peroxide in salon products. So the hardworking shuttle driver headed to a local hair salon. Surveillance videos later showed Zazi buying six bottles of a hair care product containing highly concentrated hydrogen peroxide in July and August 2009, returning to one store a few times to purchase twelve 32-ounce bottles of another hydrogen peroxide product. When one store employee commented on the volume of materials he was buying, he jokingly replied, "I have a lot of girlfriends."[36] Three other people associated with Zazi also bought acetone and peroxide products in the Denver metropolitan area during the summer of 2009.[37]

That July, his parents followed Zazi west to Aurora and moved into his apartment complex, severely restricting his ability to experiment at home.[38] So in late August he checked into a local hotel where he could test his chemical compounds removed from his family's prying eyes.[39]

On September 6 and 7, Zazi again stayed in the same hotel in Aurora. When the FBI surreptitiously searched the room, testing for explosives and chemicals, acetone residue was revealed in the vent above the stove where some of the chemicals in the bomb-making instructions were likely heated. While he was in the hotel, Zazi began contacting—although it is unclear how—a confederate for help mixing explosive ingredients. Zazi's requests became increasingly urgent and he emphasized that he needed an immediate response.[40]

The day before he drove to New York City, Zazi searched online for a home improvements store in a zip code for Flushing, Queens, where he would be able to purchase muriatic acid, a diluted form of hydrochloric acid.[41]

TRACKING ZAZI

Zazi was clearly under physical surveillance by this time. Whether by upgrade or new addition, Zazi's threat status was at a level high enough that concerns were brought to the White House's attention, and his status became the subject of a memo within the President's Daily Briefing

(PDB).[42] In this case, the FBI applied for a "roving wiretap" via the Foreign Intelligence Surveillance Act (FISA).[43] This wiretap would have allowed agents to monitor any phone or electronic communication associated with Zazi. If he had switched phones, for example, they would have been able to continue surveillance of the new phone without a new warrant.

Originally used to target the mob, roving wiretaps were expanded to include surveillance of international terrorist suspects under the authority of the FISA Court by the Uniting and Strengthening America by Providing Appropriate Tools Required to Intercept and Obstruct Terrorism Act (a.k.a. the USA-PATRIOT Act, or just "the Patriot Act"). In 2002, General Hayden argued that countering evolving national security concerns required more flexible legal tools, as terrorists could shift modes of communication just as quickly and easily as criminals. "We've gone from chasing the telecommunications structure of [the USSR] a slow-moving, technologically inferior, resource-poor nation-state, to chasing a communications structure in which an al-Qaeda member can go into a storefront in Istanbul and buy for $100 a communications device that is absolutely cutting edge, and for which he has had to make no investment for development."[44] Although Congress had originally intended the roving wiretap provision to "sunset" at the end of 2005, it has been renewed repeatedly.

The history of electronic surveillance post-9/11 also illuminates the disastrous political repercussions of ignoring checks and balances in the system. In late December 2005, a political firestorm erupted regarding electronic surveillance, but, surprisingly, it had little to do with the Patriot Act's controversial provisions. Rather, the *New York Times* broke the story that President Bush authorized the NSA to conduct a warrantless electronic surveillance program that completely circumvented the FISA process and the courts.[45] In the wake of these revelations, the White House admitted that the program allowed international communications of individuals with suspected connections to foreign terrorist organizations including al-Qaeda to be targeted without FISA warrants.

The very fact that the legal and political challenges remain years after the public learned of the program, however, provides a warning to future administrations seeking to circumvent US law. Many of the program's original detractors continue to argue that the program was illegal, and lawsuits challenging the FISA Amendments Act remain in the courts.

Still, it was the physical, not electronic, surveillance that set off the high-speed chase across the country for Najibullah Zazi. He later claimed that he was heading to New York City to resolve issues surrounding his coffee cart,[46] and his family insisted that he chose to drive in order to see the country.[47] A plausible story, perhaps, if the US hadn't been hot on his trail.

As the FBI agents following Zazi's car neared New York City, they brought New York's Joint Terrorism Task Force (JTTF) and the NYPD's Counterterrorism Division in on the case.[48] For many, this simple fact is one of the most striking in Zazi's case. After all, the relationship between the FBI and NYPD has not always been based on mutual admiration. In fact, the two organizations fought legendary turf battles in the years prior to—and immediately following—9/11.

A number of these battles resulted from decisions made by New York City police commissioner Ray Kelly. In 2001, Kelly assigned one hundred detectives to the NYC JTTF.[49] Small cells composed of special agents, linguists, law enforcement officers, detectives, and professionals from CIA and DHS, the JTTFs were the FBI's self-proclaimed frontline against terrorism in the United States. The first was established in New York City in 1980, but the FBI now has over a hundred JTTFs all over the country.[50]

More controversial, however, were some of Commissioner Kelly's other changes to the department. In 2001, he created an NYPD Counterterrorism Division and hired CIA's deputy director of operations David Cohen to lead it. The CT division worked undercover to gather human intelligence in New York City, around the nation, and even internationally—a scope of operations traditionally claimed solely by the federal government. In 2002 Kelly proposed installing a classified information vault—a sensitive compartmented information facility (SCIF)—in NYPD headquarters. The physical structure was an obvious move by the NYPD to acquire information that only belonged to federal agencies. Unsurprisingly, NYPD's aggressive posture and involvement with national and international issues rubbed many federal officials the wrong way.

Beyond the issue of perceived slights, information stove piping—one agency refusing to share information with a rival agency—has had real consequences. In 2003 the NYPD discovered that al-Qaeda operative Iyman Faris had twice traveled to New York City to case various targets during a news conference by Attorney General John Ashcroft.[51] Faris would later be arrested for trying to destroy the Brooklyn Bridge, ludicrously, with a blowtorch. The FBI refrained from publicly criticizing the NYPD, most likely to avoid exacerbating the already tense situation. "The FBI today [in 2005] wants to be seen as cooperating with local officials," said Jack Cloonan, a former agent assigned to the FBI's bin Laden investigation. "The bureau cannot afford to take issue with the city and NYPD—at least not publicly."[52]

Relations have improved in recent years. FBI director Robert Mueller has worked to advance his relationship with his counterparts in NYPD.[53] One law enforcement official told *Newsweek* that FBI and NYPD intelligence had worked together on two dozen important cases in the months preceding Zazi's 2009 arrest.[54] The Zazi case is further evidence of this improvement. The FBI not only notified local authorities and the NYPD of Zazi's arrival in their jurisdictions but also requested and received assistance in tracking him, a critical step toward information sharing.

TO STRIKE OR TO DEVELOP

By September 10, Zazi and his rental car had reached the suburban ennui of New Jersey. The NYPD and the FBI suspected he was dangerous but did not know what, exactly, was in the trunk of his car. Was it a bomb? Just twenty-five pounds of explosives could shred the car and create a lethal blast radius for any unlucky bystanders. David Cohen of the NYPD Counterterrorism Division was reportedly so worried by this case that he wanted to arrest Zazi immediately, an action that would have shut down the investigation of Zazi's contacts and activities. "I don't need to fuck around for two more weeks and learn one more fact," Cohen allegedly told federal officials. "Sometimes the search for intelligence can get you killed."[55]

To strike the target or to develop him: Cohen's statement highlighted the struggle to balance possible short-term but nonetheless dramatic

losses with plausible but not necessarily quantifiable long-term wins—
chances to gather as much evidence as possible of a suspect's activities
and associated networks, contacts, and other potential plots, thereby increasing the chance of hindering other, future plots.

The concern that Zazi might have explosives in his car led the FBI to
ask the Port Authority Police to put up a fake checkpoint on the George
Washington Bridge, which connects New Jersey to Manhattan.[56] The
police obliged, pulling over Zazi as well as several other cars under the
pretense of a random drug checkpoint, to search his vehicle for bombs or
chemicals. Discovering nothing, they let Zazi drive into the city.[57] It's
possible that Zazi knew at this point that the police were onto him, although his lawyer maintained that Zazi was unaware: "He thought this
was just one of those law enforcement things that happens every now
and then. He didn't think anything of it at that point."[58]

Later that evening, two detectives working with the NYPD's Intelligence Division visited their informants in Queens, showing them pictures of Zazi and soliciting information.[59] One informant, Imam Ahmad
Wais Afzali, told them that he knew Zazi and could identify him.

Law enforcement sources later claimed that Afzali, an imam of a local
mosque popular with Afghan immigrants, was not a paid informant but
had sometimes been asked to corroborate information provided by other
sources.[60] Afzali would later tell the press that he did not need to be paid
for his work with the FBI after 9/11, as he "was upset because the people
involved claimed to follow my faith." So when two members of the
NYPD Intelligence Division knocked on his door and asked him
whether he could identify the men in the photographs, he responded by
saying he recognized three men from his classes at his mosque when they
were boys. But he remembered little else, he claims, and the officers
would not explain to him why they were seeking Zazi and his friends,
Adis Medunjanin and Zarein Ahmedzay. The detectives instructed Afzali
to find out as much as he could about them.[61]

Such solicitations are not out of the ordinary. The FBI has sought
help from the Muslim community in identifying potential terrorists for
years and has developed relationships through advisory councils and
other contacts. Not only do the members of such communities naturally
have a better understanding of the goings-on within a certain neighbor-

hood but they also can help investigators overcome linguistic and cultural barriers.

But attempts to monitor some communities are not always welcome, and authorities struggle to gather information without alienating the locals. In early 2009, suspicion that federal officials were infiltrating mosques around the country led some Muslim charities and groups to threaten to cut ties with the FBI, and caused civil liberties and religious advocacy groups to express concern.[62] One man from Flushing told a reporter, "People are scared. They're scared that if they work with the police they'll get hurt, and if they don't work with the police they'll get hurt."[63] In the Zazi investigation, asking Afzali to serve as an informant would prove controversial and problematic.

As long as the FBI and NYPD had Zazi under constant surveillance they felt in control of the situation. But this blanket surveillance came into question when they intercepted a phone call to the Zazi household. An unidentified man apparently told Zazi's father, Mohammad Wali Zazi, that the police had questioned him about his son. One NYPD detective then left the room, listened to the call, and identified the man as Afzali.[64]

Afzali had been true to his word to the NYPD. To learn more about Zazi, he had first spoken to a distant relative of Zazi's and then to Zazi's father. The police apparently had not known the nature of the relationship between Afzali and Zazi's father—Afzali had prayed with Zazi and his family during Zazi's years in Queens.[65] According to FBI surveillance, Zazi's father talked with Afzali for twenty minutes,[66] at some point urging him to call his son.[67]

Zazi's father then called Zazi, telling him, "[Afzali] is going to call you. . . . So, before anything else, speak with [Afzali]. See if you need to go to [Afzali] or to make, make yourself aware, hire an attorney. What has happened? What have you guys done?"[68] While speaking with his father, Zazi received a second call on the other line, Afzali was again true to his word. Zazi ended his call with his father and spoke with Afzali. According to a transcript, Afzali told Zazi:

> I want to speak with you about something. . . . I want a meeting with you [and others]. You probably know why I'm calling you for this meeting. . . . I was exposed to something yesterday from the

authorities. And they came to ask me about your characters. They
asked me about you guys.

I'm not sure if somebody complained about you. I'm not sure what
happened. And I don't want to know. . . . They [the authorities] said,
"Please, we need to know who they are . . . what they're all about." . . .
And I told them that they are innocent, law abiding.

Afzali then asked Zazi when he had last traveled to Pakistan. Afzali
also said, "They [the police] came to the *masjid* to ask for help. That is a
good sign. Trust me that this a good sign. The bad sign is for them coming to you guys and picking you up automatically." Afzali told Zazi,
"Don't get involved in Afghanistan garbage, Iraq garbage" and then omi-
nously, "Listen, our phone call is being monitored."[69]

That day, Afzali tried to speak with one of Zazi's accomplices, though
he was unable to reach him. Afzali then called the police three times to
tell them what he had learned, and each time they asked him for more.
Later that day, Zazi and Afzali spoke again, and Zazi told Afzali that he
was worried that he was being watched. The individuals watching him,
he claimed, had taken his car. Afzali asked Zazi if there was "evidence in
his car," to which Zazi said no.[70]

Seeking more information, the FBI had indeed towed away Zazi's rental
car and searched it, swabbing the vehicle for various chemicals. Investigators
also mirrored Zazi's laptop's hard drive, as Zazi had left it in the car at the
time. They then carefully put everything back where they had found it.[71]

This particular search was authorized under the "sneak and peek"
provision of the Patriot Act.[72] During a sneak and peek, or in the more
official-sounding "delayed notice" search, law enforcement officials can
legally enter a place where an individual might have an expectation of
privacy, such as a car or a home, without immediately notifying him.
Although such searches have several times been challenged under the
Fourth Amendment, district courts have upheld their constitutionality. Law enforcement officials argue that they are valuable tools when
detectives do not want the targeted individual to know that he is under
investigation.

The search produced one of the most important pieces of evidence in
the case against Zazi. Authorities discovered on the hard drive a JPEG file

of nine pages of handwritten notes containing, according to Zazi's arrest affidavit, "formulations and instructions regarding the manufacture and handling of initiating explosives, main explosives charges, explosives detonators and components of a fuzing system."[73] The instructions detailed how to make triacetone triperoxide (TATP), an explosive used by so-called shoe bomber Richard Reid and the London transit bombers in 2005.

Zazi visited New York City's financial district on September 11, according to several of his former customers, who saw him there.[74] On September 12, two days before Zazi's rental car agreement expired, Zazi prepared to fly back to his apartment in Colorado, and officials debated whether to allow him on the plane. They decided to permit Zazi to fly but ensured that he was carefully screened and that he was monitored by dozens of FBI agents, including several who posed as fellow passengers.[75] It must have been a tense flight for the FBI agents, tailing an al-Qaeda terror suspect in midair over New York airspace.

Officials—or at least the FBI—still did not want to tip off Zazi to the investigation. They had probably not yet built up a full case against him[76]—they had no specific information as to when, where, or how an alleged attack might take place, or if they would need to take additional action to disrupt Zazi's plot.[77] Furthermore, they likely hoped to learn more about his contacts in the US and Pakistan.

Several FBI officials would later lambaste—anonymously of course—the NYPD for acting without FBI's knowledge in questioning Afzali and thereby compromising the investigation.[78] DHS—arriving like a dinner guest after the dishes are washed—criticized the FBI for not sharing more information with local authorities, and, according to one official, for including DHS only minimally with the investigation.[79] It's more likely that no one bothered to let DHS know, since no one took the department seriously.

These arguments highlighted yet another tension in counterterrorism operations: balancing a need for investigative secrecy with a need to empower officials to stop an attack. "Dissemination [to other agencies] guarantees release to the public," one FBI official said, while former DHS head Tom Ridge argued that information sharing is key to national security. "I don't care whether you're on the battlefield in Iraq or Afghanistan, or in the battlefield of some city in the United States," said

Ridge two months after Zazi's indictment, "having knowledge and information about a potential problem is absolutely critical . . . to making Americans more secure."[80]

Both the NYPD and the FBI publicly sidestepped questions of a ruptured relationship. "I can say without reservation that our relationships with the NYPD in this and other investigations could not be better," FBI director Robert Mueller would later tell Congress.[81]

THE FIRST SEARCHES

Two days after Zazi returned to Colorado, the New York JTTF searched four apartments in Queens. They twice searched the home of Naiz Khan, an Afghan immigrant and coffee cart owner with whom Zazi had stayed on the night of September 10, and found a calculator, several backpacks, cell phones, and a scale, all of which law enforcement claimed could potentially have been used in bomb construction—although they could equally well have been used in provisioning a coffee cart.[82] "Our homes have been destroyed," he later said. "If we go back to Afghanistan, Taliban will kill you for being American. In Pakistan, we don't have a good life. Now they say we are terrorists here? Where should we go?"[83] Questioned several times, Khan reiterated that he was just helping an out-of-town acquaintance.

The backpacks initially concerned authorities, as backpacks held the bombs used in the Madrid and London subway bombings in 2004 and 2005. Khan claimed, somewhat suspiciously, that these backpacks had been given to his uncle to take to Pakistan by a relative. That fellow had, in turn, received them from the business partner of another man who had hundreds of extra bags when he went out of business.[84] Some sources argue that the cell phones were also a cause of concern, as they could have been used as triggering devices.[85]

All sources seem equally concerned with the scale, which was found in Khan's closet although Khan claimed never to have seen it before.[86] Zazi's fingerprints were found on both the scale and its batteries, and authorities would later argue that the scale could have been used for several of the steps outlined in Zazi's bomb-making notes. According to FBI explosives experts, "With specific respect to TATP, a scale such as the one recovered would be required to weigh the hydrogen peroxide and other pre-cursor chemicals in determining the proper concentrations and ratios."[87]

Despite the suggestive evidence, FBI officials didn't think they had enough to arrest Zazi. Zazi and his lawyer, however, voluntarily met with FBI agents at the field office in Denver over the next two days. While he was being questioned, agents in Aurora evacuated his apartment building and searched his home, as well his aunt's home. Curious by-standers noticed the FBI leaving with six boxes and luggage, and direct-ing two women and one man—Zazi's brother—into separate cars, which were then driven off.[88] Around this time agents again seized and searched Zazi's laptop, though they had already copied the hard drive.[89]

During questioning, Zazi admitted that he had spent some time in an al-Qaeda training camp in Peshawar. When presented with a copy of the handwritten notes found on his hard drive, he claimed neither to have seen them nor to have written them. If they had indeed been found on his computer, he said, he must have accidentally downloaded them as an attachment to a religious book in August 2009, which he had then deleted when he saw that it spoke of jihad.[90]

By the evening of September 19, Zazi decided it was in his best in-terest to stop talking to authorities. It proved a poor choice, as the FBI arrested him just hours later.[91] The 2009 New York City subway bomb-ing was another terrorist attack that thankfully never was. Federal officers also formally arrested his father and Afzali. Four days later, a grand jury in the Eastern District of New York released an indictment charging Zazi with conspiracy to use weapons of mass destruction against persons or property within the US.

Zazi's arrest was only the beginning of a long legal process for the US government. Following Zazi's indictment, more than 120 detectives from the NYPD Intelligence Division continued to work on the case,[92] though the investigation remained under the control of the New York and Den-ver FBI JTTFs.[93]

Zazi's case had important implications for the image of the US govern-ment. As one of the FBI's highest-profile apprehensions, the case would factor in the Obama administration's public relations as well as numerous political debates. When Nigerian national Umar Farouk Abdulmutallab attempted to blow up a plane en route to Detroit on Christmas Day 2009, thwarted only by the quick actions of fellow passengers, members of the Obama administration would point to Zazi's case as an example of a successful operation, attempting to counter allegations that the administration was generally unprepared for a terrorist strike.[94]

The Zazi case would surface repeatedly throughout the end of 2009 and 2010 in reference to the reauthorization of many Patriot Act provisions. Since both the "sneak and peek" and roving wiretap provisions had been used in his case, lawmakers would repeatedly reference Zazi's case to support reauthorization of the policies of the former administration. "All the layers of defense President Bush set up after September 11 are working," said Republican congressman Peter King in September. "The FBI is working more closely with local police, the Patriot Act, which allows roving wiretaps . . . is essential."[95]

A few Democratic senators echoed this sentiment. Less than two weeks after Zazi's arrest, Senators Patrick Leahy and Dianne Feinstein proposed an amendment to the Senate's version of the reauthorization bill that significantly curtailed the increased privacy protections both had originally proposed. "The biggest investigation since 9/11 is ongoing," Feinstein said. "My concern was that nothing we do here interfere with an investigation that is going on."[96]

For almost four months following Zazi's arrest, the media would report relatively little news about the case, focusing instead on its implications for the administration and increasing "homegrown Muslim extremism." In January 2010, however, FBI agents suddenly approached two of Zazi's high school chums who had been under surveillance since his arrest. These two men, Adis Medunjanin and Zarein Ahmedzay, had traveled to Pakistan with Zazi on his final trip and had intended to join him in the unfulfilled suicide attack on the New York subway.

Medunjanin, a US citizen born in Bosnia, decided to go out in a blaze of glory. Shortly after FBI agents came to his house to take his passport, he fled, allegedly yelling, "We love death more than you love life!" to an emergency operator before crashing his car into the side of the Whitestone Bridge between Queens and the Bronx. He then attempted to flee on foot before federal agents apprehended him. Ahmedzay, also a naturalized US citizen, was apprehended later that night, though in less dramatic fashion.[97]

Soon after, the FBI charged Medunjanin with conspiring to commit murder in a foreign country and receiving training from al-Qaeda, and Ahmedzay with lying to federal agents. New charges would additionally be handed to Zazi's father and uncle—who were charged with attempting to destroy evidence. All would plead not guilty.

On February 22, 2010, Zazi pled guilty to all three counts: "conspiracy to use weapons of mass destruction (explosive bombs) against persons or property in the United States, conspiracy to commit murder in a foreign country, and providing material support to al-Qaeda."[98] A few additional details surfaced in Zazi's guilty plea, including the intended targets of the explosive bombs: New York City subway trains. When the judge asked him if he meant that he wanted to be a suicide bomber when he referred to "martyrdom activities," Zazi responded, "Yes, Your Honor. I have a different explanation to that. To me, it meant that I would sacrifice myself to bring attention to what the United States military was doing to civilians in Afghanistan by sacrificing my soul for the sake of saving other souls."[99]

Three days later, a jury indicted Medunjanin and Ahmedzay for conspiracy to use weapons of mass destruction, conspiracy to commit murder in a foreign country, providing material support to a foreign terrorist organization, receiving military-type training from a foreign terrorist organization, and making false statements to investigators.

By April, Afzali pled guilty to lying to federal officials about talking to Zazi. His residency revoked, he had to leave the country within ninety days or face deportation. "To be honest with you, the reality hasn't set in yet," Afzali later told reporters. "Anywhere I go I'm going to be known as the imam that worked with the American government . . . what country will take me in?"[100] Several weeks later, Ahmedzay pleaded guilty as well, providing additional details of the plot. In late July 2011, a Brooklyn federal jury would convict Zazi's father of destroying bomb-making materials and conspiring to obstruct a federal investigation.[101]

THE RECKONING

Zazi's case figured in one final debate in November 2009 after Attorney General Eric Holder announced that 9/11 mastermind KSM and four of his co-conspirators would be tried in federal court in Manhattan. Attorney General Holder pointed to Zazi's case as evidence of a successful trial in civilian courts. "In this case, as it has in so many other cases, the criminal justice system has proved to be an invaluable weapon for disrupting plots and incapacitating terrorists, one that works in concert with the IC and our military," Holder told the press almost immediately after Zazi's plea.[102]

The Zazi affair highlights the practical and legal difficulties the government has faced since 9/11. Attempting to provide law enforcement and intelligence agencies the tools they need to fight new threats, Congress and the executive branch have lurched toward the creation of legislation and policies that balance civil liberties and security—an ideal that arguably remains out of reach. Working to protect the public, those agencies in turn wrestle with a balance of priorities and power among themselves. But officials have to make hard choices over and over again to continue protecting the public from terrorism.

CHAPTER 10

AMERICA'S FUTURE

Shadow Wars in Yemen and Somalia

In November 2002, the deputy secretary general of Yemen's ruling party, Brigadier General Yahya al-Mutawakel, shifted uneasily in his seat in his luxurious sitting room. He was giving an interview about joint US-Yemeni counterterrorism efforts and was in a mood to vent his frustrations. "*This is why it is so difficult to make deals with the United States*," he fumed. "This is why we are reluctant to work closely with them. They don't consider the internal circumstances in Yemen."[1] Just days before, US deputy secretary of state Paul Wolfowitz confirmed that CIA killed Qaed Salim Sinan al-Harethi in Yemen via a missile fired from an American UAV. This was the first such operation outside of Afghanistan since 9/11 and the first such strike outside of a combat zone. In making this pronouncement, however, Wolfowitz apparently violated a tacit agreement with Yemeni officials that the strike would stay secret until both countries could release a joint statement. Although they would later confirm that they approved the strike, Wolfowitz's actions infuriated al-Mutawakel and the Yemeni government because they believed the US did not comprehend the implications of suggesting that the Yemeni government was complicit in the killing of a person inside a country at peace with the US.

Yemen and Somalia are considered terrorist safe havens by many—weakly governed territories that offer nominal protection of sovereignty—and the counterterrorism battlegrounds of the future. For the US, the challenge remains how to cooperate with foreign governments to finish terrorist threats within their borders—often territories they barely control—without either creating a larger problem or becoming hostage to local political concerns. This problem is not new, of course; the US has been involved in joint counterterrorism, counternarcotics, and counterinsurgency efforts for years, with many of the same problems. What is new is the way the tools have been applied since 9/11.

Sovereignty is generally understood to mean that each nation is responsible for policing and protecting its own territory. If a person, say, a known terrorist, takes refuge in a particular nation, the government of that nation has the responsibility to arrest and either extradite or prosecute the accused. If the state lacks sufficient evidence, another state or an international body such as the UN could theoretically provide the evidence to pursue or prosecute. If the host government is incapable or unwilling to carry out that responsibility, a carrot-and-stick diplomatic approach could be employed to encourage results, for instance, withholding or offering aid, trade, training, or weaponry. The process might go on for years, surviving changes in government and regimes. Even in cases of extreme injustice, however, the laborious machinations of diplomacy are generally respected.

The principle of sovereignty lies at the heart of the safe haven challenge, defining how and when the US can legitimately target and destroy terrorists in foreign territory. Unfortunately, it is difficult to define with precision—scholars list multiple possible interpretations of sovereignty.[2] One definition suggests sovereignty is a "fundamental concept underlying the system of public international law which implies the state's lawful and essentially exclusive control of its territory, with the authority to govern it and enact and enforce its laws with respect to all persons, property, and events within this territory."[3]

Under this definition, the concept includes two distinct categories: internal sovereignty and external sovereignty. Internal sovereignty is the authority of the government to exercise legal and political control within its own territory in relation to its own *people*; no other entity within the state has this right. External sovereignty is the authority of the state to exercise full and exclusive control over its own territory—and to be free from any encroachment to its authority by other states.

By this standard, an American incursion into a country without permission or notification would violate the territorial sovereignty of that particular state and United Nations Charter Article II, Section 4, which states that "all Members shall refrain in their international relations from the threat or use of force against the territorial integrity or political independence of any state."[4] But, as many are quick to point out, states have never enjoyed full territorial sovereignty and freedom from encroachment. Former UN secretary general Boutros Boutros Ghali, for example, noted, "The time of absolute and exclusive sovereignty . . . has passed; its theory was never matched by reality."[5]

Indeed, the very existence of international law is to some degree a violation of state sovereignty; most states accept that there is a trade-off between the principle of sovereignty and other principles such as self-defense. The UN Charter seems to make this exception explicit, saying that "nothing in the present Charter shall impair the inherent right of individual or collective self-defense if an armed attack occurs against a Member of the United Nations."[6] After 9/11, the US used this provision to justify its actions overseas. "There is no question but that the United States of America has every right, as every country does, of self defense, and the problem with terrorism is that there is no way to defend against the terrorists at every place and every time against every conceivable technique," remarked Donald Rumsfeld in 2001. "The only way to deal with the terrorist network is to take the battle to them."[7]

So that's what America did. The Bush Administration—staffed by highly organized, dedicated political players who believed in active US intervention overseas—decided that the attacks had occurred because the US had been too willing to accept constraints on its actions from the international system. This system, they believed, served to protect al-Qaeda and other groups with their sights set on the US. Terrorism was no longer considered a diplomatic or law enforcement problem; rather, it was a military and intelligence problem that demanded forceful action and rapid results. If another state was hosting a wanted terrorist and was unwilling or incapable of acting, the US would.

In his address to the nation on the evening of September 11, Bush explained the new approach: "I've directed the full resources of our intelligence and law enforcement communities to find those responsible and to bring them to justice. We will make no distinction between the terrorists who committed these acts and those who harbor them."[8] Nine days later, in his address to a joint session of Congress, he made the new Bush Doctrine even more explicit:

> Our war on terror begins with al-Qaeda, but it does not end there. It will not end until every terrorist group of global reach has been found, stopped and defeated. . . . And we will pursue nations that provide aid or safe haven to terrorism . . . any nation that continues to harbor or support terrorism will be regarded by the United States as a hostile regime.[9]

This message conveyed the US belief that the international rules had changed: the United States would no longer accept sovereignty as inviolable, and terrorists in safe havens would be eliminated with or without the help of local governments. Undoubtedly, this was intended to send a powerful message to spur new cooperation from foreign governments previously reticent to comply with US demands. Countries as diverse as Russia, Uzbekistan, and Mongolia contributed aid and assistance to US counterterrorism efforts, and Yemen, Sudan, and Pakistan, which had tolerated terrorist groups within their borders, began to reevaluate their positions. However, the international system was not going to change overnight, and America's new unbounded position changed nothing about the reality on the ground. All politics is local—even in the roughest patches of the globe.

The ambitious global reach of the project quickly illuminated its limitations: the US, while powerful, still needed to negotiate with small, poor nations for access, intelligence, and aid. As time went by, progress became caught up in the process of diplomatic communiqués, negotiation, and compromise. The US had changed, but the rules that governed international behavior in the world were still firmly in effect.

THE LAST RIDE OF SALIM AL-HARETHI

In late 2002, Bush administration officials wanted concrete, public examples of success in the new fight against al-Qaeda and the so-called global war on terror; the strike in Yemen against Qaed Salim Sinan al-Harethi seemed a prime example. Al-Harethi had been a major player in the 2000 attack on the USS *Cole* that killed seventeen American sailors and, at the time of his death, was a senior al-Qaeda operative.

The US and Yemen had worked together to track al-Harethi but had to wait until intelligence revealed his exact location. As before, America found him through a smart combination of intelligence resources—including a dramatic secret mission by the US ambassador to Yemen, who traveled into the desert with intelligence officials to bribe Yemeni tribe members for information on his whereabouts. The move was risky; Yemeni officials were infuriated that the US had undertaken a "diplomatic journey" to speak to the local tribesmen on their own,[10] but the information seemingly proved useful.

With information on his general location, the US fixed al-Harethi by tracking his satellite phone.[11] Al-Harethi was well aware of US capabilities—he reportedly had five phones on him when he was killed.[12] He was already on a high-value target list, and some believed that al-Harethi was probably on his way to an operation.[13] Empowered to act, a CIA officer across the Bab-el-Mandeb strait at a ███████████ base in Djibouti flew a Predator over Yemeni airspace, tracked the car carrying al-Harethi away from populated areas, and then, with prior approval, fired its lethal payload and incinerated al-Harethi and his passengers with a single Hellfire missile.[14]

Pictures of the aftermath show only a heavy black stain in the sand; Yemeni security officials attempted to identify the corpses and then took them to a military hospital in Sana'a to collect DNA, which they then shipped to the US.[15] From the American perspective, it was a brilliant success: not only had no US personnel been put at risk, but all six passengers in the car—including one US citizen—were most likely enemy combatants.

Senior (and unnamed) US officials began notifying the media the day after the strike and, not coincidentally, the day before the 2002 congressional midterm elections. When questioned, Donald Rumsfeld refused to confirm or deny any US role in the death of al-Harethi but commented that "it would be a very good thing if he were out of business."[16] Meanwhile, Yemeni press and government officials reported only that al-Harethi and the others had been killed when their car exploded in remote Marib province, and claimed the car had been carrying explosives that had detonated accidentally.[17] The following day, however, Wolfowitz seemed to confirm US involvement in an interview with CNN, saying that the hit was "a very successful tactical operation" and emphasizing that the US must continue to act against terrorist safe havens. "We have just got to keep the pressure on everywhere we're able to and we've got to deny the sanctuaries everywhere we're able to, and we've got to put pressure on every government that is giving these people support to get out of that business."[18] The Yemeni government remained silent for weeks, however, before finally confirming that the strike had in fact been a joint operation, later saying improbably that the US had acted at their request.[19]

Unsurprisingly, many of the same elements of the strike that US officials extolled as groundbreaking made it the subject of condemnation. First, the strike had occurred in the territory of a state not involved in armed conflict with the United States, and was therefore criticized as a violation of national sovereignty. Yemeni opposition parties immediately denounced both the attack and the government's refusal to condemn it: "Yemen's silence in this regard confirms an official collusion to squander national sovereignty and the blood of Yemenis."[20] Second, although the Yemeni government would eventually and reluctantly suggest that it had a hand in the strike, the symbolic violation fueled anti-US sentiment within the country. Third, critics alleged that the US operation, by eliminating al-Harethi without due process, set a dangerous precedent by which any country could justify targeting its enemies throughout the world. Swedish foreign minister Anna Lindh suggested it was "a summary execution that violates human rights." Lindh added that "even terrorists must be treated according to international law, otherwise any country can start executing those whom they consider terrorists."[21]

Back in the US, most of the American public, including those aware of this new way of conducting foreign policy, seemed to shrug off the strike, either not realizing the implications or just accepting that the rules against fighting terrorism had changed. Still, some people raised troubling questions about how a "finishing" policy could be distinguished from an assassination.[22] Even if the US president authorized al-Harethi's elimination—a new legal justification in itself—the five other people in the car had not undergone any sort of rudimentary legal process before being incinerated by US ordnance. There was also the question of how the US government applied the term "enemy combatant," since in Yemen almost anyone could possess murky "links to terrorism." Furthermore, there was no effort to prove that the others were actively engaged in combat or posed an immediate threat when they were killed.

These questions became even more pointed in the case of Kamal Derwish, the American citizen who had been one of the passengers in the car. US officials claimed they had the authority kill Derwish under a secret finding signed by President Bush immediately after 9/11, authorizing CIA to pursue al-Qaeda members around the world, not specifically excluding US citizens. "I can assure you that no constitutional questions are raised here," said national security adviser Condoleezza Rice after the strike. "[The president] is well within the balance of accepted practice and the letter of his constitutional authority."[23] The US also stressed that the CIA had not known Derwish was in the car and therefore had not targeted him specifically.[24]

Any hand-wringing over the death of this American citizen at the time was likely muted by the arrest of the so-called Lackawanna Six, a group of young Yemeni Americans who had participated in a training camp in Afghanistan; Derwish was probably their ideological mentor as well as their recruiting agent.[25] For the purposes of establishing a precedent in the new kind of war, the US had succeeded without much blowback. The strike had successfully penetrated one of the world's safe havens—hundreds of miles away from the front lines in Afghanistan—and proved that the US could truly combat terrorists globally.

The Yemeni government's eventual admission that it had requested US assistance and firepower undermined the most obvious argument that its sovereignty had been violated, since the operation threatened neither its territorial integrity nor political authority to police its own borders. But the question of whether self-defense provided sufficient justification for targeting substate actors in another sovereign state has not been clearly resolved, as most existing international law applies to state-to-state relationships. Colombia, Israel, Turkey, and the US, among other nations, have all attacked substate terrorist groups and have defended the legitimacy of such actions.

In al-Harethi's case, US officials determined that the Yemeni government had failed to exert sovereignty over its own territory. In November 2001, one year before the drone strike, Yemeni president Ali Abdullah Saleh had flown to Washington to meet with President Bush and discuss the problem. Fearing that Yemen would become the next Afghanistan, Saleh expressed his support for US counterterrorism policy and declared Yemen an ally of the US in fighting terrorism. As a "good first step" toward the development of this relationship, President Bush asked President Saleh to direct Yemeni forces to find al-Harethi and Muhammad Hamdi al-Ahdal, also wanted in connection with the USS *Cole* bombing. Stalling for time, President Saleh asked for patience, but more or less agreed to help.[26]

Saleh and the Yemeni government had to overcome difficult challenges in order to fulfill the US request. First, Yemen includes vast tracts of uninhabited or sparsely inhabited land where individuals can hide with some ease from government and its intelligence services. Second, the modern state of Yemen has been embroiled in conflict since unification between the northern and southern sections of the country; the settlement that ended the 1994 civil war was tenuous at best. Third, many of the country's powerful tribes wield more authority than the central government and deny officials access to their territory when they see fit—even attempting to broker separate agreements with the US. As the American ambassador in 2004 remarked, "If the Yemeni tribes are with us, the terrorists can't win. If they are with the terrorists, we can't win."[27]

Finally, although the government in Sana'a had declared its support of US counterterrorism efforts, the country had strong historic ties to some extremist groups—ties that did not disappear with an official declaration. Osama bin Laden's father hailed from Yemen, and during the 1990s the Yemeni government had welcomed mujahideen returning from Afghanistan with open arms, allowing them to establish training camps and recruit fighters. Al-Qaeda and affiliated groups such as Egyptian Islamic Jihad, al Gamaa al-Islamiyya, and the Algerian Armed Islamic Group had all found a degree of safety in Yemen.[28]

The Yemeni government probably knew al-Harethi was in Hosun al-Jalal, a village in Marib province, even though he was in hiding.[29] He and his terrorist colleagues did not fit in and were "not very sociable," according to Ali Saleh, the nephew of a man who rented one of them a house. "They did not pray at the mosque, they always seemed to be together, and the only times they would leave their homes would be to go buy food." In November 2001, following Saleh's meeting with Bush, the Yemeni government sent three officials to the village to ask the residents to turn over the men. When the residents asked the men to turn themselves in, they refused, and there was no follow-up.[30] The officials claimed they did not have the power to detain al-Harethi since they could only act with the permission of local chiefs. Despite the fact that it was Yemeni territory, government officials risked provoking a violent retaliation by the locals if they acted against their wishes.[31]

President Bush next offered to send elite US troops to Yemen to face the tribal leaders, but Saleh refused, fearing that such an action might spark additional violence against the government.[32] Instead, he decided to send in Yemen's own special military forces.[33] Unfortunately, Yemen's tough tribal militias completely outmatched the Yemeni government troops. The Yemeni-led operation in December 2001 was a disaster. Government forces located al-Harethi in the village where he was hiding, but were beaten back by local village militias. Accounts vary as to whether the victors were actual followers of al-Harethi or simply tribe members angered by the government incursion.[34] The Yemeni government had found and fixed al-Harethi but could not finish him.

In February 2002, two months after the failed raid, Saleh reiterated his commitment to fighting terrorism and warned his countrymen, "We will strike with an iron fist anyone who is involved in terrorism. We will not tolerate kidnappings and bombings." But Saleh never authorized another mission to capture the men. Instead, his government attempted to convince the tribes to surrender al-Harethi, promising he would be kept outside of US custody and would be considered innocent until proven guilty.[35] The tribes went on the offensive, saying in a joint statement that they were not sheltering al-Harethi and warning against allowing the US into their territory: "The involvement of any foreign force, especially the United States of America, in what is being circulated about a possibility of a military strike against specific areas will, for sure, be a grave strategic mistake and does not come in the frame of fighting terrorism."[36]

To complicate matters further, the Yemeni government now believed that the wanted man and his colleagues were moving in and out of the Empty Quarter, or Rub' al-Khali, a massive desert straddling the borders of Saudi Arabia, Yemen, Oman, and the United Arab Emirates.[37] Covering a quarter of a million square miles—an area larger than France—the Empty Quarter is virtually uninhabited. "If that is where they are, looking for them is like trying to find a needle in a haystack," commented one local governor.[38] The fact that the Saudi-Yemen border straddles the Empty Quarter was also problematic, since it could allow movement between the two countries without much detection. In fact, the car al-Harethi was traveling in when he was killed possessed Saudi license plates.[39]

The Yemeni government's thwarted attempts to finish al-Harethi clearly revealed that certain sections of the country were beyond the reach of the nation's security forces. It was at this point that President Saleh signaled his willingness to accept greater US assistance and a more robust (but secret) American presence.[40] Yemen's ungoverned spaces allowed terrorist groups to organize, raise funds, recruit, train, and operate in relative security. Saleh understood that if a second attack on the US were to link back to Yemen's terrorist safe havens and its inability to control its own territory, the consequences could be significant. The Rubicon was crossed; the decision was made, and the US moved in.

The 2002 strike on al-Harethi became a crude blueprint for how the US could penetrate foreign safe havens through multilateral engagement without explicitly violating sovereignty or putting US troops at risk. Yemeni government cooperation was critical to both fixing the target and avoiding serious legal questions in the wake of his elimination. At the same time, engagement with local assets—the tribal members who described al-Harethi's whereabouts to the US ambassador—contributed crucial intelligence. This two-pronged effort demonstrated the seriousness of US intent and ultimately reinforced, rather than undermined, the importance of diplomacy and liaison relationships. Both governments enjoyed their greatest successes in late 2002 and early 2003. In addition to supporting the strike on al-Harethi, Yemen arrested two wanted militants in April 2003, attacked an al-Qaeda hideout in June, and continued to arrest suspects in the USS *Cole* bombing. To foster this cooperation, the US provided almost $100 million in counterterrorism aid to Yemen[41] and encouraged Yemeni officials to recruit local tribal chiefs as informants on al-Qaeda, referring to them as "sheikhs against terror."[42]

The systemic problems facing Yemen were deeper than simply running down a few top terrorists, however, and the US quickly realized that enhanced liaison relationships do not guarantee effective action against terrorist threats. Some already believed that some Yemeni officials were actively supporting al-Qaeda and other militant groups, even after 9/11 and despite their pledges of support to the US. In April 2003, for example, ten suspects held in the bombing of USS *Cole* simultaneously escaped from a Yemeni prison, an event so implausible that it suggested official involvement. The same year, President Saleh announced plans to release 146 militants with suspected ties to al-Qaeda as long as they "pledged to respect the rights of non-Muslim foreigners living in Yemen or visiting it." At one point, some 8 percent of foreign-born fighters in Iraq fighting US and Iraqi forces hailed from Yemen, despite the country's small population, according to captured al-Qaeda in Iraq (AQI) records.[43]

In 2005, US officials were further stunned to learn that Abdul Majid al-Zindani, whom both the UN and the US had designated as a terrorist with ties to bin Laden, had traveled to a conference in Mecca as part of President Saleh's official delegation. A year later, twenty-three accused terrorists again escaped from a jail in Sana'a.[44] Some of these individuals would later coalesce into al-Qaeda in Yemen (AQY) and then morph into the much more lethal al-Qaeda in the Arabian Peninsula (AQAP) group. By 2008 the situation became so dangerous that the US embassy was forced to close its doors, after the building was attacked twice with rocket-propelled grenades, automatic rifles, and car bombs.[45]

Yemen's terrorist activity began to spill out of its borders. On Christmas Day 2009, an AQAP suicide bomber, Nigerian national Umar Farouk Abdulmutallab, tried to detonate explosives in his undergarments aboard a Northwest Airlines flight between Amsterdam and Detroit. Several months later, in late October 2010, AQAP tried to smuggle explosives aboard cargo planes in order to detonate them over US airspace. A tip-off from Saudi intelligence thwarted this operation.

Publicly, the US voiced support for Yemen and the US-Yemeni relationship, but sharp words of warning were packaged with the praise. In January 2010, Secretary of State Hillary Clinton praised the Yemeni government for its efforts, but also said it was "time for the international community to make it clear to Yemen that there are expectations and conditions on our continuing support for the government."[46]

Realizing that this constituted a dramatic escalation, President Saleh responded by declaring "open war" on al-Qaeda and sending thousands of soldiers to battle the group in the provinces, amid fears that the organization would attack Yemen.[47] In return, the US continued to increase military aid to Yemen from $70 million in 2009[48] to $150 million in 2010,[49] and worked with local authorities to launch air strikes and raids against al-Qaeda sites in Yemen.

The fierce fighting within Yemen during the spring and summer of 2011, during which Saleh was badly wounded and fled from Sana'a, showed that fighting al-Qaeda in Yemen had become a headache for the US and raised uncertainty about who is really in charge of the increasingly fractured nation. AQAP seemed to be gaining actual territory in addition to ideological control over certain parts of the nation. Although the US scored some successes in late September 2011, killing both US-born cleric Anwar al-Awlaki and AQAP online magazine (*Inspire*) editor Samir Khan in a dual drone strike, whether the old and now new front on the war on terror will ultimately prove fruitful for America's counterterrorism strategy remains up in the air.

BACK TO THE FUTURE:
SOMALIA AND SALEH ALI SALEH NABHAN

In 2002, a Pentagon consultant told journalist Seymour Hersh that the program of targeted killings would not last long. "You might be able to pull it off for five or six months," he believed, but then the intelligence would eventually prove wrong and civilians would get killed. "And then they [the operators] will get hung."[50] But the consultant's dire predictions have not yet come to pass; in fact, targeted killing has become a favorite tool in the counterterrorism operations toolbox, executed through overhead drone strikes and small, lethal Special Forces operations.

On September 14, 2009, US Special Forces prepared to launch yet another find-fix-finish operation, this time in southern Somalia. Their target was Saleh Ali Saleh Nabhan, a Kenyan citizen wanted in connection with the 1998 African embassy bombings and the 2002 bombing of an Israeli-owned hotel in Kenya. Nabhan, already wanted in Kenya, had been hunted by the US since 2006, who considered him one of the "big three" al-Qaeda members enjoying refuge in chaotic neighboring Somalia. The mission to finish Nabhan was groundbreaking; Special Forces had not conducted operations in the country since the early 1990s. By this point, however, Special Forces had been operating against terrorist targets around the world for eight years, fostering a new culture and outlook, and they were determined to get their man.

Of Yemeni descent, Nabhan (a.k.a. Abu Yousef al-Nabhani) was born in Mombasa, Kenya, in 1979.[51] Details of his early life are sketchy; he reportedly grew up in Mombasa's Majengo slum and received a primary education through several years of high school.[52] According to a biography of his life published on a jihadist website, he married a woman from one of the city's nearby villages.[53] By 1998, he had left Mombasa for Afghanistan with Fazul Abdullah Mohammed, an al-Qaeda member who would assist in the attacks against the US embassies later that year.[54] He later served as a guard at the al Farouq camp at the time of the 1998 US cruise missile strikes, launched as a part of Operation Infinite Reach in retaliation for al-Qaeda's bombing of the US embassies.[55]

How close Nabhan was to al-Qaeda prior to 9/11 remains uncertain, although some reports call him one of the first members of al-Qaeda's East Africa cell.[56] Although many news sources would later claim he was somehow connected with the US embassy bombings in Africa, US officials never publicly fingered him for the attack, as they did many of the other perpetrators. Even vague allegations of a connection to the attacks would not surface prior to 2002.[57] Some sources have claimed that Nabhan served as a go-between for Fazul Abdullah Mohammed—at the time the secretary of al-Qaeda's Kenyan leader Wahid el Hage—and bin Laden and others propose that Nabhan may also have been a trainer at the camps by this point.[58] His jihadist biography even claims that he trained the "19 Heroes of Manhattan Battle: Muhammad Atta and his companions" and helped forge their documents.[59] There is no corroboration of this claim, however.

What is clear is that Nabhan participated in a series of attacks that made him one of the most wanted terrorists in East Africa, setting off a local manhunt within Kenya. At 8:00 AM on November 28, 2002, two or three suicide bombers drove a Mitsubishi Pajero toward the Israeli-run Paradise Hotel, accelerated, and rammed the car through the front entrance.[60] Several dozen tourists had just checked in, and the resulting explosion demolished much of the structure, killing three Israelis and eleven Kenyans and injuring eighty more.[61] At roughly the same time, two shoulder-launched Strela 2 surface-to-air missiles were aimed at an Israeli-owned Boeing 757 as it took off for Tel Aviv from Mombasa. The missiles narrowly missed their target, leaving its 261 passengers shaken but unharmed.[62]

The US, Kenya, and Israel immediately condemned the attacks, and the countries each began their own separate investigations. Although an obscure Lebanese group initially claimed responsibility, Israeli and Kenyan officials agreed that al-Qaeda was behind the attacks.[63] Al-Qaeda later claimed responsibility, and most of the suspects eventually named were somehow linked to that group.[64]

In the months following the bombing, officials would publish the name of only one individual in connection to the investigation—Nabhan— as he had left behind the most direct evidence of involvement. Kenyan investigators traced the purchase of the green all-terrain Mitsubishi used in the bombing back to Nabhan, and soon arrested his mother and brother.[65] Subsequent interrogations led investigators to Nabhan's seventeen-year-old wife, Fatuma Saleh, who had disappeared along with their young child before the bombing and was found living with her parents on Lamu, a small, laid-back tourist island near the Somali border. Saleh claimed that Nabhan had instructed her to return to her parents shortly before the bombing. She did not know her husband's whereabouts but suggested that he might have gone to Somalia.

She pointed authorities to a home in Mombasa where neighbors reported having seen a car like the one used in the attack. Investigators found bomb materials in the home and concluded on the basis of this evidence that Nabhan and two other suspects had resided there four months prior to the bombing to construct the car bomb.[66] Authorities also concluded that Nabhan was one of the two individuals who had fired missiles at the Israeli airplane as it departed Kenyan airspace.[67]

Nabhan's wife further revealed to Kenyan police that her husband had called her on December 11 and told her he was in Baidoa, a city in southern Somalia.[68] Kenyan authorities later discovered that Nabhan had been seen in a town near the border soon after the attacks but were frustrated in attempts to track him further.[69] Their investigation took a turn for the comical after it was discovered that the Kenyan police might have arrested both Nabhan and an accomplice four months before the attacks but then lost track of them.

Nabhan's accomplice, Fazul, had indeed been arrested after attempting to use a stolen credit card to purchase jewelry sometime in July 2002, along with Nabhan, who was posing as Fazul's taxi driver at the time. The fact that Nabhan had escaped by jumping bail caused less of a stir than the fact that Fazul had escaped several armed police officers. According to one officer, the Kenyan police had considered Fazul "a normal robbery suspect" at the time of his arrest and had escorted him to what he claimed was his apartment in their search for stolen goods; they clearly did not expect that he would flee the apartment and evade them in the streets below. They apparently did not realize that their escaping detainee was also a key terrorist suspect, despite the decaying wanted posters of Fazul plastered on the walls of police stations throughout the country.[70]

That Nabhan had disappeared into Somalia was particularly problematic for the Kenyans, as well as the Americans, for no single force had been able to maintain control of the chaotic country since 1991. And no local force was available to help Kenyan, US, or Israeli forces track him down, as there had been in Yemen and Pakistan. Somalia is an extreme libertarian's dream—the entire country is an ungoverned space not accountable to a central government.

Somalia's decades-long descent into chaos was a complex tale of cruelty, international neglect, and greed. Guerrillas led by Somali warlords in 1991 ousted dictator Siad Barre, forcing US officials—who had not really cared much about Somalia in the first place—to look at the question of succession. "We hazarded a few guesses," according to Frank Crigler, the US ambassador to Somalia during the late 1980s. "But we never came close to imagining the scenario that eventually unfolded or the humanitarian nightmare."[71] The next year, several hundred thousand Somalis died due to famine. The country likely had plenty of food, but sparring warlords blocked shipments to the country's interior. Responding to the crisis, the US initially deployed troops to ensure food deliveries and provide security in what would eventually become part of a UN peacekeeping mission. After 1993, however, President Clinton announced the withdrawal of all US forces from Somalia. UN forces withdrew by March 1995, amid the country's highest level of chaos.[72]

Although the northern regions of Somalia enjoyed a degree of stability, in the southern regions virtually all economic institutions collapsed during the early 1990s. The UN classified Somalia as a "least developed country," and the inter- and intraclan warfare so devastated the south that the malnutrition rate reached 90 percent in some regions and displaced persons camps.[73] The chaos of anarchy eventually gave way to the reemergence of traditional clan structures and Islamic courts, but Somalia remained a shattered country with no real central government.[74]

Although the scene was ripe to provide terrorist groups some measure of refuge, there were impediments to this process. Some analysts have argued that Somalis were traditionally "suspicious of politically active Islam and remained attached to the clan as the sole source of protection."[75] Others, seeking to explain why al-Qaeda failed to establish a base in Somalia during the 1990s, have suggested that the country may have been too chaotic even for the terrorist group to handle. A report by West Point's Combating Terrorism Center, for example, argued that al-Qaeda operatives in Somalia fell victim to many of the same challenges that plague Western interventions—they were "prone to extortion and betrayal, found themselves trapped in the middle of incomprehensible clan conflicts, faced suspicion from the indigenous population, had to overcome significant logistical constraints and were subject to a constant risk of Western military interdiction."[76] By this logic, states such as Yemen and Kenya, with relatively weak central governments offering minimal stability, are preferable terror safe havens to anarchic states like Somalia.

This argument has some merit. Nabhan's East Africa cell initially chose Kenya over Somalia as a base of operations, and even after the Islamic Courts Union (ICU)—a coalition of conservative religious groups seeking to establish a unified Somali state under Islamic law—came to power, al-Qaeda did not develop as large a presence in Somalia as it did in many other countries. Still, Somalia offered a refuge from governments of all kinds, and many analysts have linked bin Laden and al-Qaeda to various Islamist groups in the country.[77]

With no stable government, there was no partner for the US to pressure or work with to pursue its targets. But when the ICU took over much of the country in 2006, the international community and the US quickly turned their attention to Somalia. The US had already labeled the head of the ICU's consultative council, Sheikh Hassan Dahir Aweys, a specially designated global terrorist in September 2001, citing his links to al-Qaeda. Some information claimed that the ICU was allegedly sheltering both Nabhan and Fazul in Mogadishu.[78]

By the end of 2006, the US had joined with Ethiopia to reverse the ICU's territorial gains and reassert the authority of the Transitional Federal Government (TFG). When Ethiopian troops, at great cost, pushed the ICU from Mogadishu in early 2007, Nabhan fled with them to a nebulous "Islamist stronghold" near the Kenya-Somalia border.[79] Lacking a reliable local partner, US officials began to work closely with Ethiopian intelligence agencies to obtain information to hunt Nabhan and other al-Qaeda associates. However, the Muslim Somalis' hostility toward Christian Ethiopian troops and the civilian casualties resulting from US attacks led to few actionable leads, intensifying the debate in Washington over US counterterrorism policy in the region. Ethiopia had traditionally been a strong US ally in the Horn of Africa and was viewed by many in the Bush administration as a key proxy in preventing a complete Islamist takeover of Somalia. Yet even with this partnership, determining Nabhan's exact location proved extremely difficult.

The US soon added Nabhan to the FBI's "Seeking Information—War on Terrorism" list, suggesting that the search for him was being stepped up. This may have also indicated that the evidence against him in the 1998 embassy bombings was not particularly strong, as only his colleague Fazul was on the FBI's list of most wanted terrorists.[80] During this time Nabhan felt free enough to serve as the liaison between militants in East Africa and al-Qaeda leaders in Pakistan and became an important instructor in the country's terrorist camps.[81]

Whether he was now a member of al-Shabaab—a splinter wing of the ICU, and the primary al-Qaeda-linked organization in the country—or was simply "on loan" to the group is unclear. But in 2008 Nabhan released a video showcasing an al-Shabaab training camp in Somalia. While Nabhan explicitly solicited assistance from the peoples of "Kenya and Tanzania, and Nigeria and Uganda and Chad" in the video, he was in fact training militants from around the world—including several from the United States.

His solicitation did not fall on deaf ears. A group of Somali Americans from Minneapolis, arrested in early 2009 after they allegedly returned from a terrorist training camp in Somalia, claimed that Nabhan had been one of their trainers. Two months before Nabhan's death, one of the group's members pleaded guilty to terrorism-related charges; his lawyer claimed that he had been trained in Somalia to be a suicide bomber. More disturbingly, another Somali American from Minnesota who had been at the training camps at the same time as Nabhan drove a truck bomb in November 2008 in northern Somalia; he was identified by a finger found at the explosion site.[82] By October 2009, National Counterterrorism Center (NCTC) director Michael Leiter claimed that dozens of Somali Americans and Muslim converts had trained at al-Shabaab camps.[83]

US operatives continued to track Nabhan, often relying on local warlords for information, but the effort produced little actionable intelligence. Funding brutal, untrustworthy warlords seemed to highlight America's shortsighted policy of prioritizing the fight against Islamic extremists above all else. Furthermore, Somali officials in the fledgling US- and UN-backed TFG argued that American support for the warlords hindered the effort to build a strong central government, undermining the long-term effort to deny terrorists a safe haven. "They [the US] really think they can capture al-Qaeda members in Somalia . . . but the Americans should tell the warlords they should support the government, and cooperate with the government," commented former Somali president Abdullahi Yusuf Ahmed.

On March 2, 2008, the US took its first shot at eliminating Nabhan. A US submarine off the Somali coast fired at least two missiles, destroying a house in the village of Dobley only a few miles from the Kenyan border. Dobley, together with the surrounding southern region of Somalia, had been a focal point of al-Shabaab and other insurgent group activities—most notably suicide bombs and hit-and-run attacks to rid the country of Ethiopian troops and regain territory. Although the casualties included suspected militants, they also included civilians, raising further questions about Washington's narrow focus on suspected Islamic militants versus stabilizing the country to deny terrorist groups refuge. The strike also failed to reach its true target; Nabhan either escaped or had never been there.

By 2009, Nabhan had built a militia of over 180 foreigners in Somalia, aptly calling themselves al-Muhajirun, or "the Emigrants." These battle-hardened jihadists fought alongside Somali insurgents, coordinating their efforts with al-Qaeda leadership. Through al-Muhajirun, Nabhan was able to recruit young extremists from around the globe—in Kenya, Uganda, Saudi Arabia, Europe, and the US—reportedly bringing in some of the group's most experienced fighters from outside the country. The growth of al-Muhajirun contributed to the growing concern over al-Qaeda links to militants in Somalia, with at least one security analyst suggesting that "Nabhan was a high-enough target within the al-Qaeda organization that his elimination could seriously disrupt the command structure of al-Qaeda in Somalia."[84]

The US concluded that Nabhan was commuting regularly between the cities of Merka and Kismayo on the southern coast of Somalia, and a military operation—code-named Celestial Balance—was readied. Surveillance confirmed a pattern of activity for Nabhan, providing American officials sufficient time to develop the operation. And several strategies were presented, including an air strike, a helicopter raid, and a capture attempt. While the planning stages—verifying and confirming the intelligence, determining which forces should be used, and nailing down other operational details—were conducted under the US Central Command, the operation was handed over to the US Africa Command (AFRICOM) for execution.

The NSC received a detailed outline of each option. Detaining Nabhan for interrogation was appealing, but President Obama's advisers promptly rejected the capture option, likely remembering the brutal political fallout from the 1993 Somalia incursion. The risk to US troops on the ground in such a volatile region of Somalia was enough to outweigh the potential benefits, they believed. Finally, advisers presented the air strike option to Obama, which he approved, but the weather on the day of the attack forced commanders to green-light the helicopter mission instead. While there were risks associated with putting US troops inside hostile territory, it uniquely allowed America to verify Nabhan's death.

On the afternoon of September 14, 2009, less than two weeks after the White House approved the operation, four US military helicopters flew into Somalia with a force of elite US commandos.[85] According to witnesses near Baraawe, a port town a little over a hundred miles south of Mogadishu, helicopters appeared over the horizon in hot pursuit of a convoy speeding down a highway through the desert.[86] They began firing .50-caliber machine guns and other automatic weapons at the convoy, while their targets attempted to return fire.[87] The car's occupants were quickly overwhelmed and killed. US troops the fastroped from one of the helicopters into a swirling cloud of red dust and removed the bodies for identification.[88] The operation was a success: US troops had finally identified and eliminated Nabhan and set a precedent for a different kind of "finish" operation inside a terrorist safe haven.

AMERICA'S ELIMINATION of a high-level al-Qaeda personality is good news for the US and its counterterrorism strategy, but a single killing neither changes the overall societal narrative of a region, nor is it an effective substitute for dealing with the larger issues of creating effective control over the region. Liquidating Nabhan did not bring stability to Somalia; similar successes had similar effects on Yemen, Pakistan, and other countries with weak or nonexistent government institutions.

These moves are, however, critical to achieving certain goals if they serve a larger purpose. General David Petraeus acknowledged as much in an interview in mid-August 2010: "Operations by counterterrorist forces—in other words, by our special-mission-unit elements, which will remain nameless but which you know are absolutely part of a comprehensive civil-military counterinsurgency campaign. Not only are those [operations] not at odds with counterinsurgency, they're a very important element in the overall approach."[89]

America will continue to grapple with the demons that emerge from shattered countries for years to come. As of this writing, Somalia remains a wrecked shell of a country, ranked by *Foreign Policy* magazine as the top "failed state" for three years running. The radical Islamist groups that emerged when the ICU crumbled a few years ago seem to be growing stronger by the month, and the coastlines are continuously plagued by well-armed pirates. More alarmingly, small groups of American citizens—mostly young Somali Americans—are still joining these organizations.[90] Of those American citizens who do not meet a sticky end on distant shores, several have returned to the US to wreak havoc, perhaps on al-Qaeda's behalf.

America's aggressive moves in terrorist safe havens can also produce tragic, counterproductive, unintended consequences. In May 2010, in Yemen's Marib province—where al-Harethi had met his fiery end eight years earlier—a US aerial assault killed several suspected al-Qaeda operatives.[91] However, this strike accidentally killed the deputy governor of the province, who, due to his standing among the local tribes, had been trying to convince the militants to surrender to government forces. This official's accidental death at the hands of the US prompted local tribesmen to attack an oil pipeline in revenge, and handed AQAP a propaganda victory, overshadowing the deaths of a number of low-level, easily replaceable operatives.

Firing missiles at houses and vehicles containing suspected terrorists in faraway lands from the comfort of a US base of operations has a certain visceral, short-term finishing quality to it, as a bad guy is eliminated. Ultimately, targeting individuals for death in distant blighted lands is a short-term tactical maneuver. It is not a coherent enough strategy to achieve mission-critical US national security goals. A decade after 9/11, playing whack-a-mole with al-Qaeda operatives has not proven to be an effective eradication strategy.

CHAPTER 11

GERONIMO

There are worse places than Abbottabad to meet one's end. Named after James Abbott, a resourceful British officer who gained notoriety in the region during the Sikh wars of the late 1840s, this pleasant Raj-era hill station retreat a few hours north of Islamabad is nestled between the pine forests of the surrounding Shimla and Sarban peaks. The truck-congested Karakoram Highway, a ribbon of gravel and asphalt that stretches from Pakistan to China through the Khunjerab pass, runs through the center of town. Abbottabad is a good stopping-off point for travelers to spend a night, enjoy a meal, or stretch their legs.

Abbottabad is home to the Pakistan Military Academy, the training grounds for Pakistan's junior military officers. Many military men retire to this part of the country, taking advantage of the cool air and one of the best golf clubs in the nation. Abbottabad also has a fairly large Christian community, and a few notable churches dot the city's landscape. But for all its beauty, it is perhaps best known as the final home for the most hunted man of the twenty-first century, Osama bin Laden.

In the early morning darkness of May 2, 2011, America came to collect its due.

At the end of a dirt road on the outskirts of town, inside a heavily secured multistory compound built specifically for him, the al-Qaeda leader went about his daily routine surrounded by a small group of confidants and family members. Guarded by barbed wire–topped walls, the compound was cut off from the outside world. The residents lived off the grid, burned their own trash, and were singularly unfriendly to the locals, even confiscating a soccer ball that some neighborhood kids had accidentally kicked into the compound.[1]

Around 1:00 AM on a pitch-black night, at least two specially rigged MH-60 Blackhawk helicopters flown by the 160th Special Operations Aviation Regiment, informally known as the Night Stalkers, descended on the one-acre structure.[2] Two dozen members of the elite Naval Special Warfare Development Group (DEVGRU)—commonly known as the Navy SEALs—accompanied by an interpreter and a dog named Cairo, emerged with one target in mind. They were willing to take him dead or alive. Sweeping through the compound with silenced weapons, the elite troops cleared one room after another, eliminating threats with gruesome efficiency. Finally, in a hallway outside the main bedchamber, three officers saw enemy number one rush into another room.[3] They followed him in.

President Barack Obama and other top American officials anxiously sat in the White House Situation Room thousands of miles away and listened to their secure communications. An anonymous message finally crackled over the line: "Geronimo E-KIA." America's bête noire—the individual responsible for killing thousands of innocent people worldwide and the bogeyman who animated a radical shift in US society—was dead. The president translated the message simply, saying to no one in particular, "We got him."

The United States would not have been able to eliminate bin Laden without having refined and rehearsed the updated find-fix-finish counterterrorism doctrine. Many of the tools and techniques brought to find, fix, and finish the al-Qaeda leader—advanced technology, integrated military/analytical forces, and a robust HVT interrogation program, to name a few—barely existed prior to 9/11. Furthermore, the larger legal, political, military, and intelligence effort that contributed in its own inexorable way to the hunt for the most wanted man on the planet mostly evolved after al-Qaeda's attack against the US homeland. Bin Laden's eventual death showed that the US could be grimly dedicated and relentless in the pursuit of its goals and the destruction of its enemies.

THE CHEST-THUMPING operational details of the night raid on bin Laden's compound have been widely, if not always accurately, reported in the press. But the underlying mechanisms that allowed the US to arrive in Abbottabad are much less well understood.

America was able to raid bin Laden's compound because of the tactical and strategic knowledge that US and allied countries had generated about the al-Qaeda organization since 9/11. One of the major multiagency efforts focused on how al-Qaeda leaders communicated with their followers and with each other. Top leaders needed to issue orders, and they usually did so via a complex, multilayered human courier network. To preserve operational security, this network consisted of trusted human runners who physically transmitted important messages between points in the network or, perhaps for the most secret and critical messages, from memory.[4] This system provided the protection that al-Qaeda's leaders needed—many of them entirely distrusted electronic communications, with good reason—but it was laboriously slow. Relaying a message could take as long as a month.

Some members of al-Qaeda found this terribly annoying. In a declassified letter recovered from the house of Abu Musab al-Zarqawi, bin Laden's emissary in Iran, Libyan national Atiyah Abd al-Rahman—killed in a drone strike in Pakistan in late August 2011—described his difficulties in communicating and urged Zarqawi to send a human messenger to Pakistan to establish a reliable communications line with the top leadership.[5] Pakistani president Pervez Musharraf divulged in his memoir that Pakistani intelligence intercepted some of the courier traffic and that the system included distinct layers for administration, operations, media support, and the top leadership.[6]

Surprisingly, bin Laden continued to play the role of a hands-on CEO, using a simple—and hardly NSA proof—means of communicating with the outside world.[7] After writing out his notes and uploading them onto a USB drive, he would turn it over to a courier, a trusted al-Qaeda

member, who would then head to one of the thousands of Internet cafés
in Pakistan to disseminate the leader's commands. It remains unclear
whether bin Laden received messages in this manner as well.

The main lead to locating bin Laden came from one of these trusted
couriers, Abu Ahmed al-Kuwaiti. Abu Ahmed was a Kuwait-bred Pakistani national, and was one of the last individuals at large with ties to
al-Qaeda's pre-9/11 leaders. He was a trusted confidant of KSM and
later Abu Faraj al-Libi.[8] Despite the fact that the US had detained KSM
and al-Libi since 2003 and 2005, respectively, they obscured Abu
Ahmed's pivotal role in al-Qaeda. Another al-Qaeda courier, Hassan
Ghul, captured in Iraq in 2004, shed a little more light on al-Kuwaiti's
identity.[9] Within America's robust overt and covert detention facilities,
spread across continents, certain pieces of the puzzle were waiting to be
unearthed.

In the movies, information leads logically and inexorably toward a
conclusion, but in the real world, intelligence analysis is more of a mun-
dane activity performed by low- and mid-range bureaucrats sitting in
Beltway Brutalist–style buildings synthesizing thousands of documents of
mostly useless material. Various classified and unclassified databases
feed this fire hose of information, but at the end of the day, it is a person or a team of persons who have to make sense of the story—if indeed
there is any.

If you listened to George W. Bush's last attorney general, Michael
Mukasey, you might have believed that "enhanced interrogation techniques" were vital to gaining the information that allowed bin Laden to
be located:

> Consider how the intelligence that led to bin Laden came to hand. It
> began with a disclosure from Khalid Sheikh Mohammed (KSM), who
> broke like a dam under the pressure of harsh interrogation techniques
> that included waterboarding. He loosed a torrent of information—
> including eventually the nickname of a trusted courier of bin Laden.[10]

John Yoo, who helped author the 2002 OLC memos outlining the
contours of harsh interrogation at the Department of Justice, glossed

over the subtleties of intelligence gathering in the *Wall Street Journal*: "The United States located al-Qaeda's leader by learning the identity of a trusted courier from the tough interrogations of Khalid Sheikh Mohammed, the architect of the 9/11 attacks, and his successor, Abu Faraj al-Libi."[11]

But if harsh interrogations, as opposed to other means of intelligence gathering, could elicit excellent and time-sensitive information that decisively led to bin Laden, the US would have arrived in Abbottabad many years earlier. KSM certainly provided his interrogators with a great deal of information—including crazy, incomplete, false, and misleading scraps of data along with some good bits. But the rough interrogation seemed to have more or less ceased by 2005–2006, which means all the drips and drabs of information gained by these controversial mechanisms were consigned to the proverbial back of the classified database by the time the SEALs descended into bin Laden's compound.

As has been noted time and again, prisoners under physical duress often say anything to stop the coercion, but the lines between truth and untruth can be blurry. Even the CIA director seemed to be operating in the fog of uncertainty whether harsh techniques led to tangible information that may have led the US to Abu Ahmed. In an interview by NBC's Brian Williams, then-CIA director Leon Panetta could not give a clear answer, even if he, perhaps, wanted to:

> I think some of the detainees clearly were, you know, they used these enhanced interrogation techniques against some of these detainees. But I'm also saying that, you know, the debate about whether—whether we would have gotten the same information through other approaches I think is always going to be an open question.[12]

Senator John McCain, long an opponent of waterboarding and other violent interrogation techniques, put another stake into the coercive interrogation argument soon after the raid when he stated that in fact a foreign intelligence service had produced the first tantalizing slivers of data to Abu Ahmad's identity and whereabouts:

I asked CIA Director Leon Panetta for the facts, and he told me the following: The trail to bin Laden did not begin with a disclosure from Khalid Sheik Mohammed, who was waterboarded 183 times. The first mention of Abu Ahmed al-Kuwaiti—the nickname of the al-Qaeda courier who ultimately led us to bin Laden—as well as a description of him as an important member of al-Qaeda, came from a detainee held in another country, who we believe was not tortured. None of the three detainees who were waterboarded provided Abu Ahmed's real name, his whereabouts or an accurate description of his role in al-Qaeda.

In fact, the use of "enhanced interrogation techniques" on Khalid Sheik Mohammed produced false and misleading information. He specifically told his interrogators that Abu Ahmed had moved to Peshawar, got married and ceased his role as an al-Qaeda facilitator—none of which was true. According to the staff of the Senate intelligence committee, the best intelligence gained from a CIA detainee—information describing Abu Ahmed al-Kuwaiti's real role in al-Qaeda and his true relationship to bin Laden—was obtained through standard, noncoercive means.[13]

It remains unclear whether harsh techniques indeed led to bits and pieces of possibly relevant information but one thing is certain: brutal interrogations certainly did not lead directly to bin Laden's compound. A leaked letter from Panetta to McCain said as much: "In the end, no detainee in CIA custody revealed the facilitator/courier's full true name or specific whereabouts. This information was discovered through other intelligence means."[14]

Legal commentator Dahlia Lithwick summed up the larger inherent problems with using torture, and why many apologists come out of the woodwork to defend it long after it occurred:

That's the problem with doing stupid things: You spend the rest of your life trying to convince yourself that maybe they weren't so stupid after all. Had we not water-boarded prisoners eight years ago, nobody would be making the argument that water-boarding "worked." The reason you don't order up torture in the first place is that once you do, it stays on the menu for years.[15]

LEANING FORWARD

The White House began to consider more expansive options in South Asia in late 2006 and early 2007. President Bush was determined to capture or kill bin Laden before his term in office expired in January 2009. One result was a plan to rejuvenate the hunt for bin Laden by aggressively "flooding the zone" in Pakistan and Afghanistan with CIA personnel and resources, cultivating new human sources, and setting up new bases and further streamlining cooperation with the military.[16] US forces would be authorized to cross over into Pakistan from Afghanistan when there was credible and actionable intelligence on al-Qaeda HVTs, without notification to Islamabad.[17] This plan was known as Operation Cannonball.[18]

Part of the argument for the new strategy was that bin Laden would only be apprehended if America caught one of his senior lieutenants alive.[19] Apparently the plan was approved in theory, but implementation was paralyzed as top Bush officials argued bitterly over the risk calculus for conducting ground raids inside Pakistan.[20] Pursuing a parallel path, the Bush administration also backed a proposal to enhance, train, and supply Pakistan's military and intelligence units, especially the ethnic Pashtun-dominated Frontier Corps, which would be largely responsible for combating the resulting insurgency in the tribal areas. Since 2006 or 2007, small teams of US Special Forces had been permitted to go inside Pakistan to work with their Pakistani counterparts on counterinsurgency tactics.[21]

In 2008, Pakistan agreed to expand the initiative to about a hundred American and British military trainers, and the Pentagon drafted plans to spend $75 million for new body armor, vehicles, radios, and surveillance equipment.[22] Small military intelligence teams began working with Pakistani intelligence to share techniques on reading satellite imagery and responding to requests for more advanced technical equipment,[23] while US-trained Pakistani commando units began carrying out missions in northern Pakistan.[24] Officials hoped that they could eventually ramp up assistance and cooperation with Islamabad to the point of joint combat operations.[25]

Indicating some degree of cooperation at the frequent urging of Washington, Islamabad in late 2007 and 2008 launched a series of major offensives into South Waziristan to combat the increasing encroachment of Pakistani Taliban leader Baitullah Mehsud. Pakistani forces killed hundreds of Mehsud's forces, but ended their advance with a negotiated deal. In June 2008, the military started a similar offensive to blunt Taliban advances in the north. According to press reporting, however, there was no sign anywhere of the offensive and a local warlord, Haji Namdar, told a reporter it was for show: "The army comes in, and they fire at empty buildings. It is a drama—it is just to entertain . . . America."[26]

The focus on Afghanistan and Pakistan intensified once the Obama administration took over. During his campaign, Barack Obama had vowed to shift resources away from the Iraq conflict and back to the fight against al-Qaeda in Afghanistan and Pakistan. As president, he moved quickly to fulfill that pledge. The Obama administration stepped up armed remote-piloted attacks, increased the budgets for operations in Afghanistan and Pakistan, and gave CIA license to redouble its efforts to hunt for bin Laden. At the same time, US policymakers vowed to boost development aid to Pakistan and threatened to cut off military aid unless more efforts went toward tracking down al-Qaeda.[27] While bin Laden remained out of reach for much of the decade, these overall efforts began to narrow the gap between the hunted and the hunters.

The actual physical gap began to narrow as well. After learning about Abu Ahmed's critical position within al-Qaeda, in August 2010 the CIA established a base in Abbottabad near the suspected compound. Officers there began to search for signs of life that would confirm bin Laden's actual whereabouts. As one American official later put it, "The CIA's job was to find and fix . . . the intelligence work was as complete as it was going to be, and it was the military's turn to finish the target."[28] Evidently the CIA operated under the ISI's collective noses, despite the fact that Americans deployed sensitive surveillance equipment like radar to search for subterranean escape tunnels, as well as less esoteric devices like cameras equipped with telephoto lenses.[29] Despite the best efforts of the

CIA team, however, it found no conclusive proof that bin Laden was actually there.

Beyond the assistance provided by CIA case officers, analysts, and small armies of contractors working in forward operating bases in Afghanistan, and those plying their trade in offices scattered throughout South Asia, the responsibility fell to a small number of individuals to actually breach the compound and kill bin Laden. While Navy SEALs received the glory, it was the larger JSOC organization that fused the intelligence with the so-called trigger pullers. Although the war in Iraq had been a squalid, ill-conceived mess of an operation, costing lives, money, and political prestige, it was also a living laboratory for the evolving find-fix-finish paradigm.

The high tempo of operations fused with analysis—a bureaucratic evolution honed in Iraq and Afghanistan under General Stanley McChrystal and then under his successor, General William McRaven—allowed JSOC personnel to develop an impressive ability to take on terrorist adversaries. Still, JSOC troops operate in uniform, and committing to armed incursions inside a country that the US is not at war with (i.e., Pakistan or Somalia) posed certain complex Title 10 versus Title 50 legal conundrums. When it came to targeting bin Laden in Abbottabad, President Obama sidestepped this problem by authorizing JSOC operators to work under CIA direction, which under US law allowed them to pursue covert actions within Pakistan.[30] As the intelligence began to coalesce around a particular compound, the individuals tapped for the mission prepared in duplicate buildings in California and North Carolina especially built for the takedown.[31] Through meticulous planning and drilling, drilling and planning, JSOC officers readied themselves for all sorts of contingencies, such as what would happen if the helicopters developed problems in the thin mountain air or if the SEALs failed to successfully rappel from the ropes inside the compound.

Both mishaps occurred. The tail on one of the Blackhawks clipped the twelve-foot outer wall, cracking the helicopter in two and forcing the pilot to ditch, nose first, inside the compound. The other landed outside the walls, obliging the troops to blast their way into bin Laden's concrete fortress.[32] Some forty minutes later, after engaging in firefights and disposing of the crippled helicopter, the team dragged bin Laden's body to the remaining chopper and took off into the night sky.

To neutralize bin Laden, a priority of the first order for President Obama, required cutting-edge technology and the US had such tools and technology in hand. Unmanned aircraft were generously utilized, although the drones might have been there to neutralize a different sort of adversary: the Pakistani military. The White House deployed the Lockheed Martin RQ-170 Sentinel drone, a grayish aircraft that suspiciously looks like a mini B-2 bomber, to avoid radar detection and surveillance by Pakistan's air force. Despite the tacit understanding between Washington and Islamabad that drones could operate in the tribal areas of northern Pakistan, this new aircraft could penetrate deep into Pakistan itself, operating over extremely sensitive areas without being noticed by radar.

The helicopter used in the raid may have been a recent technological breakthrough. According to *Aviation Week*, the Blackhawks utilized various noise-muffling technologies, infrared suppression finishes as well as other modifications that were publicly unknown until then.[33] Political considerations notwithstanding, US soldiers could now appear anywhere, at any moment, without the host country realizing its airspace had been penetrated.

But the helicopters and the drones would not have arrived over Abbottabad had it not been for a lethal slip-up: Abu Ahmed al-Kuwaiti decided to use the telephone. His phone call to another al-Qaeda–related individual sealed his fate when he uttered the words, "I'm back with the people I was with before."[34] US officials who had been monitoring the call from the other side realized they were listening to something important.[35] Despite knowing that phone conversations could be compromised—a fact that bin Laden himself seems to have known since 1998—electronic communications within the group did not cease entirely. Al-Qaeda personnel, including Abu Ahmed, did their best to thwart eavesdropping and ensure basic operational security by traveling a long way away from their base before putting the batteries into the cell-or satellite phone before making the call.[36]

Still, Abu Ahmed was human, and in August 2010 he wanted to touch base with an old friend. The recipient of the call was a known al-

Qaeda comrade in arms, a fact, combined with painstaking analysis several years prior, that led US officials to believe that this might be their lucky break, almost ten years in the making. America's powerful ability to track satellite phones and long-standing intelligence acquisition had finally penetrated bin Laden's personal network. By following Abu Ahmed back to the Abbottabad compound, the US was able to fix his position and then position itself to finish the job.

Finally, as with much in life, the success of this operation depended on political leadership and chance. For all the tens of billions of dollars that the US has spent on intelligence, it is worthless if leaders are unwilling to act on it. As military historian John Keegan reflected in his book, *Intelligence in War*, "Knowledge, the conventional wisdom has it, is power; but knowledge cannot destroy or deflect or damage or even defy an offensive initiative by an enemy unless the possession of knowledge is also allied to objective force."[37] Collecting, processing, and disseminating intelligence, despite the earnest efforts of its producers, is often a murky business, contradictory and sometimes just plain wrong. It is up to the leaders, often the commander in chief, to determine whether to act on this information and roll the dice on a risky operation.

President Obama received conflicting advice whether to strike the Abbottabad compound. Some advisers were convinced that an attack would come at too great a cost and the political blowback would be intolerable. Others suggested a missile strike would accomplish the end goal and pose little risk to US personnel. The debate went back and forth.

What weighed on the president was the enormous political risk he was taking, not to mention the lethal dangers elite troops would face if the operation went poorly. The images of an enraged mob dragging American servicemen through the streets were almost overpowering; a week after the raid, he told the television program *60 Minutes* that "you think about Black Hawk Down. You think about what happened with the Iranian rescue . . . the day before, I was thinking about this quite a bit."[38] Complicating things was that, despite the evidence, it was all circumstantial: no American *had actually seen* Osama bin Laden at the compound. As the president later noted, "If it turns out that it's a wealthy, you know, prince from Dubai who's in this compound and, you know, we've sent Special Forces in, we've got problems."[39]

But as his predecessor was wont to say about himself, President Obama at the time was "the decider," and he authorized a ground assault on the compound. Relying on the best efforts of the intelligence community and the best troops on the planet, he took his chance on the wheel of fortune. The Pakistani government was left out of the loop, most likely because its discretion was, to put it charitably, questionable.

And thousands of lives and billions of dollars later, America finally got its man.

CHAPTER 12

TO THINE OWN SELF BE TRUE

During the decade following the attacks on New York and Washington, Americans gradually returned to a pre-9/11 state of mind. Polling just prior to the November 2010 midterm elections showed that Americans ranked terrorism low on a laundry list of other concerns, including health care, the economy, and immigration.[1]

But the threat of terrorism is now imprinted on the front of the US policymaking cerebral cortex. The American national security apparatus today is different from the one in place on September 11, 2001, and radically so. Brand-new bureaucracies now command sizable chunks of the federal budget; US military forces have been involved in continuous irregular warfare for a decade; dozens if not hundreds of individuals are held under strained international legal standards; and despite the death of al-Qaeda's leader in Pakistan, the conflict against his organization grinds on. The US has spent hundreds of billions of dollars on homeland defense, counterterrorism efforts, emergency response and other countermeasures, not to mention the invasion and occupation of that graveyard of empires, Afghanistan.

Despite its missteps and errors, the US has radically shifted its fighting doctrine to the new find-fix-finish model. It has evolved and adapted to meet the real needs of today's geopolitical environment and take advantage of advances in technology. In the words of one former intelligence analyst, Cameron Middleton, the US has been generally "able to maintain an open society and safeguard civil liberties, even in the presence of a heightened security posture."[2]

What lessons have we learned, and where can the US go from here?

The find-fix-finish model is effective as part of a larger strategy. The US has greatly improved the art of hunting individuals in out-of-reach areas, but this process must ultimately serve a larger strategic effort. Taking pivotal individuals off the battlefield may be satisfying to policymakers and the public alike, but without a strategic vision to finish conflicts in enormously complex parts of the world such as Pakistan's tribal lands, Iraq's Anbar province, Yemen's hinterlands, and elsewhere, the find-fix-finish model will encounter certain hard limitations.

In 2001, the US proved it could wage a mobile war against an unconventional enemy. Small teams of CIA and Special Forces, combined with local allies, routed Taliban and al-Qaeda forces in Afghanistan in a matter of weeks. However, with a battered al-Qaeda on a precipice— perhaps literally—the US shifted resources away from South Asia for a costly and counterproductive invasion of Iraq. Operation Iraqi Freedom and its aftermath was a grievous, self-inflicted diplomatic, military, and intelligence wound from which the US is still recovering, and a godsend to the perpetrators of 9/11.

By the time the US refocused on the remnants of al-Qaeda's core in Afghanistan and elsewhere, the organization had spread and scattered to the winds. The US could not go to war against Sudan, Yemen, Pakistan, Iran, and other nations all at once. Instead, the fight against al-Qaeda became a search in the cracks and seams of these countries. Essential to the implementation of the find-fix-finish model is the ability to find and fix the target, two actions only possible with a strong, coordinated intelligence effort. The most effective counterterrorism reform of the last ten years has been the improved coordination between intelligence agencies, especially in conflict zones.

America needs help from other countries, whether it likes it or not. Despite its $80 billion intelligence system, the US still requires assistance from other countries to fight terrorism, as international partnerships continue to play a central role in thwarting terror plots. Just about every foreign-hatched plot against the US has required intelligence cooperation from foreign intelligence services. In 2005, CIA operations director Jose Rodriguez informed Congress that nearly every capture or killing of a suspected terrorist outside Iraq since 9/11—more than 3,000 in all—was the result of CIA cooperation with foreign intelligence services.[3] In late October and early November 2010, Saudi intelligence alerted their American counterparts that al-Qaeda in the Arabian Peninsula (AQAP) had sent explosives-filled packages to the US.[4] These warnings were accurate and probably saved many lives in the air and on the ground.

Although some believe that working with foreign countries is an encumbrance, maintaining robust liaison relationships with many countries around the world is critical to fighting terrorism. Working with other services provides US intelligence several direct benefits, including access to specific information about areas denied to large-scale US penetration, as often is the case in the Middle East and South Asia. Foreign services also can provide direct force to solve a particular problem—such as battering down terrorists' front doors and making arrests. Finally, other intelligence services can mask American actions as local ones, obscuring otherwise obvious US interventions on distant shores.

At the same time, foreign services may harm US interests. They may have conflicting political missions, may attempt to gain insight into American intentions, sources, and methods via covert means, or may provide poor or mistaken information.[5] Finally, working with liaison often opens the US to moral hazards. Foreign intelligence services are not bound by the peculiarities of the American legal system, may be involved in unethical or illegal activities, or may utilize methods not in consonance with US practice. This could be a positive or a negative aspect of international relations, depending on the perspective.

Further, counterterrorism efforts are not pursued in an international relations vacuum. In exchange for fighting al-Qaeda, the US has been obliged to overlook other thorny diplomatic issues such as prisoner abuse, clandestine nuclear deals, and human rights violations. The US continues to do business with many unpleasant regimes in exchange for information and direct action. For example, the US has partnered with the Sudanese regime—an active supporter of the genocide in Darfur—to track al-Qaeda operatives in its country. Of course, the Washington-Khartoum relationship continues to be strained due to serious and legitimate concerns about the government and its intelligence apparatus. Fighting terrorism, it seems, sometimes comes at a hefty diplomatic and moral price.

Most terrorism, like politics, is local. Most terror groups have narrowly defined parochial interests and have little interest in attacking the US homeland—or anywhere outside a small, coveted patch of earth. For example, neither Hamas nor Hizbollah has specific agendas to attack the US. As such, these groups do not immediately jeopardize the American homeland.

What makes al-Qaeda the foremost challenge to the US is the transnational nature of the group. That this organization is willing to strike the US and other countries' interests worldwide makes it a threatening presence. But its transnational behavior and desire to showcase the gruesome attack distinguish it from other extremist organizations. For example, Hamas—theoretically al-Qaeda's Sunni brothers-in-arms—has a low opinion of al-Qaeda and vice versa, which has led to violent clashes of words and arms between the two groups.[6] Al-Qaeda has had great difficulty in gaining a toehold in Gaza due to Hamas's actions—even the "al-Qaeda inspired" Jund al-Islam organization that kidnapped BBC reporter Alan Johnston in 2007 was quickly and brutally suppressed by Hamas.[7]

Al-Qaeda's utopian ideology has been inhibited by the desires of other extremist groups around the world. Before his death, Abu Musab al-Zarqawi attempted to fuse AQI with the more established Ansar al-Sunnah, a Kurdish terrorist outfit that had a long-standing relationship with al-Qaeda prior to 9/11.[8] Despite the organizations' shared goals, mutual enemies, religious outlook, and the best efforts by some in al-Qaeda's leadership, Ansar al-Sunnah declined to formally join forces with AQI.[9] Why? Probably because Zarqawi—a Jordanian Arab with no familial ties to Iraq—was an outsider, an arriviste upstart in their long fight.

Al-Qaeda has benefited from the destruction of other extremist groups. It expanded its presence in Somalia only after Ethiopia, with heavy US assistance, destroyed the conservative Islamic Courts Union. Al-Shabaab—which in early December 2011 renamed itself "Imaarah Islamiyah"—exploited the political vacuum and has proven itself more violent and vicious than its predecessor. More disturbingly, al-Shabaab seems to have attracted numerous US citizens to its banner. The US has thus empowered an enemy much more likely to strike at vital US interests than the one displaced.

Establishing a thoughtful counternarrative is the key to undermining al-Qaeda's appeal. Al-Qaeda serves its adherents an intoxicating stew of otherworldly ideology fused with petty national grievances. Through the use of imagery, violence, and martyrdom, the organization created a worldview that distorts reality. It takes the tropes of religious learning and exploits the emotional pull of communal identity for its own political ends.

However, US experiences in Iraq, Afghanistan, and elsewhere have indicated that many of the foot soldiers and midlevel cadres in the organization are not true believers in al-Qaeda's global cause or its hall-of-mirrors Islam. Rather, they join the organization because of the promises of employment, money, and power. Worldwide jihad does not seem to interest many of its own adherents. Although they are willing to fight under its banner in their nation, many choose not to fight so-called infidels elsewhere. For example, the number of Iraqis that have left Iraq to do damage outside of the country despite years of fighting and grievance can be counted on one hand.

Al-Qaeda's quasi-religious ideology is based on wobbly foundations. One common strand in al-Qaeda and other extremist groups is that the leadership possesses little religious training. KSM, for example, did not claim to have much formal training in Islam despite his father's teachings. Neither did bin Laden (a rich man's idle son), Zawahiri (a lackluster surgeon), Zarqawi (a thug and ne'er-do-well), or Mohammad Atef (a police officer). Al-Qaeda's leaders are ideological charlatans, religious hucksters who wear the robes of learned scholars but in actuality have little patience for serious religious study.

Sun Tzu said, "The highest realization of warfare is to attack the enemy's plans."[10] Hence, an effective counternarrative campaign—known to varying audiences as public relations, information operations, or covert influence—is one of the core needs currently lacking in the global effort to defeat al-Qaeda. The organization is clearly open to such critiques, and it is partially up to the US to take advantage of this opportunity.

Indeed, the writings of various highly regarded jihadist intellectuals in recent years, such as Sayyid Imam al-Sharif (a.k.a. Dr. Fadl) in Egypt,

Abu Muhammad al-Maqdisi in Jordan, or the various LIFG members in Libya, have all attacked al-Qaeda's global campaign of terror. Their critiques have been profoundly unsettling to al-Qaeda's leadership, forcing it to produce intricate refutations.[11] Many of these battles are still jihadist inside baseball, opaque to most outside observers. Still, the counternarrative produced by these credible voices combined with an aggressive US effort may be the best means to undermine al-Qaeda's morale and moral foundations.

Too much bureaucracy impedes counterterrorism efforts and harms national security. The government's answer to a new challenge is often to create new organizations and bureaucracies. And yet bureaucracy, like too many cooks in the kitchen, can greatly hinder agility, responsiveness, and speed in the fight against terror.

Anecdotally, the best time to have worked in CIA's Counterterrorism Center (CTC) and similar organizations was during the weeks following 9/11, when the system was so scrambled by the attacks that bureaucratic impediments were removed and creative thinking was encouraged. Unfortunately for those energized by the opportunities afforded, the system soon returned to its normal, sclerotic self. The way things are now, according to Professor Richard Russell of the National Defense University, is that the intelligence community and the CIA are reminiscent of a "1950s bureaucracy. It's far too hierarchical, and the top-down style of bureaucracy in place [is] just added fat and infrastructure."[12]

Some counterterrorism experts additionally suggest that the US government squanders resources and provides ineffective defenses against terrorist attacks. According to Ishmael Jones, a pseudonym for a former CIA officer who worked for most of his career without official cover, Congress provided the CIA over $3 billion after 2001 to upgrade its abilities to fight terrorism. But the funding was instead spent on domestic bureaucracy and new buildings, items that do not inherently generate foreign intelligence.[13] He noted in mid-October 2010 that, "We need financial accountability and whistle blower systems to stop tremendous waste and theft."[14]

Theft is a strong charge and a bureaucratic affection for red tape may not necessarily rise to a criminal act. Bureaucracy and administration are, after all, necessary for the functioning of the modern national security apparatus. Nonetheless, former and current officials agree that the multiple layers of bureaucracy have been an impediment to doing their job and defending the nation. The system by its very nature forces many talented, creative people out the door because they challenge assumptions, attempt to change established norms, and oblige the slothful to perform their job more adequately. Few sharp, smart people will put up with eight or nine layers of bureaucracy, even in the interest of national security, for very long.

The ODNI must have a real mandate or be eliminated. Looking for something positive to say about the role of the Office of the Director of National Intelligence (ODNI), which was founded in 2005, may be a fruitless effort. There are talented individuals staffing its ranks but the function these people are meant to play is, at best, unclear and, at worst, destructive. Beyond its information-sharing and relationship-building abilities—two areas that the intelligence bureaucracy has improved apart from the ODNI's efforts—the office has not added value in the fight against al-Qaeda. The ODNI—and its subcomponent, the National Counterterrorism Center (NCTC)—has yet to take center stage in thwarting an attack or identifying a critical node in a terror plot, despite multiple chances to do so. Rather, organizations with clearly defined missions—the FBI, CIA, the military, even local police—have actually made things happen.

In late 2008 the ODNI inspector general blasted his own organization, stating that "the majority of the ODNI and IC employees (including many senior officials) . . . were unable to articulate a clear understanding of the ODNI's mission, roles, and responsibilities with respect to the IC."[15] Furthermore, the ODNI's authority remains unclear, encouraging some agencies "to go their own way, to the detriment of the unified and integrated intelligence enterprise envisioned by [the Intelligence Reform and Terrorism Prevention Act] IRTPA."[16]

The Director of National Intelligence (DNI) has a broad job description but little actual power. He is held hostage by twin roles: top intelligence officer and theoretical manager of sixteen disparate, often warring intelligence agencies, many of which take their marching orders from other leaders, including the DNI's boss, the president of the United States. Being CEO of the intelligence community is an all-consuming task; having one individual absorb and synthesize all the intelligence issues facing the country on top of that is well-nigh impossible.

The ODNI's inability to hire and fire heads of organizations and the problems that result has been well documented. But the difficulty runs deeper than the bureaucratic imperatives of the day. Twenty-three-year CIA veteran and former director of intelligence and counterintelligence at the US Department of Energy Rolf Mowatt-Larssen argues that the IC needs "genius, great ideas, great concepts . . . that's the edge to cut through all the red tape. . . . The world is changing so rapidly. We need to transform to keep up with the world."[17] But as of now, Mowatt-Larssen sadly remarked, there seems to be "no sense of urgency—the urgency that fuels successful transformation. Whenever there's a change of culture, the bureaucracy protects itself."[18]

Still, beyond its role as the political fall guy in the event of another catastrophic terror attack, the ODNI can be an interagency umpire. In the event that two agencies are at odds with each other over policy, the ODNI can serve as a neutral arbiter. For example, in 2008 CIA and Saudi security services covertly ran a jihadist website intended to lure extremists in order to gather intelligence, thwart terror plots, and make arrests before anything became operational.[19] However, the US military became concerned that the website was being used to facilitate fighters entering Iraq and shut it down—despite the intelligence lost. In this case, the ODNI could have refereed this high-stakes interagency conflict to some sort of conclusion instead of one bureaucracy forcibly getting its way over another.

Another way the ODNI could provide value is through real strategic intelligence. It doesn't need to redraft the tactical and pseudo-strategic memos drawn from the same information streams exploited by every open source analysis shop in the intelligence community. As of now, the slurry porridge that is "finished intelligence"—especially counterterrorism analysis—is crafted by multiple government agencies with varying degrees of competence, accuracy, and creativity. But it remains unclear whether the redundant analysis provided by the ODNI, the "house that al-Qaeda built," is superior, or even on par, with what their colleagues in long-established organizations produce. Of course, a certain amount of redundant analysis can be an important check, but multiple redundancies can often lead to bureaucratic constipation and paralysis.

In this light, ODNI could remove itself from the day-to-day tactical analysis churned out by other mission-focused organizations, and develop a prestigious cadre of "superanalysts"—the US government's foremost experts in a given national security field—who can focus on the big picture and remain above the fray of the timid, lowest-common-denominator analysis common in communally created products. As the WMD Commission (among other commissions and studies) noted a few years ago, "Analysts cannot maintain their expertise if they cannot conduct long-term and strategic analysis," but the demand for "current intelligence" consumes the majority of government analysts' time and energy.[20] By creating a cadre of first-among-equals analysts, the ODNI could capitalize on the creative energies of its working population. This effort would be separate from the occasional strategic-level papers produced by the National Intelligence Council (NIC) because these particular thinkers would be encouraged to challenge conventional wisdom.

Nothing remains secret forever; intelligence activities must be defensible in the court of public opinion. Denying actions that are legally or morally questionable does not make them go away. America's robust drone-based strikes against al-Qaeda and Taliban-linked individuals in countries with whom we are not at war has been a firm policy since 9/11, yet the US government will not officially confirm that these actions are taking place.

The US exploits numerous new counterterrorism tactics, including some extremely controversial ones. The White House–sanctioned, Department of Justice–certified use of so-called black sites, enhanced interrogation techniques, warrantless electronic surveillance, and targeted killings were once closely guarded secrets. Not only was the public kept in the dark but most people in the intelligence community knew nothing of these efforts. But most secrets eventually become public; it was only a matter of time before the information inevitably leaked.

For reasons as varied as disgruntlement, fame-seeking, political mischief, or a troubled conscience, US policymakers and intelligence officials have brought these controversial practices to light. Furthermore, detainees treated to stepped-up methods of information extraction have and will likely continue to talk about their treatment in detention. And the media and public are always hungry for a good story.

These morally gray areas would benefit from debate and consensus, as a number of counterterrorism techniques raise troubling moral, ethical, and legal questions. The targeted killings of terrorists as a function of state policy has been one of the clearest reversals of American foreign policy behavior stemming from the 9/11 attacks. As late as July 2001, US ambassador to Israel Martin Indyk specifically condemned Israel for its policy of targeting specific terrorist leaders for death, stating "the United States government is very clearly on the record as against targeted assassinations. They are extrajudicial killings, and we do not support that."[21]

Clearly the US has set upon a difficult path. The list of individuals slated for elimination seems to be growing. At first al-Qaeda top leaders were the only ones on the list, then Taliban leaders, and now other individuals such as drug lords in Afghanistan—not direct combatants—are marked.[22] This "target creep" is dangerous and its implications are dizzying.[23] There must be a sober discussion in America to determine whether this road is worth traveling down in the future, long after al-Qaeda is dead and gone.

Pakistan is a critical but deeply unreliable ally in the fight against al-Qaeda. As the Taliban ambassador to Pakistan—Islamabad being one of three capitals that recognized the Taliban as the rightful rulers of Afghanistan prior to 9/11—once remarked, "[The Pakistanis] have two tongues in one mouth, and two faces on one head, so that they can speak everybody's language. They use everybody, deceive everybody."[24]

On one hand, Pakistani assistance is essential to destroying al-Qaeda. Bin Laden lived and died there, as have most of the major personalities in the organization. Pakistan's government and security services are on the forefront of the conflict with al-Qaeda; they also supply and support US efforts in Afghanistan. Hundreds of al-Qaeda and Taliban leaders are now dead or imprisoned because of Pakistani efforts. Most top al-Qaeda leaders in American custody today are sitting in Guantanamo Bay today because of the ISI's partnership.

On the other hand, almost all major terrorist attacks against the West in the modern era—9/11, the 2003 Madrid train bombings, the 2005 London transit attacks, as well as several botched attacks, including Operation Overt and the Zazi plot—are intimately connected to Pakistan. In fact, the case can be made that Pakistan is a state sponsor of terrorism.

Admiral Mike Mullen, chairman of the Joint Chiefs of Staff, in September 2011 called the Haqqani network, the terrorist family-cum-criminal syndicate operating in northwestern Pakistan, a "veritable arm" of the ISI. The Haqqanis, responsible for many operations against US and allied forces in Afghanistan, including an attack against the US embassy in Kabul in late 2011, are part and parcel of Pakistan's strategy "to use violent extremism as an instrument of policy," as Mullen noted in congressional testimony, in order to take advantage of Afghanistan after the US pulls out of the country.[25]

Pakistan allows a permissive environment and some security assistance to the Afghan Taliban and other vicious terrorist organizations like Lashkar-e-Taiba and Jaish-e-Mohammed as well as al-Qaeda. There are persistent rumors that members of the security and military establishment have no small degree of personal sympathy for the extremists in their borderlands fighting US forces in Afghanistan. The tension in the bilateral military relationship can be seen in a number of tragic events that have occurred between American and Pakistani forces—many of which are charitably characterized as "friendly fire" but are more accurately expressions of the frustration that each side feels with the other. For instance, in June 2008, a US air strike killed eleven Pakistani Frontier Corps soldiers in what American officials later described as a "tragic mistake." However, according to local observers, it was anything but: US forces called in the strikes because Pakistani border guards were shooting at them. "When the Americans started bombing the Taliban, the Frontier Corps started shooting at the Americans," said one observer. "They [the Frontier Corps] were trying to help the Taliban. And then the American planes bombed the Pakistani post.'"[26]

After the May 2010 car bombing attempt in New York City's Times Square—carried out by an individual who colluded with TTP operatives and trained in a camp in Pakistan—the White House considered options for unilateral strikes in the event that a successful attack on American soil was traced back to Pakistan's tribal areas.[27] The context of this message suggests that what officials were discussing was a larger retaliatory strike—versus a surgical capture/kill operation—sending the message that the US was prepared to take stronger actions if Pakistan's actions (or inaction) resulted in US civilian casualties in the homeland.

The crux of the problem is that Pakistan—a country chronically just three days from total collapse—has fundamentally different geopolitical priorities than the US. A segment of Pakistan's military and civilian leaders see the cultivation of extremist organizations as part of a larger strategic game that ensures the stability of the Pakistani state. By assuring the US that attacking Islamic extremists is a priority, while at the same time tolerating and occasionally assisting the same militants, the Pakistani government has successfully secured a continuous flow of billions of dollars in aid to boost the economy, military, and the leaders' personal coffers.[28] In a country where less than 5 percent of the population pays income tax and where the ruling elite has created a system that protects them from paying anything at all, the jihadist threat is essential to keeping the economy afloat.[29] "Pakistan is dependent on the American money that these games with the Taliban generate," a Pakistani official once told journalist Dexter Filkins. "The Pakistani economy would collapse without it."[30]

Pakistan is a deeply corrupt country and the American largesse flowing in does little to ameliorate this endemic problem. Transparency International's 2010 Corruption Perceptions Index rated Pakistan the 143rd most corrupt country (out of 178), making it more corrupt than such legendary kleptocracies such as Zimbabwe and Nigeria.[31] The ravaging floods in mid-2010, affecting tens of millions of people and destroying hundreds of miles of land, only worsened the teetering financial state of the country.

Since Pakistan's civilian government and the semi-autonomous ISI have little interest in bringing down their dangerous extremist groups, the US may have to act unilaterally. Pakistan has repeatedly pushed back against proposals for the US to conduct boots on the ground operations inside Pakistan, warning that failing to respect the country's sovereignty could result in armed resistance by Pakistani troops. Still, to fulfill US national security requirements, at least one major foreign policy player with long-term experience in South Asia suggested that the US should conduct operations with or without Islamabad's acquiescence. George W. Bush's ambassador to Iraq, Afghanistan, and the United Nations, Zalmay Khalilzad, wrote in late October 2010 that "the United States should demand that Pakistan shut down all sanctuaries and military support programs for insurgents or else we will carry out operations against those insurgent havens, with or without Pakistani consent. Arguments that such pressure would cause Pakistan to disintegrate are overstated. Pakistan's institutions, particularly the country's security organs, are sufficiently strong to preclude such an outcome."[32]

The bin Laden raid was the clearest example of successful American intervention. Using the tools at hand, including intense overhead reconnaissance, forward bases along the Afghanistan border, and tactical ground maneuvers, is extremely risky and probably cannot be sustained over a long period of time. The strategy is hamstrung by the fact that US combat troops in Pakistan would incite a strong response within the country, marginalizing any supporters still left in the country and the military. Despite their decade-long involvement, American forces are still alien to the region, while the adversary has walked these ancient pathways for generations. The possibility of American blood being shed in Pakistan remains high. Khalilzad's comments notwithstanding, a hard political shove by America could result in Pakistan's complete disintegration of the tenuous grip on stability that Islamabad maintains, leading to a revolt most likely ending with one of two terror-inducing possibilities: a hard-line, half-cocked, nuclear-armed Islamic state or total anarchy.

Beyond Pakistan, Yemen in recent years has become a growing concern for American policymakers. The Fort Hood shootings, the attempted Christmas Day 2009 bombing, and the October 2010 cargo plane attacks were all traced back to the unstable nation. However, these terror attempts, while potentially lethal, are not yet on the level and complexity of the plots emanating from Pakistan. Yemen is a failed state and a definite cause of concern. But Pakistan is a country of nearly 200 million people—almost ten times the size of Yemen—with a much greater global reach. If Pakistan implodes it would become a menace to the US of a wholly different order.

Deploying elite forces, however effective, is not a substitute for a reasonably articulated counterterrorism strategy. During a decade of asymmetric conflicts, special military forces, backed with overwhelming air power, have fought in a multitude of different environments. Further, one of the great successes of the last decade has been the strengthening of the relationship between the military and intelligence services when combating threats.

However, these special units cannot address nation-building issues on their own without the rest of government providing a large measure of support. Ultimately, the use of special forces as a lethal counterterrorism force—mostly though the auspices of JSOC and its 5,000 personnel—and the preeminent national military resource carries its own set of challenges, both in the way the combat is conducted and in the manner in which policymakers utilize these forces in the conflicts of the future.[33]

America will likely shelve the model of full-scale ground invasion of ramshackle nations for a generation or longer, given the recent US experiences in Iraq and Afghanistan. Still, the US military's role has significantly expanded in the last decade to include not only fighting America's wars but also maintaining America's peacekeeping obligations, nation building, and other quasi-diplomatic missions. The niche roles that these special military forces occupy may draw away the best and brightest people at the expense of other critical missions. JSOC may be "the instrument of choice," according to one Pentagon official in September 2010, but it is the regular military units that are doing much of the hard work of rebuilding Afghanistan.[34]

By placing the hunter-killers in a vaunted position, the US military as a whole may be weighting their efforts more heavily than the efforts of the rest of the armed forces. Even though elite troops are asked to perform a spectrum of issues beyond capturing and killing terrorists, the trigger pullers alone get the glory. This is some cause for concern, as retired Special Forces officer Mark Haselton commented: "If we spend the rest of our lives 'capturing and killing' terrorists at the expense of those SF missions that are more important—gaining access to the local population, training indigenous forces, providing expertise and expanding capacity—we're doomed to failure."[35]

Trends in military spending highlight the growth of Special Forces: Special Operations Command's (SOCOM) budget has been increased from $3.8 billion to almost $10 billion over the last decade.[36] And the Special Forces community is expected to grow significantly larger in the next decade. By 2015, SOCOM will be putting another 10,000 people on its payroll.[37] This may be the most significant threat to its current strength. The close-knit nature of these groups may be eroded if a hum-drum, stultifying bureaucratic class of desk-bound warriors rises in their place. After all, SOF personnel cannot be mass-produced.[38]

Finally, there will remain a strong bureaucratic temptation to search for other targets beyond those in the Iraq and Afghanistan conflict zones. The possible spillover of sending elite military forces into places that have some degree of al-Qaeda presence—such as Algeria or Mali—is a troubling issue for the future. Indeed, as JSOC is already participating in an expanding conflict in Yemen, Somalia, and elsewhere, the potentially destabilizing effect of inserting these elite military forces into countries across the globe remains unclear.[39]

America's legal system can handle the challenge posed by captured al-Qaeda operatives. The battle against individual al-Qaeda leaders can be resolved on the battlefield or in a courtroom. When top leaders, such as Abu Musab al-Zarqawi or Mohammad Atef, die in combat, their ability to foment political violence ends, martyrdom notwithstanding. But the lives of other terror suspects like KSM do not end with a lethal last stand. Much ink has been spilled over whether these people should spend a lifetime in legal limbo or be prosecuted in civilian or military courts, but trying these individuals in a legitimate and legitimating court of law would be most beneficial to the fabric of American society. Individuals who have been successfully tried in American courts include KSM's nephew Ramzi Yousef (convicted 1997), the twentieth hijacker Zacarias Moussaoui (convicted 2006), Najibullah Zazi (convicted 2010), and a host of lesser-known terrorists and terrorist wannabes.

Some argue that the legal means of "finishing" al-Qaeda might not work. What if the suspect is not convicted? Detainees, in many cases, are truly awful terrorists, but the evidence against them may have been received through sensitive intelligence methods or coercion, neither being admissible evidence in open court. Respected conservative jurists Benjamin Wittes and Jack Goldsmith argued in March 2010 that, given the harshly partisan climate and the Gordian knot that America's national security detentions provide, the US should sidestep the issue of the courts and detain these individuals indefinitely. "Don't bother trying them at all," they wrote, "the politically draining fight about civilian vs. military trials is not worth the costs. It also distracts from more important questions in the legal war against terrorism."[40] The KSM affair is perhaps the best example (but not the only one), as the information he provided was valuable, but it was extracted through means debatably outside the bounds of US legal code.

But detaining people indefinitely—their presumed guilt or potential innocence notwithstanding—rubs most Americans the wrong way. Arriving at an appropriate conclusion through a legitimate court proceeding is the best way to finish this problem once and for all. But the manner in which the government handled individuals such as KSM has unfortunately allowed these people to use their incarceration to publicly highlight their slow-motion martyrdom, as well as reinforce the nagging feeling that the US engages in acts that it would roundly condemn if carried out by other nations.

As David Frakt of the Air Force Reserve JAG Corps and a professor of law at Western State University College of Law has stated, "Nearly everyone agrees that [9/11] was one of the most monstrous single crimes ever committed. Whether one views KSM and his alleged co-conspirators as war criminals or simply mass murderers, there needs to be a criminal trial in some forum."[41] The civilian court system is certainly no friend to terrorist suspects. According to the New York University School of Law's terrorist trial report card, "The overall conviction rate for prosecutions involving terrorism charges rate now stands at 89%."[42] In large part due to post-9/11 reforms, civilian prosecutors now have a number of tools to use when trying suspected terrorists. Moreover, civilian judges generally hand down stiff sentences in terrorism cases.

So, how can the US proceed? There may be a "least worst" option available. One way to pursue justice while calming political winds is to try KSM and others for different charges in *both* military commissions and federal court. Wittes advanced this idea several months after publishing his "do nothing" thesis, arguing this method would "provide a valuable fail-safe against the possibility of total system failure. . . . Military commissions remain something less than ready for prime time, and federal court trials can go bad, too."[43] His optimism notwithstanding, there are unfortunately no true fail-safes since evidence derived from coercion could poison all the trials. Given the legal mess that the government has created and the fear of a precedent that would undermine the sanctity of the US legal system, however, this might be the best, if not the most satisfying, way to finish the job.

People whose hearts burn with the fires of jihad aren't automatically blessed with the know-how to produce mass destruction. As cases like 9/11, the Zazi affair, the 2005 London transit attack, and Operation Overt suggest, most complex attacks against Western targets are conceived, planned, and trained for by strategic-minded leaders and competent personnel. Meanwhile, untrained attackers tend to slip up because of ill-preparedness, general stupidity, and skittishness. For example, the 2010 Times Square bomber-wannabe left the keys to his getaway car in the car that he was going to detonate and, despite paying for the car in cash, used his actual name in the e-mail used to contact the car's seller.[44] In 2007, a British-Iraqi medical doctor, with the help of radicalized compatriots, tried to set off a series of vehicle-borne explosive devices in central London; they failed due to mechanical problems.

Without competent operational leaders like KSM, Rashid Rauf, or even Hizbollah's Imad Mughniyah, the planning and execution of complex attacks can be stopped by security services. In the future, the US will likely see more of these wild, relatively simple one-off attacks that are thwarted by poor planning and human error. They may still be lethal, but they will not be as catastrophic as a well-laid plan.

An invested, educated populace is essential to protect against attack. In *The Death and Life of Great American Cities,* Jane Jacobs wrote "the first thing to understand is that the public peace—the sidewalks and street peace—of cities is not kept primarily by the police, necessary as police are. It is kept primarily by an intricate, almost unconscious network of voluntary controls and standards among the people themselves, and enforced by the people themselves."[45] This analysis is as true in fighting terrorism as it is in fighting street crime; if regular citizens are invested in the upkeep of their society, then they can help thwart terrorism. Within walking distance of Jacobs's former home, a T-shirt vendor proved her theory; Lance Orton noticed a smoking SUV and alerted local cops, thereby blocking Faisal Shahzad's effort to blow up Times Square.[46]

To this effect, America should avoid scapegoating Muslims in a misguided attempt to damage the terrorist impulse, since it merely feeds al-Qaeda's narrative that the West is reflexively anti-Islam. If Islam does indeed drive violent behavior, or if none of the 1.5 billion Muslims in the world can be trusted, then the US is in an exceptionally dire security position. This is especially true, given that some of America's critical counterterrorism relationships—from Turkey to Jordan to Saudi Arabia to Iraq to Afghanistan to Pakistan to Indonesia—are with Muslim-majority nations. The US relies on these nations among many others for assistance in the fight against al-Qaeda and its extremist allies, and dismissing the countries' majorities because of their faith is reckless and ignorant.

Furthermore, Muslim Americans help identify individuals with a propensity for violent behavior cloaked in religious fervor. MI5 and Scotland Yard discovered this when British-Pakistani neighbors tipped off local cops to the Op Overt hideout. Closer to home, cops in Portland, Oregon, received a tip-off from within the Muslim community in November 2010 that thwarted a car bomb attack.[47]

It goes against smart national security precautions—not to mention a violation of American neighborliness—to marginalize citizens for their faith and cast them into the rhetorical and political darkness. To those who disagree with this sentiment, President George W. Bush responded, a week after the 9/11 attack:

> America counts millions of Muslims amongst our citizens, and Muslims make an incredibly valuable contribution to our country. Muslims are doctors, lawyers, law professors, members of the military, entrepreneurs, shopkeepers, moms and dads. And they need to be treated with respect. In our anger and emotion, our fellow Americans must treat each other with respect. . . . Those who feel like they can intimidate our fellow citizens to take out their anger don't represent the best of America, they represent the worst of humankind, and they should be ashamed of that kind of behavior.[48]

Only Americans have the power to destroy American civilization. America is a nation defined as much by its national mentality as by its borders. In this regard, decisions made by the American public and its elected leaders will advance or hinder the country. For all its technical prowess and good intentions, America can be its own worst enemy, as the largest threats to US security stem from overreaction to terrorist provocations. Terrorism—even WMD-enabled terrorism—will not cause the systemic destruction of American society. Extremists can blow up buildings, crash civilian airplanes, and kill scores of people, but they will not cause the downfall of a country of some 310 million citizens. It is, instead, the reactions to violent provocations that will undermine the American system of government, social structures, and way of life.

More often than not, regular police officers, customs officials, security guards, transit workers, and concerned citizens play critical roles in thwarting terrorism. Local Manila cops who responded to an apartment fire in 1995 apprehended a key player in the Bojinka case. Similarly, in 1999 alert customs officials in bucolic Port Angeles, Washington, helped apprehend Ahmed Ressam, an Algerian al-Qaeda member en route to attack Los Angeles International Airport.[49] In 2005 firefighters in Diyarbakir, Turkey, responding to an apartment fire found chemicals and explosives that eventually led to the capture of the Zarqawi-linked terrorist Luay Sakka, a ringleader in the lethal series of attacks in November in Istanbul that killed twenty-seven people, including the British consul general to Turkey.[50] Passengers on both Richard Reid's and Umar Farouk Abdulmutallab's flights tackled both men before they could destroy the aircraft.

Policymakers, legislators, and jurists all along the political spectrum will stumble and continue to make ill-advised choices in the nebulous fight against terrorism. Despite the efforts of hundreds of thousands of law enforcement officials, case officers, analysts, military personnel, customs officials, diplomats, and others, people with violent tendencies will attack civilian targets for political reasons. Some of them will succeed. But terrorists are not lurking behind every wall, around every corner, or up every tree. As John Brennan, Obama's deputy national security adviser for homeland security and counterterrorism, wrote in February 2010, "[Al-Qaeda does not] deserve the abject fear they seek to instill . . . and the notion that America's counterterrorism professionals and America's system of justice are unable to handle these murderous miscreants is absurd."[51]

The US has the tools at its disposal and the political will to grapple with and attack the murderous group called al-Qaeda. The true test will nevertheless come not from finding, fixing, or finishing the terrorist threat, but instead from the way we accomplish this goal. President John Adams quipped two centuries ago that government is "little better practiced now than three or four thousand years ago," and his deeply cynical insight may well be true.[52] It is, however, this system of government that offers the best chance of keeping America and Americans safe from the protean menace of terrorism.

In this imperfect vessel, for better or for worse, we place our trust.

ACKNOWLEDGMENTS

This book is the product of many people generously providing their time, expertise, and good humor. Certain individuals prefer to remain anonymous for personal and professional reasons, but they have our sincere thanks. We would like to thank our agent, Matthew Carnicelli, for his ability to navigate the choppy waters of the publishing world, as well as the hardworking folks at PublicAffairs who made this book possible: Clive Priddle, Jaime Leifer, Melissa Raymond, and Chrisona Schmidt. We gratefully acknowledge the assistance of Ingrid Gustafson and David Millar, who performed months of research in service of this publication.

We would also like to thank Spencer Ackerman, Dick Best, Dick Clarke, Jack Cloonan, Charles Cogan, Ken Dilanian, Senator Bob Graham, Jack Goldsmith, Senator Chuck Hagel, Blake Hall, Ishmael Jones, Eric Joyce, Nicholas Karnaze, Juliette Kayyem, John McLaughlin, Renny McPherson, David Mesrobian, Cameron Middleton, Heba Morayef, Rolf Mowatt-Larssen, John Paine, Piers Platt, Jessica Reitz, Richard Russell, and James Wolfe. Special thanks go to Mieke Eoyang, Matt Bennett, Sean Gibbons, Jill Pike, and Bill Rapp at Third Way for their support of this project.

Finally, I (Aki) would like to thank my wonderful wife, Dana, who stayed up night after night to edit draft upon draft of this book. Without her assistance and encouragement, *Find, Fix, Finish* would not have seen the light of day.

APPENDIX I:
LIST OF ACRONYMS

AFRICOM Africa Command

AQAP Al-Qaeda in the Arabian Peninsula

AQI Al-Qaeda in Iraq

AUMF Authorization for Use of Military Force

BSS British Security Service

CIA Central Intelligence Agency

COS Chief of Station

CSG Counterterrorism Security Group

CTC Counterterrorism Center

DCI Director of Central Intelligence

DEVGRU Naval Special Warfare Development Group

DHS Department of Homeland Security

DIA Defense Intelligence Agency

DITSUM Defense Intelligence Terrorism Summary

DNI Director of National Intelligence

EIJ Egyptian Islamic Jihad

EIT Enhanced Interrogation Technique

FBI Federal Bureau of Investigation

FISA Foreign Intelligence Surveillance Act

FM Field Manual

GCHQ Government Communications Headquarters

GID General Intelligence Department

HAMAS Harakat al-Muqāwamah al-Islamiyyah

HUMINT Human Intelligence

HVD High Value Detainee

HVT High Value Target

IC Intelligence Community

ICU Islamic Courts Union

IIS Iraqi Intelligence Service

IRA Irish Republican Army

IRTPA The Intelligence Reform and Terrorism Prevention Act

ISI Inter-Services Intelligence

JAG Judge Advocate General

JeM Jaish-e-Mohammed

JSOC Joint Special Operations Command

JTAC Joint Terrorism Analysis Centre

JTJ Jama'at a-Tawhid wa Jihad

JTTF Joint Terrorism Task Force

KSM Khalid Shaykh Mohammed

LeT Lashkar-e-Taiba

LIFG Libyan Islamic Fighting Group

MI5 Military Intelligence-5

MI6 Military Intelligence-6

MNF-I Multi-National Force–Iraq

MON Memorandum of Notification

NCA&T North Carolina Agricultural & Technical State University

NCTC National Counterterrorism Center

NIC National Intelligence Council

NIE National Intelligence Estimate

NRO National Reconnaissance Office

NSA National Security Agency

NSC National Security Council

NYPD New York Police Department

ODNI Office of the Director of National Intelligence

OIF Operation Iraqi Freedom

OLC Office of Legal Counsel

OSP Office of Special Plans

PCTEG Policy Counter Terrorism Evaluation Group

PDB President's Daily Brief

PDD Presidential Decision Directive

QJBR Tanzim Qa'idat al-Jihad Fi Bilad al-Rafidayn

SAR Synthetic Aperture Radar

SCIF Sensitive Compartmented Information Facility

SCIRI The Supreme Council for the Islamic Revolution in Iraq

SDR Surveillance Detection Route

SEAL Sea, Air, and Land Teams

SF Special Forces

SIGINT Signals Intelligence

SIS Secret Intelligence Service

SOCOM Special Operations Command

SOF Special Operations Forces

SSCI Senate Select Committee on Intelligence

SSE Sensitive Site Exploitation

TATP Triacetone Triperoxide

TFG Transitional Federal Government

TTP Tehrik-e-Taliban Pakistan

TTP Tactics, Techniques, and Procedures

UAV Unmanned Aerial Vehicle

UCMJ Uniform Code of Military Justice

UNSC United Nations Security Council

USA-PATRIOT Act Uniting and Strengthening America by Providing
    Appropriate Tools Required to Intercept and Obstruct Terrorism Act

WMD Weapons of Mass Destruction

APPENDIX II:
IBN SHAYKH AL-LIBI TIMELINE

- September 11, 2001—Al-Qaeda attacks NYC and Washington DC
- September 20, 2001—President Bush declares "war on terror"
- October 2001—US-led coalition invades Afghanistan
- October 2001—USA-PATRIOT Act passes Congress
- November 2001—Al-Libi is captured in Pakistan
- December 2001—Pakistan turns al-Libi over to US at Kandahar air base
- December 2001—Al-Libi is transferred to Bagram air base
- January 2002—The CIA transfers al-Libi to the USS *Bataan*
- Late January 2002—The CIA transfers al-Libi to Egyptian custody
- Late January 2002–February 2002—Al-Libi provides information that al-Qaeda agents traveled to Iraq for training
- February 2002—The DIA publishes DITSUM 044–02, which casts doubt on the truth of al-Libi's testimony
- March 2002—The CIA establishes the first "black sites"
- Summer 2002—Support builds for the Iraq War
- August 1, 2002—John Yoo writes the "torture memo"
- September 2002—The CIA's *Iraqi Support for Terrorism Report* casts doubts on al-Libi's statements
- September 2002—DCI Tenet and National Security Adviser Rice use al-Libi's statements as proof of an Iraq-al-Qaeda link in testimony
- September 2002—Undersecretary of Defense Feith and Deputy Secretary of Defense Wolfowitz found the Office of Special Plans
- October 1, 2002—The IC delivers the Iraq NIE to Congress

- October 7, 2002—Bush references al-Libi's testimony in his Cincinnati speech
- October 10, 2002—Congress authorizes the use of military force against Iraq
- November 8, 2002—The UNSC releases Resolution 1441, which claims that Iraq is in breach of cease-fire agreements
- January 2003—The CIA's *Iraqi Support for Terrorism* report is updated and more broadly disseminated
- February 5, 2003—Secretary of State Powell presents the US case for war with Iraq to the UN
- Early 2003—Egypt returns al-Libi to US custody; he is reportedly detained in Afghanistan
- March 19, 2003—Operation Iraqi Freedom begins
- June 2003—The Office of Special Plans is dissolved
- October 2003—Undersecretary Feith sends *Summary of Body of Intelligence on Iraq–Al-Qaeda Contacts,* which references al-Libi's testimony, to members of Congress
- January 2004—Al-Libi recants his testimony and alleges torture by the Egyptians
- February 2004—Al-Libi is reportedly transferred to Guantanamo Bay, Cuba; CIA learns of his recantation
- February 2004—Senior administration officials learn of al-Libi's recantation
- April 2004—News of abuse at Abu Ghraib breaks
- June 2004—In an interview with CNBC, Vice President Cheney argues that an al-Qaeda–Iraq connection exists
- June 2004—The torture memo is leaked to the press; CIA suspends the use of enhanced interrogation techniques
- July 2004—The media first publishes accounts of al-Libi's recantation
- July 9, 2004—The SSCI releases its first assessment of prewar intelligence on Iraq
- September 2004—The Iraq Survey Group concludes that Iraq did not have an active WMD program
- October 2005—DITSUM 044–02 is declassified
- Early 2006—The US transfers al-Libi to Libyan custody

- September 6, 2006—President Bush orders the CIA to transfer fourteen HVDs from black sites to Guantanamo Bay
- September 8, 2006—The SSCI releases its Phase II reports, which include descriptions of al-Libi's recantation and harsh interrogation
- November 2006—The Democrats gain a congressional majority in the midterm elections
- February 9. 2007—The Pentagon's inspector general releases a report on the Office of Special Plans that finds the organization's work "inappropriate"
- May 24, 2007—Four members of Congress request information on al-Libi's whereabouts from President Bush
- November 2008—Democrat Barack Obama is elected president
- January 2009—President Obama signs executive orders shutting down Guantanamo and all CIA black sites
- May 11, 2009—Al-Libi reportedly commits suicide in Libyan custody

APPENDIX III:
TARGETED FLIGHTS

The targeted flights for Op Overt plotters were:

1. 1415 UA931 LONDON-SAN FRANCISCO (United Airlines)
2. 1500 AC849 LONDON-TORONTO (Air Canada)
3. 1515 AC865 LONDON-MONTREAL (Air Canada)
4. 1540 UA959 LONDON-CHICAGO (United Airlines)
5. 1620 UA925 LONDON-WASHINGTON (United Airlines)
6. 1635 AA131 LONDON-NEW YORK (American Airlines)
7. 1650 AA91 LONDON-CHICAGO (American)[1]

British authorities found this information on a USB drive.

APPENDIX IV:
POSSIBLE TARGETS

Other Possible Targets for Op Overt plotters:

1. Canary Wharf
2. The national grid
3. A gas pipeline between Britain and Belgium
4. UK airports, including Heathrow's new control tower
5. Oil and gas refineries at Bacton, Fawley, Correton, and Kingsbury
6. Several UK power plants, including nuclear stations
7. Companies that store and process hydrogen peroxide[2]

APPENDIX:
PUPPET THEATER

NOTES

CHAPTER 1: FIRE FROM THE SKY

1. Declan Walsh, "Air Strike Kills Taliban Leader Baitullah Mehsud," *Guardian*, August 7, 2009; Peter Bergen and Katherine Tiedemann, *Revenge of the Drones: An Analysis of Drone Strikes in Pakistan*, New America Foundation, October 19, 2009.

2. Jane Mayer, "The Predator War," *New Yorker*, October 26, 2009; Joby Warrick, "CIA Places Blame for Bhutto Assassination," *Washington Post*, January 18, 2008.

3. Mayer, "Predator War."

4. "Obama: 'We Took Out' Pakistani Taliban Chief," Reuters, August 21, 2009.

5. Joby Warrick, Josh Partlow, and Haq Nawaz Khan, "A Psychological Blow to Pakistani Taliban," *Washington Post*, August 8, 2009.

6. Ibid.

7. US Department of State, "Rewards for Justice: Baitullah Mehsud," March 25, 2009.

8. Matthew B. Ridgeway, *The Korean War* (Garden City, NY: Da Capo Press, 1967), 89.

9. Michael Hayden, "Intelligence in the 21st Century," *Air Force Speeches,* June 19, 2007.

10. James R. Clapper Jr., "Intelligence Transformation: Meeting New Challenges in the Middle East and Beyond" (address presented to the Washington Institute, Washington DC, May 19, 2009).

11. Dana Priest, "Foreign Network at Front of CIA's Terror Fight," *Washington Post*, November 18, 2005.

12. "CIA Pays for Support in Pakistan," *Los Angeles Times*, November 15, 2009.

13. Dana Priest and Ann Scott Tyson, "Bin Laden Trail 'Stone Cold,'" *Washington Post,* September 10, 2006.

14. George Tenet, *At the Center of the Storm* (New York: HarperCollins, 2007), 254.

15. Elizabeth Bumiller, "Later Terror Link Cited for 1 in 7 Freed Detainees," *New York Times*, May 20, 2009.

16. Rolf Mowatt-Larssen, *Al Qaeda Weapons of Mass Destruction Threat: Hype or Reality?* Belfer Center for Science and International Affairs, Harvard Kennedy School, January 2010.

17. Ibid., 1.

18. Alexander Mooney, "Obama Says Time to Rid World of Nuclear Weapons," CNN, July 16, 2008.

CHAPTER 2: ATROPHY

1. *9/11 Commission Report: Final Report of the National Commission on Terrorist Attacks Upon the United States* (Washington, DC: US Government Printing Office, 2004), 131.

2. Ibid.

3. From August 1998 until July 1999, President Clinton signed a series of memorandums of notification (MON) authorizing the CIA, the CIA's tribal assets, and later the Northern Alliance to run capture and kill operations against bin Laden.

4. See the 9/11 Commission report for further explanation. In 1998, director of central intelligence George Tenet canceled a capture plan that was opposed by Richard Clarke, chair of the NSC's Counterterrorism Security Group, and national security adviser Sandy Berger. In August 1998, members of the Office of the Secretary of Defense opposed follow-on strikes. In 1999, all principals struck down a cruise missile proposal. Clarke stood in the way of U2 flights over Afghanistan in 1999. CENTCOM commander general Anthony Zinni halted a proposal to deploy AC-130 gunships in 1999. That same year, both Clarke and Tenet opposed a plan to target bin Laden in fear that it could also strike representatives of the United Arab Emirates (UAE). It is unclear whether the "best chance" strike on bin Laden in 1999 was canceled by Tenet or the Pentagon. CIA leadership would halt all of the Agency's own plans until 2001.

5. *9/11 Commission Report,* 115.

6. *9/11 Commission Report,* 112–113.

7. "Military Bases That U.S. Could Use," Associated Press, September 26, 2001.

8. Christopher O'Sullivan, *Colin Powell: American Power and Intervention from Vietnam to Iraq* (Lanham, MD: Rowman & Littlefield, 2009), 60.

9. Barbara Slavin, "Threats Blurred for U.S. After Cold War," *Washington Times,* November 9, 2009.

10. Richard Clarke, *Against All Enemies: Inside America's War on Terror* (New York: Free Press, 2004), 74.

11. *9/11 Commission Report,* 105–107.

12. John Goldman, "Yousef, Driver Guilty in Trade Center Bombing," *Los Angeles Times,* November 13, 1997.

13. Clarke, *Against All Enemies,* 78.

14. "Missed Signals: Many Say U.S. Planned for Terror but Failed to Take Action," *New York Times,* December 30, 2001.

15. *The CIA: History and Performance,* interview with R. James Woolsey, June 20, 2006, www.pbs.org/wgbh/pages/frontline/darkside/themes/cia.html.

16. *Terrorism Project, In the Spotlight: Aum Shinrikyo,* Center for Defense Studies, July 23, 2002; William Broad, "Sowing Death: How Japan Germ Terror Alerted World," *New York Times,* May 26, 1998.

17. William Clinton, Presidential Decision Directive 39, June 21, 1995.

18. Ibid.

19. John Deutch, "Worldwide Threat Assessment Brief to the Senate Select Committee on Intelligence by the Director of Central Intelligence," February 22, 1996, www.cia.gov/news-information/speeches-testimony/1996/dci_speech_022296.html.

20. Richard Clarke, *Your Government Failed You: Breaking the Cycle of National Security Disasters* (New York: Harper Perennial, 2009), 158.

21. William Clinton, Statement on Signing the Antiterrorism and Effective Death Penalty Act of 1996, April 24, 1996, www.presidency.ucsb.edu/ws/index.php?pid=527 13#axzz1cVMxVsde.

22. William Clinton, PDD 62, May 22, 1998.

23. Ibid.

24. Gary Berntsen and Ralph Pezzullo, *Jawbreaker: The Attack on Bin Laden and Al-Qaeda by the CIA's Key Field Commander* (New York: Three Rivers, 2006).

25. Farhan Haq, "Politics-U.N.: Sudan, Afghanistan Struggle for Response to Attacks," Inter Press Service.

26. James Risen, "To Bomb Sudan Plant, or Not: A Year Later, Debates Rankle," *New York Times,* October 27, 1999.

27. "A Question of Credibility," *Economist,* September 8, 1998.

28. Byron York, "The Facts About Clinton and Terrorism," *National Review Online,* September 11, 2006.

29. *9/11 Commission Report,* 213.

30. Richard Miniter, *Losing Bin Laden: How Bill Clinton's Failures Unleashed Global Terror* (Washington, DC: Regnery, 2003), 222–227.

31. Ted Bridis, "Before 9–11, Terror Was a Low Priority," Associated Press, June 29, 2002.

32. Condoleezza Rice, "Campaign 2000: Promoting the National Interest," *Foreign Affairs,* January–February 2010.

33. Daniel Benjamin and Steven Simon, *The Age of Sacred Terror: Radical Islam's War Against America* (New York: Random House, 2003), 336.

34. Jim Mann, "Post–Cold War CIA Fighting for Its Future," *Los Angeles Times,* January 3, 1993.

35. George Tenet, "Written Statement for the Record of the Director of Central Intelligence Before the National Commission on Terrorist Attacks Upon the United States," March 24, 2004.

36. Tenet, *At the Center of the Storm,* 15.

37. Robert Dreyfuss, "Orbit of Influence: Spy Finance and the Black Budget," *American Prospect,* March 1, 1996.

38. Douglas Jehl, "Campaign Is Begun to Protect Money for Spy Agencies," *New York Times,* March 14, 1993; Walter Pincus, "Spy Agency Hoards Secret $1 Billion; Satellite Managers Did Not Tell Supervisors Of Classified 'Pot of Gold,' Hill Sources Say," *Washington Post,* September 24, 1995.

39. Elaine Sciolino, "Clinton Offering Few Hints of His Plans for Spy Agency, *New York Times,* November 29, 1992.

40. *Phase III Report: Road Map for National Security: Imperative for Change,* United States Commission on National Security/21st Century, February 15, 2001.

41. Walter Pincus, "CIA Plans to Close 15 Stations in African Pullback," *Washington Post,* June 23, 1994.

42. *9/11 Commission Report,* 357.

43. Tenet, *At the Center of the Storm.*

44. David Kaplan, "Playing Offense in the War on Terror," USNews.com, June 2, 2003.

45. Steve Coll, *Ghost Wars* (New York: Penguin, 2004), 456.

46. Robert Baer, "A Dagger to the CIA," *Gentlemen's Quarterly,* April 2010.

47. Clarke, *Your Government Failed You*, 107.

48. Tenet, *At the Center of the Storm*, 15.

49. *9/11 Commission Report*, 133.

50. Ibid.

51. Coll, *Ghost Wars*,

52. *9/11 Commission Report*, 211.

53. Coll, *Ghost Wars*, 550.

54. Tenet, *At the Center of the Storm*; *9/11 Commission Report*.

55. Coll, *Ghost Wars*, 550.

56. *9/11 Commission Report*, Staff Statement 9.

57. Khalid al-Midhar and Nawaf al-Hazmi were two of the nineteen terrorist hijackers in the 9/11 attacks. Zacarias Moussaoui, though he had trained to be a pilot, did not participate in the attacks and is now serving a life sentence in Florence, Colorado's federal ADX supermax prison, for conspiring to kill US citizens.

58. Attorney General John Ashcroft, testimony to the National Commission on Terrorist Attacks on the United States, April 13, 2004.

59. *9/11 Commission Report*, Staff Statement, 9.

60. Kelly Moore, "The Role of Federal Criminal Prosecutions in the War on Terrorism," *Lewis and Clark Law Review* 11, no. 4 (2007).

61. *9/11 Commission Report*, 76.

62. *9/11 Commission Report*, Staff Statement, 9.

63. Ibid.

64. Eric Lichtblau, "Threats and Responses: The Former FBI Director; Tough Security Questions Are Likely for Ex-Chief of FBI," *New York Times*, April 13, 2004.

65. Richard Schmitt, "FBI's Computer Upgrade Develops Its Own Glitches," *Los Angeles Times*, January 28, 2003.

66. Clarke, *Against All Enemies*.

67. Richard Shultz, "Nine Reasons Why We Never Sent Our Special Operations Forces After al-Qaeda Before 9/11," *Weekly Standard*, January 16, 2004.

68. *9/11 Commission Report*, 120.

69. Richard Myers, testimony to the National Commission on Terrorist Attacks on the United States, June 17, 2004.

70. Shultz, "Nine Reasons."

71. Ibid.

72. Edward F. Bruner, Christopher Bolkcom, and Ronald O'Rourke, "Special Operations Forces in Operation Enduring Freedom: Background and Issues for Congress," *Congressional Research Service Report*, October 15, 2001.

73. *9/11 Commission Report*, 98.

74. Ibid.

75. Richard Shultz Jr., "How Clinton Let Al-Qaeda Go," *Weekly Standard*, January 19, 2004.

76. "Presidential Approval and Reporting of Covert Actions," Title 50, Chap. 15, Subchapter III, Sec. 413b, www.law.cornell.edu/uscode/50/usc_sec_50_00000413 —b000-.html.

77. Shultz, "How Clinton Let Al-Qaeda Go."

78. Ibid.

79. Thomas Henriksen, *The Israeli Approach to Irregular Warfare and Implications for the United States,* Joint Special Operations University Report 07–3, 2007.

80. *9/11 Commission Report,* 189.

81. Shultz, "How Clinton Let Al-Qaeda Go."

82. *9/11 Commission Report,* 351.

CHAPTER 3: THE SEARCH FOR MR. #3

1. Interview by author, September 22, 2011.

2. Ibid.

3. Tom Daschle, "Power We Didn't Grant," *Washington Post,* December 23, 2005.

4. Tenet, *At the Center of the Storm,* 157; "Iron Fist Reaches from Far Side of the Globe," *Australian,* November 19, 2001; Daniel McGrory, "'Bear' May Lead to bin Laden," *Times of London,* June 20, 2002; Mubashir Zaidi, Paul Watson, and Josh Meyer, "Bin Laden Aide Held in Pakistan," *Los Angeles Times,* May 5, 2005; Ian Bruce, "MI6 to Interview al-Qaeda Suspect Held in Pakistan," *Herald (Glasgow),* May 6, 2005; Rana Jawad, "Pakistan Hunts Two Top al-Qaeda Masterminds," Agence France Presse, August 6, 2004; Pervez Musharraf, *In the Line of Fire: A Memoir* (New York: Free Press, 2008), 258–260.

5. Khaled Dawoud, "Mohammed Atef: Egyptian Militant Who Rose to the Top of the al-Qaida Hierarchy," *Guardian,* November 19, 2001.

6. Ibid.

7. Jean Sasson, Najwa bin Laden, and Omar bin Laden, *Growing Up bin Laden* (New York: St. Martin's, 2009), 162.

8. "Atef Linked by Terrorism and Blood to bin Laden," Agence France Presse, November 16, 2001.

9. Peter Bergen, *The Osama bin Laden I Know: An Oral History of al-Qaeda's Leader* (New York: Free Press, 2006), 211.

10. Dawoud, "Mohammed Atef."

11. Ibid.

12. Ibid.

13. "Atef Linked by Terrorism."

14. Dawoud, "Mohammed Atef"; Bergen, *Osama bin Laden,* 211; Michael S. James, "Atef Death Would Be a Major Blow," ABC News Online, November 17, 2001.

15. "Atef Linked by Terrorism"; Dawoud, "Mohammed Atef"; Bergen, *Osama bin Laden,* 255; Abdel Bari Atwan, *The Secret History of al-Qaeda,* 2nd ed. (Berkeley: University of California Press, 2008), 49.

16. Bergen, *Osama bin Laden,* 118, 255, 285.

17. "Atef Linked by Terrorism."

18. John Sullivan, "Al-Qaeda Terrorist Duped FBI, Army," *Raleigh News and Observer,* October 12, 2001.

19. Bergen, *Osama bin Laden,* 241.

20. *9/11 Commission Report,* 153.

21. Bergen, *Osama bin Laden,* 237.

22. "Analysis: Al-Qa'ida Military Training on the Internet," *Al-Sharq al-Awsat,* February 16, 2002; Bergen, *Osama bin Laden,* 237.

23. Bergen, *Osama bin Laden,* 237.

24. Judith Miller and Eric Schmitt, "A Nation Challenged: The Battle; Ugly Duckling Turns Out to Be Formidable in the Air," *New York Times,* November 23, 2001; "Iron Fist Reaches from Far Side of the Globe," *Australian,* November 19, 2001.

25. Ian Gallagher, "We've Got Bin Laden Cornered Says US," *The Mail (London),* November 18, 2001.

26. Miller and Schmitt, "A Nation Challenged."

27. Miller and Schmitt, "A Nation Challenged"; David Martin, "Secretary of War: Donald Rumsfeld's Role in Planning and Executing the Battle Against Terrorism and the Hunt for bin Laden," *60 Minutes II,* November 21, 2001.

28. "Iron Fist Reaches."

29. George Tenet, "Written Statement for the Record of the Director of Central Intelligence Before the National Commission on Terrorist Attacks Upon the United States," March 24, 2004; "Key Bin Laden Helper Reported Struck Down, Killed by US Air Strike," Associated Press, November 19, 2001.

30. "Afghan Battles; Observing Islam; Political Wrap," *NewsHour with Jim Lehrer,* November 16, 2001; John Stufflebeem, US DOD News Briefing, November 19, 2001.

31. "Afghan Battles"; Jim Mannion, "US Forces Believed to Have Killed Bin Laden Deputy: US Officials," Agence France Presse, November 16, 2001.

32. Damon Johnston, "Osama's Man in Deadly Betrayal; Deputy Killed in Air Raid," *Sunday Herald Sun,* November 18, 2001; "Iron Fist Reaches."

33. John Stufflebeem, US DOD News Briefing, November 19, 2001; "Reports Suggest al-Qaeda Military Chief Killed," CNN, November 17, 2001.

34. "Iron Fist Reaches."

35. "Iron Fist Reaches"; Gary Berntsen, *Jawbreaker: The Attack on Bin Laden and al-Qaeda* (New York: Three Rivers Press, 2006), 206.

36. Taliban Confirm Death of Top bin Laden Aide," Agence France Press, November 18, 2001.

37. Chuck Murphy, "If He's Dead, Then Why Is He Wanted?" *St. Petersburg Times,* January 3, 2002.

38. Ian Gallagher, "SAS Hunt bin Laden in Caves and Tunnels," *Courier Mail,* November 19, 2001; Ian Gallagher, "We've Got Bin Laden Cornered Says US," *Mail of London,* November 18, 2001.

39. Kathy Gannon, "Former Taliban Official Told US in 1999 That al-Qaida Had Taken Over Afghan Movement," Associated Press, June 9, 2002; Gannon, "Road Rage: Marauding Taliban and Drug-Dealing Warlords on the Road to Kandahar," *New Yorker,* March 22, 2004.

40. Berntsen, *Jawbreaker,* 118; Hugh Barnes, "Rumors of Taliban Minister's Defection Raises Coalition Hopes," Agence France Presse, November 15, 2001; Griff Witte, "Taliban Defector Is Assassinated," *Washington Post,* January 15, 2006; Peter Baker, "Defector Says Bin Laden Had Cash, Taliban in His Pocket," *Washington Post,* November 30, 2001.

41. Tim McGirk, "The Man the CIA Won't Question," *Time,* February 25, 2002.

42. Peter Bergen, "The Battle for Tora Bora," *New Republic,* December 22, 2009.

43. Hamid Mir, "The Osama bin Laden I Knew," *News International (Pakistan),* May 3, 2011.

44. Jonathan Mahler, *The Challenge* (New York: Farrar, Straus & Giroux, 2008), 30–31.

45. R. Jeffrey Smith and Dan Eggen, "Gonzales Helped Set the Course for Detainees," *Washington Post,* January 5, 2005.

46. Ibid.

47. Interview by author, September 22, 2011.

48. Ibid.

49. Anthony Shadid, "Fighting Terror/Kidnapping Victim; US Falling Short of Its War Goals, Officials Concede Qaeda Elusiveness," *Boston Globe,* February 21, 2002.

50. Juan O. Tamayo, "War on Terror Unfinished As Targets Move; Decisive Victories Remain Elusive," *Miami Herald,* September 9, 2002.

51. Ibid.

52. Ibid.

53. James Risen and Dexter Filkins, "Threats and Responses: Slippery Foe; Qaeda Fighters Said to Return to Afghanistan," *New York Times,* September 10, 2002.

54. "Al-Qaeda's New Military Chief," BBC News, December 19, 2001; "Officials, Documents Detail the Big Fish Besides bin Laden," Associated Press, December 18, 2001.

55. Dan Eggen and Michael Dobbs, "Danger Persists After Hobbling of al-Qaeda," *Washington Post,* January 14, 2002; Mary Anne Weaver, *Pakistan: Deep Inside the World's Most Frightening State* (New York: Farrar, Straus & Giroux, 2003); Eric Schmitt and Erik Eckholm, "A Nation Challenged: The Hunted; US Takes Custody of a Qaeda Trainer Seized by Pakistan," *New York Times,* January 6, 2002; Philip Shenon, "A Nation Challenged: Bin Laden's Network; A Qaeda Leader Is Reported to Plan New Raids on US," *New York Times,* February 14, 2002.

56. Jane Mayer, *The Dark Side: The Inside Story of How the War on Terror Turned into a War on American Ideals* (New York: Anchor, 2009), 139–143; Peter Finn and Joby Warrick, "Detainee's Harsh Treatment Foiled No Plots," *Washington Post,* March 29, 2009.

57. Finn and Warrick, "Detainee's Harsh Treatment."

58. "Biographies of High Value Terrorist Detainees Transferred to the US Naval Base at Guantanamo Bay," Office of the Director of National Intelligence (ODNI) website, September 6, 2006.

59. Ibid.; Verbatim Transcript of Combatant Status Review Tribunal Hearing for ISN 10016 (Zayn al Abidin Muhammad Husayn), US Naval Base Guantanamo Bay, Cuba, March 27, 2007.

60. Tenet, "Written Statement," 145.

61. "Profile: Abu Zubaydah," *New York Times,* April 20, 2009; Memorandum for John Rizzo, Acting General Counsel of the Central Intelligence Agency (Declassified), August 1, 2002.

62. James Risen, "A Nation Challenged: The Terror Network; Bombs Have Killed 3 Qaeda Leaders, US Now Believes," *New York Times,* December 13, 2001; "The Hunt for Osama bin Laden," *New York Times,* December 18, 2001.

63. Risen, "A Nation Challenged"; Stewart Bell, "'The Next bin Laden Under Arrest: Al-Qaeda's Chief Recruiter," *National Post (Canada),* April 3, 2002; "To Catch a Terrorist," *Boston Globe,* April 3, 2002.

64. Risen, "A Nation Challenged"; Jelinek, "Rumsfeld Denies Torture Rumors," Associated Press, April 3, 2002; Kevin Johnson, "Al-Qaeda Figure a 'Huge' Catch," *USA Today*, April 2, 2002.

65. "Profile: Abu Zubaydah," BBC, April 2, 2002; "Al-Qaeda Figure."

66. Finn and Warrick, "Detainee's Harsh Treatment"; Tenet, "Written Statement," 146, 240.

67. Finn and Warrick, "Detainee's Harsh Treatment"; Peter Finn and Julie Tate, "CIA Mistaken on 'High Value' Detainee, Document Shows," *Washington Post*, June 16, 2009; Scott Shane, "Divisions Arose on Rough Tactics for Qaeda Figure," *New York Times*, April 17, 2009.

68. Dan Eggen and Walter Pincus. "FBI, CIA Debate Significance of Terror Suspect," *Washington Post*, December 18, 2007; Mayer, *Dark Side*, 139–143.

69. Michael R. Gordon, "A Nation Challenged: Bin Laden Lieutenant; A Top Qaeda Commander Believed Seized in Pakistan," *New York Times*, March 31, 2002.

70. John Kiriakou, *The Reluctant Spy: My Secret Life in the CIA* (New York: Bantam, 2002), 107.

71. Tenet, "Written Statement," 240.

72. "A Master Terrorist Is Nabbed," *New York Times*, April 6, 2002.

73. The details of the raid come primarily from an account written by the lead CIA operations officer in Pakistan at the time and is generally corroborated by other accounts.

74. Mayer, *Dark Side*, 139–143.

75. Kiriakou, *Reluctant Spy*.

76. Ibid.

77. Ibid.

78. Ibid.

79. Ibid.

80. Kiriakou, *Reluctant Spy*; Gordon, "A Nation Challenged."

81. Kiriakou, *Reluctant Spy*.

82. Ibid.

83. Ibid.

84. Tenet, "Written Statement," 240.

85. "Al-Qaeda Leaders Held at British Base," *Mail on Sunday*, July 7, 2002; James Risen, *State of War: The Secret History of the CIA and the Bush Administration* (New York: Free Press, 2006), 21.

86. Kiriakou, *Reluctant Spy*, 132.

87. Tenet, "Written Statement," 242.

88. Ali Soufan, "My Tortured Decision," *New York Times*, April 22, 2009.

89. Ronald Kessler, *The Terrorist Watch: Inside the Desperate Race to Stop the Next Attack* (New York: Crown, 2007), 46–48; "Summary of the High Value Terrorist Detainee Program," Office of the Director of National Intelligence, September 6, 2006.

90. David Alexander, "CIA Briefed 68 Lawmakers on Interrogation Program," Reuters, February 23, 2010.

91. "Summary of the High Value Terrorist Detainee Program," Office of the Director of National Intelligence, September 6, 2006, www.odni.gov/press_releases_2006.htm.

92. Judith Miller and Philip Shenon, "A Nation Challenged: Plots; Qaeda Leader in US Custody Provokes Alert," *New York Times*, April 20, 2002.

93. Dan Eggen and Walter Pincus, "FBI, CIA Debate Significance of Terror Suspect," *Washington Post*, December 18, 2007.

94. McGrory, "Bear."

95. Ronald Kessler, *The Terrorist Watch: Inside the Desperate Race to Stop the Next Attack* (New York: Crown, 2007), 46–48; "Summary of the High Value Terrorist Detainee Program."

96. Memorandum for John Rizzo, Acting General Counsel of the Central Intelligence Agency (Declassified), August 1, 2002.

97. "Summary of the High Value Terrorist Detainee Program."

98. Finn and Warrick, "Detainee's Harsh Treatment"; Mayer, *Dark Side*, 141–144.

99. David Johnston, "At a Secret Interrogation, Dispute Flared over Tactics," *New York Times*, September 10, 2006.

100. "Profile: Abu Zubaydah," *New York Times*, April 20, 2009.

101. Scott Shane, "Waterboarding Used 266 Times on 2 Suspects," *New York Times*, April 19, 2009.

102. "Summary of the High Value Terrorist Detainee Program."

103. Jelinek, "Rumsfeld Denies Torture Rumors."

104. Alexander, "CIA Briefed 68 Lawmakers"; "Summary of the High Value Terrorist Detainee Program."

105. Mark Mazzetti, "CIA Destroyed 2 Tapes Showing Interrogations," *New York Times*, December 7, 2007.

106. Johnston, "At a Secret Interrogation"; Testimony of John E. Cloonan, Retired FBI Special Agent, before the Senate Committee on the Judiciary, June 10, 2008, http://judiciary.senate.gov/hearings/testimony.cfm?id=3399&wit_id=7228.

107. Ali Soufan, "My Tortured Decision," *New York Times*, April 22, 2009.

108. Scott Shane, "Divisions Arose on Rough Tactics for Qaeda Figure," *New York Times*, April 17, 2009; Finn and Warrick, "Detainee's Harsh Treatment."

109. Shane, "Divisions."

110. Finn and Warrick, "Detainee's Harsh Treatment"; "At a Secret Interrogation, Dispute Flared over Tactics"; Shane, "Waterboarding"; Tenet, "Written Statement," 146, 243; Mayer, *Dark Side*, 175–176; "Summary of the High Value Terrorist Detainee Program."

111. Jeremy Kahn, "The Next al-Qaeda? Terror Group Lashkar-e-Taiba Is Now Focusing on Foreigners and the West," *Newsweek*, March 8, 2010.

112. Ibid.

113. Mayer, *Dark Side,* 141.

114. "Biographies of High Value Terrorist Detainees."

115. "Al-Qaeda's Number-Three Leader Now in Pakistani Custody," *All Things Considered*, May 4, 2005.

116. "Biographies of High Value Terrorist Detainees"; "Summary of Evidence for Combatant Status Review Tribunal—Al Libi, Abu Faraj," United States Department of Defense, February 8, 2007.

117. Musharraf, *In the Line of Fire,* 258.

118. "Summary of Evidence for Combatant Status Review Tribunal."

119. Ibid.; Transcript of Open Session Combatant Status Review Tribunal Hearing for ISN 10017, March 9, 2007, www.defense.gov/news/transcript_ISN10017.pdf.

120. "Biographies of High Value Terrorist Detainees"; "Al-Qaeda's Number-Three Leader."

121. "Biographies of High Value Terrorist Detainees."

122. Paul Watson and Ken Silverstein, "Senior Leader of al-Qaeda Is Killed in Blast," *Los Angeles Times*, December 4, 2005.

123. Robert Windrem, "Hunt on for bin Laden's Latest No. 3 Man," MSNBC, September 7, 2004.

124. Rana Jawad, "Distinctive Skin Blew al-Qaeda Man's Cover," *Courier Mail (Australia)*, May 6, 2005.

125. Musharraf, *In the Line of Fire*, 253; Somini Sengupta, "Pakistan Reports Arrest of a Senior Qaeda Leader," *New York Times*, May 5, 2005.

126. Kamran Khan and John Lancaster, "Top al-Qaeda Figure Is Held in Pakistan," *Washington Post*, May 5, 2005.

127. Musharraf, *In the Line of Fire*, 253, 255; "Libyan al-Qaeda Mastermind Eluded Hot Chase for Two Years," Agence France Presse, May 4, 2005.

128. Musharraf, *In the Line of Fire*, 241–242; "Libyan al-Qaeda Mastermind"; Paul Haven, "Senior al-Qaeda Suspect Arrested in United Arab Emerates, Flown to Pakistan for Interrogation," Associated Press, August 8, 2004.

129. Rana Jawad, "Pakistan Hunts Two Top al-Qaeda Masterminds," Agence France Presse, August 6, 2004.

130. Musharraf, *In the Line of Fire*, 255–256; "Al-Qaeda's Number-Three Leader"; "Biographies of High Value Terrorist Detainees"; "Hunt on for bin Laden's Latest No. 3 Man."

131. Musharraf, *In the Line of Fire*, 258–260.

132. Ibid.

133. Ibid.

134. Ibid.; Somini Sengupta, "Pakistan Reports Arrest of a Senior Qaeda Leader," *New York Times*, May 5, 2005.

135. Musharraf, *In the Line of Fire*, 256.

136. "Al-Qaeda's Number-Three Leader"; "Pakistan Seizes al-Qaeda no. 3," CNN.com, May 4, 2005; Kamran Khan and John Lancaster, "Top al-Qaeda Figure Is Held in Pakistan," *Washington Post*, May 5, 2005.

137. Khan and Lancaster, "Top al-Qaeda Figure."

138. Mubashir Zaidi, Paul Watson, and Josh Meyer, "Bin Laden Aide Held in Pakistan," *Los Angeles Times*, May 5, 2005.

139. Daniel McGrory, "Bin Laden Aide Had 10-Strong British Cell," *Times (London)*, May 6, 2005.

140. Khan and Lancaster, "Top al-Qaeda Figure."

141. Musharraf, *In the Line of Fire*, 221.

142. Massoud Ansari, "Truth Drug Fails to Get al-Qaeda No. 3 to Talk," *Sunday Telegraph (London)*, May 8, 2005.

143. Ian Bruce, "MI6 to Interview al-Qaeda Suspect Held in Pakistan," *The Herald*, May 6, 2005.

144. Khan and Lancaster, "Top al-Qaeda Figure."

CHAPTER 4: THE FINISHING NEVER ENDS

1. "Khalid Shaykh Muhammad: Preeminent Source on Al-Qa'ida," Central Intelligence Agency Intelligence Assessment, July 13, 2004, 6.

2. Ibid.

3. Ibid.

4. Lawrence Wright, *The Looming Tower. Al-Qaeda and the Road to 9/11* (New York: Knopf, 2006), 100.

5. Ibid.

6. Steve Coll, *Ghost Wars* (New York: Penguin, 2004), 248; "Khalid Shaykh Muhammad: Preeminent Source on Al-Qa'ida."

7. *Ghost Wars,* 327.

8. *9/11 Commission Report,* 154.

9. Ibid.

10. Ibid., 149.

11. Ibid., 155.

12. Ibid.

13. "Khalid Shaykh Muhammad: Preeminent Source on Al-Qa'ida," 7.

14. Musharraf, *In the Line of Fire*, 240.

15. "Detainee Reporting Pivotal for the War Against Al Qa'ida," Central Intelligence Agency Intelligence Assessment, June 3, 2005, ii.

16. "Khalid Shaykh Muhammad: Preeminent Source on Al-Qa'ida," 8.

17. Yosri Fouda and Nick Fielding, *Masterminds of Terror* (New York: Arcade, 2003), 38.

18. Scott Shane, "Inside a 9/11 Mastermind's Interrogation," *New York Times,* June 22, 2008.

19. Ibid.

20. Musharraf, *In the Line of Fire*, 240.

21. Ibid.

22. Daniel Byman, Prepared Statement Before the Senate Foreign Relations Committee on Extraordinary Rendition, Extraterritorial Detention, and Treatment of Detainees: Restoring Our Moral Credibility and Strengthening Our Diplomatic Standing, July 26, 2007.

23. Steven Strasser and Craig R. Whitney, eds., *The 9/11 Investigations: The Staff Reports of the 9/11 Commission* (Washington DC: Public Affairs, 2004), 148; Byman, Prepared Statement Before the Senate Foreign Relations Committee.

24. Arthur Hulnick, *Keeping Us Safe: Secret Intelligence and Homeland Security* (Westport, CT: Praeger, 2004), 113–114.

25. James Baker, *In the Common Defense* (Cambridge: Cambridge University Press, 2007), 168.

26. Jane Mayer, "Outsourcing Torture: The Secret History of America's 'Extraordinary Rendition' Program," *New Yorker.* February 14, 2005; Robert Fisk, "Cairo's Dirty War Spills Across Europe," *Independent*, December 6, 1995.

27. Benjamin, "Rendition at Risk."

28. Ibid.

29. Daniel Benjamin and Steven Simon, *The Next Attack* (New York: Times Books, 2005), 256–257.

30. Ibid.

31. Daniel Benjamin, "Five Myths About Rendition (and That New Movie)," *Washington Post*, October 20, 2007.

32. Coll, *Ghost Wars.*

33. George Tenet, *At the Center of the Storm* (New York: Harper Collins, 2007), 254.

34. Porter Goss, Testimony Before the Senate Select Committee on Intelligence, 109th Congress, 1st sess., February 16, 2005.

35. Daniel Byman, Prepared Statement Before the Senate Foreign Relations Committee.

36. Baker, *In the Common Defense,* 167.

37. "Man Sues CIA over Torture Claims," BBC News, December 7, 2005.

38. "German Sues for CIA Extradition," BBC News, June 9, 2008; Jerry Markon, "Lawsuit Against CIA Is Dismissed," *Washington Post*, May 19, 2006.

39. Dana Priest and Barton Gellman, "U.S. Decries Abuse but Defends Interrogations," *Washington Post*, December 26, 2002.

40. Baker, *In the Common Defense,* 170.

41. Michael Scheuer, "A Fine Rendition," *New York Times,* March 11, 2005.

42. John Goetz and Britta Sandberg, "New Evidence of Torture Prison in Poland," *Der Spiegel*, April 27, 2009; Mark Mazzetti, "Portrait of 9/11 'Jackal' Emerges As He Awaits Stage in New York," *New York Times,* November 15, 2009.

43. Anthony Lake, "Joint Intelligence Committee Testimony, Testimony of Anthony Lake," September 19, 2002.

44. Michael Hayden, "A Conversation with Michael Hayden: Transcript," Council on Foreign Relations, September 7, 2007.

45. Ibid.

46. Jane Mayer, *The Dark Side: The Inside Story of How the War on Terror Turned into a War on American Ideals* (New York: Random House, 2009), 109.

47. Hayden, "Conversation."

48. Mayer, *Dark Side*, 108.

49. "Detainee Reporting Pivotal."

50. "Khalid Shaykh Muhammad: Preeminent Source on Al-Qa'ida."

51. "Special Review: Counterterrorism Detention and Interrogation Activities (September 2001–October 2003)," Central Intelligence Agency Inspector General, May 7, 2004, 87.

52. "Polish Investigation into CIA Crimes: Questions over Secrecy Remain," Amnesty.org, June 26, 2009.

53. Jane Mayer, "The Black Sites," *New Yorker,* August 13, 2007.

54. "Special Review: Counterterrorism Detention," 104.

55. "Senate Confirmation Hearings: Eric Holder, Day One," *New York Times,* January 16, 2009.

56. *U.S. Army Intelligence and Interrogation Handbook: The Official Guide on Prisoner Interrogation* (Department of the Army 2005), 8.

57. Carl W. Hoffman, *The Seizure of Tinian,* USMC Historical Monograph, www.ibiblio.net/hyperwar/USMC/USMC-M-Tinian/USMC-M-Tinian-2.html#fn94.

58. Phil Zelikow, Testimony of Philip Zelikow Before the Senate Judiciary Committee, May 13, 2009, http://judiciary.senate.gov/hearings/testimony.cfm?id=3842&wit_id=7907.

59. Glenn Fine, Testimony of Glenn A. Fine, Inspector General, U.S. Department of Justice, Before the Senate Committee on the Judiciary, June 10, 2008, www.justice.gov/oig/testimony/t0806a/index.htm.

60. John Cloonan, Testimony of John E. Cloonan, Retired FBI Special Agent, Before the Senate Committee on the Judiciary, June 10, 2008, http://judiciary.senate.gov/hearings/testimony.cfm?id=3399&wit_id=7228.

61. Gary Coh, "Torture Was Taught by CIA; Declassified Manual Details the Methods Used in Honduras; Agency Denials Refuted," *Baltimore Sun*, January 27, 1997. "The CIA also declassified a Vietnam-era training manual called 'KUBARK Counterintelligence Interrogation—July 1963,' which also taught torture and is believed by intelligence sources to have been a basis for the 1983 manual. . . . The 1983 manual was altered between 1984 and early 1985 to discourage torture after a furor was raised in Congress and the press about CIA training techniques being used in Central America."

62. "Special Review: Counterterrorism Detention," 9.

63. Ibid., 10.

64. Jack Goldsmith, *The Terror Presidency: Law and Judgment Inside the Bush Administration* (New York: Norton, 2007), 142.

65. Office of Legal Counsel, Department of Justice, www.justice.gov/olc/index.html.

66. Goldsmith, *Terror Presidency*.

67. Memorandum for Alberto R. Gonzalez, Counsel to the President, from Jay S. Bybee, Assistant Attorney General, Office of Legal Counsel, *Re: Standards of Conduct for Interrogation under 18 U.S.C. §§ 2340–2340A*," August 1, 2002.

68. Memorandum for John A. Rizzo, Senior Deputy General Counsel, Central Intelligence Agency, from Steven G. Bradbury, Principal Deputy Assistant Attorney General, Office of Legal Counsel, *Re: Application of 18 U.S.C. §§ 2340–2340A to Certain Techniques That May Be Used in the Interrogation of a High Value al-Qaeda Detainee*, May 10, 2005.

69. Jonathan Karl, "'High-Value' Detainees Transferred to Guantanamo," ABC News, September 6, 2006, http://abcnews.go.com/International/story?id=2400470; "Bush Admits to CIA Secret Prisons," BBC News, September 7, 2006, http://news.bbc.co.uk/2/hi/americas/5321606.stm.

70. Dana Priest, "CIA Holds Terror Suspects in Secret Prisons," *Washington Post*, November 2, 2005.

71. Ibid.

72. Alistair Horne, *A Savage War of Peace: Algeria 1954–1962* (New York: New York Review of Books. 2006), 204–206.

73. Suketu Mehta, *Maximum City: Bombay Lost and Found* (New York: Vintage, 2004), 132.

74. Scott Shane and Mark Mazzetti, "Advisers Fault Harsh Methods in Interrogation," *New York Times*, May 30, 2007.

75. David Rose, "Tortured Reasoning," *Vanity Fair*, December 16, 2008.

76. Mark Mazzetti and Scott Shane, "C.I.A. Abuse Cases Detailed in Report on Detainees," *New York Times*, August 24, 2009.

77. William Ranney Levi, "Interrogation's Law," 118 Yale L.J. 1434, 1436 (2009).

78. "Special Review: Counterterrorism Detention," 101–102.

79. Ibid., 105.

80. David Rose, "Tortured Reasoning," *Vanity Fair*, December 16, 2008.

81. Randy James, "A Brief History of Military Commissions," *Time*, May 19, 2009.

82. 317 U.S. 1 (1942).

83. *American Bar Association Task Force on Terrorism and the Law: Report and Recommendations on Military Commissions* (2002).

84. Victor Hansen, "The Usefulness of a Negative Example: What We Can Learn About Evidence Rules from the Government's Most Recent Efforts to Construct a Military Commissions Process," 35 *Wm. Mitchell L. Rev.* 1480, 1485 (2009).

85. 548 US 557 (2006).

86. 128 S. Ct. 2229 (2008).

87. Ibid.

88. William Glaberson, "Five Charged in 9/11 Attacks Seek to Plead Guilty," *New York Times,* December 8, 2008.

89. William Glaberson, "U.S. May Revive Guantanamo Military Courts," *New York Times,* May 1, 2009.

90. Executive Order 13492, issued January 22, 2009.

91. Glaberson, "U.S. May Revive Guantanamo Military Courts,"

92. Jane Mayer, "The Trial," *New Yorker*, February 15, 2010.

93. Statement of President Barack Obama on Military Commissions, White House Office of the Press Secretary, May 15, 2009.

94. Ibid.

95. Jim Comey and Jack Goldsmith, "Holder's Decisions on Mohammed Trial Defended," *Washington Post,* November 20, 2009.

96. "Terror Trial Switch? NYC: Not in My Backyard," *Good Morning America*, January 29, 2010; Joseph Lieberman et al., Letter to the Honorable Eric H. Holder Jr., Attorney General. Washington DC, January 26, 2010; Kasie Hunt, "Two Senate Democrats Want KSM Trial Out of NYC," *Politico*, January 26, 2010.

97. "Terror Trial Switch?"

98. Anthony M. DeStefano, "Kelly: New York 9/11 Trial 'Politically Impossible,'" *Newsday,* June 4, 2010; Suzanne Malveaux, "White House Considers Military Trial for Khalid Sheikh Mohammed," CNN, March 5, 2010.

99. Mayer, "Trial."

100. Warren Richey, "Obama Endorses Military Commissions for Guantanamo Detainees," *Christian Science Monitor*, October 29, 2009.

101. "President Obama Signs Military Commissions Changes into Law," *ACLU,* October 28, 2009.

CHAPTER 5: INTERROGATIONS, INTELLIGENCE, AND WAR

1. NEFA Foundation, *Ibn al-Sheikh al-Libi,* October 2009, 4; Jane Mayer, *The Dark Side: The Inside Story of How the War on Terror Turned into a War on American Ideals* (New York: Doubleday, 2008), 103; Edward Cody, "Pakistan Sends Ex-Taliban Envoy Back to Afghanistan," *Washington Post,* January 5, 2002.

2. The three custody exchanges would be US to Egypt, Egypt to US, and US to Libya.

3. Mayer, *Dark Side,* 119.

4. See note 150.

5. Camille al-Tawil, "US Reportedly Hands Over to Libya Ibn al-Shaykh al-Libi," *Al-Hayat,* May 3, 2006; Mayer, *Dark Side,* 134.

6. Eric Schmitt and Erik Eckholm, "A Nation Challenged: The Hunted; US Takes Custody of a Qaeda Trainer Seized by Pakistan," *New York Times,* January 6, 2002; Bill Hemmer, "Ibn al-Shaykh al-Libi Is in US Custody," CNN, January 5, 2002.

7. "Organizations with Assets Frozen by Bush's Order," *Washington Post,* September 24, 2001, http://old.911digitalarchive.org/crr/documents/1123.pdf. The list also included Osama bin Laden, Ayman al-Zawahiri, Muhammad Atif, Abu Zubaydah, Sayf

al-Adl, Abu Hafs, Shaykh Saiid, Abd al-Hadi al-Iraqi, Thirwat Salah Shihata, Tariq Anwar Al-Sayyid Ahmad, and Muhammad Salah.

8. "The Truth About Torture," *Newsweek,* November 13, 2005.

9. Senate Select Committee on Intelligence, *Postwar Findings About Iraq's WMD Programs and Links to Terrorism and How They Compare with Prewar Assessments,* September 8, 2006, 76–77, www.fas.org/irp/congress/2006_rpt/srpt109–331.pdf.

10. George W. Bush, speech in Cincinnati, Ohio, October 7, 2002, http://archives.cnn.com/2002/ALLPOLITICS/10/07/bush.transcript; Colin Powell, Presentation to the U.N. Security Council, February 5, 2003, www.cnn.com/2003/US/02/05/sprj.irq.powell.transcript.

11. David Corn and Michael Isikoff, *Hubris: The Inside Story of Spin, Scandal, and the Selling of the Iraq War* (New York: Three Rivers, 2006), 119.

12. Ibid.

13. Omar Nasiri, *Inside the Jihad: My Life with Al-Qaeda* (New York: Basic Books, 2006), 178.

14. The Libyan Islamic Fighting Group (LIFG), an al-Qaeda affiliate, was founded in the 1990s by Libyans who had fought against the Soviets in Afghanistan and were now waging jihad against Muammar Qadhafi's regime and seeking to establish an Islamic state in Libya. Nic Robertson and Paul Cruickshank, "Jihadist Death Threatened Libyan Peace Deal," CNN, November 28, 2009.

15. Mayer, *Dark Side,* 104; Nasiri, *Inside the Jihad,* 120.

16. "Rendition to Torture: The Case of Maher Arar," Joint Hearing Before the Subcommittee on International Organizations, Human Rights, and Oversight of the House Foreign Affairs Committee and the Subcommittee on the Constitution, Civil Rights, and Civil Liberties of the House Judiciary Committee, 110th Congress, 1st sess., Serial 110–118/110–52, October 18, 2007, 13; Jack Cloonan, discussion with author, April 6, 2009.

17. Bobby Ghosh, "Terror Interrogations: Can the CIA and FBI Work Together?" *Time,* July 26, 2009.

18. "Rendition to Torture."

19. Kenneth Levit, "The CIA and the Torture Controversy: Interrogation Authorities and Practices in the War on Terror," *Journal of National Security Policy and Law* 1, no. 341 (2005): 350.

20. Jack Cloonan, discussion with author, April 6, 2009.

21. Ibid.

22. Satinder Bindra, "India Identifies Terrorist Training Camps," CNN, September 19, 2001.

23. "Unclassified Verbatim Transcript of Combatant Status Review Tribunal Hearing for ISN 10016 (Abu Zubaydah)," March 27, 2007, www.defenselink.mil/news/transcript_ISN10016.pdf.

24. Omar Nasiri, *Inside the Jihad,* 179.

25. Jack Cloonan, discussion with author, April 6, 2009.

26. George Tenet, *At the Center of the Storm: My Years at the CIA* (New York: Harper Collins, 2007), 353.

27. Michael Isikoff, "Entering the Mind of a Terrorist," *Science and Spirit,* May–June 2007; Mayer, *Dark Side,* 104–106; Jack Cloonan, discussion with author, April 6, 2009.

28. Corn and Isikoff, *Hubris,* 120; Mayer, *Dark Side,* 105.

29. Jack Cloonan, discussion with author, April 6, 2009.

30. Corn and Isikoff, *Hubris*, 120; Mayer, *Dark Side*, 104–105.

31. Jack Cloonan, discussion with author, April 6, 2009.

32. Corn and Isikoff, *Hubris*, 120; Mayer, *Dark Side*, 105.

33. Mayer, *Dark Side*, 105; "Unclassified Verbatim Transcript," 10.

34. "Unclassified Verbatim Transcript," 9–10.

35. Corn and Isikoff, *Hubris*, 121; Mayer, *Dark Side*, 106.

36. "The Truth About Torture," *Newsweek*, November 13, 2005.

37. Jack Cloonan, discussion with author, April 6, 2009.

38. Ibid.

39. Transcript of "Rendition to Torture: The Case of Maher Arar," 110th Congress, 1st sess., 13.

40. Ibid.

41. Jack Cloonan, discussion with author, April 6, 2009; Mayer, *Dark Side*, 106.

42. Jack Cloonan, discussion with author, April 6, 2009; Mayer, *Dark Side*, 106.

43. The authors unsuccessfully solicited interviews from CIA officials familiar with these events in an attempt to provide a more complete understanding of these circumstances.

44. Corn and Isikoff, *Hubris*, 121; Mayer, *Dark Side*, 106; Jack Cloonan, discussion with author, April 6, 2009.

45. Jamie McIntyre, Andrea Koppel, and Barbara Starr, "Top al-Qaeda Leader Held Aboard US Warship," CNN, January 8, 2002.

46. Erik Eckholm and Eric Schmitt, "A Nation Challenged: The Hunted: US Takes Custody of a Qaeda Trainer Seized by Pakistan," *New York Times*, January 6, 2002.

47. "FBI Director Checks on His Agents Far Away from Home," *St. Petersburg Times*, January 24, 2002.

48. Kevin Johnson, Toni Locy, and Jonathan Weisman, "Officials May Transfer Al-Qaeda Figure to U.S.," *USA Today*, April 24, 2002.

49. Declassified reports released in April 2009 argue that Abu Zubaydah was not a leader in al-Qaeda but rather a training camp personnel clerk who arranged false documents and travel for mujahideen. His work enabled him to provide information about key al-Qaeda operatives. See Scott Shane, "Divisions Arose on Rough Tactics for Qaeda Figure," *New York Times*, April 17, 2009.

50. Tenet, *At the Center of the Storm*, 353; Douglas Jehl, "Qaeda-Iraq Link Cited Is Tied to Coercion Claim," *New York Times*, December 9, 2005; Omar Sinan, "Al-Qaida No. 2 Praises Dead Militant Leader," Associated Press, October 4, 2009; Tom Malinowski, "Hearing of the Senate Foreign Relations Committee," Federal News Service, July 26, 2007; Michael Hirsh et al., "The Debate over Torture," *Newsweek*, November 21, 2005; NYU School of Law, "Fate and Whereabouts Unknown: Detainees in the 'War on Terror,'" 2005, www.chrgj.org/docs/Whereabouts%20Unknown%20Final.pdf.

51. George W. Bush, News Conference on Iraq, Social Security, and the World Bank, *New York Times*, March 16, 2005.

52. Mayer, *Dark Side*, 119.

53. Mayer, *Dark Side*, 119; Stephen Grey, *Ghost Plane: The True Story of the CIA Torture Program* (New York: St. Martin's, 2006), 31–32.

54. Johnson, Locy, and Weisman, "Officials May Transfer"; John Lumpkin, "Bin Laden Lieutenant Talks and American Interrogators Listen, Mindful of Deception," Associated Press, April 24, 2002.

55. Lumpkin, "Bin Laden Lieutenant Talks."

56. Ibid.

57. Senate Select Committee on Intelligence, *Postwar Findings.*

58. Ibid., 75–77.

59. Ibid., 76.

60. Ibid., 76–77.

61. Ibid., 77.

62. Robert McCain, "Biden Sees Pre-Emptive Strike on Iraq: US Probably to go to War," *Washington Times*, August 5, 2002.

63. "Eyes on Iraq; In Cheney's Words: The Administration's Case for Removing Saddam Hussein," *New York Times*, August 27, 2002; James Crawley and Jeanette Steele, "Rumsfeld Meets the Troops: Argument Made for a Pre-Emptive Strike Against Iraq," *San Diego Union-Tribune*, August 28, 2002.

64. Dick Cheney, interview, *Meet the Press*, September 8, 2002, www.mtholyoke.edu/acad/intrel/bush/meet.htm.

65. Michael Gordon and Judith Miller, "Threats and Responses: The Iraqis; US Says Hussein Intensifies Quest for A-Bomb Parts," *New York Times,* September 8, 2002.

66. Senate Select Committee on Intelligence, *Report on the US Intelligence Community's Prewar Intelligence Assessments on Iraq,* July 7, 2004, 298–299, http://intelligence.senate.gov/pub108thcongress.html.

67. Ibid.

68. Senate Select Committee on Intelligence, Postwar Findings, 78.

69. John McLaughlin, letter to the Senate Select Committee on Intelligence, October 7, 2002.

70. Condoleezza Rice, interview, NewsHour, September 25, 2002, www.pbs.org/newshour/bb/international/july-dec02/rice_9–25.html.

71. Douglas Jehl, "Report Warned Bush Team About Intelligence Suspicions," *New York Times*, November 6, 2005; Michael Isikoff and Mark Hosenball, "Spies, Lies, and the White House," *Newsweek*, June 11, 2008; Mayer, *Dark Side*, 135–136.

72. George W. Bush, speech in Cincinnati, Ohio, October 7, 2002, http://archives.cnn.com/2002/allpolotics/10/07/bush.transcript.

73. Since retiring in 2005, Colonel Wilkerson, who was responsible for clearing the intelligence used in Secretary Powell's 2003 speech to the UN, has become an outspoken critic of the role played by the Bush administration and the intelligence community in the lead-up to the Iraq War. In a January 19, 2006, *Washington Post* article, "Breaking Ranks," Wilkerson cited intelligence failures, the detainee abuse issue, the ineptitude of post-invasion planning for Iraq, and secretive decision making as his reasons for speaking out. Wilkerson called for Bush's impeachment, scathingly criticized the administration's top officials, and left the Republican Party. Though once very close, Powell and Wilkerson have become "estranged," according to the *Post*, on account of Wilkerson's stance and allegations.

74. Larry Wilkerson, discussion with author, March 27, 2009.

75. Ibid.

76. Tenet, *At the Center of the Storm*, 374.

77. Larry Wilkerson, discussion with author, March 27, 2009.

78. Ibid. Typically, intelligence assessments must provide source notes for the underlying intelligence information.

79. The Mukhabarat, or Iraqi Intelligence Service (IIS), was the main intelligence agency in Iraq under Saddam Hussein.

80. Larry Wilkerson, discussion with author, March 27, 2009.

81. Douglas Jehl and Richard Stevenson, "Leak Case Renews Questions on War's Rationale," *New York Times*, October 23, 2005.

82. John McLaughlin, statement to the WMD Commission, April 1, 2005, www.fas.org/irp/offdocs/wmd_mclaughlin.html.

83. Tenet, *At the Center of the Storm*, 372; Senate Select Committee on Intelligence, *Report on the US Intelligence Community's Prewar Intelligence Assessments on Iraq*, 241.

84. Larry Wilkerson, discussion with author, March 27, 2009.

85. Ibid. The authors were refused an interview with former DCI George Tenet regarding Colonel Wilkerson's account. In electronic communication, however, a representative of Tenet reports that three CIA officials involved in the speechwriting process do not remember the above scene as it is described.

86. Colin Powell, presentation to the U.N. Security Council, February 5, 2003, www.cnn.com/2003/US/02/05/sprj.irq.powell.transcript.

87. "Senators Praise Powell's Presentation," Associated Press, February 5, 2003.

88. "Sen. Durbin Finds Powell Evidence 'compelling,'" Copley News Service, February 5, 2003; "Democrats Say Powell Made Compelling Case," Associated Press Online, February 5, 2003.

89. Mike Allen and Dan Balz, "Congress's Overall Opinion Is Positive: But Some Members Say It's Still Too Soon for War," *Washington Post*, February 6, 2003.

90. Ibid.

91. Ibid.

92. Kim Gamel, "Powell Evidence Gets Mixed Reviews," Associated Press Online, February 5, 2003.

93. Keith Richburg, "Speech Fails to Budge Europeans from Their Divergent Positions," *Washington Post*, February 6, 2003.

94. Kim Gamel, "Powell Evidence Gets Mixed Reviews."

95. Ibid.

96. Ibid.

97. Larry Wilkerson, discussion with author, March 27, 2009.

98. John McLaughlin, discussion with author, November 3, 2009.

99. Ibid.

100. Larry Wilkerson, discussion with author, March 27, 2009.

101. Ibid.

102. Three senior intelligence officials, interview by author.

103. Corn and Isikoff, *Hubris*, 334; Stephen Hayes, *The Connection: How al-Qaeda's Collaboration with Saddam Hussein Has Endangered America* (New York: Harper Collins, 2004), 120.

104. Department of Defense Office of Inspector General, *Review of Pre-Iraqi War Activities of the Office of the Under Secretary of Defense for Policy: Executive Summary, Report 07-INTEL-04*, February 9, 2007, www.npr.org/documents/2007/feb/dod_iog_iraq_summary.pdf.

105. Seymour Hersh, "Selective Intelligence: Donald Rumsfeld Has His Own Special Sources. Are They Reliable?" *New Yorker*, May 12, 2003.

106. Ibid.

107. Tenet, *At the Center of the Storm*, 347–348.

108. Stephen Hayes, "Case Closed: The US Government's Secret Memo Detailing Cooperation Between Saddam Hussein and Osama Bin Laden," *Weekly Standard*, November 24, 2003.

109. US Department of Defense, *DoD Statement on News Reports of Al-Qaeda and Iraq Connections*, November 15, 2003, www.defenselink.mil/releases/release.aspx?releaseid=5785.

110. Corn and Isikoff, *Hubris*, 335.

111. Douglas Jehl, "Qaeda-Iraq Link Cited Is Tied to Coercion Claim," *New York Times*, December 9, 2003; Jane Mayer, "Outsourcing Torture," *New Yorker*, February 14, 2005.

112. Jane Mayer, "Outsourcing Torture"; Douglas Jehl, "Report Warned Bush Team About Intelligence Suspicions," *New York Times*, November 6, 2005; "Libya Reports Prison Suicide of top Qaeda Man," Reuters, May 11, 2009; Nicole Gaouette, "Prewar Claims Set Off Bells," *Los Angeles Times*, November 7, 2005.

113. Stephen Grey, "CIA Rendition: The Smoking Gun Cable," ABC Newsblotter, November 6, 2007, http://blogs.abcnews.com/theblotter/2007/11/cia-rendition-t.html.

114. Senate Select Committee on Intelligence, *Postwar Findings*, 79.

115. Grey, "CIA Rendition"; Senate Select Committee on Intelligence, *Postwar Findings*, 79.

116. Senate Select Committee on Intelligence, *Postwar Findings*, 79.

117. Ibid., 80.

118. Ibid.

119. Grey, "CIA Rendition."

120. Senate Select Committee on Intelligence, *Postwar Findings*, 81.

121. Ibid.

122. Ibid.

123. Ibid.

124. Ibid., 82.

125. Douglas Jehl, "The Reach of War: Prewar Intelligence; High Qaeda Aide Retracted Claim of Link with Iraq," *New York Times*, July 31, 2004.

126. Tenet, *At the Center of the Storm*, 353.

127. Dick Cheney, interview, CNBC, June 17, 2004, http://kucinich.house.gov/UploadedFiles/artII1I.pdf.

128. Michael Isikoff, "Iraq and Al-Qaeda: Forget the Poisons and Deadly Gases," *Newsweek*, July 5, 2004.

129. Tenet, *At the Center of the Storm*, 353.

130. Ibid., 354.

131. At least four HVDs have recanted information provided under interrogation. In addition to al-Libi, they include Khalid Shaykh Mohammed. See Peter Finn, Joby Warrick, and Julie Tate, "How a Detainee Became an Asset," *Washington Post*, August 29, 2009; David Rose, "Tortured Reasoning," *Vanity Fair*, December 16, 2008; James Risen, *State of War: The Secret History of the CIA and the Bush Administration* (New York: Free Press, 2006), 33; and "Unclassified Verbatim Transcript of Combatant Status Review Tribunal Hearing for ISN 10024 (Abu Zubaydah)," 15. On Abd al-Rahim al-Nashiri, see Craig Whitlock, "Probe of USS Cole Bombing Unravels," *Washington*

Post, May 4, 2008. On Abu Zubaydah, see "Unclassified Verbatim Transcript of Combatant Status Review Tribunal Hearing for ISN 10016" (Abu Zubaydah)."

132. Tenet, *At the Center of the Storm*, 232.

133. Rolf Mowatt-Larssen, discussion with author, April 8, 2009.

134. John McLaughlin, discussion with author, November 3, 2009.

135. Senate Select Committee on Intelligence, *Report on the US Intelligence Community's Prewar Intelligence Assessments on Iraq*, 253.

136. Ibid., 363.

137. Pat Roberts and John Rockefeller, *News Conference on the Release of the Senate Select Committee on Intelligence Report*, July 9, 2004, www.washingtonpost.com/wp-dyn /articles/A38650–2004Jul9.html.

138. Ibid.

139. Dianne Feinstein, letter to Senator Pat Roberts, July 29, 2005, http://feinstein .senate.gov/05releases/r-intel-robrts.pdf.

140. Defense Intelligence Agency, letter to Senator John Rockefeller IV, October 26, 2005, levin.senate.gov/newsroom/supporting/2005/DIAletter.102605.pdf.

141. Ibid.

142. Ibid.

143. Daniel Douglass, "Democrats Seek Report on Prewar Iraq Intel," *Washington Post*, November 6, 2005.

144. Ibid.

145. Ibid.

146. Senate Select Committee on Intelligence, *Postwar Findings*, 76.

147. Ibid., 77.

148. Ibid., 78.

149. Ibid.

150. Jonathan Weisman, "Iraq's Alleged Al-Qaeda Ties Were Disputed Before War; Links Were Cited to Justify US Invasion, Report Says," *Washington Post*, September 9, 2006.

151. William Delahunt, Edward Markey, and Jerrold Nadler, letter to President Bush, May 24, 2007, http://markey.house.gov/index.php?option=com_content&task=view &id=2870&Itemid=141.

152. Camille al-Tawil, "US Reportedly Hands Over to Libya Ibn al-Shaykh al-Libi," *Al-Hayat*, May 3, 2006; Mayer, *Dark Side*, 134.

153. Peter Finn, "Detainee Who Gave False Iraq Data Dies in Prison in Libya," *Washington Post*, May 12, 2009.

154. Heba Morayef, discussion with author, July 2, 2009.

155. Ibid.

156. Ibid. See also Human Rights Watch, "World Report 2010: Events of 2009," 539, www.hrw.org/sites/default/files/related_material/wr2010.pdf.

157. Ibid.

158. Ibid.

159. Heba Morayef, discussion with author, July 2, 2009.

160. "Detainee Who Gave False Iraq Data Dies in Prison in Libya"; William Maclean, William Lamine Ghanmi, and Alison Williams, "Libya Reports Prison Suicide of Top Qaeda Man," ABC News/Reuters, May 11, 2009.

161. Mark Hosenball and Michael Isikoff, "Death in a Libyan Jail Cell," *Newsweek*, May 16, 2009; "Libya Reports Prison Suicide of Top Qaeda Man."

162. Heba Morayef, discussion with author, July 2, 2009.

163. "Death in Libya: The Reported Suicide of a Prisoner Who Falsely Linked Saddam Hussein to Al-Qaeda Surprises Human-Rights Workers and Lawyers for Other Top Terror Detainees"; Heba Morayef, discussion with author, July 2, 2009.

164. Ibid.

165. Human Rights Watch, "Libya/US: Investigate Death of Former CIA Prisoner," May 11, 2009, www.hrw.org/en/news/2009/05/11/libyaus-investigate-death-former-cia-prisoner.

166. State Department, *Daily Press Briefing*, May 12, 2009, www.state.gov/r/pa/prs/dpb/2009/05/123282.htm.

167. Richard Helms, "Intelligence in American Society," *Studies in Intelligence*, Summer 1967, 15.

CHAPTER 6: COUNTERTERRORISM IN A WAR ZONE

1. Samantha Power, *Chasing the Flame: Sergio Vieira de Mello and the Fight to Save the World* (New York: Penguin, 2008).

2. Thanassis Cambanis, "Jordan's Islamists Seek Offices Their Allies Scorn," *New York Times,* November 16, 2007.

3. Anne Marie Weaver, "The Short, Violent Life of Abu Musab al-Zarqawi," *Atlantic,* July–August 2006.

4. Jean-Charles Brisard, *Zarqawi: The New Face of Al-Qaeda* (New York: Other Press, 2005), 13.

5. Weaver, "Short, Violent Life."

6. Brisard, *Zarqawi,* 15.

7. *Militant Ideology Atlas: Executive Report,* Combating Terrorism Center, West Point, November 2006.

8. Brisard, *Zarqawi,* 31.

9. Borzou Daragahi and Josh Meyer, "Zarqawi Attack Put Jordan Hot on His Trail," *Los Angeles Times,* June 13, 2006.

10. Brisard, *Zarqawi,* 36.

11. Ibid., 41.

12. Ibid., 59.

13. Loretta Napoleoni, *Insurgent Iraq: Al Zarqawi and the New Generation* (New York: Seven Stories, 2005), 94–95.

14. Ibid.

15. Ibid., 95–96.

16. Weaver, "Short, Violent Life."

17. Ibid.

18. Don Van Natta and David Johnston, "A Terror Lieutenant with a Deadly Past," *New York Times,* February 10, 2003; "Two Killed in Amman Bomb Blast," BBC, February 28, 2002.

19. Napoleoni, *Insurgent Iraq,* 264; Van Natta and Johnston, "Terror Lieutenant."

20. Brisard, *Zarqawi,* 87.

21. Jeffrey Gettleman, "Zarqawi's Journey: From Dropout to Prisoner to Insurgent Leader," *New York Times*, July 13, 2004.

22. Colin Powell, "Transcript of Powell's U.N. Presentation, Part 9: Ties to al-Qaeda."

23. James Risen, "Split at CIA and FBI on Iraqi Ties to Al-Qaeda," *New York Times*, February 2, 2003.

24. Senate Select Committee on Intelligence, *Postwar Findings About Iraq's WMD Programs and Links to Terrorism and How They Compare with Prewar Assessments*, 109th Cong., 2d sess., 2006, 92.

25. Napoleoni, *Insurgent Iraq*, 117.

26. Napoleoni, *Insurgent Iraq*, 118; Senate Select Committee on Intelligence, *Postwar Findings*, 93.

27. Ibid., 109.

28. Ibid., 90.

29. Ibid., 91.

30. "Iraq's Links to Terrorism," www.gpoaccess.gov/serialset/creports/pdf/s108–301 /sec12.pdf.

31. "Levin Releases Newly Declassified Intelligence Documents on Iraq–al-Qaeda Relationship," press release by Senator Carl Levin, April 15, 2005.

32. Michael Gordon and Bernard Trainor, *Cobra II: The Inside Story of the Invasion and Occupation of Iraq* (New York: Vintage, 2007), 145.

33. Gordon and Trainor, *Cobra II*, 145.

34. "Levin Releases Newly Declassified Intelligence Documents."

35. Jim Miklaszewski, "Avoiding Attacking Suspected Terrorist Mastermind," *NBC News*, March 2, 2004.

36. Ibid.

37. "Bush Turned Down Chances to Kill Zarqawi: Ex-CIA Spy," Australian Broadcasting Company (ABC) News Online, May 1, 2006; Debbie Whitmont, "Interview: Michael Scheuer," Australian Broadcasting Corporation, Four Corners, May 1, 2006.

38. Miklaszewski, "Avoiding Attacking."

39. Jason Burke, "US Special Forces Take Fight to Fundamentalist Terror Group," *Observer*, March 20, 2003.

40. Barry Schweid, "Powell Renews US Demand for Recovery of Top Terror Suspects," Associated Press, October 27, 2003; Raymond Bonner, "The Struggle for Iraq: On Alert for Al-Qaeda in Iraq, US Is Tracking 2 Suspects," *New York Times*, September 28, 2003; Douglas Jehl, "Iran Said to Hold Qaeda's No. 3, but to Resist Giving Him Up," *New York Times*, August 2, 2003.

41. Bonner, "Struggle for Iraq."

42. Sean Loughlin, "Rumsfeld on Looting in Iraq: 'Stuff Happens,'" CNN, April 12, 2003.

43. Power, *Chasing the Flame*, 513.

44. Ibid., 514.

45. Philli Kurata, "U.S. Freezes Their Assets, Forbids Transactions with U.S. Nationals," US Department of State, Washington file, September 29, 2003.

46. "U.S. Offers $5 Million Bounty on Embassy Bomb Suspect," CNN, October 30, 2003.

47. "First Audio Recording by Al-Qa'ida Leader in Iraq Abu Mus'ab Al-Zarqawi," MEMRI, January 7, 2004.

48. "US Expects More Attacks in Iraq," CNN, March 31, 2004.

49. George Packer, *The Assassins Gate* (New York: Farrar, Straus & Giroux, 2005).

50. Dick Camp, *Operation Phantom Fury* (Minneapolis: Zenith, 2009), 4.

51. Ibid., 58.

52. "Fallujah Stable, 'Robust' Manhunt for Zarqawi Under Way," American Forces Press Service, April 13, 2004; "Alleged Al-Qaeda Iraq Chief Believed to Be in Fallujah: Coalition," Agence France Press, April 13, 2004.

53. "Official: Al-Zarqawi Caught, Released," CNN, December 15, 2005; "Saudi Suicide Bomber Claims Zarqawi Was Captured, Then Released," Voice of America, December 24, 2005.

54. Mark Bowden, "The Ploy," *Atlantic*, May 2007.

55. Loretta Napoleoni, "Profile of a Killer," *Foreign Policy*, December 6, 2005.

56. Piers Platt, interview, October 25, 2010.

57. "Terrorist Narrowly Eludes U.S. Troops," *Daily Telegraph*, April 27, 2005; Sean Naylor, "Closing in on Zarqawi; We Go Inside the Search for the Ringleader of al-Qaeda in Iraq," *Army Times*, May 8, 2006.

58. Naylor, "Closing in on Zarqawi."

59. "The Hunt for Zarqawi," *NBC Nightly News,* April 26, 2005.

60. Naylor, "Closing in on Zarqawi."

61. Eric Joyce, interview by author, May 5, 2010.

62. Eric Joyce, e-mail to author, May 19, 2010.

63. Eric Joyce, interview by author, May 5, 2010.

64. Ibid.

65. Ibid.

66. Eric Joyce, email to author, May 19, 2010.

67. "Terrorist Narrowly Eludes U.S. Troops."

68. Peter Grier and Faye Bowers, "US at Least Seizes Zarqawi's Laptop," *Christian Science Monitor*, April 27, 2005.

69. "Terrorist Narrowly Eludes U.S. Troops."

70. Tom Clonan, "US Offensive Informed by Intelligence Coups," *Irish Times*, May 11, 2005.

71. "Official: Al-Zarqawi Caught, Released," CNN, December 15, 2005.

72. "Hunting Zarqawi (The Last Word)," *Middle East*, April 1, 2005.

73. "Leader of Al-Qaeda in Iraq Al-Zarqawi Declares 'Total War' on Shi'ites, States That the Sunni Women of Tel'afar Had 'Their Wombs Filled with the Sperm of the Crusaders,'" MEMRI, September 16, 2005.

74. "Leader of Al-Qaeda in Iraq Al-Zarqawi."

75. Letter from al-Zawahiri to al-Zarqawi, ODNI News Release 2–05, October 11, 2005.

76. Ibid., 42.

77. Rick Jervis, "Al-Qaeda Claims Hotel Bombings; Jordanians Show Resolve," *USA Today,* November 11, 2005.

78. "Zarqawi Gunfight Kept from US Hero's Widow," *Sunday Times*, June 25, 2006.

79. "Al-Qaeda Explains Amman Bombings Threatens: 'In a Few Days, the Infidel Leaders Will Witness an Event That Will Make [the Amman Bombings] Seem Insignificant,'" MEMRI Translation Service, December 8, 2005.

80. Ibid.

81. "Inside a Manhunt: Abu Musab al-Zarqawi," *World News Tonight*, November 21, 2005; Ellen Knickmeyer, "Officials Probing Whether Raid in Mosul Killed Zarqawi," *Washington Post*, November 21, 2005.

82. Michael Howard, "Zarqawi Family Disown Him After Bombings," *Guardian*, November 21, 2005.

83. Ibid., 44.

84. "Iraqi FM: Al-Zarqawi Thought to Be Dead," Associated Press, November 11, 2005.

85. Anthony Cordesman, quoted in "War in Iraq; Al-Qaeda Raid," *ABC News*, November 20, 2005; Ellen Knickmeyer, "U.S. Raid 'Didn't Get' al-Zarqawi," *Washington Post*, November 22, 2005; Knickmeyer, "Officials Probing Whether Raid in Mosul Killed Zarqawi," *Washington Post*, November 21, 2005.

86. Kim Sengupta, "Iraq Awaits Verdict of DNA Test on Zarqawi 'Corpse,'" *Independent (London)*, November 22, 2005.

87. Knickmeyer, "U.S. Raid 'Didn't Get' al-Zarqawi."

88. Gordon and Trainor, *Cobra II*, 585.

89. Thomas Ricks, *The Gamble* (New York: Penguin, 2009), 55.

90. Ibid., 37.

91. Andy Mosher, "Baghdad Morgue Tallies 1,815 Bodies in July," *Washington Post*, August 10, 2006.

92. Ricks, *The Gamble*, 32.

93. Jane Arraf, "Two Iraq Al-Qaeda Leaders Killed: Did They Really Get Abu Omar al-Baghdadi?" *Christian Science Monitor*, April 19, 2010.

94. Naylor, "Closing in on Zarqawi."

95. Ibid.

96. Ibid.

97. Ibid.

98. Chris Cuomo and Eamon McNiff, "The Men in the Shadows: Hunting al-Zarqawi," *ABC News*, June 9, 2006.

99. Naylor, "Closing in on Zarqawi."

100. Ibid.

101. Robert Kaplan, "Man Versus Afghanistan," *Atlantic*, April 2010.

102. Naylor, "Closing in on Zarqawi."

103. Mark Bowden, "The Ploy," *Atlantic*, May 2007.

104. Naylor, "Closing in on Zarqawi"; "Efforts to Capture Abu Musab al-Zarqawi Intensify," *CBS Morning News*, May 3, 2006.

105. "Task Force 145 Leads Hunt for Abu Musab al-Zarqawi," *CBS News*, May 2, 2006.

106. "Special Report," *Fox News*, May 1, 2006.

107. Borzou Daragahi and Josh Meyer, "Zarqawi Attack Put Jordan Hot on His Trail," *Los Angeles Times*, June 13, 2006.

108. "New Video by Al-Qaeda Commander in Iraq Abu Mus'ab Al-Zarqawi," MEMRI, April 26, 2006.

109. Daragahi and Meyer, "Zarqawi Attack."

110. Joel Roberts, "What's Next After Zarqawi's Death?" CBS/Associated Press, June 8, 2006; George Pascoe-Watson, "MI6 Helped Nail Zarqawi," *The Sun*, June 9, 2006.

111. Hamza Hendawi and Jim Krane, "Long, Costly Hunt Finally Ends," *Winnipeg Free Press*, June 9, 2006.

112. Scott Horton, "The American Public Has a Right to Know That They Do Not Have to Choose Between Torture and Terror: Six Questions for Matthew Alexander, Author of *How to Break a Terrorist*," *Harper's*, December 18, 2008; Bowden, "The Ploy."

113. Horton, "The American Public Has a Right to Know."

114. "How Iraq's Ghost of Death Was Cornered," *Sunday Times*, June 11, 2006; Dexter Filkins, Mark Mazzetti, and Richard Oppel, "How Surveillance and Betrayal Led to a Hunt's End," *New York Times*, June 9, 2006; Bowden, "The Ploy."

115. Bowden, "The Ploy."

116. "How Iraq's Ghost of Death Was Cornered."

117. Naylor, "Inside the Zarqawi Takedown"; "How Iraq's Ghost of Death Was Cornered."

118. Naylor, "Inside the Zarqawi Takedown."

119. Robert Granacher, *Traumatic Brain Injury: Methods for Clinical and Forensic Neuropsychiatric Assessment* (Boca Raton, FL: CRC Press, 2004), 11–12.

120. Naylor, "Inside the Zarqawi Takedown."

121. "How Iraq's Ghost of Death Was Cornered"; Filkins, Mazzetti, and Oppel, "Surveillance and Betrayal."

122. Evan Thomas and Rod Nordland, "Death of a Terrorist," *Newsweek*, June 19, 2006.

123. David Gerlach, "How They Got Him," *Newsweek*, June 19, 2006.

CHAPTER 7: BOJINKA REDUX

1. "New Al-Jazeera Videos: London Suicide Bomber 'Before Entering Gardens of Paradise,' and Ayman Al-Zawahiri's Threats of More Bombings in the West," MEMRI, September 2, 2005.

2. Terry McDermott, "The Plot: How Terrorists Hatched a Simple Plot to Use Planes As Bombs," *Los Angeles Times*, September 1, 2002; Steve Coll, *Ghost Wars* (New York: Penguin, 2004), 274.

3. Matthew Brzezinski, "Bust and Boom," *Washington Post*, December 30, 2001.

4. Christopher Wren, "Plane Bombing Is Described in Terror Trial," *New York Times*, June 4, 1996.

5. Ibid.

6. McDermott, "The Plot"; Coll, *Ghost Wars*, 274.

7. Philip Shenon, "Traces of Terrorism: The Warnings; FBI Knew for Years About Terror Pilot Training," *New York Times*, May 18, 2002.

8. "Al-Qaeda's Global Context," *Frontline*, www.pbs.org/wgbh/pages/frontline/shows/knew/etc/cron.html.

9. Coll, *Ghost Wars*, 272.

10. US official, interview, March 2010.

11. Pervez Musharraf, *In the Line of Fire* (New York: Free Press, 2006), 260.

12. Duncan Campbell, "Pakistan Says al-Qaida Link to Plot Found," *Guardian*, August 17, 2006.

13. John Burns and Elaine Scolino, "No One Convicted of Terror Plot to Bomb Planes," *New York Times*, September 8, 2008.

14. US Department of the Treasury, "Treasury Designates Individual Supporting Al Qaida, Other Terrorist Organizations," December 19, 2006.

15. Cahal Milmo et al., "From Birmingham Bakery to Pakistani Prison: The Mystery of Rashid Rauf," *Independent*, August 19, 2006; Ian Fisher and Serge Kovaleski, "In British Inquiry, a Family Caught in 2 Worlds," *New York Times*, August 20, 2006.

16. Question and answer session, Pakistani Ministry of Foreign Affairs, December 19, 2007.

17. Asif Farooqi, Carol Grisanti, and Robert Windrem, "Sources: UK Terror Plot Suspect Forced to Talk," *NBC News*, August 18, 2006. Farooqi also took part in the two assassination attempts on Pakistani president Pervez Musharraf in 2003.

18. NEFA Foundation, "Bojinka II: The Transatlantic Liquid Bomb Plot," April 2008, www.nefafoundation.org, 15.

19. Cahal Milmo, "How the Web of Intelligence Led to Pakistan," *Independent*, September 8, 2009.

20. Francie Grace, "Terror Mastermind in Afghanistan?" *CBS News*, August 18, 2006.

21. David Williams and Rebecca Camper, "Liquid Bomb Terror Plot That Changed Air Travel Forever: How Gang of Fanatics Planned Britain's 9/11," *Daily Mail*, September 8, 2009.

22. Duncan Gardham, "Airline Bomb Plot: Investigation 'One of the Biggest Since WW2,'" *Independent*, September 8, 2009.

23. Ibid.

24. Paul Cheston, "Heathrow Liquid Bomb Plot Bigger Than 9/11," *London Evening Standard*, September 8, 2009.

25. Don Van Natta, Elaine Sciolino, and Stephen Grey, "Details Emerge in British Terror Case," *New York Times*, August 28, 2006.

26. Craig Whitlock and Dafna Linzer, "Tip Followed '05 Attacks on London Transit," *Washington Post*, August 11, 2006.

27. Ibid.

28. Dominic Casciani, "Liquid Bomb Plot: What Happened," BBC, September 7, 2009.

29. Peter Walker and Vikram Dodd, "Video Tirades That Sealed Case Against Liquid Bomb Plotters," *Guardian*, September 9, 2008.

30. Richard Greenberg, Paul Cruickshank, and Chris Hansen, "Inside the Terror Plot That 'Rivaled 9/11,'" *Dateline NBC*, September 14, 2009.

31. Van Natta, Sciolino, and Grey, "Details Emerge."

32. Van Natta, Sciolino, and Grey, "Details Emerge"; Allison Barrie, "Tang Bomb: Liquid Explosives Are the New 'Weapon of Choice,'" *Fox News*, May 17, 2008.

33. Ibid.

34. Greenberg, Cruickshank, and Hansen, "Inside the Terror Plot."

35. Richard Norton-Taylor, "MI5: 30 Terror Plots Being Planned in UK," *Guardian*, November 10, 2006.

36. Sean O'Neill, "Airline Bomb Plot: Coded E-Mail Trail Exposed Plan," *Times* Online, September 7, 2009.

37. "Operation Overt Uncovered 2006 Terrorist Plot Against Airliners," *Daily Telegraph*, September 9, 2009; Greenberg, Cruickshank, and Hansen, "Inside the Terror Plot."

38. O'Neill, "Airline Bomb Plot."

39. Simon Hughes and Mike Sullivan, "British Bomb Plot Traitors," *Sun*, September 8, 2009.

40. Dafna Linzer, "Airliner Plot Had Support in Pakistan, Officials Say," *Washington Post,* August 12, 2006.

41. Greenberg, Cruickshank, and Hansen, "Inside the Terror Plot."

42. Don Van Natta, Elaine Sciolino, and Stephen Grey, "Seven Martyrdom Videos Uncovered: Suspects Not Ready for Immediate Strike," *New York Times,* August 28, 2006.

43. Vikram Dodd and Rachel Williams, "Jury Shown Martyrdom Videos Promising Revenge for Oppression of Muslims in Aircraft Bombs Plot Trial," *Guardian*, April 5, 2008.

44. Ibid.

45. Cahal Milmo, "Police Watched the Plotters, Then Pounced," *Independent,* September 8, 2009.

46. Justin Davenport, "Airport Bomb Plot: Three Guilty," *London Evening Standard,* August 9, 2008.

47. Aram Roston and Lisa Myers, "Disagreement over Timing of Arrests," *NBC News*, August 14, 2006.

48. Barrie, "Tang Bomb."

49. "Would Have Killed Thousands," *ABC News,* August 6, 2007.

50. Sidney Alford explains: http://news.bbc.co.uk/2/hi/uk_news/7536167.stm.

51. Jim Popkin, "Rail Security: Gov't Warns of Terror Threat to Trains," MSNBC.com, March 4, 2008.

52. Cahal Milmo, "How Web of Intelligence Led to Pakistan," *Independent*, September 8, 2009.

53. Chris Greenwood, "Soft Porn and Condoms to Throw Security Off Scent," *Birmingham Post*, April 5, 2008.

54. "Keelty Shocked at Suicide-Baby Bomb Plot," AAP/*Daily Telegraph*, August 14, 2006.

55. Julie Hyland, "Contradictions, Anomalies, Questions Mount in UK Terror Scare," *Global Research (Canada),* August 18, 2006.

56. Milmo, "How Web of Intelligence Led to Pakistan."

57. Ron Suskind, *The Way of the World* (New York: HarperCollins. 2008), 43–45.

58. Ibid.

59. Carlotta Gall, "Pak confirms JeM, Qaida Links of Rauf," *Times of India*, August 17, 2006.

60. US official, interview, August 24, 2009.

61. Kim Zetter, "NSA-Intercepted E-Mails Helped Convict Would-Be Bombers," *Wired*, September 8, 2009.

62. "U.S.: 'Do Your Attacks now' Message Triggered Arrests," CNN, August 11, 2006.

63. "Airline Terror Plot Foiled in UK Soon Before Planned Bombings," *NewsHour*, August 10, 2006.

64. David Leppard et al., "Focus: Terror in the Skies," *Sunday Times*, August 13, 2006.

65. Ibid.

66. Haroon Siddique, "Timeline: Transatlantic Airline Bomb Plot," *Guardian,* September 8, 2009; Leppard et al., "Focus: Terror in the Skies."

67. Joel Roberts, "Italy Arrests 40 in Security Crackdown," *CBS News*, August 11, 2006; "UK/US Airliner Bomb Plot (UKUS-ABP) v1.5," US Embassy-Paraguay, August 11, 2006. http://paraguay.usembassy.gov/uploads/UT/an/UTanq3kpNUaoeZq7SnbJUw/UKUS-ABP-PUB-v1–5.pdf.

68. Glenda Cooper, "British Charge 11 Suspects in Airliner Plot," *Washington Post,* August 22, 2006.

69. Ibid.

70. "Agency Adjusts Liquid Ban, Aviation Threat Level Remains High," TSA press release, September 25, 2006.

71. Richard Curran, "Will It Ever Be Safe to Fly Again?" *Sunday Business Post (Ireland),* August 20, 2006.

72. Michael Holden, "Airline Bombings Were Just Days Away: UK Police," Reuters, September 7, 2009.

73. "Airliners Bomb Plot: The Verdicts," *BBC News*, September 7, 2009.

74. Zetter, "NSA-Intercepted E-Mails."

75. Andrew Alderson, "British Terror Mastermind Rashid Rauf 'Killed in US Missile Strike,'" *Telegraph*, November 22, 2008; "UK Militant 'Killed in Pakistan,'" BBC, November 22, 2008.

76. "Airline Liquid Bomb Plotters Jailed for 108 Years for Planning 'Most Wicked Crime in Britain's History,'" *Daily Mail*, September 14, 2009.

77. "Three Guilty of Airline Bomb Plot," *BBC News*, September 7, 2009.

78. "Airline Liquid Bomb Plotters Jailed for 108 Years."

79. David Byers, "Missionary Mohammed Gulzar 'Was Airline Terror Plot Ringleader,'" *Times of London*, April 7, 2008.

80. Remarks by CIA director at DNI headquarters, January 19, 2007, https://www.cia.gov/news-information/speeches-testimony/2007/remarks_012207.htm.

81. US official, interview, August 24, 2009.

82. Ibid.

83. Jon Clements, "Liquid Bomb Plot: US Spies Gave Key Evidence . . . After Killing," *Mirror,* September 8, 2009.

CHAPTER 8: AN INCREASING PREFERENCE FOR LETHAL ENDS

1. "Osama No Longer in Control of al-Qaeda: US Ambassador," *Pajhwok Afghan News*, December 12, 2005.

2. Susan B. Glasser, "Review May Shift Terror Policies: US Is Expected to Look Beyond Al-Qaeda," *Washington Post*, May 29, 2005.

3. Ibid.

4. "Key Al-Qaeda Figure Died in Blast, Pakistan Says," *Star Telegram*, December 4, 2005.

5. Craig Whitlock and Kamran Khan, "Blast in Pakistan Kills Al-Qaeda Commander," *Washington Post*, December 4, 2005.

6. "Key Al-Qaeda Figure Died in Blast."

7. Ibid.

8. James Meek, "CIA Missile Strike Kills Key Qaeda Thug," *Daily News*, December 4, 2005.

9. Sarah Baxter, "Al-Qaeda Chief Killed in Pakistan," *Sunday Times (London)*, December 4, 2005.

10. Paul Watson and Ken Silverstein, "Senior Leader of Al-Qaeda Is Killed in Blast," *Los Angeles Times,* December 4, 2005; Zeeshan Haider, "Terror Kingpin Killed: Blow to Al-Qaeda as Blast Claims Its No. 3," *Daily Telegraph (Sydney)*, December 5, 2005; Meek, "CIA Missile Strike Kills Key Qaeda Thug."

11. "Questions Surround al-Qaeda Leader's Death," *Voice of America News,* December 6, 2005.

12. Whitlock and Khan, "Blast in Pakistan Kills Al-Qaeda Commander"; "Al-Qaeda No. 3 Dead, But How?" CNN, December 4, 2005.

13. Sarah Baxter, "Al-Qaeda Chief Killed in Pakistan," *Sunday Times (London)*, December 4, 2005; "Sources Say Key Al-Qaeda Operative in Pakistan Still Alive: Paper," *Pakistan Observer*/BBC Monitoring South Asia, December 8, 2005; "Al-Qaeda No. 3 Dead, But How?"; "Senior Leader of Al-Qaeda Is Killed in Blast."

14. Zulfiqar Ali and Paul Watson, "Pakistani Journalist Abducted from Northern Tribal Area,*" Los Angeles Times*, December 8, 2005.

15. Whitlock and Khan, "Blast in Pakistan Kills Al-Qaeda Commander."

16. Zeeshan Haider, "Terror Kingpin Killed: Blow to Al-Qaeda as Blast Claims Its No. 3," *Daily Telegraph*, December 5, 2005; Munir Ahmad, "Al-Qaeda Commander Killed in Pakistan," *Independent,* December 4, 2005; Gretchen Peters, "Drone Said to Have Killed Al-Qaeda's No. 3," *Christian Science Monitor*, December 5, 2005.

17. "Pakistani Tribe Shows US-Marked Missile They Claim Killed Two Boys," *Irish Times*, December 5, 2005; Whitlock and Khan, "Blast in Pakistan Kills Al-Qaeda Commander," *Washington Post,* December 4, 2005; Ali and Watson, "Pakistani Journalist Abducted"; Haider, "Terror Kingpin Killed."

18. Kim Pilling, "British Muslim Is Convicted of Being Mastermind for al-Qa'ida: Mancunian Was So Vital He Recruited Another Man to Carry Incriminating Files," *Independent (London),* December 19, 2008; Russell Jenkins, "Diaries in Invisible Ink Help to Convict British Muslim Intent on Mass Murder," *Times (London)*, December 19, 2008.

19. Jenkins, "Diaries in Invisible Ink."

20. "Journalist Missing After Reporting al-Qaeda Death," National Public Radio, December 9, 2005.

21. Whitlock and Khan, "Blast Killed al-Qaeda Commander," *BBC News*, December 3, 2005; "Al-Qaeda No. 3 Dead, But How?"

22. "Al-Qaeda No. 3 Dead, But How?"; "Pakistani Tribe Shows US-Marked Missile"; "Evidence Suggests US Missile Used in Strike," MSNBC, December 5, 2005.

23. Whitlock and Khan, "Blast in Pakistan Kills Al-Qaeda Commander."

24. "Sources Say Key Al-Qaeda Operative in Pakistan Still Alive"; Peters, "Drone Said to Have Killed Al-Qaeda's No. 3."

25. Peters, "Drone Said to Have Killed Al-Qaeda's No. 3."

26. "Questions Surround al-Qaeda Leader's Death," *Voice of America News,* December 6, 2005.

27. Whitlock and Khan, "Blast in Pakistan Kills Al-Qaeda Commander."

28. Gretchen Peters, "Violence Grows in Pakistan's Tribal Zone, Despite Army Presence," *Christian Science Monitor*, December 12, 2005.

29. Whitlock and Khan, "Blast in Pakistan Kills Al-Qaeda Commander."

30. Ibid.

31. "Interview with Stephen Hadley; Interview with Hoshyar Zebari," *CNN Late Edition with Wolf Blitzer*, December 4, 2005; "Al-Qa'ida Boss Dead, Insists Pakistan," Associated Press, December 6, 2005.

32. Peters, "Violence Grows in Pakistan's Tribal Zone."

33. Whitlock and Khan, "Blast in Pakistan Kills Al-Qaeda Commander"; Rana Jawad, "Al-Libi, the 'Face of Al-Qaeda,'" Agence France Press, February 1, 2008; "Senior al-Qaeda Member Reported Dead," CNN, January 31, 2008.

34. DCI Michael McConnell, "Hearing of the House Permanent Committee on Intelligence, Annual Worldwide Threat Assessment," February 7, 2008.

35. Ibid.

36. US Air Force, "Air Force's Hunter-Killer UAV Now Flying in Afghanistan," Press Release, October 11, 2007.

37. US Air Force, *Factsheet: MQ-1 Predator;* and *Factsheet: MQ-9 Reaper.*

38. "Reaper Scores Insurgent Kill in Afghanistan," *Air Force Times*, October 29, 2007.

39. Jeremy Page, "Google Earth Reveals Secret History of US Base in Pakistan," *Times of London*, February 19, 2009; Tom Coghlan, Zahid Hussain, and Jeremy Page, "Secrecy and Denial As Pakistan Lets CIA Use Airbase to Strike Militants," *Times of London,* February 17, 2009.

40. Imtiaz Ali and Massoud Ansari, "Pakistan Fury as CIA Air Strike on Village Kills 18," *Telegraph*, January 15, 2006.

41. "Qaeda Vows to Fire Pakistan Nukes at US," english.aljazeera.net, June 22, 2009.

42. Ali and Ansari, "Pakistan Fury"; Josh Meyer, "CIA Expands Use of Drones in Terror War," *Los Angeles Times,* January 29, 2006; Craig Whitlock, "The New Al-Qaeda Central," *Washington Post*, September 9, 2007.

43. Meyer, "CIA Expands Use of Drones in Terror War"; Daniel Byman, "Targeted Killing, American-Style," *Los Angeles Times*, January 20, 2006; Griff Witte and Kamran Khan, "Attacks Strain Efforts on Terror," *Washington Post,* January 23, 2006.

44. Silvestre Reyes, "Hearing of the House Permanent Committee on Intelligence, Annual Worldwide Threat Assessment," February 7, 2008; John D. Rockefeller, "Hearing of the Senate Select Committee on Intelligence, Annual Worldwide Threat Assessment," February 5, 2008.

45. Imtiaz Ali and Craig Whitlock, "Al-Qaeda Commander Moved Freely in Pakistan; Libyan Killed Last Week Operated Openly," *Washington Post*, February 4, 2008.

46. Jawad, "Al-Libi, the 'Face of Al-Qaeda.'"

47. Ibid.

48. Craig Whitlock and Munir Ladaa, "Abu Laith al-Libi," *Washington Post*, February 1, 2008.

49. Eric Schmitt, "Senior Qaeda Commander Is Killed by US Missile Strike in Pakistani Tribal Area," *New York Times*, February 1, 2008.

50. Whitlock and Ladaa, "Abu Laith Al-Libi."

51. Jawad, "Al-Libi, the 'Face of Al-Qaeda.'"

52. Ibid.

53. Simon Santow, "Top al-Qaeda Operative Killed in Air Strike: Report," Australian Broadcasting Corporation, February 1, 2008.

54. Schmitt, "Senior Qaeda Commander Is Killed"; "Al-Qaida Figure Killed in Pakistan Attack," National Public Radio, February 1, 2008.

55. Ali and Whitlock, "About Laith Al-Libi"; "Al-Qaeda Commander Moved Freely in Pakistan."

56. Ali and Whitlock, "About Laith Al-Libi."

57. Jawad, "Al-Libi, the 'Face of Al-Qaeda.'"

58. Craig Whitlock and Karen DeYoung, "Al-Qaeda Figure Is Killed in Pakistan; Senior Commander Blamed in Bombing at US Afghan Base," *Washington Post,* February 1, 2008.

59. Schmitt, "Senior Qaeda Commander Is Killed"; Jawad, "Al-Libi, the 'Face of Al-Qaeda.'"

60. Ali and Whitlock, "Al-Qaeda Commander Moved Freely in Pakistan."

61. Ibid.

62. Joby Warrick and Robin Wright, "Unilateral Strike Called a Model for US Operations in Pakistan," *Washington Post,* February 19, 2008.

63. Schmitt, "Senior Qaeda Commander Is Killed."

64. Warrick and Wright, "Unilateral Strike Called a Model."

65. Ibid.

66. Declan Walsh, "Mysterious Chip Is CIA's Latest Weapon Against al-Qaida Targets Hiding in Pakistan's Tribal Belt," *Guardian,* June 1, 2009.

67. Ibid.

68. Walsh, "Mysterious Chip"; Anthony Lloyd, "Drones Take a Heavy Toll on Hearts and Minds; Pakistan," *Times of London*, March 10, 2010.

69. Warrick and Wright, "Unilateral Strike Called a Model."

70. Ibid.

71. "Libi Was on Satellite Phone When Missile Hit," Associated Press, February 1, 2008; Warrick and Wright, "Unilateral Strike Called a Model."

72. Warrick and Wright, "Unilateral Strike Called a Model."

73. Eric Schmitt and David Sanger, "Pakistan Shift Could Curtail Drone Strikes," *New York Times*, February 22, 2008.

74. Ibid.

75. Jane Perlez and Ismail Khan, "Air Strikes Kill 9 in Pakistan Region That Harbors Militants," *New York Times*, March 17, 2008.

76. Robin Wright and Joby Warrick, "US Steps Up Unilateral Strikes in Pakistan; Officials Fear Support from Islamabad Will Wane," *Washington Post,* March 27, 2008.

77. Schmitt and Sanger, "Pakistan Shift Could Curtail Drone Strikes."

78. Wright and Warrick, "US Steps Up Unilateral Strikes."

79. Schmitt and Sanger, "Pakistan Shift Could Curtail Drone Strikes"; David Cloud, "CIA Drones Have Broader List of Targets," *Los Angeles Times*, May 5, 2010.

80. Wright and Warrick, "US Steps Up Unilateral Strikes."

81. Jane Perlez and Ismail Khan, "Air Strikes Kill 9 in Pakistan Region That Harbors Militants," *New York Times*, March 17, 2008.

82. Michele Norris, "Attack Reveals Snags in US Terror Fight in Pakistan," *All Things Considered,* February 19, 2008.

83. Warrick and Wright, "Unilateral Strike Called a Model."

84. Warrick and Wright, "Unilateral Strike Called a Model"; David Ignatius, "Terrorists in the Crosshairs," *Washington Post,* February 17, 2010.

85. Peter Bergen and Katherine Tiedemann, "The Drone War," *New Republic,* June 3, 2009.

86. Matthew Rosenberg, "Pakistan Lends Support for US Military Strikes," *Wall Street Journal,* February 18, 2009.

87. Bergen and Tiedemann, "The Drone War"; Walsh, "Mysterious Chip Is CIA's Latest Weapon."

88. Michael Scheuer, "Al-Qaeda's New Leader in Afghanistan: A Profile of Abu al-Yazid," *Terrorism Focus,* July 3, 2007.

89. Steven Emerson, statement before the Committee on House Select Intelligence, April 9, 2008; Scheuer, "Al-Qaeda's New Leader in Afghanistan."

90. Scheuer, "Al-Qaeda's New Leader in Afghanistan"; Mohamed al Shafey, "Sheikh Said: Al-Qaeda's Financier," *Asharq Al-Awsat,* August 8, 2008.

91. Scheuer, "Al-Qaeda's New Leader in Afghanistan."

92. Jake Tapper, "Officials: Al-Qaeda No. 3 Killed," ABCNews.com, May 31, 2010; *9/11 Commission Report,* 251.

93. Shafey, "Sheikh Said: Al-Qaeda's Financier"; Greg Miller and Craig Whitlock, "Al-Qaeda No. 3 Yazid Reported Killed by U.S. Drone," *Washington Post,* June 1, 2010.

94. Shafey, "Sheikh Said: Al-Qaeda's Financier"; "Al-Arabiya Talk Show Discusses Al-Qa'idah's 'Third Man,'" *Al Arabiya*/BBC Monitoring, August 31, 2008.

95. "Al-Qaeda's Closer Ties with Pasdarans," Intelligence Online, July 20, 2007; "Al-Qa'idah Leader for Afghanistan Sees US Suffering More Defeats, Losses," *Today's Encounter,* Al-Jazeera/BBC Monitoring, June 21, 2009.

96. Shafey, "Sheikh Said: Al-Qaeda's Financier"; "Qaeda Says Top Leader Yazid Dead: Monitors," Agence France Presse, June 1, 2010.

97. "Little-Known Egyptian Is Key Al-Qaeda Figure," Associated Press, October 15, 2009.

98. Katarina Kratovac, "Afghan al-Qaida Commander Warns of Attacks on West," Associated Press, September 5, 2008; Eric Schmitt, "Top Militant Killed by US in Pakistan, Qaeda Says," *New York Times,* June 1, 2010.

99. Shafey, "Sheikh Said: Al-Qaeda's Financier"; Kratovac, "Afghan al-Qaida Commander Warns of Attacks."

100. Ibid.

101. "Qaeda Vows to Fire Pakistan Nukes at US," english.aljazeera.net, June 22, 2009; "Al-Qa'idah Leader for Afghanistan Sees US Suffering."

102. Adam Goldman and Brett J. Blackledge, "AP Sources: Al-Qaida's Afghan Head Contacted Zazi," Associated Press, October 14, 2009.

103. Schmitt, "Top Militant Killed by US in Pakistan"; "Al-Qa'idah Leader for Afghanistan Sees US Suffering."

104. Schmitt, "Top Militant Killed by US in Pakistan."

105. Miller and Whitlock, "Al-Qaeda No. 3 Yazid Reported Killed"; Kimberly Dozier, "Al-Qaida: No. 3 Official Killed with Family," Associated Press Online, June 1, 2010.

106. Greg Miller and Craig Whitlock, "Al-Qaeda's Third-Ranking Leader Is Reported Dead; U.S. Officials Believe Statement from Terrorist Group Is Accurate," *Washington Post,* June 1, 2010; "Third-Ranking al-Qaida Leader Killed in Pakistan," *Voice of America News,* June 1, 2010.

107. Dozier, "Al-Qaida: No. 3 Official Killed."

108. Ravi Velloor, "Al-Qaeda's No. 3 Killed in Drone Attack; Announcement by Terror Group, If Confirmed, Marks Huge US Success," *Straits Times (Singapore),* June 2, 2010.

109. Jake Tapper, "Officials: Al-Qaeda No. 3 Killed," ABCNews.com, May 31, 2010.

110. Stuart Levey, "How al-Qaeda Will Miss Its Moneyman," *Washington Post,* June 6, 2010.

111. Kim Sengupta, "Al-Qa'ida's No 3 Killed by Drone Strike," *Independent,* June 2, 2010.

112. Joby Warrick, "Jan 1 Attack by CIA Killed Two Leaders of Al-Qaeda," *Washington Post,* January 9, 2009; "Official: Hotel Blast 'Biggest Attack' in 7 Years for Pakistan," CNN, September 21, 2008.

CHAPTER 9: THE ENEMY WITHIN

1. Catherine Tsai and P. Solomon Banda, "Najibullah Zazi Terror Probe: A Timeline of Events," Associated Press, September 21, 2009.

2. David Johnston and William Rashbaum, "Rush for Clues Before Charges in Terror Case," *New York Times,* September 30, 2009.

3. "Inside the Zazi Takedown," *Newsweek,* September 26, 2009. If—or how much—authorities knew of these activities at this point or if they learned of them immediately prior to his arrest remains unknown. Some sources claim authorities did not know.

4. Anne Kornblut, "Obama Team Says Zazi Case Illustrates Balanced Approach to Terror Threat," *New York Times,* October 6, 2009.

5. Victoria Cavaliere, "Zazi Plot Planned Attacks on Busiest Subway Stations," *NBC New York,* April 12, 2010.

6. Robert Kaplan, "Afghanistan Post Mortem," *Atlantic,* April 1989.

7. "Did Zazi Heed Call to Terrorize Americans?" Associated Press, October 3, 2009.

8. Michael Wilson, "From Smiling Coffee Vendor to Terror Suspect," *New York Times,* September 25, 2009.

9. Wilson, "From Smiling Coffee Vendor to Terror Suspect."

10. Ibid.

11. "Did Zazi Heed Call to Terrorize Americans?"

12. Ibid.

13. Wilson, "From Smiling Coffee Vendor to Terror Suspect."

14. Ibid.

15. Samantha Gross, David Caruso, and Michael Rubinkam, "Radical Influences All Around NYC Terror Suspect," Associated Press, October 3, 2009.

16. Robert Boczkiewicz, "Bomb Plot Suspect Said to Have Eyed 9/11 Attack," Reuters, September 25, 2009.

17. Gross, Caruso, and Rubinkam, "Radical Influences."

18. Wilson, "From Smiling Coffee Vendor to Terror Suspect."

19. Ibid.

20. Tsai and Banda, "Najibullah Zazi Terror Probe."

21. "United States of America Versus Najibullah Zazi," Transcript of Criminal Cause for Pleading, February 22, 2010, http://www.cbsnews.com/htdocs/pdf/USvZazi.pdf.

22. "United States of America Versus Najibullah Zazi."

23. Ibid.

24. Department of Justice, Office of Public Affairs, "Najibullah Zazi Pleads Guilty to Conspiracy to Use Explosives Against Persons or Property in U.S., Conspiracy to Murder Abroad and Providing Material Support to Al-Qaeda," February 22, 2010.

25. Sebastian Rotella, "Fear of Homegrown Terror Up," *Chicago Tribune*, December 7, 2009.

26. Michael Powell, "US Recruit Reveals How Qaeda Trains Foreigners," *New York Times,* July 23, 2009.

27. Jerry Markon, "Al-Qaeda Leaders Said to Have Ordered Attack on New York Subway System," *Washington Post*, April 24, 2010.

28. Department of Justice, Office of Public Affairs, "Najibullah Zazi Pleads Guilty to Conspiracy."

29. "British Spies Help Prevent Al-Qaeda-Inspired Attack on New York Subway," *Telegraph*, November 9, 2009.

30. Wilson, "From Smiling Coffee Vendor to Terror Suspect."

31. Dina Temple-Raston, "Terrorism Case Shows Range of Investigators' Tools," NPR, October 3, 2009.

32. Michael Wilson, "Who Is Najibullah Zazi?" *Denver Post*, September 27, 2009.

33. Tsai and Banda, "Najibullah Zazi Terror Probe."

34. Wilson, "From Smiling Coffee Vendor to Terror Suspect."

35. US Department of Justice, "Memorandum of Law in Support of the Government's Motion for a Permanent Order of Detention," September 23, 2009.

36. Wilson, "From Smiling Coffee Vendor to Terror Suspect."

37. US Department of Justice, "Memorandum of Law in Support of the Government's Motion for a Permanent Order of Detention."

38. Ibid.

39. "United States of America Versus Najibullah Zazi."

40. US Department of Justice, "Memorandum of Law in Support of the Government's Motion for a Permanent Order of Detention."

41. Ibid.

42. Anne Kornblut, "Obama Team Says Zazi Case Illustrates Balanced Approach to Terror Threat," *Washington Post*, October 6, 2009.

43. Temple-Raston, "Terrorism Case Shows Range of Investigators' Tools."

44. Mark Hosenball, "Hold the Phone," *Newsweek*, May 22, 2006.

45. James Risen and Eric Lichtblau, "Bush Lets U.S. Spy on Callers Without Courts," *New York Times*, December 16, 2005.

46. Wilson, "From Smiling Coffee Vendor to Terror Suspect."

47. Tsai and Banda, "Timeline of Events in NYC Terror Probe."

48. "Inside the Zazi Takedown."

49. Michael Sheehan, "The Hatfields and the McCoys of Counterterrorism," *New York Times,* September 26, 2009.

50. Department of Justice, Office of the Inspector General, "The Department of Justice's Terrorism Task Forces," June 2005, www.justice.gov/oig/reports/plus/e0507/final.pdf.

51. Ibid.

52. "NYPD's Voice Loud and Clear," *NYPD Confidential*, October 14, 2005, http://nypdconfidential.com/columns/2005/051014.html.

53. "Inside the Zazi Takedown."

54. Ibid.

55. Ibid.

56. Ibid.

57. David Johnston and William Rashbaum, "Rush for Clues Before Charges in Terror Case," *New York Times,* September 30, 2009.

58. Temple-Raston, "Terrorism Case Shows Range of Investigators' Tools."

59. "Inside the Zazi Takedown."

60. Ibid.

61. A. G. Sulzberger, "Imam and Informant Tells Why He Lied," *New York Times,* April 15, 2010.

62. Carrie Johnson and Robin Shulman, "Probes Test Trust That Authorities Strove to Win from US Muslims," *Washington Post,* October 5, 2009.

63. Ibid.

64. "Inside the Zazi Takedown."

65. "Probes Test Trust That Authorities Strove to Win from US Muslims."

66. "The United States of America Versus Mohammad Wali Zazi," criminal complaint for the US District Court for the District of Colorado, September 16, 2009, www.npr.org/blogs/thetwo-way/M%20Zazi.pdf.

67. "The United States of America Versus Ahmad Wais Afzali," criminal complaint for the United States District Court Eastern District of New York, http://cryptome.org/zazi/usa-v-zazi.htm#Ahmad Wais Afzali.

68. "The United States of America Versus Najibullah Zazi."

69. Ibid.

70. Ibid.

71. Temple-Raston, "Terrorism Case Shows Range of Investigators' Tools."

72. Furthermore, Section 213 of the act allowed for such searches while making no explicit references to terrorism, clearing the path for use in a range of federal cases. A 2009 report by the Administrative Office of the US Courts noted that, of the 763 requests in 2008, only three dealt with terrorism, while 65 percent were requested for drug-related investigations. By 2009, relatively little controversy surrounded the revelations that terrorism concerns played only a minor part in these requests, despite the fact that the bill that birthed this law had the word "terrorism" in the title. Administrative Office of the United States Courts, *Report of the Director of the Administrative Office of the United States Courts on Applications for Delayed-Notice Search Warrants and Extensions,* July 2, 2009.

73. "The United States of America Versus Najibullah Zazi."

74. Wilson, "From Smiling Coffee Vendor to Terror Suspect."

75. Johnston and Rashbaum, "Rush for Clues Before Charges in Terror Case."

76. Bobby Ghosh, "NYPD Denies It Botched a Terrorism Probe," *Time,* September 22, 2009.

77. Bobby Ghosh, "Spotlight: The Zazi Terrorism Case," *Time,* October 5, 2009.

78. Ibid.

79. Mike Levine, "White House Wades into Terror Intel Dispute Between FBI, Homeland Security," FOX News.com, December 17, 2009, www.foxnews.com/politics/2009/12/16/white-house-intervenes-dispute-fbi-homeland-security.

80. Ibid.

81. Al Baker and Karen Zraick, "FBI Searches Colorado Home of Man in Terror Inquiry That Reached Queens," *New York Times,* September 16, 2009.

82. Karen Zraick, "A Man Under Watch, but Not Under Wraps, in a Terrorism Case," *New York Times,* October 8, 2009; "Facts and Fictions About Alleged Zazi Plot," NPR, September 28, 2009.

83. Zraick, "A Man Under Watch."

84. Ibid.

85. "Facts and Fictions About Alleged Zazi Plot."

86. Zraick, "A Man Under Watch."

87. US Department of Justice, "Memorandum of Law in Support of the Government's Motion for a Permanent Order of Detention."

88. See www.thedenverchannel.com/news/20949911/detail.html.

89. US Department of Justice, "Memorandum of Law in Support of the Government's Motion for a Permanent Order of Detention."

90. "The United States of America Versus Najibullah Zazi."

91. Kirk Mitchell et al., "Zazi, Father held in Terror Probe," *Denver Post,* September 20, 2009.

92. "Inside the Zazi Takedown."

93. Department of Justice, Office of Public Affairs, "Najibullah Zazi Indicted for Conspiracy," September 24, 2009.

94. John Brennan, "State of the Union," CNN, May 9, 2010, http://transcripts .cnn.com/TRANSCRIPTS/1005/09/sotu.01.html.

95. Michael Farrell, "Zazi Case: How Far should FBI Go in Tracking Muslims?" *Christian Science Monitor,* September 30, 2009.

96. David Kravets, "Lawmakers Cave to FBI in Patriot Act Debate," *Wired,* October 1, 2009.

97. William Rashbaum, "After Months of Scrutiny in Zazi Terrorism Case, Two Arrests Came as a Surprise," *New York Times,* January 8, 2010.

98. Department of Justice, Office of Public Affairs, "Najibullah Zazi Pleads Guilty to Conspiracy."

99. "The United States of America Versus Najibullah Zazi."

100. Sulzberger, "Imam and Informant Tells Why He Lied."

101. "Father of Would-Be Suicide Bomber Convicted of Obstructing Terrorism Investigation," FBI press release, July 22, 2011.

102. Carrie Johnson and Spencer Hsu, "Najibullah Zazi Pleads Guilty in New York Subway Bomb Plot," *Washington Post,* February 23, 2010.

CHAPTER 10: AMERICA'S FUTURE

1. Philip Smucker, "The Intrigue Behind the Drone Strike," *Christian Science Monitor,* November 12, 2002.

2. Winston Nagan and Craig Hammer, "The Changing Character of Sovereignty in International Law and International Relations," www.law.ufl.edu/faculty/publications /pdf/sov.pdf.

3. Boczek Boleslaw, *International Law: A Dictionary* (Lanham, MD: Scarecrow, 2005).

4. UN Charter, Article 2, Section 4, www.un.org/en/documents/charter/chapter1 .shtml.

5. See www.un.org/Docs/SG/agpeace.html.

6. UN Charter, Article 51, www.un.org/en/documents/charter/chapter7.shtml.

7. Donald Rumsfeld, "Remarks at Stakeout Outside ABC TV," October 28, 2001, www.defense.gov/Transcripts/Transcript.aspx?TranscriptID=2225.

8. George W. Bush, "Statement by the President in His Address to the Nation," September 11, 2001, http://georgewbush-whitehouse.archives.gov/news/releases/2001/09/print/20010911–16.html.

9. Ibid.

10. Smucker, "Intrigue Behind the Drone Strike."

11. Smucker, "Intrigue Behind the Drone Strike"; Seymour Hersh, "Manhunt: The Bush Administration's New Strategy in the War Against Terrorism," *New Yorker*, December 23, 2002.

12. Hersh, "Manhunt."

13. James Risen and David Johnston, "Bush Has Widened Authority of C.I.A. to Kill Terrorists," *New York Times*, December 15, 2002; Hersh, "Manhunt."

14. Risen and Johnston, "Bush Has Widened Authority of C.I.A."; Hersh, "Manhunt."

15. Ibid.

16. Ahmed al Haj, "Blast Said to Kill Bin Laden Aide," Associated Press, November 4, 2002.

17. Ibid.

18. Deputy Secretary Wolfowitz, interview by CNN International, November 5, 2002, www.usatoday.com/news/world/2002–11–04-yemen-explosion_x.htm.

19. Ahmed al Haj, "Yemen Acknowledges U.S. Role in Attack Against al-Qaida but Criticizes One-Sided Announcement," Associated Press Worldstream, November 19, 2002.

20. "Yemeni Parties Condemn US Killing of Six Nationals on 3 November," *Yemen Times*, November 18, 2002.

21. Matt Kelley, "Unmanned Craft a Terror War Tool," Associated Press, November 5, 2002.

22. Hersh, "Manhunt."

23. Sue Chan, "CIA's License to Kill: CIA Agents Authorized to Kill Americans Working for Al-Qaeda," CBS, December 4, 2002, www.cbsnews.com/stories/2002/12/03/terror/main531596.shtml?tag=mncol;lst;1.

24. Ibid.

25. David Ensor, "U.S. Confirms Death of Man Linked to Alleged Buffalo Terror Cell," CNN, November 12, 2002. http://articles.cnn.com/2002–11–12/us/yemen.blast.us_1_ahmed-hijazi-kamal-derwish-men-of-yemeni-descent?_s=PM:US.

26. Patrick Tyler, "Yemen, an Uneasy Ally, Proves Adept at Playing Off Old Rivals," *New York Times*, December 19, 2002.

27. Jim Landers, "U.S. Officials Say Group Hasn't Been Able to Gain Firm Foothold," *Dallas Morning News*, May 6, 2004.

28. Jonathan Schanzer, "Aid to Yemen: Throwing Good Money After Bad?" House Committee on Foreign Affairs, Written Testimony, February 3, 2010.

29. Anwar Faruqi, "Suspect Was on the Run for Months in Yemen," Associated Press, November 6, 2002.

30. Anwar Faruqi, "Al Qaida Suspects Sought in Yemen," Associated Press, February 4, 2002.

31. "U.S. Kills Al-Qaeda Suspects in Yemen," Associated Press, November 5, 2002.

32. Tyler, "Yemen, an Uneasy Ally."

33. Kimberley Dozier, "U.S. Leading Assaults on al-Qaeda in Yemen: Cruise Missile Strikes, Military Units on Ground Exemplify American Actions in Country," CBS, January 3, 2010, www.cbsnews.com/stories/2010/01/02/eveningnews/main6048291.shtml ?tag=contentMain;contentBody.

34. Dozier, "U.S. Leading Assaults"; Landers, "U.S. Officials Say Group Hasn't Been Able to Gain Firm Foothold"; Tyler, "Yemen, an Uneasy Ally"; Faruqi, "Suspect Was on the Run."

35. Ahmed al Haj, "President: Yemen to Fight Terrorism," Associated Press, February 28, 2002.

36. Ahmed al Haj, "Yemeni Tribes Warn U.S. Against Attack," Associated Press, May 17, 2002.

37. Anwar Faruqi, "Al Qaida Suspects Sought in Yemen," Associated Press, February 4, 2002.

38. Faruqi, "Suspect Was on the Run."

39. Hersh, "Manhunt."

40. Tyler, "Yemen, an Uneasy Ally."

41. Schanzer, "Aid to Yemen."

42. Andrew Buncombe and Raymond Whitaker, "Silent Killer Changes Rules of Engagement," *Independent*, November 6, 2002.

43. West Point Combating Terrorism Center, "Al Qa'ida's Foreign Fighters in Iraq: A First Look at the Sinjar Records," December 2007, http://brianhowesfishman.files .wordpress.com/2009/12/sinjar-records_final.pdf.

44. Ian Black, "Yemen Terrorism: Soft Approach to Jihadist Start to Backfire as Poverty Fuels Extremism," *Guardian*, July 30, 2008.

45. Shane Bauer, "U.S. Embassy Hit in Yemen, Raising Militancy Concerns," *Christian Science Monitor,* September 18, 2008.

46. "Yemeni Troops Target al-Qaeda," english.aljazeera.net, January 5, 2010, http://english.aljazeera.net/news/middleeast/2010/01/201015132832598600.html.

47. "Yemen in War with al-Qaeda, Urges Citizens to Help," Reuters, January 14, 2010.

48. Christa Case Bryant, "Yemen Air Strike on Al-Qaeda: Was Cleric Linked to Fort Hood Shooting Killed?" *Christian Science Monitor*, December 24, 2009.

49. Adam Entous, "Gates Backs Big Boost in U.S. Military Aid to Yemen," Reuters, February 22, 2010.

50. Hersh, "Manhunt."

51. Jeffrey Gettleman and Eric Schmitt, "U.S. Kills Top Qaeda Militant in Southern Somalia," *New York Times,* September 14, 2009.

52. *Profile: Saleh Ali Saleh Nabhan,* BBC, September 15, 2009. According to one of his sisters, however, Nabhan grew up in a well-off neighborhood north of Mombasa. See "Concerns Grow Over Rising Militancy Among Kenyan Muslims," Associated Press, January 10, 2003.

53. *Profile: Saleh Ali Saleh Nabhan.*

54. "Kenya's Most Dangerous Al-Qaeda Terrorist," *Daily Nation*, June 21, 2009.

55. Raymond Bonner and Steve Levine, "'We Are Freedom Fighters,' Says a Leader of Militants," *New York Times,* August 27, 1998; NEFA Foundation, *Biographical Sum-*

mary of the Martyred Commander, Allah-willing, Abu Yusuf al-Nabhani, October 12, 2009.

56. *Profile: Saleh Ali Saleh Nabhan.*

57. Ibid.

58. Stephen Mburu, "Kenya: How the Nairobi Terror Attack Was Planned," *Daily Nation,* August 6, 2008; "Kenya's Most Dangerous Al-Qaeda Terrorist," *Daily Nation,* June 21, 2009.

59. NEFA Foundation, *Biographical Summary.*

60. Marc Lacey, "Same Suspects Tied to Mombasa and '98 Embassy Attacks," *New York Times,* February 22, 2003.

61. "Israel Evacuates Tourists from Kenya," BBC, November 29, 2002.

62. "The Threat from Portable Missiles," BBC, November 29, 2002; "Israel Evacuates Tourists."

63. "Israel Evacuates Tourists."

64. Lacey, "Same Suspects Tied to Mombasa and '98 Embassy Attacks."

65. Lubaina Kher, "Kenyan Police Question Bomb Suspect's Kin," Associated Press, December 11, 2002.

66. Lacey, "Same Suspects Tied to Mombasa and '98 Embassy Attacks"; Matthew Rosenberg, "Concerns Grow Over Rising Militancy Among Kenyan Muslims," Associated Press, January 10, 2003.

67. Andrew England, "FBI's Most Wanted Leader of al-Qaida Cell Indicted for U.S. Embassy Bombings Escaped," Associated Press, June 13, 2004.

68. Lubaina Kher, "Kenya Attacks Suspect May Be in Somalia," Associated Press, December 17, 2002.

69. Rosenberg, "Concerns Grow over Rising Militancy among Kenyan Muslims."

70. England, "FBI's Most Wanted Leader."

71. Jeffrey Gettlemen, "In Somalia, a New Template for Fighting Terrorism," *New York Times,* October 17, 2009.

72. "Key Events in the Recent History of the African Nation of Somalia," Associated Press, September 15, 2009.

73. "The Situation in Somalia," www.forces.gc.ca/somalia/vol1/v1c11e.htm#14.

74. Daveed Gartenstein-Ross, "The Strategic Challenge of Somalia's Al-Shabaab: Dimensions of Jihad," *Middle East Quarterly,* Fall 2009, 25–36.

75. Ibid.

76. Combating Terrorism Center, *Al-Qa'ida's (Mis)Adventures in the Horn of Africa,* www.ctc.usma.edu/aq/aq_exsumII.asp.

77. Ross, "Strategic Challenge."

78. Paul Haven, "The Death of al Zarqawi; Tracking the Fates of Members of the Terrorist 'Class of 2004' Gives Glimpse of Short Life Expectancy of Those Who Take Up Arms; New Jihadist Generation Dead, Hiding," Associated Press, June 10, 2006.

79. Alisha Ryu, "Kenyan Officials Deny Reports of Arrest of Terror Suspect," *Voice of America,* March 14, 2007.

80. FBI, "Fazul Abdullah Mohammed," www.fbi.gov/wanted/terrorists/termohammed.htm.

81. Gettleman and Schmitt, "U.S. Kills Top Qaeda Militant."

82. Dina Temple-Raston, "Dead Al-Qaida Suspect Tied to Somali Youths in U.S.," NPR, September 16, 2009.

83. Spencer Hsu, "Concern Grows Over Recruitment of Somali Americans by Islamists," *Washington Post*, October 4, 2009.

84. Scott Baldauf, "Obama's First Somalia Strike Hits Al-Qaeda Suspect," *Christian Science Monitor*, September 15, 2009.

85. "Slain al-Qaida Suspect's Mother Asks to See Body," Associated Press, September 16, 2009.

86. Gettleman and Schmitt, "U.S. Kills Top Qaeda Militant"; Maamoun Youssef, "Al-Qaida Group in Somalia Confirms Leader's Death," Associated Press, September 16, 2009.

87. Tristan McConnell, "Terrorist Saleh Ali Saleh Nabhan Killed by US Commandos in Somalia," *Times*, September 16, 2009.

88. Mohamed Olad Hassan, "US Special Forces Targeted al-Qaida in Somalia," Associated Press, September 15, 2009.

89. Spencer Ackerman, "David Petraeus: The Danger Room Interview," *Wired*, August 18, 2010.

90. "14 Charged with Aiding Terror Group Al-Shabab," Associated Press, August 5, 2010.

91. Scott Shane, Mark Mazzetti, and Robert F. Worth, "Secret Assault on Terrorism Widens on Two Continents," *New York Times*, August 14, 2010.

CHAPTER 11: GERONIMO

1. White House, Press Briefing on the Killing of Osama bin Laden, May 2, 2011; www.whitehouse.gov/the-press-office/2011/05/02/press-briefing-senior-administration-officials-killing-osama-bin-laden; Nic Robertson Twitter account, May 3, 2011, https://twitter.com/#!/NicRobertsonCNN/status/65377085165813760.

2. Lolita Baldor, "Pentagon: US Has Questioned bin Laden's Widows," Associated Press, May 13, 2011.

3. Kimberley Dozier, "Sources: Raiders Knew Mission a One-Shot Deal," *Navy Times*, May 17, 2011.

4. Jane Mayer, "The Search for Osama: Did the Government Let bin Laden's Trail Go Cold?" *New Yorker*, August 4, 2003; Pervez Musharraf, *In the Line of Fire: A Memoir* (New York: Free Press, 2008), 220–221.

5. Combating Terrorism Center, *Letter Exposes New Leader in al-Qaeda High Command*, www.ctc.usma.edu/aq/pdf/CTC-AtiyahLetter.pdf.

6. Musharraf, *In the Line of Fire*, 220–221.

7. Spencer Ackerman, "Osama's Diabolical Plan for Secure E-Mail: Thumb Drives," *Wired*, May 13, 2011.

8. Laura Rozen, "The Courier: The Multiple Identities of the Man Who Led U.S. to bin Laden," Yahoo News, May 4, 2011; http://news.yahoo.com/blogs/envoy/courier-multiple-identities-man-led-u-bin-laden-133835572.html; Michael Isikoff, "How Profile of Bin Laden Courier Led CIA to Its Target," *NBC News*, May 4, 2011.

9. Farah Stockman, "Harsh Tactics May Have Aided US Raid," *Boston Globe*, May 4, 2011.

10. Michael Mukasey, "The Waterboarding Trail to bin Laden," *Wall Street Journal*, May 6, 2011.

11. John Yoo, "From Guantanamo to Abbottabad," *Wall Street Journal*, May 4, 2011.

12. Leon Panetta, interview, MSNBC, May 3, 2011, www.msnbc.msn.com/id/4288 7700/ns/world_news-death_of_bin_laden/t/transcript-interview-cia-director-panetta.

13. John McCain, "Bin Laden's Death and the Debate over Torture," *Washington Post*, May 11, 2011.

14. Greg Sargent, "Exclusive: Private Letter from CIA Chief Undercuts Claim Torture Was Key to Killing bin Laden," Washington Post Plum Line, May 16, 2011, http://tinyurl.com/44rlvlq.

15. Dahlia Lithwick, "Still Stupid, Still Wrong, Still Immoral," *Slate*, May 4, 2011.

16. Mark Mazzetti and David Rohde, "Amid US Policy Disputes, Qaeda Grows in Pakistan," *New York Times*, June 30, 2008; Julian Borger and Declan Walsh, "The Never-ending Manhunt," *Guardian*, July 10, 2009; "TV Show Discusses US Charges Against Pakistan Intelligence Agency," *Today with Kamran Khan*, Karachi Geo News Television in Urdu/BBC Monitoring South Asia, August 2, 2008.

17. Mazzetti and Rohde, "Qaeda Grows in Pakistan"; Borger and Walsh, "Never-ending Manhunt."

18. Ibid.

19. Ibid.

20. Ibid.

21. Eric Schmitt and Thom Shanker, "US Plan Widens Role in Training Pakistani Forces," *New York Times*, March 2, 2008.

22. Ibid.

23. Ibid.

24. Khalid Hasan, "US-trained Pakistani Commandos to Be Deployed in Tribal Areas," *Daily Times (Pakistan)*/BBC World Monitoring, August 4, 2008.

25. R. Jeffrey Smith, Candace Rondeaux, and Joby Warrick, "2 US Air Strikes Offer a Concrete Sign of Obama's Pakistan Policy," *Washington Post*, January 24, 2009.

26. Dexter Filkins, "Right at the Edge," *New York Times*, September 7, 2008.

27. Smith, Rondeaux, and Warrick, "2 US Air Strikes."

28. Greg Miller, "CIA Spied on bin Laden from Safe House," *Washington Post*, May 6, 2011.

29. Declan Walsh, "Osama bin Laden Monitored for Months Before Raid," *Guardian*, May 6, 2011.

30. Marc Ambinder, "Then Came Geronimo," *National Journal*, May 12, 2011.

31. Ibid.

32. Dozier, "Raiders Knew Mission a One-Shot Deal."

33. Bill Sweetman, "Bin Laden Raid May Have Exposed Stealth Helo," *Aviation Week*, May 5, 2011, http://tinyurl.com/3dywvaw.

34. Bob Woodward, "Death of Osama bin Laden: Phone Call Pointed U.S. to Compound and to 'the Pacer,'" *Washington Post*, May 6, 2011.

35. Ibid.

36. Ibid.

37. John Keegan, *Intelligence in War* (Toronto: Vintage Canada, 2002), 348.

38. "Obama Talks Risks, Payoffs in Making bin Laden Decision," Agence France Press, May 8, 2011, http://tinyurl.com/5vfwea4.

39. Ibid.

CHAPTER 12: TO THINE OWN SELF BE TRUE

1. Pew Research Center for the People and the Press, *GOP Likely to Recapture Control of House,* October 31, 2010.

2. Cameron Middleton, interview, November 15, 2010.

3. Dana Priest, "Foreign Network at Front of CIA's Terror Fight," *Washington Post,* November 18, 2005.

4. Joseph Berger, "Nations Halt Air Cargo From Yemen," *New York Times,* November 1, 2010.

5. George Tenet, *At the Center of the Storm* (New York: Harper Collins, 2007).

6. Ali Waked, "Hamas Crushes al-Qaeda Uprising," *YNet News,* August 14, 2009.

7. "Meshal: Johnston's Release Shows Hamas Brought Order to Gaza," *Haaretz,* July 4, 2007.

8. Ansar al-Sunnah used to be known as Ansar al-Islam. It has since resumed using its original name.

9. Ansar al-Sunnah was until 2003 known as Ansar al-Islam. Ansar al-Sunnah changed its name back to Ansar al-Islam several years later in an effort to return to its Kurdish roots. See Department of State, *Country Reports on Terrorism: Ansar al-Islam,* April 30, 2008.

10. Sun Tzu, *The Art of War* (Taipei: SMC Publishing, 1994), 177.

11. MEMRI, "Major Jihadi Cleric and Author of Al-Qaeda's Shari'a Guide to Jihad: 9/11 Was a Sin," \December 14, 2007, www.memrijttm.org/content/en/report.htm?report =2636&param=AJT; Abdul Hameed Bakier, "Al-Qaeda's al-Zawahiri Repudiates Dr. Fadl's Rationalization of Jihad," Jamestown Foundation Terrorism Focus, April 30, 2008.

12. Richard Russell, interview, June 29, 2009.

13. Pam Benson, "Former Spy Sued by CIA for Publishing Without Permission," CNN.com, October 20, 2010, http://articles.cnn.com/2010–10–19/us/spy.cia.suit _1_cia-employees-cia-statement-prb?_s=PM:U.S.

14. Office of the Director of National Intelligence, Office of the Inspector General, "Critical Intelligence Community Management Challenges," November 12, 2008.

15. Ibid.

16. Ibid.

17. Rolf Mowatt-Larssen, interview, June 29, 2009.

18. Ibid.

19. Ellen Nakashima, "Dismantling of Saudi-CIA Web Site Illustrates Need for Clearer Cyberwar Policies," *Washington Post,* March 19, 2010.

20. Commission on the Intelligence Capabilities of the United States Regarding Weapons of Mass Destruction, *Report to the President of the United States,* March 31, 2005.

21. Marjorie Cohn, "Assassination and Display in Iraq: The Killings of Uday and Qusai Hussein in International Law," *Jurist,* July 29, 2003.

22. James Risen, "US to Hunt Down Afghan Drug Lords Tied to Taliban," *New York Times*, August 9, 2009.

23. Alan Dershowitz, "Double Standard Watch: Targeted Killings OK for US but Not for Israel," *Jerusalem Post,* August 16, 2009.

24. Anatol Lieven, "Five Myths About Pakistan," *Washington Post*, June 3, 2010.

25. "Pakistan Backed Haqqani Attack on Kabul: Mike Mullen," BBC, September 22, 2011.

26. Dexter Filkins, "Right at the Edge," *New York Times*, September 7, 2008.

27. Ibid.

28. Ibid.

29. Akbar Zaidi, *Pakistan's Roller-Coaster Economy: Tax Evasion Stifles Growth,* Carnegie Endowment for International Peace, Policy Brief 88, September 2010.

30. Filkins, "Right at the Edge."

31. Transparency International, *Corruption Perceptions Index 2010.*

32. Zalmay Khalilzad, "Get Tough on Pakistan," *New York Times*, October 19, 2010.

33. Sean Naylor, "JSOC Task Force Battles Haqqani Militants," *Army Times*, September 14, 2010.

34. Ibid.

35. Sean Naylor, "More Than Door Kickers," *Armed Forces Journal*, March 2006.

36. Michele Malvesti, *To Serve the Nation: US Special Operations Forces in an Era of Persistent Conflict,* Center for a New American Strategy, June 2010, 32.

37. Ibid.

38. *USSOCOM Fact Book,* 14; www.fas.org/irp/agency/dod/socom/factbook-2010.pdf.

39. Dana Priest, "US Military Teams, Intelligence Deeply Involved in Aiding Yemen on Strikes," *Washington Post*, January 27, 2010.

40. Benjamin Wittes and Jack Goldsmith, "The Best Trial Option for KSM: Nothing," *Washington Post*, March 19, 2010.

41. William Fisher, "Wittes, Goldsmith, and KSM: Absurd, Cynical," *Huffington Post*, March 22, 2010, www.huffingtonpost.com/william-fisher/wittes-goldsmith-and-ksm_b_508175.html.

42. New York University Center on Law and Security, *Terrorist Trial Report Card: September 11, 2001–September 11, 2009,* www.lawandsecurity.org/Portals/0/documents/02_TTRCFinalJan142.pdf.

43. Benjamin Wittes, "The Right Way to Try KSM," *Washington Post*, October 28, 2010.

44. Catherine Philip, "Faisal Shahzad's Basic Errors Led Police to His Last-Minute Arrest," *Times of London*, May 6, 2010.

45. Jane Jacobs, *The Death and Life of Great American Cities,* Modern Library ed. (New York: Random House, 1993), 40.

46. Michael Schmidt, "T-Shirt Vendor Takes on New Persona: Reluctant Hero of Times Square," *New York Times*, May 2, 2010.

47. Jerry Markon, "FBI Foils Elaborate Bomb Plot in Oregon," *Washington Post*, November 28, 2010.

48. "Islam Is Peace," Says President. Remarks by the president at Islamic Center of Washington, DC, September 17, 2001, http://georgewbush-whitehouse.archives.gov/news/releases/2001/09/20010917–11.html.

49. Mike Carter, "Ressam Gets 22 Years for Millennium Bomb Plot," *Seattle Times*, December 3, 2008.

50. Chris Gourlay and Jonathan Culvert, "Al-Qaeda Kingpin: I Trained 9/11 Hijackers," *Times of London*, November 25, 2007; US Department of State Country Reports on Terrorism 2005, www.state.gov/s/ct/rls/crt/c17689.htm.

51. John Brennan, "Opposing View: 'We Need No Lectures,'" *USA Today*, February 9, 2010.

52. Thomas Jefferson and H. A. Washington, eds., *The Writings of Thomas Jefferson: Autobiography, Correspondence, Reports Messages, Addresses, and other Writings, Official and Private* (New York: Derby & Jackson, 1859), 159.

APPENDICES

1. "'Airliners Plot': The Allegations," *BBC News*, April 3, 2008.

2. Richard Edwards, Gordon Rayner, and Duncan Gardham, "Terror Suspects 'Planned Nuclear Station Strike,'" *Telegraph*, April 4, 2008.

INDEX

Abbottabad, Pakistan, 54, 207–208
  Central Intelligence Agency (CIA) base in,
    214–215
Abdel-Rahman, Omar ("The Blind Sheik"), 27
Abdullah II, King of Jordan, 110–111
Abdulmutallab, Umar Farouk, 181–182, 195,
  237
Abidin, Muhammad Husayn, al- (Abu
  Zubaydah), 45–46
Abu Amina, see Rahman, Shaykh Abd al-
Abu Ahmed al-Kuwaiti. see Kuwaiti, Abu Ahmed al-
Abu Faraj al-Libi. see Uzayti, Mustafa Muhammad
  al-
Abu Hafs al-Masri. see Atef, Mohammad
Abu Hamza Rabia. see Shuayb, Muhammad Rabia
  Abdul Halim
Abu Layth al-Libi. see Rufayi, Ali Ammar Ashur al-
Abu Muhammad al-Maqdisi. see Maqdisi, Abu
  Muhammad Asem al-
Abu Musab al-Zarqawi. see Khalayleh, Ahmad
  Fadil Nazal Al-
Abu Salim prison, 104
Abu Talha. see Khan, Muhammad Naeem Noor
Abu Ubaydah al-Masri, 139, 164
Abu Umar al-Baghdadi. see Zawi, Hamid Daoud
  Muhammad Khalil al-
Abu Zubaydah. see Abidin, Muhammad Husayn, al-
Adams, John, 237
Adams, John Quincy, 10
Adel, Saif al-, 44–45, 111
Afghanistan
  al-Qaeda in, 37, 39, 59, 111
  civil war, 1991, 45, 110
  Northern Alliance (anti-Taliban group), 14, 15,
    26, 41
  Pakistan border, 37, 42, 44, 60
  Soviet occupation, 45, 59, 82, 168
  Taliban. see Taliban
  U.S. invasion of, 3–4, 37, 40–44, 79, 220, 232
  U.S. relations with, 15, 59, 236
AFRICOM (U.S. Africa Command), 203

Afzali, Imam Ahmad Wais, 176, 177–178, 181, 183
Ahmedzay, Zarein, 176, 182–183, 183
Ain Zara prison, 104
Air Force 24th Special Tactics Squadron, 128
Air Force Reserve JAG Corps, 234
Air Force's School of Advanced Airpower Studies,
  44
Al-Aksari Golden Dome shrine, Samarra, 127
Albania, response to Powell's UN address, 92–93
Alec Station, Central Intelligence Agency, 24–25
Alfred P. Murrah federal building, 18
Algeria, 71, 72, 193, 233, 237
Al-Hussein Ben Ali mosque, 109–110
Ali, Abdulla Ahmed, 139, 140, 141, 144, 145,
  146, 147
Al-Khalayleh, Ahmad Fadil Nazal (Abu Musab
  al-Zarqawi). see Zarqawi, Abu Musab
Allen, George, 101–102
Al-Qaeda
  before 9/11, 13–16, 19
  in Afghanistan, 82–83, 111, 220
  appeal, to recruits, 223, 235–236
  attacks USS Cole. see USS Cole attacked
  attempts on Pervez Musharraf, 53
  bombs U.S. Embassies. see Terrorist attacks,
    U.S. embassies
  and the CIA, 45, 191
  communication systems, 55, 149–150, 151,
    173, 209–210, 216
  couriers, 210
  double agent, 54–55
  funding, 163–164
  and Hamas, 222
  in Iran, 162
  and Iraq, 84, 86–87, 88–90, 94, 95, 96, 97, 98,
    112, 113–114, 115–116
  in Kenya, 197
  and KSM, 60–61
  in London, 135–148
  millennium plot, 45, 112
  nuclear weapons, 162

Al-Qaeda (*continued*)
   organization, 37, 38, 39–40, 41–42, 44–45, 53,
      80, 149, 150–151, 161–162, 163–164, 212
   and other groups, 222–223, 223–224
   in Pakistan, 37, 46–48, 51, 53–54, 79, 111,
      138–139, 140, 143–144, 146–147, 150–158,
      162, 170, 228
   propaganda videos, 162, 165
   religious training, 223
   security, 40
   in Somalia, 197–206, 200–201, 203
   and the Taliban, 37, 40, 162
   training camps, 45, 79, 80, 82, 84, 170–171, 202
   undermining appeal of, 223–224, 235–236
   uranium procurement, 10
   weapons training, 170
   widespread nature of, 220, 222
   and WMDs, 10, 86–87, 99, 162
   in Yemen, 189–196
Al-Qaeda in Iraq (AQI) (Tanzim Qa'idat al-Jihad
      Fi Bilad al-Rafidayn (Organization of Jihad's
      Base in the Country of the Two Rivers
      (QJBR), 108, 121, 195
   online political front, 127–128
   safe houses raided, 129
   after Zarqawi, 133
Al-Qaeda in the Arabian Peninsula (AQAP), 9,
      195, 221
Al-Qaeda in Yemen (AQY), 195
American Airlines Flight 63, 83
American Civil Liberties Union (ACLU), 77
Amina, Abu (Shaykh Abd al-Rahman), 130, 131
Amnesty International, 68
Ansar al-Islam/Ansar al-Sunnah (Kurdish terrorist
      organization), 112, 115, 222–223
Anthrax, 116
Antiterrorism and Effective Death Penalty Act, 20
Aqrab, al-(Scorpion) detention center, Egypt, 85–86
Arcadia 8 military raid, 130
Armed Services Committee, 100
Armitage, Richard, 94
Army Rangers, 122
Army Times, 128
Ashcroft, John, 27–28, 73, 175
Assassinations, targeted. *see* Killings, targeted
Atef, Mohammad (Abu Hafs al-Masri), 38–40,
      42, 44–45, 58, 92, 233
Atiyah, Abd al-Rahman, 209
Atta, Muhammad, 161, 198
Aum Shinrikiyo, 10, 18
Aurora, Colorado, 168, 171–172, 181
Authorization of Military Force (AUMF), 35–36,
      42
Aviation Week magazine, 216
Azzam, Abdullah, 59

Baath Party, 118
Baer, Robert, 25
Baghdadi, Abu Umar al- (Zawi, Hamid Daoud
      Muhammad Khalil al-), 127–128
Bagram air base, 81, 84
Baluchi, Ammar al-, 75
Baluchs, 62
Bani Hassan tribe, 109
Barbary pirates, 3
Barre, Siad, 199
Bataan, USS, 85
Bayat, 60, 61, 114
Beheadings, of hostages, 121
Benjamin, Daniel, 64
Berg, Nicholas, 121
Berger, Sandy, 31
Bhatti, Salahuddin, 53
Bhutto, Benazir, 1, 164
Biden, Joe, 87
bin Laden, Osama, 78, 150
   before 9/11, 13–16
   after 9/11, 36–37
   in Afghanistan, 42, 44, 59
   al-Zarqawi pledges *bayat*, 121
   and the CIA, 24, 25, 26, 213–215
   communication systems, 209–210
   family, 39–40
   gives interview, 42–43
   kill mission, 207–209
   legal status of, 9, 10
   meets Abu Faraj al-Libi, 52
   meets Abu Zubaydah, 45
   meets Zarqawi, 111
   as military target, 29–30
   in Pakistan, 37, 160, 228
   personal security, 39
   religious training, 223
   and Shaykh Said, 162
   takedown, 215–217
   Tarnak Farms compound, 26
   ties to Yemen, 192
   tracking, 209, 210
   and U.S. embassy bombings, 20–21
Biological weapons, 86, 113, 116
Black, Cofer, 25, 69
Black Hawk Down, 217
Black Hawk Down (book and film), 15
Black sites, 70, 227
Blackhawk helicopters, 208, 216
Blair, Tony, 143, 144
Bloomberg, Michael, 76
Bojinka conspirators, 136–137, 138, 237
Bombs, making, 139, 140, 140–141, 142,
      171–172, 179, 180–181
Boren, David, 23

Borger, Gloria, 98
Bosnia, 45
Boumediene v. Bush, 75
Brennan, John, 237
Britain
  al-Qaeda in, 135–148
  British Security Service (BSS, MI5), 136
  forces in Iraq, 120
  intelligence gathering in, 171
  intelligence organizations, 135, 136, 140, 141, 144
  London transit system attacks, 2005, 135, 139, 140, 179, 228
  Operation Overt (plot to blow up commercial flights). *see* Operation Overt (plot to blow up commercial flights)
  response to Powell's UN address, 93
Britain's, Joint Terrorism Analysis Centre (JTAC), 144
British School, Lahore Pakistan, 47–48
British Secret Intelligence Service (SIS, MI6), 136, 143, 148
British Security Service (BSS, MI5), 136, 141, 147, 236
Brooklyn Bridge, as terrorist target, 175
Bulgaria, response to Powell's UN address, 92–93
Bureaucracy, of intelligence organizations, 18, 38, 65, 106, 116, 224–227
Burjak, Ali and Yasmin, 112
Bush, George H. W.
  assassination plot, 32
  rendition under, 64
Bush, George H. W. administration, 16
Bush, George W., 46, 70, 74, 80, 87, 93
  and bin Laden, 213–214
  defends rendition, 85
  elected president, 22
  and Guantanamo prison, 43–44
  meets with Yemeni president, 192, 193
  and Operation Overt, 143
  public confidence, post-9/11, 89
  response to 9/11 attacks, 35, 188, 236
  response to civilian attacks, 120
  on war on terror, 9
  and warrantless searches, 173
Bush, George W. administration, 6, 22–23
  2004 reelection campaign, 53–54
  and al-Qaeda, 36, 150
  defends Iraq-al-Qaeda connection, 98, 113
  expansion of presidential power, 43–44
  intelligence analysis, 95–96
  legacy, 182
  and Libya, 103–104
  misuse of intelligence, 100–102, 108, 116–117
  and Operation Cannonball, 213–214

  public confidence, post-9/11, 89
  response to 9/11 attacks, 35–36, 187–188
  on war on terror, 9
Bush Doctrine, 188
Byman, Daniel, 65
Bybee, Jay, 50
Byrd, Robert, 92

Caldwell, William, 131
Canal Hotel, Baghdad, 107
Capitol Report (CNBC TV show), 98
Cartoon, of Prophet Mohammad, 162
"Case Closed" (*Weekly Standard* article, Hayes), 96
Centennial Olympic Park bombing, 132
Central Intelligence Agency (CIA)
  budget, 19–20, 23–24, 224
  as bureaucratic, 224–225
  and Clinton administration, 18
  Counterterrorist Center (CTC), 24–25, 90, 98, 224
  Directorate of Intelligence, 115
  errors in intelligence, 94–95
  errors in rendition, 65–66
  and the FBI, 27–28, 84–85
  internal investigation, 94–95, 99
  interrogation methods, 49–51, 69–70, 72–73, 104
  investigation of, 25
  Iraq and al-Qa'ida, 115–116
  Iraqi Support for Terrorism report, 86, 115–116
  Khost, Afghanistan base bombed, 163
  Office of General Counsel, 67
  paper on Iraq–al-Qaeda connection, 90
  and PDD 39, 19
  Special Activities Division, 15
  traditional role, 81
Chemical and biological weapons (CBW), 86, 113, 116
Cheney, Dick, 87, 98, 143, 157
Chertoff, Michael, 148
Chowan University, 59
Church committee, 25
Civil liberties, 77, 173–174, 178, 182, 184
Clarke, Richard, 16, 17, 20, 25, 160
Clinton, Bill, 14, 17–18, 18–19, 19–20, 21, 26, 32, 63, 200
  plan to assassinate, 58, 137
  targets al-Qaeda, 81–82
Clinton, Hillary, 196
Clinton administration, 14, 16, 17, 17–18, 23, 27
  and the CIA, 18
  rendition under, 63–64
Cloonan, Jack, 81, 82, 82–83, 85, 175
Cohen, David, 174, 175
COIN (counterinsurgency), 3, 3–4

Cold war, 4–5, 7, 16, 59
Cole, USS (naval destroyer), 22, 30, 76, 189, 192, 195
Colombia, 192
Columbia Law School, 67
Combating Terrorism Center at West Point, 110
Commission on the Roles and Capabilities of the United States Intelligence Community, 23
The Creed of Abraham (al-Maqdisi), 110
Cressey, Roger, 113, 150
Crigler, Frank, 199–200
Croatia, 63, 92–93
Crocker, Peter, 150
Cruise missiles, 21, 32, 34

Danish embassy, bombed, 162
Darfur genocide, 221–222
Darkness at Noon, 68
Daschle, Tom, 36, 92
Davidson, Lynne, 90, 91
Death and Life of Great American Cities (Jacobs), 235
Debriefing, 42, 49, 129, 138, 152, 156
Defense Intelligence Agency (DIA), 85–86, 86, 94–95, 96, 115
Delahunt, William, 103
Delayed notice search, 178
Delta Force, 128
Democratic Party, 103
Denmark, cartoon scandal, 162
Department of Defense, 19, 34. *see also* Pentagon, Military plans to combat terrorism
Department of Homeland Security (DHS), 6, 86, 148, 179
Department of Justice (DOJ), 50, 69, 72
Deportation, of terrorists, 9
Derwish, Kamal, 191
Desert One operation, 31
Detainee Treatment Act, 72, 74
Detainees
  high-value, 80, 84, 98
  intelligence from. *see* Debriefing; Torture
  legal status of. *see* Terrorists, legal status
  suicide, 79, 105
  tried in U.S. courts, 233
Deutch, John, "Worldwide Threat Assessment Brief," 19
Diego Garcia (island), 48
Director of National Intelligence (DNI), 6, 225–226
Disco bombing, Germany, 32
Drones, 149, 216
Drug lords, as targets, 228
Durbin, Dick, 87

Economist, The (magazine), 21
Egypt, 39, 66, 85–86, 97–98

Egyptian Islamic Jihad (EIJ), 10, 39, 161, 192–193
Egyptian nationals, 44–45, 63, 150
EITs (enhanced interrogation techniques), 68, 69, 73
Electronic surveillance, 38, 46–47, 55, 130, 140, 189
  detected by subjects, 141
  effect on al-Qaeda, 149–150, 151
  limitations of, 7
  Predator UAVs, 40–41
  warrantless, 6, 20, 154–155, 173–174, 227
  wiretaps, 177–178
Embassy bombings, in Kenya and Tanzania in 1998, 14–15, 21, 28, 197, 201
Emigrants, the (al-Muhajirun), 203
Enhanced interrogation techniques, 50, 51, 58, 68, 70, 72, 210, 211, 212, 227
Eoyang, Mieke, 36, 43
Estonia, response to Powell's UN address, 92–93
Ethiopia, 201
European Union, 103
Ex Parte Quirin, 73–74
Executive Order 13492, 75

Fadl, Doctor (Sayyid Imam al-Sharif), 223
Faisalabad, Pakistan, 46–47
Fakhiri, Ali Abdul-Hamid al- (ibn al-Shaykh al-Libi)
  on bin Laden, 84
  death, 79, 105
  interrogation of, 79–80, 83–86, 97–98
  life before al-Qaeda, 80–81
  recants statements, 96–98
  rendition, 85–86, 103
  role of, 82, 83
  seen by human rights workers, 104–105
  statements, declassified, 101
  statements on Iraq–al-Qaeda link, 88–89, 91, 92, 94–95, 97, 102
  tried in Libyan State Security Court, 104
  whereabouts, after recanting, 103
Fallujah, Iraq, 119–120
Faris, Iyman, 68, 175
Farooqi, Amjad Hussein, 139
Federal Bureau of Investigation (FBI)
  before 9/11, 17–18, 27–29
  9/11 Commission on, 27
  budget, 19–20, 23
  and the CIA, 84–85
  counterterrorism center, 18, 28
  Counterterrorism Division, 81–82
  focus, of agent activities, 28–29
  information sharing, 27–28, 28, 29, 84
  interrogation methods, 81, 83–84

Joint Terrorism Task Force (JTTF), 174–175, 180, 181
  meets with Zazi, 181
  and NYPD, 174, 175, 179, 180
  and Operation Overt, 141
  in Pakistan, 47, 48
  position on torture, 50
  surveillance of Zazi, 167, 168, 172–173, 174, 177–178, 179
  "the wall," 27–28
  Trilogy project, 29
Feinstein, Dianne, 87, 88, 100, 182
Feith, Douglas, 95, 96
Filkins, Dexter, 230
Fincher, Russell, 81, 83–84, 85
Find, fix, finish strategy, 4–9
  applied to terrorists, 5–9, 51, 219–221
Finishing
  vs. targeted killing, 191
  and collateral damage, 191
  targeted killing. see Killings, targeted
Fischer, Joschka, 93
Flight 103 bombing, by Libya, 27
Foley, Laurence, assassination, 112, 115
Foreign Affairs (magazine), 22
Foreign Intelligence Surveillance Act (FISA), 27, 140, 154, 173, 174
Foreign Policy magazine, 205
Forensics Explosives Laboratory, London, 142
Fort Hood shootings, 231
Fourth Amendment, United States Constitution, 178
France, 71, 72, 93
Freeh, Louis, 28, 29
Front de Libération Nationale, Algeria, 71
Frontier Corps, 213, 229

Gamaa al-Islamiyya, 193
Geneva Conventions, 43, 72, 74
Geo TV (Pakistani TV), 162
Germany, 32, 93
Ghabrah, Mohammad al-, 138, 140, 147
Ghali, Boutros Boutros, 187
Ghul, Hassan, 210
Ghulzar, Muhammad, 145, 147
Goldsmith, Jack, 76, 233
Gonzales, Alberto, 43, 73
Gorbachev, Mikhail, 16, 168
Goss, Porter, 65
Government Communications Headquarters (GCHQ), 140
Grant, Ulysses S., 4
Great Britain. see Britain
Guantanamo Bay, Cuba, 8, 9, 43–44, 67, 68, 70, 75–76, 79, 96–97, 104

Hakim, Ayatollah Muhammad Baqir al-, 118
Hamas, 222
Hamdan v. Rumsfeld, 70, 72, 74
Haqqani network, 229
Harethi, Qaed Salim Sinan al-, 185, 189–190, 191, 192, 193, 193–194, 195, 205
Hastert, Dennis, 92
Hatch, Orrin, 101
Hayden, Michael, 5, 66, 147, 159, 160, 173
Hekmatayar, Gulbuddin, 169
Hellfire missiles, 11, 40, 158, 189
Helms, Dick, 106
Hersh, Seymour, 196
High-value detainees (HVDs), 50, 69, 70, 84, 98
High-value targets (HVTs), 80, 108, 120, 132, 160, 165, 189, 213
Hijacking, 27, 40, 60, 63
Hizbollah, 20, 222, 235
Hoffman, Bruce, 56
Holder, Eric, 76, 183–184
Holy Tuesday operation. see World Trade Center attacks, 9/11/2001
Homeland Security (DHS), 6, 86, 148, 179
Homing devices, electronic, 158
Hostage, beheaded, 121
Hostage crisis, Iran 1980, 15, 31, 217
Human intelligence, 7, 23–24, 108, 130, 132
Human Resource Exploitation program, CIA, 69
Human rights, 90, 103
Human rights organizations, 44, 68, 103, 104, 105
Human Rights Watch, 44, 104–105, 105
HUMINT (human intelligence), 7, 23–24, 130, 132
Hussain, Tanvir, 145, 146
Hussein, King of Jordan, 110
Hussein, Saddam, 8, 16, 87, 89, 92, 94, 108, 113
  and al-Zarqawi, 115
  captured, 118
  secular government, 115

Ibn al-Shaykh al-Libi, see Fakhiri, Ali Abdul-Hamid al-
Ikegami, Haruki, 137
Imaarah Islamiyah. see al-Shabaab
Indonesia, U.S. relations, 236
Indyk, Martin, 228
Inquisition, 68
Intelligence
  analysis of, 210
  and military operations, 215
  and U.S. invasion of Iraq, 80
  use and misuse of, 105–106
Intelligence gathering, 7, 23–24
  cooperation between domestic agencies, 27–28, 175, 179–180, 225

Intelligence gathering (*continued*)
  cooperation with foreign intelligence services, 6,
     38, 46–48, 55, 55–56, 99, 108–109, 136,
     140, 141, 143, 147–148, 153, 165, 171,
     194–195, 220–221, 226
  and corroboration, 98–99
  curtailed with kill missions, 155–156, 165,
     175–176
  and debriefing, 42, 49, 129, 138, 152, 156
  electronic surveillance. *see* Electronic
     surveillance
  and elimination of bin Laden, 209, 210
  and information stove piping, 175
  in the Muslim community, 176–177
  by NYPD, 174–175
  and organic integration, 132
  Pakistani intelligence. *see* Inter-Services
     Intelligence Directorate (ISI), Pakistan
  quality, and torture, 99, 210–213
  sensitive site exploitation (SSE), 130
  and Special Operations Forces (SOF). *see*
     Special Operations Forces (SOF)
  techniques, morally questionable, 227–228
  and technology, 108
  torture. *see* Torture
  voice and video analysis and, 165
Intelligence in War (Keegan), 217
Intelligence Reform and Terrorism Prevention Act
  (IRTPA), 225
Intelligence Science Board, 71–72
International Committee of the Red Cross, 50
Internet presence, of AQI (al-Qaeda in Iraq),
  127–128
Interrogation, goal of, 68
Interrogation methods, 8, 42, 49–51, 68–70, 81
  and counterinterrogation training, 49
  enhanced interrogation techniques (EITs). *See*
     Torture
Inter-Services Intelligence Directorate (ISI),
  Pakistan, 6, 46, 47, 51, 53, 54–55
IRA (Provisional Irish Republican Army), 135
Iran
  1980 hostage crisis, 15, 31, 217
  al-Qaeda in, 162
  Desert One operation, 31
  and Hizbollah, 20
  and Khobar Towers attack, 20, 31
  and the Taliban, 40
  U.S. relations with, 15, 31
Iraq
  and al-Qaeda, 84, 86–87, 88–90, 94, 95, 96,
     97, 98, 113–114, 115–116
  and al-Zarqawi, 115
  American contractors, murdered, 119–120
  and nuclear weapons, 87, 94

  Shia vs. Sunni, 117
  Samarra attack, 127
  and WMDs, 86–87, 93–94, 95, 99, 113
Iraq, U.S. invasion of, 8, 69, 80, 215
  al-Zarqawi in, 117–119
  and anarchy, 118
  begins March 19, 2002, 93
  as counterproductive, 220, 232
  death toll, 127
  and internal conflicts, 117, 118, 119, 127–128,
     133
  justifying, 87–96
Iraq and al-Qa'ida (CIA), 115–116
Iraqi Intelligence Service (IIS), 32, 112, 115
Iraqi Support for Terrorism report (CIA), 86,
  115–116
Isikoff, Michael, 98
Islam
  Shia vs. Sunni, 117, 118, 119, 120, 123–124,
     127, 133, 222
  and suicide, 105
  scapegoating, 235–236
Islamabad, Pakistan, 214
Islamic Courts Union (ICU), 200–201, 202, 205,
  222
Islamic State of Iraq, 127–128
Israel, 192, 197, 198, 228
Italian intelligence, 144
Itihad-e-Islami, 59

Jacobs, Jane, *The Death and Life of Great American
     Cities*, 235
Jaish-e-Mohammed (JeM), 138, 139, 229
Jama'at a-Tawhid wa Jihad (JTJ), 108
Japan, sarin gas attack, 18
Jarad, Yasin, 118
Jaysh al-Mahdi (Shia militant group), 133
Al Jazeera, 2, 62, 121, 157, 162
Jefferson, Thomas, 3
Jemaah Islamiya, 8, 10, 65
Jihad, 59, 82, 84, 111, 224
John Paul II (Pope), 58, 137
Johnston, Alan, 222
Joint Chiefs of Staff, 30, 34, 229
Joint Special Operations Command (JSOC), 7,
  15, 128–129, 215, 232
Joint Terrorism Analysis Centre (JTAC), Britain,
  144
Joint Terrorism Task Force (JTTF), 174–175,
  180, 181
Jones, Ishmael, 224
Jordan, 66, 109–110, 111, 112, 125
  General Intelligence Department (GID), 110
  hotel attacks in 2005, 124–126
  Zarqa, 109

Joyce, Eric, 122, 123
Jund al-Islam, 222
Justice Department, 72. *see also* Department of
    Justice
Justice Department's Office of Legal Counsel
    (OLC), 50, 69

Karakoram Highway, 207
Keegan, John, *Intelligence in War*, 217
Kelly, Ray, 76, 174
Kennedy, Ted, 36
Kenya, 13, 20–21, 61
    Mombasa attack, 197–198
Kenyan nationals, 164, 197–205, 203
Khaksar, Mohammed, 41
Khalden training camp, Afghanistan, 79, 80,
    82–83, 84
    Federal Bureau of Investigation (FBI), 82
Khalilzad, Zalmay, 230
Khan, Mohammad Siddique, 135, 139
Khan, Muhammad Naeem Noor (Abu Talha), 53
Khan, Samir, 196
Khmer Rouge, 68
Khobar Towers complex attack, Saudi Arabia, 14,
    20, 30, 31
Khost, Afghanistan base, CIA, 163
Khurmal, Northern Iraq, 113, 117
Khushali Torikel, North Waziristan, 158
Kidnappings, 121, 222
Killings, targeted, 1–2, 8, 202–203, 203–204,
    227, 228
    importance of, 204
    Osama bin Laden, 207–209
    policy of, 228
    and target creep, 228
    unintended consequences, 205
King, Peter, 148, 182
Korean War, 4
KSM (Khalid Shaykh Mohammed), 8, 9, 57–63,
    137, 138, 233, 234, 235
    and al-Qaeda, 60–61
    captured, 62–63
    early life, 58–59
    education, 59
    interrogation of, 65, 67–68, 69, 210, 211, 212
    as martyr, 78
    meets Osama bin Laden, 60
    religious training, 223
    venue, for trial, 75, 76–77, 183–184
KUBARK manuals, 69
Kurdistan, 112, 115
    Ansar al-Sunnah/Ansar al-Islam (Kurdish
    terrorist organization), 222–223
Kurram valley, Pakistan, 79
Kuwaiti, Abu Ahmed al-, 210, 211–212, 216–217

Lackawanna Six, 174, 191
Laden, Osama bin. *see* bin Laden, Osama
Lake, Anthony, 29–30
Lashkar-e-Taiba (LeT), 51, 229
Lebanon, 7, 33
Legal changes, instituted by Bush administration,
    43–44
Legal status, of terrorists. *see* Terrorists, legal status
Leiter, Michael, 202
Levin, Carl, 87, 101, 102–103
Lewinsky, Monica, 21
Libby, Scooter, 90
Libya, 27, 32, 66, 103, 104
Libyan Islamic Fighting Group (LIFG), 80, 104,
    157, 224
Lindh, Anna, 190
Lithwick, Dahlia, 212–213
Lockerbie bombing, 27
Lockheed Martin RQ-170 Sentinel drone, 216
London transit system attacks, 2005, 135, 140,
    164, 179, 228
Los Angeles International Airport, 112, 140, 237

MI5 (British Security Service), 136, 141, 147, 236
MI6 (British Secret Intelligence Service), 136,
    143, 148
M249 SAW (squad automatic weapon), 129
Macedonia, response to Powell's UN address, 92–93
Machain, Dr. Humberto Alvarez, 64
Madrid train bombings, 2003, 228
Mahmood, Awwaz Abd al-Aziz (al-Kurdi), 118
Mahon, Marty, 81, 85
Manila, Philippines, 237
Manningham-Buller, Eliza, 144
Marine Corps, United States, 68–69
Markey, Edward, 103
Martyrdom, and terrorism, 5, 60
Martrydom videos, 141, 144, 145
Masjid Hazrat Abu Bakr mosque, 169
Masood, Ahmad Shah, 61–62
Maqdisi, Abu Muhammad Asem al-, 110, 224
Maximum City: Bombay Lost and Found (Mehta), 71
McCain, John, 211–212
McChrystal, Stanley, 128–129, 215
McLaughlin, John, 48, 88, 90, 91, 94, 99
McVeigh, Timothy, 18, 27, 78
Medunjanin, Adis, 176, 182–183, 183
Meet the Press (TV show), 87
Mehsud, Baitullah, 1–2, 8, 214
Mehsud, Hakimullah, 2
Mehta, Suketu, *Maximum City: Bombay Lost and
    Found*, 71
de Mello, Sergio Vieira, 107
Mexican-American War, 73
MH-60 Blackhawk helicopters, 208

Middleton, Cameron, 220
Military, 81, 82, 84, 232. *See also* Air Force, Navy
Military commissions, 73–75, 76, 77
Military Commissions Act of 2006, 74
Military Commissions Act of 2009, 77
Military plans to combat terrorism, 29–34, 36–38
Millennium plot, 45, 112
Mogadishu, 15, 33, 201
Mohammed, Ali (double agent), 40
Mohammed, Fazul Abdullah, 197, 199, 201
Mohammed, Shaykh Khalid (KSM). *see* KSM (Khalid Shaykh Mohammed)
Morayef, Heba, 104–105
Morocco, 49, 66
Moussaoui, Zacarias, 28, 83–84, 233
Mowatt-Larssen, Rolf, 98–99, 226
MQ-1 Predator UAV, 155
MQ-9 Reaper UAV, 155
Mueller, Robert, 72, 84, 175, 180
Muhajirun, al- (the Emigrants), 203
Mukasey, Michael, 210
Mukhtar, 49
Mullah Omar, 157, 162
Multi-National Force Iraq (MNF-I), 120
Murad, Abdul Hakim, 137
Musharraf, Pervez, 53, 55, 150, 152, 154, 156, 159, 160, 209
Muslim Americans, 176–177, 236
Muslim Brotherhood, 59, 126
Muslims, scapegoating, 235–236
Muslims, Shia vs. Sunni, 117
Mutawakel, Yahya al-, 185

Nabhan, Saleh Ali Saleh, 197–199, 202–205
    forces in Somalia, 203
    hotel suicide bombing, Kenya, 198–199
    killed, 204
    military strikes, 202–203, 203–204
Nasiri, Omar, 80–81, 82
Nation building, 232
National Counterterrorism Center (NCTC), 6, 202, 225
National Defense Authorization Act of 2010, 77
National Defense University, 224
National Intelligence Council (NIC), 227
National Intelligence Estimate (NIE), on Iraq, 88, 90, 99–100
    request for, 87–88
National Reconnaissance Office (NRO), 23
National security
    before 9/11, 13–34
    and bureaucracy, 224–227
    controversy over, 10–11
    lack of terrorism policy, 16–18, 22
    and political concerns, 31

post-9/11, 219–221
    strengthening, 19–20
National Security Council (NSC), 50, 116, 150, 203–204
    bombs al-Qaeda camps, 21
    Counterterrorism Security Group, 14, 16
    lack of terrorism policy, 22
    and Osama bin Laden, 13–16, 21
    and PDD 39, 19
Naval forces, 40
Navy SEALs (Naval Special Warfare Development Group (DEVGRU, Navy SEALs), 122, 128, 208, 215
New York Police Department's Counterterrorism Division, 174, 174–175, 175, 179
New York Police Department's Intelligence Division, 176
New York subway system, as target, 163–174
New York Times, 87, 173
New York University School of Law's terrorist trial report card, 234
New Yorker magazine, 151
Newsweek (magazine), 98, 175
Nicaragua, CIA in, 25
Nichols, Terry, 18
Nigerian nationals, 181–182, 195
Night Stalkers (160th Special Operations Aviation Regiment), 208
9/11 attacks. *see* World Trade Center attacks, 9/11/2001
9/11 Commission, 17, 27, 32, 34
North Carolina Agricultural & Technical State University (NCA&T), 59
North Waziristan, 158, 163
Northern Alliance, 14, 15, 26, 41, 42, 61–62, 111
NSA (National Security Agency), 140, 141, 146, 147
Nuclear weapons, 10, 87, 162

Oae (Libyan newspaper), 105
Obama, Barack, 1, 3, 10, 18, 167–168, 208
    on *60 Minutes*, 217
    and al-Qaeda, 214, 215
    and bin Laden takedown, 217–218
    on military commissions, 75–76
Obama, Barack administration, 9, 68, 75, 181–182, 203–204, 214
Office of General Counsel, CIA, 67
Office of Legal Counsel (OLC), Justice Department, 64, 69
Office of Special Plans (OSP) (Policy Counter Terrorism Evaluation Group), 95–96
Office of the Director of National Intelligence (ODNI), 225, 226–227

Oklahoma City bombing, 18
160th Special Operations Aviation Regiment
    (Night Stalkers), 208
Operation Cannonball, 213–214
Operation Celestial Balance, 203
Operation Enduring Freedom (U.S. invasion of
    Afghanistan). *See* Afghanistan, U.S. invasion
Operation Infinite Reach, 197
Operation Infinite Resolve, 21
Operation Iraqi Freedom. *See* Iraq, U.S. invasion of
Operation Overt (plot to blow up commercial
    flights), 136, 138–148, 164, 228
    cost of, 144
    failure of, 235, 236
    prosecution, of conspirators, 144–148
Operation Pathway, 171
Operation Phantom Fury, 120
Operation Vigilant Resolve, 120
Orton, Lance, 235

Padilla, José, 49
Pakistan
    Abbottabad, 54, 207
    Afghanistan border, 37, 42, 44, 60
    al-Qaeda in, 37, 46–48, 51, 52–53, 138, 140,
        143–144, 146–147, 150–158, 170, 188, 228
    Central Intelligence Agency (CIA) in, 163, 213,
        214–215
    intelligence gathering in, 38, 46–48, 136, 143
    internal conflicts, 230
    Inter-Services Intelligence Directorate (ISI), 46,
        47, 51, 53, 54–55, 143, 148, 152, 213–214,
        214–215, 228, 229, 230
    Shamsi air base, 155, 159
    as state sponsor of terrorism, 228–229
    and the Taliban, 1, 2, 40, 51, 153, 159, 161,
        214, 228, 229
    TV station, 162
    as unreliable ally, 228, 230
    U.S. operations in, 150–159, 213–214, 230
    U.S. relations with, 21, 47, 51, 53, 55, 156,
        160, 165–166, 213–214, 228, 229–231, 236
Pakistan Military Academy, 207
Pakistani Taliban (TTP, Tehrik-e-Taliban Pakistan),
    1, 2, 40, 51, 153, 159, 161, 214, 228, 229
Palacio, Ana, response to Powell's UN address, 93
Palestine, 45, 222
Panetta, Leon, 17–18, 211, 212
Paradise Hotel, Kenya, bombed, 198
Patriot Act, 173, 178, 182
Pelosi, Nancy, 92
Pentagon, 21, 44, 96, 116
    attacked, on 9/11/2011, 35–36
Petraeus, David, 204
Philippines Airlines Flight 434, 137

Pirates, 3, 205
Platt, Piers, 121
Policy Counter Terrorism Evaluation Group
    (PCTEG) (Office of Special Plans), 95–96
*Postwar Findings about Iraq's WMD Programs and
    Links to Terrorism and How They Compare
    with Prewar Assessments* (SSCI), 102, 114–115
Powell, Colin, 16, 30, 80, 89–90, 90, 91, 94
    before United Nations, 91, 94–95, 99,
        113–114
Predator UAVs, 26, 40–41, 130–131, 189
Presidential Decision Directive (PDD) 19, 20, 39,
    62, 63
Presidential power, expansion of, 43–44
President's daily briefing (PDB), 172–173
Protect America Act of 2007, 154
Provisional Irish Republican Army (IRA), 135

Qadhafi, Muammar, 32, 103, 156, 157
Qaeda, al-. *see* Al-Qaeda

Rabia, Abu Hamza (Muhammad Rabia Abdul
        Halim Shuayb), 150–152
    killed, 152–154
Rahman, Shaykh Abd al- (Abu Amina), 130, 131
    letter to al-Zarqawi, 209
Rashidi, Ali Amin, 39
Rauf, Rashid, 138–141, 143–148, 171
Reagan, Ronald, 32, 63
Red Cross, International Committee, 50
Reid, Richard (shoe bomber), 77–78, 83, 138,
        179, 237
Rendition, 8, 63–67
    definition, 63
    errors in, 65–66
    to foreign countries, 70
    and PDD 39, 19
    prevention of, 103
Republican Party, 89
Ressam, Ahmed, 237
Rice, Condoleezza, 22, 45, 88–89, 191
Ricin, 113, 116
Ridge, Tom, 179–180
Ridgway, Matthew, 4
Roberts, Pat, 100, 103
Rockefeller, Jay, 100, 101, 103
Rodriguez, Jose, 6, 143–144, 221
Romania, response to Powell's UN address, 92–93
Roving wiretaps, 173, 182
RQ-1 Predator UAV, 40
Rub' al-Khali (The Empty Quarter), 194
Rudolph, Eric, 132
Rumsfeld, Donald, 41, 50, 87, 95, 118, 120, 187,
        190
Russell, Richard, 224

Rufayi, Ali Ammar Ashur al- (Abu Layth al-Libi),
    156–159
  killed, 158–159

Sadat, Anwar, 63, 161
Sadr, Moqtada al-, 133
Salafists, 109–110
Saleh, Ali Abdullah, 192, 193, 194, 195, 196
Samarra, al-Aksari Golden Dome shrine, 127
Sarwar, Assad, 139, 140, 144, 145, 146
Satellite phones, tracking, 189
Satellite systems, 7, 23, 149
Saudi Arabia
  funds Afghanistan's war against USSR, 59
  intelligence service, 221, 226
  Khobar Towers complex attack, 14, 20, 30, 31
  U.S. relations with, 236
Saudi-Yemen border, 194
School of Advanced Airpower Studies, U.S.
    Airforce, 44
Schroen, Gary, 13
Scotland Yard, 236
Scowcroft, Brent, 16
Search, warrantless, 178
Security, national. *see* National security
Senate Select Committee on Intelligence (SSCI),
    23, 87–88, 95, 101
  Phase I report, 99–100
  Phase II report, 100, 101, 102–103, 114–115
Sensitive site exploitation (SSE), 130
September 11, 2001. *see* World Trade Center
    attacks, 9/11/2001
Seven dwarves, 59
Shabaab, al-, 202, 203, 222–223
Shamsi air base, Pakistan, 155, 159
Sharif, Sayyid Imam al-(Doctor Fadl), 223
Shaykh Said al-Masri. *see* Yazid, Mustafa Ahmed
    Muhammad Uthman Abu al-
Sheehan, Michael, 22, 30
Shibh, Ramzi bin al-, 61, 62, 75
Shoe bomber (Richard Reid), 77–78, 83, 138,
    179, 237
Shuayb, Muhammad Rabia Abdul Halim (Abu
    Hamza Rabia), 150–152, 152–154
SIGINT (United Kingdom's intelligence
    collection organization), 140
Site X, 47–48
60 Minutes (TV program), 217
Sneak and peek, 178, 182
Snow, Tony, 102
Somali Americans, 202, 205
Somalia, 15, 31–32, 33, 120, 196–205
  al-Qaeda in, 39, 197–206, 200–201, 203
  as failed state, 199–201, 205
  famine, 200

pirates, 205
  as terrorist safe haven, 186
  Transitional Federal Government (TFG), 201
  U.S. forces in, 200, 202–204, 217, 233
Sovereignty
  and the Bush Doctrine, 187–188
  definitions, 186
  internal vs. external, 186–187
  and international law, 187, 191–192
  respecting, through cooperation, 194–195
  violations of, 190–191, 230
Soviet Union (USSR), 4–5, 16
  collapse of, 16, 23
  occupation of Afghanistan, 45, 59, 82, 168
Spain, 93, 228
Special Operations Command (SOCOM),
    31–32, 232–233
Special Operations Forces (SOF), 31, 33–34,
    128–129
  160th Special Operations Aviation Regiment
    (Night Stalkers), 208
  failures, 44
  growth of, 232–233
  and intelligence, 33–34
Straw, Jack, response to Powell's UN address, 93
Strike versus develop dilemma, 143
Subway gas attack, Japan, 18
Sudan, 21, 29–30, 33, 39, 188, 221–222
Suicide bombers, 5, 53, 108, 118, 124, 125, 168, 198
  martyrdom videos, 141
  plan to bring infant as cover, 142
The Sullivans, USS, 112
*Summary of Body of Intelligence on Iraq–al-Qaeda
    Contacts* (PCTEG), 95
Supreme Council of the Revolution in Iraq
    (SCIRI), 118
Supreme Court, United States, 70, 72
  Boumediene v. Bush, 75
  Ex Parte Quirin, 73–74
  Hamdan v. Rumsfeld, 74
Surveillance, electronic, 38, 46–47, 55, 130,
    130–131, 140, 189
  effect on al-Qaeda, 149–150
  limitations of, 7
  Predator UAVs, 40–41
  telephone, 216
  warrantless, 6, 20, 154–155, 173–174, 227
  wiretaps, 177–178
Surveillance, physical, 130, 141–142, 174
  detected by subjects, 141, 178
Surveillance detection route (SDR), 130
Suskind, Ron, 143
Swedish foreign minister, on sovereignty, 190
Synthetic aperture radar (SAR), 155
Syria, 11, 66

Taliban, 157, 220
  and al-Qaeda, 37, 39, 40, 162
  ambassador to Pakistan, 228
  leadership, analyzed, 40
  in Pakistan, 1, 2, 40, 51, 153, 159, 161, 214, 228, 229
  and U.S. invasion of Afghanistan, 44, 48
Tanzania, U.S. embassy bombed, 13, 20–21, 61
Tanzim Qa'idat al-jihad Fi Bilad al-Rafidayn (Organization of Jihad's Base in the Country of the Two Rivers (OJBR) (al-Qaeda in Iraq (AQI), 108
Targeted killings. *see* Killings, targeted
Tarnak Farms (bin Laden compound), 26
Technology
  for bin Laden takedown, 216
  importance of, 132
  shortcomings of, 132
  surveillance. *see* Surveillance, electronic
  and U.S. dominance, 149, 165
Tehrik-e-Taliban Pakistan (TTP, Pakistani Taliban), 1, 2, 40, 51, 153, 159, 161, 214, 228, 229
Tenet, George, 21, 23, 24, 25, 49, 51, 62, 65, 85, 87, 90, 91, 94
  on al-Libi, 98
  on Office of Special Plans, 96
  before SSCI, 88, 102
Terrorist attacks
  failed, 116, 136, 136–148, 163–174, 168, 198, 229, 231, 235, 237
  as inevitable, 30–31
Terrorist Surveillance Program, 6
Terrorists
  domestic, 18, 27, 78, 231. *see also* Zazi, Najibullah
  legal status of, 9, 20, 58, 65, 72–73, 74–75, 76, 77–78, 190, 233, 234–235
  trial by military commission, 73, 74
  tried in U.S. courts, 234
  United States citizens, 18, 27, 78, 191, 202, 205, 223, 231
Thani, Shakyh Abdullah bin Khalid al-, 60
Times Square car bomb, 229, 235
Title 10, U.S. Code, 33, 215
Title 50, U.S. Code, 33, 215
Tomahawk cruise missiles, 21, 32, 34
Tora Bora, 37, 42, 44, 60
Torture, 8, 50–51, 58, 67–68, 85–86, 227
  effectiveness of, 71, 210–213
  of Ibn al-Shaykh al-Libi, 97–98
  and intelligence, 99
  legal cover for, 70
  political fallout, 71, 72–73, 227–228
  and rendition, 66, 70
  United Nations Convention against Torture, 66

Torture Outsourcing Prevention Act, 103
Transportation Security Administration (TSA), 144
Transitional Federal Government (TFG), Somalia, 201
Transparency International's 2010 Corruption Perceptions Index, 230
Trilogy project, FBI, 29
TTP (Tehrik-e-Taliban Pakistan, Pakistani Taliban). *see* Pakistani Taliban (TTP, Tehrik-e-Taliban Pakistan)
Turkey, 192, 236, 237
TWA Flight 847, hijacked, 63

UAV (unmanned aerial vehicle), 1, 26, 38, 40, 152, 158, 189
  and bin Laden takedown, 216
  MQ-1 Predator, 155
  MQ-9 Reaper, 155
Uniform Code of Military Justice (UCMJ), 74
United Kingdom (UK). *see* Britain
United Nations, 44
  Baghdad compound bombed, 107
  Charter Article II, Section 4, 187
  Colin Powell addresses, 91–92
  in Somalia, 200
United Nations Convention against Torture, 66
United Nations Security Council
Resolution 1441, 89, 93
United States Constitution, Fourth Amendment, 178
Uniting and Strengthening America by Providing Appropriate Tools required to Intercept and Obstruct Terrorism Act (USA-PATRIOT Act), 173
  sneak and peek, 178, 182
Universal Declaration of Human Rights, 72
Uranium procurement, 10
Usama al-Kini, 164
U.S. Africa Command (AFRICOM), 203
US Agency for International Development (USAID), 112
U.S. Airforce's School of Advanced Airpower Studies, 44
U.S. Code, Titles 10 and 50, 33, 215
The Use by the Intelligence Community of Information Provided by the Iraqi National Congress (SSCI), 102
U.S. embassies, bombed. *see* Embassy attacks
U.S. Marine Corps, 68–69
U.S. Special Forces. *see* Special Operations Forces (SOF)
U.S. Supreme Court, 72
  Boumediene v. Bush, 75
  Ex Parte Quirin, 73–74
  Hamdan v. Rumsfeld, 70, 74

USS *Bataan*, 85
USS *Cole* attacked, 22, 30, 76, 189, 192, 195
USS *The Sullivans*, 112
USSR (Soviet Union), 4–5, 16
  collapse of, 16, 23
  occupation of Afghanistan, 45, 59, 82, 168
Uzayti, Mustafa Muhammad al- (Abu Faraj al-Libi),
    51–56, 79, 138–139, 150, 151, 152, 156
  captured, 55
  interrogation of, 55, 210, 211
  in Pakistan, 52, 139
  personal appearance, 52–53

Videos, terrorist, 129–130, 141, 144, 145, 162,
    165, 202
Vietnam War, 43, 68

Wall Street Journal, 31, 211
War Crimes Act, 72
Warrantless electronic surveillance, 6, 20, 227
Warrantless search, 178
Washington Post, 2, 23
Waterboarding, 50, 68, 69, 210, 212
Weekly Standard, 31, 96
West Point, Combating Terrorism Center, 110, 200
Wilkerson, Larry, 89–90, 91, 92, 93–94, 94–95
Wilson, Woodrow, 3
Wiretaps, roving, 173, 182
Wittes, Benjamin, 233
WMD Commission, 227
WMDs (weapons of mass destruction), 10
  and al-Qaeda, 86–87, 162
  and U.S. invasion of Iraq, 80, 87–88, 89, 90,
    93–94, 95, 97, 113
Wolfowitz, Paul, 95, 185, 190
Woolsey, James, 18
World Trade Center attack, 1993, 14, 17, 27, 28
World Trade Center attacks, 9/11/2001, 3,
    35–36, 137–138
  eighth anniversary, 167–168
  funding, 161
  George W. Bush's response, 35, 188, 236
  law reforms, post-, 234
  planning, 45, 49, 57, 59, 60, 197–198
  and sovereignty, 187–188
  terrorists watch, 61
World War II, 68–69

Yazid, Mustafa Ahmed Muhammad Uthman Abu
    al- (Shaykh Said al-Masri), 160, 161–164, 170
Yemen, 33
  al-Qaeda in, 189–196
  geography of, 192, 194

  intelligence gathering in, 7, 38
  internal conflicts, 192, 193–194, 196
  as terrorist safe haven, 185–186, 188, 192–193,
    195, 231
  and the United States, 194–195, 196, 233
  U.S. embassy attacked, 85, 195
Yoo, John, 210–211
Yousef, Ramzi, 17, 27, 59, 60, 63, 77, 136–137,
    233

Zarqa (town), 109
Zarqawi, Abu Musab al-, 6, 108, 150, 222, 233
  in Afghanistan, 111
  and al-Qaeda, 111, 114
  audio messages, 119, 123–124, 125–126, 129
  blooper reel video, 129–130
  and Colin Powell's UN address, 113–114
  death falsely claimed, 126
  early life, 109–110
  eliminated, 130–131
  founds training camp, 111
  and Iraq under Saddam Hussein, 115, 116,
    120–121
  and Jordanian intelligence, 110, 111, 112
  kidnaps and beheads foreign nationals, 121
  letter from Atiyah, 209
  meets bin Laden, 111
  message from al-Zawahiri, 124
  military attempts capture, 121–124
  orders hotel attacks, 124–126
  in Pakistan, 110, 111
  plans bioterrorism, 113, 116
  pledges *bayat* to bin Laden, 121
  property recovered, 123
  pursued by U.S. intelligence, 128–132
  religious training, 109–110
  and Shaykh Said, 162
  strategy, in U.S.-occupied Iraq, 117–119,
    123–124
Zawahiri, Ayman al-, 36–37, 37, 39, 44–45, 78,
    81–82, 139, 150, 156, 161
  in Afghanistan, 110
  message to al-Zarqawi, 124
  religious training, 223
Zawi, Hamid Daoud Muhammad Khalil al- (Abu
    Umar al-Baghdadi), 127–128
Zazi, Mohammad Wali, 177, 183
Zazi, Najibullah, 163, 167–182, 228, 233, 235
Zubaydah, Abu (Zayn al-Abidin Muhammad
    Husayn), 42–47, 61, 69, 82, 84, 85, 86, 105
  captured, 48, 154
  and the CIA, 45–48
  interrogated, 49–51

Aki Peritz is the senior national security advisor to the Third Way think tank. He is the author, or coauthor with Eric Rosenbach, of a wide range of publications on security issues through Harvard University's Belfer Center. Before joining the Belfer Center, he worked for several years at the CIA's Counterterrorism Center.

Eric Rosenbach is deputy assistant Secretary of Defense. He has taught courses on counterterrorism at the Harvard Kennedy School, and served as a professional staff member on the Senate Select Committee on Intelligence, where he led oversight of U.S. counterterrorism programs.

PublicAffairs is a publishing house founded in 1997. It is a tribute to the standards, values, and flair of three persons who have served as mentors to countless reporters, writers, editors, and book people of all kinds, including me.

I.F. STONE, proprietor of *I. F. Stone's Weekly*, combined a commitment to the First Amendment with entrepreneurial zeal and reporting skill and became one of the great independent journalists in American history. At the age of eighty, Izzy published *The Trial of Socrates*, which was a national bestseller. He wrote the book after he taught himself ancient Greek.

BENJAMIN C. BRADLEE was for nearly thirty years the charismatic editorial leader of *The Washington Post*. It was Ben who gave the *Post* the range and courage to pursue such historic issues as Watergate. He supported his reporters with a tenacity that made them fearless and it is no accident that so many became authors of influential, best-selling books.

ROBERT L. BERNSTEIN, the chief executive of Random House for more than a quarter century, guided one of the nation's premier publishing houses. Bob was personally responsible for many books of political dissent and argument that challenged tyranny around the globe. He is also the founder and longtime chair of Human Rights Watch, one of the most respected human rights organizations in the world.

·   ·   ·

For fifty years, the banner of Public Affairs Press was carried by its owner Morris B. Schnapper, who published Gandhi, Nasser, Toynbee, Truman, and about 1,500 other authors. In 1983, Schnapper was described by *The Washington Post* as "a redoubtable gadfly." His legacy will endure in the books to come.

Peter Osnos, *Founder and Editor-at-Large*